ELEMENTS

OF

INTELLECTUAL PHILOSOPHY.

DESIGNED

FOR A TEXT BOOK

AND

FOR PRIVATE READING.

BY

HUBBARD WINSLOW,

AUTHOR OF PHILOSOPHICAL TRACTS, SOCIAL AND CIVIL DUTIES, YOUNG MAN'S AID, CHRISTIAN DOCTRINES, ETC.

"*THE PROPER STUDY OF MANKIND IS MAN.*"

BOSTON:

JENKS, HICKLING, & SWAN.

NEW YORK: A. S. BARNES & CO.; PRATT, WOODFORD, & CO.; CADY & BURGESS.
PHILADELPHIA: THOMAS, COWPERTHWAIT, & CO.; LIPPINCOTT, GRAMBO, & CO.; PECK & BLISS. — BALTIMORE: CUSHINGS & BAILEY. — WASHINGTON: ROBERT FARNHAM. — CINCINNATI: J. F. DESILVER; H. W. DERBY & CO.; MOORE & ANDERSON. — LOUISVILLE: MORTON & GRISWOLD. — ST. LOUIS: JOHN HALSALL. — CHARLESTON: McCARTER & ALLEN. NEW ORLEANS: T. L. WHITE.

1853.

PREFACE

TO THE SECOND EDITION.

The favor with which the first edition of this work has been received, has conspired, with a desire to give it an extensive and enduring circulation as a text book, to induce the author carefully to revise and to stereotype it for a second and enlarged edition. Great pains have been taken to render the statements and discussions as thorough, luminous, and condensed as the nature of the work admits. Technical terms are mostly avoided; quotations from foreign languages are introduced only in English; and every sentence in the book is studiously brought within the apprehension of all who are accustomed to reflect.

Having devoted several years to teaching, the author has realized the difficulty of interesting the minds of the young, and of conducting them to sound and discriminating views on subjects of this nature. This difficulty it has been his special effort to remove; and he has been induced to believe, both from his own experience and the assurance of distinguished teachers, that the effort has not been in vain.

The author is now preparing a work on MORAL PHILOSOPHY, similar in size and plan to this, and intended to succeed it in a course of study, which may be expected within a few months. In the mean time, he respectfully dedicates this volume to his fellow-teachers and their pupils, for whom it is especially designed, with the earnest desire that those who use it as a text book may realize as much satisfaction and profit in the study of it as he has in its preparation.

BOSTON, May 1, 1852.

CONTENTS.

PART I.

PSYCHO-PHYSIOLOGY.

CHAPTER I.

LIFE.

CHAPTER II.

DIFFERENCE BETWEEN MEN AND ANIMALS.

CHAPTER III.

INSTINCT.

CHAPTER IV.

NATURE OF THE HUMAN MIND.

CHAPTER V.

IMMORTALITY OF THE HUMAN MIND.

CHAPTER IV.

SENSATION.

CHAPTER V.

IMPROVEMENT OF OUR SENSATIONS.

CHAPTER VI.

PERCEPTION.

CHAPTER VII.

CONCEPTION.

CHAPTER III.

MEMORY.

CHAPTER IV.

MEMORY CONTINUED.

PART IV.

DISTINGUISHING POWERS OF THE HUMAN INTELLECT.

CHAPTER I.

GENERAL VIEWS OF MAN'S SUPERIORITY.

CHAPTER II.

ABSTRACTION.

CHAPTER III.

CLASSIFICATION.

CHAPTER IV.

INDUCTION.

CHAPTER V.

REASON.

CHAPTER VI.

MORAL REASONING.

CHAPTER VII.

JUDGMENT.

CHAPTER VIII.

IMAGINATION.

CHAPTER IX.

IMAGINATION AS RELATED TO MORALS AND RELIGION.

CHAPTER X.

DREAMING.

PART V.

ABNORMAL MENTAL STATES.

CHAPTER I.

INSANITY.

CHAPTER II.

MESMERISM.

CHAPTER III.

SUSPENDED ANIMATION.

CHAPTER IV.

TRANCE.

PART VI.

SUMMARY VIEW OF THE LEADING PHILOSOPHICAL SCHOOLS.

CHAPTER I.

PHILOSOPHICAL SCHOOLS.

CHAPTER II.

THE GERMAN SCHOOL.

CHAPTER III.

THE BRITISH SCHOOL.

INTRODUCTION.

A BOOK ON INTELLECTUAL PHILOSOPHY should not only furnish lessons, but elicit inquiry, excite the reasoning powers, enkindle original thought, and guide to well-formed, independent conclusions. Dogmatism, always odious, is particularly so upon this subject. He who sets our minds upon a track of successful inquiry, does a more valuable service than he who puts authoritatively forth the stereotype lessons of the schools.

All who have had valuable experience in teaching will agree, also, that a great book is ordinarily a great evil. A text book, especially, should be mostly filled with "the seeds of things." These thoughts have been much in the author's mind, while preparing the following pages; to what effect, others must judge.

Briefly to exhibit the most important principles of Intellectual Philosophy, as acknowledged by the best authorities, in language as plain and free from technicalities as possible; to elicit free inquiry, and give reasons for differing from others, in cases of dissent; to show wherein the human powers transcend those of the animal, and to point out their relations to Christianity; to trace the mental phenomena, so far as present science conducts, to their physical source; finally, to adapt the subject both to the popular and the educated mind, — are the leading objects of this volume.

This subject encounters several popular objections, of which the following are the most prominent: Want of confidence in it, resulting from differences of opinion among its professed teachers; the abstruse and scholastic manner in which it has been often discussed; the violence which it has sometimes offered to common sense; and the absence of any perceived connection between it and the practical interests of life. These objections can here receive but a passing notice.

Differences of opinion cannot impair the value of the truths to which they relate. Indeed, the most valuable truths often come to light amidst the conflict of opinions. But many of the differences now in question are more apparent than real. Some of them are resolvable into mere logomachies. Such terms as "innate," "idea," "original," "reason," have occasioned volumes of controversy. Such controversies are upon the mere surface; they do not disturb the vital truths of mental science.

Writers have differed, also, respecting the *number* of the mental *powers;* some, like Kaims and Reid, allowing many; others, like Hartley and Brown, allowing only a few.

Now the mind is ONE. The *powers* of the mind are only the mind's *ability or propensity to perform certain acts.* When we speak of attention, perception, abstraction, memory, as mental powers, we only mean to say that the mind can attend, perceive, abstract, remember: one and the same intellect exerts itself in these several ways. Strictly speaking, the powers of the mind are as numerous as its acts. Classification of the mental powers is, then, a mutual convenience for the interchange of thought; and the fact that some philosophers adopt more than others, is no more an objection to mental philosophy than the fact that some merchants pack their goods in larger boxes than others is an objection to merchandise.

Yet the question, whether a power is *constitutional* or *acquired*, is of considerable interest; as it involves other questions, touching the true end and right culture of the mind. Nor must it be supposed that the classification of the mental phenomena is *merely* a conventional arrangement, having no foundation in nature. Psychological facts, as well as all others in creation, are so related to each other as to form a natural basis for scientific classification.

To avoid circumlocution, writers often use the same word in different senses. Thus *perception* may denote either the *power* of perceiving, or the *act* of perceiving, or the *idea* obtained by the act. Physical *taste* may denote the *power* of tasting, or the *act* of tasting, or the *quality* of the thing tasted, or the *effect* on the sense. The taste of an orange may indicate a quality in the *fruit*, independently of its being tasted, or that quality as *experienced* by him who tastes it. The former is called the *objective* use of the term, the latter the *subjective*. By carefully observing in which sense terms are used, we reconcile many apparent differences, and find the work of mental analysis less perplexing than is usually supposed.

It must be conceded, that mental philosophers have too often written in an abstruse and scholastic manner. They have employed strange words, learned definitions, abstruse arguments, when those more obvious might have been used. They have done this, not to appear profound, nor to cover ignorance with mysticism, but because they have written only for the more highly educated, or have not duly considered the capacities of their readers. This, however, is no valid objection to the subject itself, and should only stimulate our endeavors both to understand it ourselves and to render it plain to others.

But even after the writer has done the best he can to be understood, his object may be defeated by the reader. He who would read a book on this subject as he would a novel, has mistaken his business. He must address himself to it as a *labor*, not as a pastime. He must pause, and converse much with his own experience and reflections; he must compare with them what he reads. The rapid and superficial manner in which most reading is now done, peculiarly unfits the mind for the investigation of grave subjects.

The remark often quoted from Cicero, that the human mind is like the eye, which sees every thing but itself, relates to the difficulty of demonstrating facts not cognizable by the senses. When the chemist analyzes a glass of water, our eyes tell us, at once, into what parts he resolves it. But when the philosopher analyzes the human mind, we must refer to our personal experience for the facts in question, and are liable to mistake his meaning. Hence this is a peculiarly difficult subject upon which to write intelligibly. On none ought the reader to exercise more caution, reflection, patience.

To the objection, that philosophy sometimes contradicts common sense, assuming that it is wiser to trust the latter than the former, I reply, if by common sense be meant the mere vulgar apprehension, irrespective of inquiry and reflection, sound philosophy must needs sometimes contradict it. The great principles of truth lie below the surface. The celestial orbs roll in their paths, not as the vulgar mind apprehends, but as searching science demonstrates. In most of the natural sciences, principles are reached only by a process of experiment and induction beyond the reach of many minds.

But if by common sense be meant the sober sentiment of mankind in general, relating to subjects which they examine and understand, the above objection has weight. Every person is constantly making experiments upon his own mind, and may thus learn its powers and propensities. He needs books, not so much to teach him the mental faculties as to inform him how to designate and classify them, how to improve them, and to what ends to apply them. Hence common sense has here an important service. Her sober decisions are of the highest authority, and no philosophy can permanently stand against them.

The philosophy of the human mind is not truly taught by bewildering abstractions and scholastic refinements, much less by bold hypotheses and doubtful speculations, but by a simple and plain exposition of the *mental facts,* leaving the reader, for the proof of them, to his own experience and reflection. As all minds are cast in the same mould of humanity, he who thus studies his own mind becomes acquainted with those of the whole human race. He is a mental philosopher.

The alleged want of a perceived connection between mental philosophy and the practical interests of life is more relevant to writers of continental Europe than to those of Great Britain and America. The former are the more contemplative, the latter the more practical. It is desirable to combine the two. The deep, rich undercurrent of thought and emotion, which habits of profound contemplation tend to produce, gives great strength and beauty to the mental character. Indeed, it is only the contemplative man that is in the true sense a philosopher. Still it must be acknowledged that even the English and Scotch authors, notwithstanding their strong utilitarian tendencies, have failed to make sufficiently prominent the practical bearings of this subject. It sustains a most important relation to our highest interests as social, moral, and religious beings, which no effort should be wanting to render obvious.

The study of man as a *physical* being has perhaps, also, in this connection, received too little attention. The metaphysical has been kept too widely apart from the physical. They unite in the same being; the spiritual beginning where the physical ends, and carrying out the same wise design. We trace the operations of matter so far as we can; all beyond we refer to spirit. The facts of the physical philosophy of man thus underlie those of mental philosophy, and their relation to it should be carefully examined. Yet I am far from believing that a sound and entire system of mental science can ever be erected upon a mere physical basis. It has been said, with perhaps too much assurance, that "if we are to have a correct philosophy of the human mind, it must come from physicians." The true philosopher of the mental must study also the physical in man; but if he study *only* the latter, I am afraid that it will cost him more than one lifetime to educe from nerves, brains, fibres, tissues, ganglia, and vital fluids, a perfect system of mental philosophy.

Let anatomy carry its dissecting process to the extreme limit of possibilities, minutely tracing the nervous fibrile of each muscle to its termination in the cerebral mass; let surgery thrust its glittering blade into the living flesh, and search, amid palpitating muscles and throbbing nerves, for the pathological phenomena in their most hidden retreats; let physiology appropriate each demonstrated fibre for its sensitive and motor functions; let it diligently pursue the wonderful movements of life, as it outspeeds the lightning in its courses around and through the human frame, until it escapes and is there no more; let it place itself as near as possible to the mechanism of thought, and claim to possess the narrow isthmus which unites the luminous and mental way; let phrenology next come forth to fix the seat of consciousness in the sensorium, explain how impulses are communicated to the mind from without, and sent forth from the mind by the motor nerves to the muscles, through the nervo-galvanic circuits of the brain; let it even definitely indicate the organ of every mental faculty, and take its precise gauge and dimensions; finally, let etheropathy come to the service; let it hypothesize the existence of an all-pervading *ethereum*, by which bodies and minds act upon each other; let it show how the human mind, like the magnet, may, by this ethereum, pierce through solid masses, may send forth its impulse, and even its vision, to distant beings and things; let it thus reveal, if possible, the mysteries of a supposed clairvoyance, — all these may serve to throw light upon mental philosophy. Still, we ere long reach the inevitable point, where neither one nor all of them avail — where we must take naked facts as they rise up, unexplained, from the spirit world.

Those who make no account of physical inquiries on the one hand, and those who admit nothing but what they explain on the other, are alike in fault. Let them proceed together. What neither can do alone, they may unitedly accomplish. Let them bring their respective offerings to the same altar. All their demonstrations may yet be seen to harmonize and to confirm each other. Such an event would be a beautiful triumph of truth. That investigations of a subject so profound, commenced at opposite points, and pursued by ways so different, should finally reach the same conclusions, would not be unlike those sublime triumphs in astronomy won by the united demonstrations of the calculus and of the telescope.

I have endeavored to make the work strictly progressive, like a mathematical treatise, commencing with the origin of intellect, and conducting it through its several stages of growth up to its highest earthly development. The interest and profit with which subjects like this are studied eminently depend on such an arrangement. The human mind loves order; it looks for a beginning, a progress, and an end; every step in the course being necessary to a clear understanding of what follows.

The first part is devoted to psycho-physiology, or the mutual relations of life, mind, and matter. The design is to explore the physiological sources of the mental phenomena, to show wherein the intellectual is dependent on the physical, and the physical on the intellectual, to examine the evidence for the mind's immortality, and to point out the origin of its knowledge. The way is thus prepared for our strictly psychological inquiries.

We proceed, in the second part, to examine the nature and sources of our primary knowledge. The distinction usually made by the terms *original* and *acquired* is here indicated by the terms *primary* and *secondary*. The reason is, that I consider *all* knowledge acquired. To speak of original knowledge, comports with the theory of innate ideas. By primary knowledge, I mean that which the mind has first. It is that which we obtain without any reasoning process, being received in the form of simple and direct cognitions. The reader's particular attention is here requested to the important distinction between cognitions and suggestions, and to the means by which we may know whether our perceptions are true.

In the third part, we consider the nature and sources of our secondary knowledge, or that which we obtain by a process of reasoning. This is the most trodden part of the path in mental science. Averse to needless innovation, I have endeavored, so far as justice to the subject allows, to abide by the classification and the use of terms adopted by the most approved authors, and have never materially differed from them without carefully stating their views and the reasons for dissent. I have felt constrained, however, to differ materially on some points, especially upon the subject of memory. It is hoped the reader will not pass slightly over this subject.

In the fourth part, we advance to a consideration of those intellectual faculties which distinguish man from the brute creation, and place him in relation to a higher order of beings. It is by virtue of these that, in an intellectual view, he is rendered, unlike the mere animal, capable of morality and religion. Philosophical writers have ever failed to point out this distinction with the clearness and fulness which it deserves. It is one of great interest and importance, both in its philosophical and religious aspects. It will be perceived that I differ from most writers respecting reason and judgment; still more respecting imagination.

Having thus accompanied the mind through its various stages of normal development, we notice, in the fourth part, its most important abnormal states. Respecting mesmeric states, I adopt no theories and profess no belief. To do thus, in a work like this, would be premature. My only aim has been briefly to state what may be considered as known on this subject. For this I rely, not on the declarations of professed "believers," much less on any observations of my own, but on the authority of eminently scientific physiologists. The facts relating to suspended animation and trance cannot fail to interest those who are disposed to know what powers the human soul is capable of exerting independently of the body.

The sixth part is devoted to a summary review of the leading philosophical schools. Every pupil ought, before leaving school, to obtain a correct general view of the history of philosophy, as an incentive and guide to future reading upon the subject. But it is nearly impossible to obtain this from any available sources. And even if the sources were available, so many volumes, in various languages, replete with technical terms and conflicting theories, present too formidable a task for most young minds. It is hoped, therefore, that this brief compend will be found an acceptable article with which to conclude our study.

No person of taste can be indifferent to the ornaments of style. Indeed, in some works they are indispensable; success depends upon them. But in a work like this, the writer must strive, mainly, to be understood. If ornament is sometimes sacrificed to perspicuity, some indulgence is expected. Few are aware how difficult it is to write on subjects of this nature, in language intelligible to all, without using the same words more frequently, and sometimes adopting more familiar illustrations, than a refined literary taste would dictate.

That the philosophy of the human mind should constitute a part of the study of every person, is undeniable. Some have thought it too elevated a subject, however, for youth at school. It ought, undoubtedly, to be one of the later in course, but should never be finally omitted. Every youth of decent attainments, under the guidance of a suitable teacher, is competent to understand its most essential truths; and unless he studies it at school, he ordinarily *never* does. Lighter reading, amusements, business, passing events engross his attention.

He accordingly goes through life ignorant of even the *terms* which define the powers and operations of his mind. When he hears or reads them, they convey to him no distinct meaning; when he employs them, he does not definitely know what he says. He listens to lectures, addresses, sermons relating to philosophy, morals and religion, under serious disadvantages. Sometimes an entire argument or illustration hinges on a single term of which he is ignorant. No defining dictionary can supply the place of that clear and enlarged knowledge of terms which is obtained by a thorough and systematic study of the subjects to which they relate.

When we further consider that the mind is to live forever; that, forsaken of the world, it is soon to be thrown upon its personal resources; and that its present training is preparatory to its future welfare, — those clear and earnest views of its powers, duties, and destinies, which this study affords, appear to be of the highest importance.

To all who are invested with the high and responsible office of teaching, I would therefore most respectfully and earnestly say, Inspire your pupils with a taste for this ennobling study; secure in them a fondness for it, while they are yet under your culture; arouse them to a wakeful consciousness of their powers, and to a stirring sense of their responsibilities; teach them to define and trace the operations of their minds, and to refer them to their appropriate objects. You will thus lay the foundation, and form the habits, favorable to an enduring progress in true knowledge. The study of the human mind, thus auspiciously commenced, prepares the way for the most sublime and glorious of all knowledge — THE SCIENCE OF GOD AND ETERNAL LIFE.

INTELLECTUAL PHILOSOPHY.

PART I.

PSYCHO-PHYSIOLOGY.

CHAPTER I.

LIFE.

Respecting the mysterious principle which we call *Life*, there have been various speculations. Some have identified it with *caloric*, meaning by the term, not *heat*, but the *cause* of heat. Heat is an *effect*, of which caloric, acting through a material substance, is the *cause*. That all the effects produced by life cannot be referred to this, will appear evident when we shall notice the peculiar operations of the vital principle. But even if it could be shown that life is caloric, the question returns, What is *caloric?* All we have gained is an exchange of names.

THE ATHEISTIC THEORY.

Some atheistic theorists have considered *Life*, and what we call *Mind* or *Spirit*, the same thing, and to be nothing more than the *heat* or *agitation* resulting from the action of caloric on elementary atoms. To this cause they would refer all the wonders of wisdom and goodness in the living creation! "There is nothing," says the learned Cudworth, "in fire and flame, or a kindred body, different from other bodies, but only the motion or mechanism and fancy of it. And, therefore, it is but a crude conceit, which the atheists and corporealists of former times have been always so fond of, that souls are nothing but fiery or flammeous bodies. For though heat in the bodies of animals be a necessary instrument for the soul and life to act by in them, yet it is a thing really distinct from life; and a red-hot iron hath not, therefore, any nearer approximation to life than it had before, nor the flame of a candle than the extinguished snuff or tallow of it; the difference between them being only in the agitation of the insensible parts." * Thales, on the other hand, and the disciples of his school, supposed the principle of all life to reside in *water*.

It was, doubtless, from observing the important uses of heat and water in the processes of organized life, that men were led to such theories.

LIFE WIDELY DIFFUSED.

Matter may be either inert or animated, dead or alive. But life is more widely diffused through the material world than is generally supposed. Indeed, some philosophers, both of ancient and modern schools, have considered every *atom* of matter instinct with life. Such was one of the conceits of the ancient atomic theory, which made every atom a living thing. A modern writer on Dynamical Physiology says, "The elements of dust are the elements of life; for there is no substance, however inert or passive its atoms may be, whose combinations are not governed by a force common to all vital structures. The very debris of the soul, that lies mouldering in the grave, moved only by the worm, has generated the force that moves it, and testifies that all matter is vital, and ever ready to animate all other atoms

* Intellectual System of the Universe, vol. i. p. 108.

with which it comes in contact with a higher degree of life. Death is but a comparative term; in a world where there is *nothing fixed but change*, death has no reality." *

That ingenious and observing minds should have adopted such sweeping theories, is accounted for only by the fact that life is so eminently all-pervading. Wherever we look, whether with the microscope or with the unaided eye, we see life every where at work. Still, there is a state of matter, in which it is subject only to the laws of gravitation, chemistry, and mechanical forces. This we call a state of *inertia*. There is another state, in which it passes from under their sovereignty, and becomes subject to the dominion of a higher power, which we call *Life*.

Life is not itself an intelligent being, nor is it of itself intelligent; for the vegetable has life, without intelligence. But life *sustains* intelligent beings, as truly as vegetables. It is a power imparted by God, the source of all life, sustaining alike the vegetable, animal, and rational creations. All hold it at his pleasure; when he withdraws it, by whatever means, they cease to be.

PHENOMENA OF LIFE.

Although entirely ignorant of the *essence* of life, we know something of its *phenomena*. If we cannot tell what it *is*, we can tell what it *does*. It would be out of place here to discuss the subject of dynamics, but some notice of the phenomena of life will assist our inquiries respecting the nature and relations of the human mind. Of the effects of life upon matter, or the particulars in which matter *alive* differs from matter *dead*, we observe the following: —

1. Living matter is ORGANIZED. It is *formed into a union of parts, each contributing to sustain all the others.* The organism becomes more simple, the lower we descend on the scale of living things; still it exists, and, so

* Laws of Causation, p. 81.

far as we can trace with the microscope, the line of demarcation is every where the same between living and dead matter.

A marble statue is *not alive*, for *each part is independent of all the others.* Take off the head, and the rest remains as before. Not so with a living being — the removal of *any part* more or less affects the *whole.* While a tree is alive, the excision or mutilation of a single *branch* produces some effect upon the *whole tree;* when the tree is dead, it may be hacked into a thousand pieces, without producing any effect excepting what is merely mechanical.

Life, then, as related to matter, is an *organizing* power. It lays hold of ultimate atoms, establishes mutual relations between them, and unites them in a bond of common interest.

2. When matter thus comes under the power of life, it is PERPETUALLY CHANGING. The effect of life upon its subject is, to cause a continuous *removal* of matter, and to supply its place by the introduction of other matter.

When the matter introduced exceeds in quantity the matter removed, the subject is said to *grow.* Physiologists have shown, that the substance of a living human body is ordinarily thus changed once in about seven years; but a marble statue may stand for thousands of years, and, through the whole period, its substance will remain essentially unchanged. Whatever of change is ever effected in it, is the result of *chemical* and *mechanical* agencies, not of *life.*

The manner in which the change produced by life is effected, varies with the subject. The plant, by its roots and leaves, absorbs those elements which its nature demands; while by its exhalations and deposition of withered leaves and branches, it rids itself of what is no longer wanted. Thus it may be said, in its own way, to eat, drink, breathe, and perform all the offices of life. With the animal, some voluntary movement must subserve the vital. The food must be voluntarily consigned to its place, or the vital principle cannot reach it.

3. Every species of organized life has the POWER OF SELF-PROPAGATION. The law of reproduction extends

alike through all the vegetable and animal creations. No lump of dead matter produces any thing, from which another lump, like itself, is formed. But in the flower of the vegetable is a globular fluid, which, as the flower matures and dies, becomes gradually hardened, and is finally ejected from the parent plant, to furnish the germ of another plant like its parent. And thus does every species of organized life, animal as well as vegetable, perpetuate its own.

Nothing that lives *begins* to be by a mere chemical or mechanical combination of its parts. It springs into being, and grows, by virtue of an embodying vitality, of which the parent, under God, is the occasion. This principle of vitality is coeval with the first embryonic existence, and forms the organized body. The various members of an automaton are formed, before they are united and made to operate; they are then moved by some *foreign power;* but the various members of a human body are formed by the inherent action of LIFE — the same that perpetuates their existence and growth.

4. All living things RECEIVE THEIR SUBSTANCE AND SHAPE FROM WITHIN. Stones and other masses of dead matter increase by mere *accretion.* The force of attraction, chemical affinity, or mechanical pressure, attaches additional matter to the mass. And if that mass is ever wrought into any form of beauty, according to the fancy of the artist, it is by a *mechanical action from without.* But the substance which enlarges whatever lives is not thus attached. It enters through roots and leaves, through stomach and lungs, and is conveyed by a *circulating system* to the various parts. The power of life is greater than that of attraction and of chemical affinity, so that, in *opposition* to them, it often causes the sap and the blood to flow. And further, whatever of form and beauty appertain to the subjects of organized life, are by the hand of no *external artist.* The magnificent branching elm, the blooming tulip, the beauties of the human form and countenance, which art strives in vain to rival, are all, under God, the work of the *vital power within.*

5. Every living thing ASSIMILATES TO ITSELF THE MATTER BY WHICH IT GROWS. Whatever is united to a life-

less mass, is the same after being united that it was before. Uniting brass with gold does not make it gold. Chemical agencies may neutralize or change the nature of the substances on which they act; but there is no *assimilating* power in chemical combinations like that of life. "It is therefore correct to say, that in a living being the matter does not precede its form. The air we exhale is no longer what it was when we inhaled it; the light absorbed by the plant is changed into color, and consequently does not exist in it as pure light; and this change begins when the element is received by the plant. The wormwood, the rose bush, the tube rose, may all of them stand on the same soil, receive the same moisture, the same atmosphere, and the same degree of heat, and consequently live on the same elements; yet the different taste and medical power of their sap, the different color of their leaves, the different fragrance of their flowers, sufficiently show, that, while the same elements enter into their nature, they do not remain the same, but are changed and peculiarly modified by the form under which they enter it." *

Such are the *most manifest* particulars in which matter, under the power of life, differs from matter inanimate. Life, then, as applied to matter, is eminently a PLASTIC power. It *organizes, changes, reproduces, moulds by an inward force, and assimilates to itself the material subject to its agency.* It does not operate in a mere general way, but by specific methods to specific ends. Not more definite and individual is the potter's power in reference to the clay, which rises under his hand into vessels of every description, than is that of the Almighty, in reference to the clay, which rises under the plastic agency of life into every thing that lives upon the earth. The humble *lichens*, in which the feeblest symptoms of vegetable life appear, not less than the sturdy oaks; the minute *infusoria*, the lowest class of animals, so small that five thousand millions may live in a drop of water,† as well as the proud lords of creation, *are alike produced by the plastic power of life.*

* Ranch's Psychology, p. 25. † See Ibid. p. 30.

It is thus evident, that there is a wide distinction between living and dead matter; that the various forms of organization are not produced by matter, nor by chance, but by a *plastic power*, which we call LIFE, placed in matter by the Creator — a power by which he creates, upholds, and perpetuates all beings.

VEGETABLE LIFE.

This is the lowest order of life, and makes the *first step* above the mineral creation. It is that plastic power which the Almighty places in connection with matter, to fashion it into the various herbs, plants, trees, that adorn and bless the earth. The peculiarity of this life is, that it is connected with no sensation nor will — all of its movements, involving design, *being directly referable to an intelligence above it.*

The life of the vegetable dates from the first movement of the organizing power, by which a living embryo is formed from the parent, and terminates with the destruction of that power. The vegetable body, then, becomes, like the forsaken human body, subject to mere natural laws. The principle of life perishes with the vegetable, because its object is accomplished.

Now, it is evident that neither *heat* nor *water* furnishes this principle. They are only *food*, by which life makes the vegetable grow. The seed of a plant may lie dormant thousands of years. If the principle of life is still there, we have only to furnish the appropriate food, — heat and water, — and the process of growth recommences. If the seed is *dead*, no power of heat or water can quicken it into life.

That *life* is actually in the seed during all this time, and not subsequently infused by heat or water, is certain from the fact that the seed does not *perish*. Take *life* from that seed, and it instantly becomes subject to the law of chemistry, and begins to be *disintegrated*. The same power that *brought* the atoms into an organized body *holds* them there.

It is equally certain that life cannot be mere *motion;*

for, during the thousands of years in which the seed lies embedded, it is motionless. Life is there, but no motion; life is there, but not in action. The same mysterious principle, by which the great UNSEEN first *formed* the seed from the parent, and set it apart as a new living organization, still *remains* with it, and is ever ready, until it is forcibly expelled,* or its mission is accomplished, to go on perfecting and maturing its work, as fast as the materials are furnished.

ANIMAL LIFE.

Animal life is of a *higher order* than vegetable. It is, like vegetable life, a plastic power; but it performs a more complicated and finished work; and it differs infinitely from mere vegetable life, in being connected with *sensation.* Bichat has distinguished between *animal* and *organic* life, making the latter respect the functions of the various parts; the former, the general principle of life, pervading them all, and uniting them in one living being. Organic life is only *functionary,* or subservient to animal life. The whole, therefore, may be included under the general term.†

As the Creator has ordained that the life of the vegetable shall perish with the body, because its object is accomplished, for the same reason he has ordained a similar end to the life of the animal. Hence Solomon says, "Who knoweth the spirit of man, that goeth upward," — that is, does not perish with the body, but ascends to a higher state, — "and the spirit of the brute, that goeth downward to the earth," — that is, perishes with the body.

* When Christ, by his miraculous power, destroyed the fig tree, he does not appear to have *touched* the body. The same invisible almightiness, which originally *put* life in connection with the material of that tree, to organize and perfect it, *withdrew* the vital principle, and "*instantly the fig tree withered away.*"

† See General Anatomy, by Xavier Bichat. Persons not familiar with the French may avail themselves of an excellent translation of this great work, by George Hayward, M. D., of Boston.

RATIONAL LIFE.

But there is a still higher order of life, that of a *rational being*, created in the "image of God," and destined, like the Being in whose image he is made, to an endless existence. Life, in man, is a higher order of the same plastic power, which moulds the vegetable and the animal, forming a more exquisite and beautiful frame.

But its chief glory is its relation to a rational and immortal nature. Considered in this relation, or as involving this nature, it is known by the various names, soul, spirit, ghost, mind.* When this has finally forsaken the body, the body is *dead.* Whatever is *merely animal* perishes with the body; the *rational soul* returns "to God who gave it."

AT WHAT PERIOD DOES HUMAN LIFE BECOME RATIONAL AND IMMORTAL?

The first man had no human parentage; he was created by the immediate agency of God. But it is not philosophical to suppose that God first formed a lifeless body by mechanical or miraculous power, and then put life into it. It is more consistent to suppose that here, as elsewhere, he worked like himself; that he put the principle of life in connection with matter to form a body; but whether that life was, from its first move-

* These terms, as applied to man, are nearly synonymous. When writers have more particular reference to *intellect,* they commonly use the term *mind;* when to the *moral* or the *vital* powers, *soul, spirit,* or *ghost.* Some apply the term *mind* to the vital power of the *vegetable,* and hence speak of the mind of a plant or tree. But as this term is usually associated with some kind of intelligence, I prefer restricting it to the animal and rational creations.

Mr. Francis Bowen, author of the "Application of Metaphysical and Ethical Science to the Evidences of Religion," supposes that life in man may be an *entirely different thing* from what it is in the brute. His views of the distinction between the human and the brute mind, and on the direct agency of God in all of the movements of the brute, are somewhat in advance of the present state of science, but deserving of the highest regard. The reader is referred to the above work, comprising his Lectures before the Lowell Institute, as one in which he cannot fail to find both interest and instruction.

ment upon matter, rational and immortal, or whether this higher nature was imparted at a certain development of bodily organization, we are left to conjecture. The language of the sacred historian is popular, and throws no light on this curious point.

And so also in the case of all others coming into the world by the ordinary laws of generation. Whether from the first moment of embryonic life that life is the life of a rational and immortal being, so that in case of death the soul survives; or whether the high prerogatives of rationality and immortality are subsequently bestowed at such a stage of development as Divine Wisdom sees best; is a point on which I confess myself unable to throw a ray of light.*

THE EXISTENCE OF THE SOUL NOT DEPENDENT ON THE BODY.

Some have supposed that the existence of the soul depends upon the body. Such were the ancient Sadducees, who denied angel and spirit; such are all atheists, who deny both the existence of God as a spirit, and the spiritual nature of man; and such are all materialists, who either take the bold ground of atheism, or deny the conscious existence of the soul betwixt death and the resurrection. But a bright African lad, of a Sabbath school, might teach all such persons a truthful lesson. On being asked, "What is the soul?" after a moment's pause, he replied with kindling eye, "I do not exactly know what it is, but it is *something that lives without the body.*"

We have seen that life is a plastic power, put in relation to matter to organize it. It is, then, not dependent on the organization; for a cause cannot depend upon its effect. *Organization depends upon life, not life upon organization.* The human body may have the same

* Beausobre speaks of three opinions held by the fathers respecting the origin of the soul: "First, that souls were created when the body was ready to receive them; second, that they came from God, and are enclosed in the male seed; third, that the first soul, namely, that of Adam, was made of nothing, and that all the rest came from this by ordinary generation." — See also Priestley's Disquisitions, vol. i. p. 248.

organization the moment after life has fled as the moment before. Whatever difference there may be is occasioned by the presence or absence of life. This is proved by what has been previously shown, but the evidence will be more distinctly stated.

THE SOUL PRECEDES AND FORMS THE BODY.

If the plastic power, which we call *life*, precedes and forms the *vegetable* and the *animal* body, no less does the same power precede and form the *human* body. Whether this life or soul is from the first rational and immortal, or is endowed with these attributes subsequently, is a question that we have felt compelled to waive; but that it precedes and forms the body, is clearly demonstrable from the following facts: —

1. It is the *controlling agent over the body.* The soul is active; the body passive. The soul acts directly upon the body; the body only reacts upon the soul. The heart beats, the blood flows, the lungs play, the body grows, only as operated upon by the power of life. The muscles move as the will moves them. Whether we are awake or asleep, the soul is still animating and controlling the body in all its movements, both involuntary and voluntary. The body is, then, the soul's *instrument*, and hence *cannot produce the soul.* An instrument cannot operate without an agent to operate it; hence, to suppose that the body produces the soul, is an absurdity. The soul, the agent, *must* exist, before the body, the instrument, *can* operate. "God did not create the soul posterior and junior," says Plato; "for he would not have suffered an elder thing to be ruled by a younger. Wherefore he constituted the soul, both by excellence and by birth, to be prior to and older than the body, as the mistress and ruler thereof." *

2. *Physiological facts* prove the same. The minutest examinations which physiologists have been able to

* On this point Plato has many excellent thoughts, in his argument against atheism. See Plato Contra Atheos; edited by Taylor Lewis, D.D., New York edition, 1845, p. 19. This is a valuable selection in the original Greek, and ably edited.

make with microscopes upon embryonic life, in fishes and other animals, demonstrates *that the ultimate material of which all bodies are formed* IS PRECISELY THE SAME.* Why, then, the difference in the bodies formed? If not found in the *material*, it must be sought in the *formative* principle, the *living soul.* Created directly by God, or proceeding from the parent by the laws of propagation, it forms to itself a body suited to its nature. The living soul or spirit of the fish forms to itself the body of a fish; that of the animal, the body of an animal; and that of the man, the body of a man. Let it not be supposed that we overlook the sovereign agency of God in the formation of the body. It is HE that, directly or indirectly, *creates and empowers the living spirit, and guides all its movements.* Viewed in its relation to the *body*, the soul is an *agent;* viewed in its relation to GOD, an *instrument.* As it is thus through the instrumentality of the soul that God begins, forms, and sustains the body, so, when he withdraws the soul, the body falls back under natural agencies, and is gradually resolved to dust.

"The matter which composes organic bodies," says the author of the Laws of Causation, "consists of precisely the same materials as that of inorganic matter, differing only in the number and intensity of its combinations." This must, of course, depend upon the nature of the organizing agent. "The proximate elements peculiar to animal life are fibrine, albumen, and gelatin: these are found to be the elements of our own framework, and chemical analysis reduces them all to the same simple elements which constitute mineral bodies. Seventeen mineral substances, or twenty, are found in vegetables, and fifteen in animals and man. All these substances more or less commingle, and each is promiscuously found both in vegetable and animal life, as well as in mineral bodies. Chemical analysis reduces these bodies still further into oxygen, nitrogen, carbon, and hydrogen, the primitive elements of inorganic matter, which brings them into dust, the starting point of man." †

* For this fact, the reader is referred to the Lectures of Professor Agassiz, before the Lowell Institute, of Boston, 1848–49, on Embryonic Life.

† Laws of Causation, p. 82.

QUESTIONS ON CHAPTER I.

What is the first-mentioned theory of life? Distinction between heat and caloric? Objections to this view? The atheistic theory? Cudworth's reply? Theory of Thales? Of what two conditions is matter susceptible? Opinions of some philosophers respecting the diffusion of life? What has led them to such sweeping theories? What is a state of *inertia?* What is the other state called? What is said of life? What do we know of it? What is the *first* peculiarity of living matter? Illustrations. Inference. *Second* peculiarity? Remarks. How is the change effected in plants? Animals? *Third* peculiarity? Illustrate. By virtue of what do living things spring into being and grow? Illustrate. *Fourth* peculiarity? Facts in proof? *Fifth* peculiarity? Remarks. What then, eminently, is *Life?* *Vegetable* life? Its peculiarity? Origin and end? Does heat or water produce it? Why not? Is life mere *motion?* Why not? *Animal* life? Wherein different from vegetable? Bichat's distinction between animal and organic life? When does animal life end? *Rational* life? Its chief glory? Subsequent remarks. Have any supposed the soul dependent on the body? Who? Anecdote? Why is not the soul dependent on the bodily organization? Which precedes and forms the other, the soul or the body? *First* proof of this? Remarks. *Second* proof? Remarks.

CHAPTER II.

DIFFERENCE BETWEEN MEN AND ANIMALS.

The first difference that strikes us between man and the brute creation is found in the *body*. This should be particularly noticed, as it throws light upon their points of difference in respect to mind. There is a perfect adaptation of body to mind through the whole range of organized beings. It may assist us in tracing these analogies, to start below the animal, with the vegetable creation.

DIFFERENCE BETWEEN THE VEGETABLE AND THE ANIMAL.

The vegetable has *no apparatus for locomotion;* and if it had, it has no intelligence nor will *with which to move it.* All of its movements are, therefore, *passive.* It is tossed by the winds, bowed by the dews and rains, borne to different places by human hands — the mere passive subject of extraneous forces. The simple principle of life, the plastic power alone, can develop itself, and accomplish all its ends, in the mere vegetable organization.

The limbs of animals *point downwards*, and are furnished with various firm fixtures at the bottom, to be moved along by a motive power *in the mind.* But the limbs of vegetables point *upwards*, and, by unfolding a wide surface to the heavens, invite the winds to move them. Both the vegetable and the animal, then, have a moving apparatus; but the one is moved by a power *within*, the other by a power *without.*

Something more than the mere plastic power of life is

needed to accomplish the ends of the animal. Possessed of a moving *apparatus*, he has a *mind*, a *will*, to move it. The distinction between the vegetable and the animal is thus clearly marked. The one has intelligence, and a body adapted to it; the other has neither. Hence, the animal is *not*, as some assert, a higher order of vegetable. Elevate the vegetable infinitely, it is still a vegetable, and not an animal. There is not an unbroken chain of degrees running upwards from the vegetable to the animal; the animal is a *new creation*. Each has life; each is truly organized; each begins, grows, dies, by a similar process; but here the analogy ends.*

Nor do we annihilate the generic distinction between the vegetable and the animal by facts deduced from the "countless tribes of atomic life" called animalcules. Chemical experiments have proved that the germ of animalcules is abundantly found in vegetable and mineral bodies; and microscopic observation has detected myriads of these living mites in a drop of water. But the germs, or eggs from which they spring, have their unequivocal animal parentage: these creatures live and breathe, eat, drink, move, suffer, and enjoy, and finally die, in their appropriate elements, like their larger brethren of the various animal tribes. Although they are generated, live and die, in the vegetable, the mineral, the water, they are as distinct from either as is the ox from the air in which he moves and the ground on which he treads. They are not themselves a "constituent property" of the vegetables, the minerals, the water in which they are found; for these may exist without them. It is

* The infusoria, or moulds, that grow upon damp walls, are said to have sensation, but no voluntary motion. If no desire or will to move exists, a moving apparatus would of course be useless; but if there be *sensation* only, there is a new creation, a new order of being. It is not certain, however, that infusoria *have* sensation; if not, they are mere vegetable, and furnish no exception to our law.

"The simplest combination of animal life, where sensation first manifests itself in matter, is found in mines, where, 'unmolested by winds or changing temperature, the *infusoria*, or *moulds*, cover the damp wall.' The proper element of the infusoria, or moulds, is albumen, which they receive from the mineral body to which they adhere; the mineral being the matrice of the mould. Its delicate tissue is composed chiefly of water, eighty-five per cent. of which is oxygen; they have a feeble circulation, with *little or no sensation*." — *Laws of Causation, Sensational Physiology*, p. 102.

only the *matter* of which their bodies are organized that is a constituent property of these several substances.*

DIFFERENCE BETWEEN THE ANIMAL AND MAN.

The difference between the animal and man is of a similar nature. It is not a difference of mere *degrees*, but of KIND. Elevate the animal infinitely, it is still an animal. The essential prerogatives of the man are not there, and only a new creation can impart them. In their organizations, physical functions, sensations, diseases, processes of growth, and of dissolution, man and animals are analogous; beyond this, the analogy fails. However nearly some of the more curious animals, as the orang outang and the monkey, may seem to approach man, they are yet heaven-wide distant from him; the distinguishing glory of man, the rational and immortal nature, they have not.

In the vast and complicated work of creation, God moves from the lower to the higher, with as few abrupt changes as possible. Angular transitions are not common in his works; and when they must needs be, they are gracefully disguised. Across every chasm he throws a bridge, that human philosophy may find a path from the humblest point of creation up to the highest order of being. As he ascends in the work of creation, he avails himself of all possible relations to the lower orders; never passing from the lower to the higher, without binding them together by some common bonds. Hence, the vegetable is by various ties united to the animal, and the animal to the rational; but we must not infer that, therefore, the one is a *mere continuation* of the other. This is a mistake which philosophy has too often made.

* "Chemical experiments have decided that the element or germ of animalcules is found as a constituent property, not only of vegetable, but as far back as that of mineral bodies. Fibrin, albumen, and gelatin — the elements which compose our own bodies — are properties and constituent principles of mineral substances." — *Laws of Causation.* But there is this important difference: fibrine, albumen, and gelatin are *essential parts* of our bodies. Our bodies *cannot* exist with them. But animalcules are *not* essential parts of vegetables, animals, and water, for these *can* exist *without* them

The *psychological* distinctions between men and animals will be considered hereafter; it is only their *physical* differences with which we are particularly concerned at this moment. Man differs from the brute, physically, in the following particulars: —

1. Erectness of Position. Man was made *upright* not less in body than in soul. He is the only being that was made to look *upwards* towards his home in heaven; all animals look *downwards* towards the earth, to which they are going. Few animals ever saw the sun, moon, or stars; the glorious arch of heaven spreads over them unobserved; they look ever towards the earth, and care only for the earth, which feeds their bodies.

The body of man is so formed that it is *unnatural* and *very difficult* for him to walk in any other than an *erect position.* His legs are much longer than his arms, and his *knee joints so project* as to render it impossible for him to plant the bottom of his feet upon the ground, as animals do, with the body in a horizontal position. Moreover, the *muscles* that support the head *are so inserted* as to be incapable of sustaining it in this position but for a short time. The *eyes* of the animal are so situated that he sees the path before him when walking on all fours, or with his body balanced horizontally on his two feet, like the barn fowl; but the eyes of man are so situated that he can see in the distance *only as he moves erect.* "Man," says Ranch, "is made to turn his head from the earth to the sky, from the right to the left, to view, now the crawling insect beneath his feet, and now the millions of stars above his head. To the fish it is natural to swim, to the bird to fly, to man to walk upright. The Greek word for man, signifying a being that can look upwards, indicates the difference between man and animals in this respect. It influences our whole being and nature. Even the bees, when they have lost their queen bee, cause the larva of a future laboring bee to be transformed into a queen by changing its horizontal to an upright position, and giving it food." *

2. Covering. The outer covering of animals is *hair*,

* Ranch's Psychology, p. 14.

fur, *feathers*, *bristles*, *scales*, and other insensible substances, which are a kind of *substitute for clothes.* In this respect, the animal approaches nearer to the vegetable than to man. The rough bark, the prickles, thorns, &c., serving to protect and defend the vegetable, are like the various coverings, and the horns and claws, which protect and defend the animal.

These animal coverings change with seasons and climates, thus protecting their subjects from the extremes of cold and heat. Hair, wool, feathers, &c., are put off in spring, and gradually resumed at autumn; and if we transport a woolly animal from frigid to torrid zones, the hotter clothing — wool — is soon exchanged for the cooler clothing — hair.

Because the animal has no *reason to contrive*, and no *hands to make*, a covering for himself, the all-wise Creator makes it *for* him. But while it serves to protect him, it deprives him of those delicate sensations to which man is perpetually subject over the entire surface of his body. The only natural covering of man is a highly sensitive, smooth, delicate *skin*, to be protected by artificial means. Even the first pair, untaught as they were, were yet left in this condition, until reason and industry placed the rude dress upon them. Since man has these, by which to clothe himself as he needs and desires, his natural covering is so made as to answer a superior, beneficent design.

While his skin serves, in common with that of the animal, to limit and protect the muscular system, it is, at the same time, of so refined a structure as to be almost transparent. Through it we see the various channels of the blood, the boundaries of chords and muscles, the precise points where to apply the surgical instrument; through it we see the healthy or diseased condition of every limb and muscle; blooming vigor, burning fever, wasting consumption, are all seen through the skin,* in every part of the human frame. It is far otherwise with animals.

* Although this remark is less applicable to the colored than to the white races, yet in many respects it applies to all.

3. The Head and Face. The head of man is symmetrical, lofty, and balanced erect. The largest part is the forehead and upper portions, the organ of the rational powers. His face is also the expression of beauty, intelligence, dignity, feeling. Thought sparkles in the eye, modesty blushes on the cheek, passion plays upon the lip; hope, love, courage, anger, joy, mirth, and sorrow come and go upon the countenance, as the soul bids. We see the man in the face. He is the only being upon earth, that, in strict language, can laugh and cry — although deer, and some other animals, indicate sorrow, in ways resembling those of man. The head of the animal pitches downwards, and converges towards the mouth, the sensual part being most prominent. The mouths of animals are much larger, relatively, than those of men. The face is hairy and almost motionless. As the mind of the brute is very limited in its operations, so the face, the index of the mind, is equally limited. The innumerable thoughts and emotions to which the human countenance gives expression could not be indicated by the face of the animal.

The lower part of the human face, in the male sex, is covered with hair, to distinguish it from the other sex; but as this is not needed for covering, like that of the head, men usually find all its purposes answered in a shorn condition, excepting those who would retain it for the sake of ornament. But the more intellectual and beautiful parts, the forehead, cheeks, nose, mouth, refuse all covering, and conspire with the eyes to give perpetual utterance to the mind. Even the Jew and the Mormon, with the full growth of hair dangling on the chin, cannot prevent the soul from making herself manifest in the countenance.

4. The Hand. This has justly been considered *the wonder of our frame*. The thoughtful study of this member, alone, would seem to be a cure for atheism. Animals have paws, hoofs, claws, proboces, and other substitutes for the human hand; it was for man alone to possess that perfect instrument, by which the blessings of civilization and religion are extended over the earth. The delicate touch and finished mechanism of this organ

give it a versatility and power of execution, equalled only by the multitudinous thoughts and promptings of the mind that moves it.

It hews down the forest, and converts its savage wildness into fields of blooming beauty and waving harvests. It bores through the mountains, lifts up the valleys, constructs bridges for the oceans, and makes highways around the globe. It builds houses and cities ; it raises temples of worship, pointing their pinnacles to the heavens, whither the mind aspires.

The same instrument performs the lighter and more delicate works of art. It digs the minerals from the earth, and subjects them to the various purposes of utility and ornament. It clothes our persons with fabrics of strength and beauty, adapted to all climates, seasons, and conditions. It wields that little but mighty instrument, the pen, by which the mind throws its thoughts upon paper; it constructs and operates a printing apparatus, by which those thoughts are transferred, multiplied, and sent breathing over the world.

The *fine arts*, strictly so called, are indebted to this same wonderful instrument. Its delicate pencillings animate the canvas ; repeat the verdant landscape, the winding river, the ragged cliff, the towering mountain; array our absent friends, and illustrious men of other lands and other ages, in living forms before us ; and portray, in varied light, the brilliant and wondrous workings of imagination. The same hand, with the chisel it has wrought, puts life into the dull, cold rock, and can " almost make the marble speak." Its flexible joints and nimble muscles dance over the chords and keys of the musical instrument, and make it " discourse sweet harmonies."

The hand is the instrument, too, by which the soul impresses its *moral sentiments and emotions*. Desire and aversion, supplication and resistance, animation and distress, are expressed by the hand. It is the instrument of *affection*. Its warm embrace communicates the soul of friendship, and sends a thrill of joy into the heart.

5. ORGANS OF SPEECH. Animals have organs suited to utter all their minds dictate; this is only a few inarticulate though significant sounds. Besides the purpose

of breathing, the mouth and throat of the animal seem, by their structure, to have contemplated scarcely any higher end than seizing, eating, and swallowing their food. Their projecting jaws, with hooked or cutting teeth, and the strong muscles that operate them, and their large, open throats, eminently and almost solely adapt them to seize and hold their prey, to clip the grasses and twigs, and greedily to devour whatever their stomachs crave. Many of the ends to which the animal subjects his mouth are, by man, secured with the hand.

The mouth and throat of man have their importance as an *eating apparatus*, but they also subserve *other purposes, more directly relating to his higher nature.* So great is the number and flexibility of muscles connected with his organs of speech, that their utterances well nigh keep pace with the lightning-like flashes of his thoughts. A language of eighty thousand significant words, with their infinitude of combinations, pours from his lips with a rapidity and ease at which nothing but familiarity saves us from utter amazement. Seriously considered, no miracle is more wonderful. Its muscles are so movable, that, according to Haller's calculation, it may pronounce in one minute fifteen hundred letters. The contraction of a muscle forming the letter must consequently take place in the three thousandth part of a minute, and the vibrations of the stylopharyngean muscle, in pronouncing a letter, in the thirty thousandth. "No bird flies as fast as the winged words fall from the lips of man." The human voice can be made not only to express all the sounds of all human languages, in every conceivable tone, but to mimic the language of every irrational creature upon the earth.

6. Digestive Functions. Man is said to be the only creature strictly *omnivorous*. The range of animals in respect to food, especially those of the lower order, is extremely limited. Some reptiles subsist, like the vegetable, on mud alone; some fishes, like certain vegetables, on mere water. The higher we rise in the scale of being, the more varied we find the food. But even the horse, the ox, the elephant is confined to vegetables, while the lion and the tiger are confined to flesh. But man spreads

his table from the flesh of all animals and the fruits of all climes. There is no flesh which he cannot eat and digest; no vegetable, not poisonous, to which he cannot adapt his appetite and his taste. Even grass and leaves, in the absence of all other food, will sustain his life for a season. The kind of flesh selected by different people is, in a great measure, conventional; what some reject, others consider their richest dainty. The same is true of vegetables. But it is not so with the animal races. The animal of a certain species selects the same food, the world over, in all ages — any essential deviation occasions sickness and death.

This omnivorousness of man eminently *fits him to inhabit all countries, at all seasons;* to endure all climates; to live on sea and on land; to dwell in cities and in forests, in deep ravines and on mountain tops; to range the world at large, and lord it over creation.

Some have considered it an argument for man's *servility* and *dependence*, that he partakes of so many kinds of food. But they should consider that he is not *dependent* on all these. He *can* subsist, like the animal, on *one* or *two*, and hence has the twofold advantage of living when and where the animal cannot, and of feasting upon all kinds, where they are at his service. From the oyster, the turtle, the frog; from the hosts of the finny tribes, in waters salt and fresh; from all the animals that graze the fields, range the forests, and climb the mountains; from all the "winged racers of the sky," he gathers the smoking viands of his board. To the substantial gifts of the earth, the corn, rice, and esculent roots, he adds the savory spices of India, the luscious fruits of sunny climes, and cools his tongue in summer with the crystal ice dug from the heart of winter. It is, then, no poetry, but severe truth, to say that man makes the whole living world subserve his purposes; that all the fish of the sea, all the fowls of the air, all the beasts of the field, and all the vegetable creation lay their united offerings upon his board; and to all he is prepared to give a cordial reception.

Having thus seen the superiority of man's *body* over that of the animal, we are the better prepared to trace the corresponding superiority of his *mind.* In the mean time, there is one quality in respect to which, in the absence of reason, the animal has the superiority — I refer, of course, to *instinct.* Having taken some notice of this, in the next chapter, we shall proceed to the main subject.

QUESTIONS ON CHAPTER II.

What is the first difference that strikes us between men and brutes? Why deserving of notice? What is said of the vegetable? Of the animal? Of the distinction between them? Of animalcules? Distinction between men and animals? How does God move in the work of creation? What may we not infer? *First* particular difference between men and brutes? Remarks. How is man formed? In reference to walking? The animal? *Second* particular difference? The covering of animals? Its resemblance to that of trees? Its changes? Of what does it deprive the animal? What superior advantages has man in this respect? *Third* particular difference? What of man's head and face? Of the animal's? What of the lower parts of the human face? Of the upper? *Fourth* particular difference? Remarks. What have animals in place of the human hand? What does the human hand do? Give particulars. In what lies the *fifth* difference between man and brutes? What is said of the mouth and throat of animals? Particulars. Those of man? Particulars. What is the *sixth* difference between men and brutes? What is man said to be? The range of animals in respect to food? Particulars. The range of man? To what does this adapt him? How does it appear that this does not render him servile? Remarks.

CHAPTER III.

INSTINCT.

INSTINCT, in brutes, is a *substitute for human reason.* As this subject has but an incidental connection with intellectual philosophy, it will here receive but a brief notice. Some allow no instinct to man, and no intelligence to the brute; referring *all* the actions of the one to *instinct*, and *all* those of the other to *intellect.** However this may be, the brute has certainly a much larger endowment of instinct than man; and that, evidently, because destitute of reason.

DEFINITION OF INSTINCT.

"AN INSTINCT *is a propensity prior to experience, and independent of instruction.*" This is the definition given by Paley, and perhaps the best that can be framed. He adds, "We contend that it is by *instinct* that the sexes of animals seek each other; that animals cherish their offspring; that the young quadruped is directed to the teat of its dam; that birds build their nests, and brood with so much patience upon their eggs, deposit them in those particular situations in which the young, when hatched, find their appropriate food; that it is instinct which carries the salmon, and some other fish, out of the sea into rivers, for the purpose of shedding their spawn in fresh water." †

* See Bowen on Metaphysical and Ethical Science, p. 222.
† Paley's Natural Theology; chapter on Instinct.

DISTINCTION BETWEEN INSTINCT AND REASON.

As these are set off against each other, in the animal and human races, it will further our inquiries to notice their most material points of difference. We shall find that animals have, in common with man, to some extent, sensation, perception, memory; all these are implied in many of their instinctive acts. As they pertain to man, they will be considered in their appropriate place. Over and above these, man has *rational* powers to guide him, while animals have those of *instinct*. They differ in the following particulars: —

1. Instinct is MATURE AT ONCE; reason matures GRADUALLY. So progressive is reason, that philosophy is puzzled to tell *when it commences*. The first developments of reason are exceedingly feeble, and it is a long time before it can go alone. Through the whole period of infancy, little or no reliance can be placed upon the rational powers; nor is it until a process of training has been realized, that the child is competent even to select appropriate food, and use the other essential means of life.

But no sooner is the chicken hatched than it seeks a proper shelter, and, at the right time, looks around for food, selects only appropriate kinds, and practises, skilfully, all the arts of self-preservation and self-nutrition which we see in the older and more experienced. This is true of a solitary chicken, hatched by artificial means, and never seeing any other fowl. If it does this by reason, then its rational powers far transcend those of man; if by instinct, then instinct is mature at once, and independent of all instruction.

2. Instinct is a BLIND IMPULSE; reason is a REFLECTIVE POWER. The one qualifies the mind to think and judge *for itself;* the other is the mind of the Creator, operating through that of the animal. The instinctive movements of the animal are those of a *mere instrument*, operated by divine wisdom; the rational movements of man are those of a *responsible agent*. The animal knows not *why* he does thus and so; he cannot interpret his own

acts; he can give no reason for them. Man, on the contrary, knows what he does, and can *give a reason* for his conduct. "However it may be with the brute," says Bowen, "reason is not united with instinct (properly so called) in man. The human intellect is pure and unmixed. It may be obscured by appetite, or stormed by passion; habit may render its operations so swift and easy that we cannot note and remember their succession. But when free from these disturbing forces, it acts always with a full perception of the end in view, and, by a deliberate choice of means, aims at its accomplishment. We have the immediate testimony of consciousness that we never select means until experience has informed us of their efficacy, and never use them but with a full knowledge of their relation to the end." *

3. Instinct is LIMITED, reason is UNIVERSAL. Indeed, the entire range of instinct embraces only *four objects — nutrition, protection, motion, propagation;* and these might, perhaps, be further reduced to two or three. Each animal has its own specific instinct, beyond the range of which it is utterly incompetent. Each species has its own kinds of food and ways of receiving it; its own method of locomotion; its own manner of propagating, cherishing, nourishing, training its young. Left to itself, each will take a particular course, and no other; and if we undertake to force it into another, we soon find that we are contending against nature. The eagle, the swallow, the ground bird, will each build its nest in its own way and place; the gosling and the duck, hatched by the hen, and knowing no other parent, will disregard her call, and plunge into the water, and act just like all other goslings and ducks. The cat has her peculiar ways, and can never be forced into those of the dog. Thus does the Creator, by specific instincts, limit and mark the several species of the animal creation.

Reason, on the contrary, is applied *in all directions, and embraces all subjects.* It can regard all possible objects, appropriate all possible means, and sweep the entire compass of human interests and relations, as they

* Lowell Lectures, p. 242.

respect both the body and the soul, the present life, and the life to come.

EXAMPLES OF INSTINCT.

A few examples of instinct will be here subjoined.

Bees. The manner in which bees construct their comb and deposit their honey furnishes one of the most wonderful illustrations of this power. The comb is constructed upon the exact mathematical principle, by which the greatest possible strength is secured, in connection with the greatest possible capacity. The base of each cell is so placed upon the rim of the cell beneath as both to impart strength to the vessel on which it rests, and secure the greatest strength to itself. If one corner rested perpendicularly upon another, the sides would be weak, and the whole mass would soon crush. A round figure would occasion loss of room; a square figure is weak; the only one by which all the surfaces could be made exactly to coincide, while yet the sides and corners alternate in the way most conducive to strength, is that which the bee has selected.* And if we separate bees from the parent hive at the earliest possible moment, and keep them ever by themselves, they construct their comb and deposit their honey in the same way. The principle on which they do it, subjected to reason, involves some of the highest mathematical calculations, such as only a Euclid or an Arkwright can appreciate or understand. Here, then, we have the alternative — either the untaught bee is a mathematician, deserving a place by the side of Newton and La Place, or she is a mere *instrument* in the hands of her Creator, acting out

* I have to-day attended the hiving of a swarm of bees. About a peck of them hung from a branch, which was placed under the new hive, into which they are now fast entering. The intelligent gentleman who has the care of them says, "I consider bees a miracle." This living mass moves in a solid body up into the hive. After remaining in this condition four and twenty hours, you begin to see the beautiful white comb occupying the place where they have been. They go in laden with the material for building; and the interior bees, in total darkness, with thousands hanging around them, construct vessels for their nectar, which, for beauty, skill, strength, and mathematical accuracy, far transcend the highest powers of human ingenuity.

his wisdom, and *not her own.* The latter is our conclusion, and this brings us to our explanation of instinct. The bee *knows not what she does,* nor *why she does it.* She acts only as she is *acted upon.*

BUTTERFLIES. It is known to all that these beautiful creatures are transformed caterpillars. The two creatures are as much unlike as can be well conceived. We can hardly suppose it possible that the butterfly ever recognizes the caterpillar as sustaining the relation to her which it does. Butterflies associate together, but we never see them associating with caterpillars. We should as soon think of seeing doves and snakes herding together. The butterfly deposits her eggs, and that is the last of them to her, unless, at some future day, she meets them in the form of kindred butterflies. But there is this curious fact: they "deposit their eggs," says Paley, "in the precise substance — that of a cabbage, for example — from which, not the butterfly herself, but the caterpillar which is to issue from her egg, draws its appropriate food. The butterfly cannot taste the cabbage. Cabbage is no food for her; yet in the cabbage, not by chance, but studiously and electively, she lays her eggs. There are, amongst many other kinds, the willow caterpillar and the cabbage caterpillar; but we never find upon the willow the caterpillar which eats the cabbage; nor the converse. This choice, as appears to me, cannot, in the butterfly, proceed from instruction. She had no teacher in her caterpillar state. She never knew her parent. I do not see, therefore, how knowledge acquired by experience, if it ever were such, could be transmitted from one generation to another. There is no opportunity either for instruction or imitation." *

SPIDERS. All who have studiously watched the spider in constructing her web, must have been struck with the wonderful ingenuity of that animal. The object is to catch flies for food, to secure protection in an elevated position, and to construct a convenient bridge for service, when not in a condition to spin. Availing herself of her resources at the right time, she spins and so weaves

* Natural Theology; chapter on Instinct.

the web as to secure the greatest strength and widest surface with the smallest amount of material; and so arranges the entire network, as to have it under the direct control of her fingers. She renders the trap invisible to its victims, and at the same time sufficiently strong to hold them. She thus sits securely in her central position, commanding the whole web, and feasting her eye upon the poor insects insnared by her cunning.

No less marked is the ingenuity of those spiders which bore into the earth. "The mining spider," says Ranch, "digs a channel into the earth about two feet deep, and closes it very artificially by a trap door. This door is round, formed of different layers of earth, which are held together by threads; its outside is rough, but the inside smooth and lined with a thick texture, from the upper part of which threads run to the surface of the channel, so that the door hangs on a string, and falls by its own weight into a fold, as accurately as if the whole had been effected by mathematical skill. This door the spider has the skill to keep shut by its bodily exertions, when an enemy tries to open it." *

Fishes and Amphibious Animals. The manner in which *fishes deposit their spawn*, so as to secure for it a suitable place and element, is a striking example of instinct. The salmon and the shad, for instance, make long pilgrimages up rivers, surmounting rapids and other difficulties, for the sole purpose, so far as appears, of finding a proper deposit for their spawn. Having done this, they immediately return to the sea, having no further concern with their issue. Other animals, again, make journeys from the mountains to the salt water, to find the element congenial to their spawn. "The violet crab of Jamaica performs a fatiguing march of some months' continuance, from the mountains to the seaside. When she reaches the coast, she casts her spawn into the open sea, and sets out upon her return home." † In the one case the sea, in the other the land, is the only suitable place for hatching the spawn. How do the respective animals

* Psychology, p. 34.
† Paley's Natural Theology; chapter on Instinct.

know this? Not by having been taught; for they do thus when kept always by themselves; not by experiment, for all do so from the first; not by reason, for it is a thing not within the province of reason, until taught by facts. These animals know what no human being, under the circumstances, *possibly could know;* or they do not understand their own conduct, but are *under direction of a wisdom acting through them*, by a law which we have termed *instinct.*

BARN FOWLS. The above examples suffice to illustrate and confirm our definition; but for the sake of calling the attention of the young to the operations of instinct, let us observe them as illustrated in an animal with which all are familiar.

1. Why does the hen provide a *nest* for her eggs? Why does she not drop them about promiscuously? What has taught her to attach any value to them, or, if she value them, so to arrange them in a nest as to be able to cover them all with her feathers? Here, certainly, is *design;* but not springing from any wisdom in the untaught animal, for no reason, until taught by observation, could explain the means of hatching eggs. Here animal instinct *first taught human reason.*

2. Why does the hen, having filled her nest with eggs, incline to *set* upon them? It is a most self-denying business for the hen, which delights in roving about in quest of food, to be confined to a single spot. She could not, ordinarily, be made to stay there a moment. Scarcely a cord would suffice to bind her there. But here is something stronger than any cord. It holds her, night and day, for three long weeks, to her chosen prison; from which she departs only at intervals long enough to get the food and drink essential to life. Sometimes she wastes away, and even dies of starvation, upon the nest. This cannot be explained by affection for her eggs, nor by any "pleasure which the bird is supposed to receive from the pressure of the smooth convex surface of the shells against the abdomen," for she often continues to set, *after the eggs are removed;* nor is it referable to *example* or *instruction;* for a hen raised by herself from a chick artificially hatched will do the same.

3. Why is the hen careful, when she leaves her nest for food, to return to it before the eggs *become cold?* What has taught her that a chill upon the egg destroys the chick? If food is not so accessible as to fill her crop within her time, she returns to the nest hungry, imparts a fresh warmth to the eggs, and goes again. If she cannot obtain food without leaving her nest too long, she ordinarily pines with hunger.

4. After the chickens are hatched, why does the hen *brood over and protect them?* At all other times, when not setting, she perches upon a pole; nothing would induce her to expose herself upon the ground. She seems to prize the comfort and protection of her young above her own safety. How does she know that they *require* covering? She does not need any herself. Such a covering spread over her would be very oppressive. What has taught her, that the same genial warmth which *hatched* the chickens is, for a time, required to *cherish* them?

5. How is it that all hens have the same method of *calling* their chickens? They can make a variety of other noises; but when they call their young, they uniformly *cluck.* It is not because they remember that their parent clucked to them, when they were young; for those hatched and raised artificially do thus. And this cluck, all chickens, from the first, readily understand. If there be ducks or goslings among them, to these the cluck is unnatural. Slow to regard it, they stray from their guardian and plunge into the water, despite of her entreaties. Hens cluck *only* while setting and brooding, the ordinary cluck seeming designed to inform others of their engagement; and their peculiar rapid cluck, to call their chickens to food or from danger.

6. Why do hens and all other animals, after cherishing their young till they are able to take care of themselves, *become as indifferent towards them as to all others of their species?* We can readily see, that if the parental and filial affection were *retained* among them, as it is among human beings, it would become a source of immense evil to man; and perhaps, as animals have not reason to control it, lead to their ultimate extermination. The

answer must be found, where we must look for the answers to all our inquiries upon this point, in that power or law of instinct which we interpret *the wisdom of the Creator, operating through animal mind as its instrument.*

QUESTIONS ON CHAPTER III.

What place does instinct hold in brutes? Has man instinct? Define instinct. What have animals in common with man? What has man which the brute has not? What is the *first* distinction between instinct and reason? Illustrate this in the case of the *child.* In the case of the *chicken.* The *second* distinction between instinct and reason? Explain this. The *third* distinction? What does the entire range of instinct embrace? What is said of each species — the eagle, the duck, the cat, &c.? How is it with *reason?* What is said of *Bees? Butterflies? Spiders?* The *mining* spider? *Fishes?* The violet crab? Queries concerning the *hen* — providing a *nest* — *setting* — not allowing the eggs to become *cold* — *brooding* — *clucking* — becoming alienated from her offspring? Where must the answer be found?

CHAPTER IV.

NATURE OF THE HUMAN MIND.

INQUIRIES concerning the human mind are of two kinds, *ontological* and *psychological*. The former respect its *substance;* the latter its *phenomena*. As we can know little or nothing of the former, true philosophy is mostly concerned with the latter. Some would reject or postpone all ontological inquiries; but when we are about to discourse upon any subject, it is of some importance to settle, so far as possible, what cannot, as well as what can, be known of it.

DEFINITION OF THE MIND.

What, then, is the mind? It is not a property, or appendage; it is a *living and conscious being*. It is not something that man *possesses;* it is what he *is*. It is that which he designates when he says *I*. Annihilate the mind, and you annihilate the man. The body is an instrument; it is a *tool*, a *thing*. The mind is an *intelligent agent*. In popular language, a man speaks of his mind as something distinct from himself. He then means to designate his mental powers, or to speak of the mind in distinction from the body. But, in strict philosophical accuracy, the mind is the man. "Do you think," said Socrates, after he had swallowed the fatal cup, "that the body which you will soon see laying here, cold and stiff, is myself? I shall be gone."

CREATION OF THE HUMAN MIND.

However curiously the Creator's hand might have wrought the *frame* of the first man, had not the more wonderful work been performed, the essential prerogatives of the man would have been wanting. There might have been an eye, wrought in the most finished style of artistic skill, but that eye could not see; an ear, but it could not hear; a hand, but it could have no cunning; a tongue, but it could not speak: there would have been only a mass of senseless, organized matter. But the breath of the Almighty rendered that matter instinct with *living mind;* it was by virtue of this that those eyes opened on creation, and a world of wonders burst on the vision. Those ears were saluted with the melodies of rejoicing nature; the taste was gratified with delicious fruits; the thirst assuaged with crystal waters; the touch saluted with downy carpets and soft breezes; the smell regaled with spicy breezes and sweet odors, *because the living mind was there.* Lifting the kindling eye upon this bright creation, every part of which, like a polished mirror, reflected its Maker's image to the sinless mind, man awoke to those exalted strains in which the morning stars sang together, and the sons of God shouted for joy.

THE ESSENCE OF MIND.

By the *essence* of mind we denote its *substance*, or that of which it is *made.* Respecting this, philosophy is at a stand. The learned and the ignorant are alike at fault here. Indeed, the more we truly learn, the more are we convinced of our utter ignorance on this point. "He, indeed, it may always safely be presumed, knows least of the mind, who thinks that he knows its substance best. '*What is the soul?*' was a question once put to Marivaux. 'I know nothing of it,' he answered, 'but that it is spiritual and immortal.' 'Well,' said his friend, 'let us ask Fontenelle, and *he* will tell us what it is.' 'No,' cried Marivaux; 'ask any body but Fontenelle, *for he has* *too much good sense to know any more about it than we do.'"* *

Equally ignorant are we respecting the essence of *matter*. Here is, perhaps, a lesson for us, in some future stage of being. To resolve the *essence* of mind, or of matter into its *properties*, is unphilosophical. It is confounding cause with effect. Yet some philosophers have perpetrated this blunder—they have made the mind a string of *exercises*, a rope of sand. Others have supposed the essence of the mind to be *caloric*. This theory was, for a time, popular with some of the French naturalists; but it is liable to the same objection which exists against the theory that caloric is life.

Nor does the theory of *monads*, held by Leibnitz,—that supposes ultimate elementary living atoms or beings, without divisions, all their qualities being strictly internal,—make a single advance in solving the problem in question. Even if the theory be admitted, it is a mere solution of phenomena; it does not reach the point which its distinguished advocate contemplated—the *essence* of being. This theory, in some form, has a much higher antiquity than Leibnitz. "This atheistic system of the world," says Cudworth, "that makes all things to be materially and mechanically necessary without a God, is built upon a peculiar physiological hypothesis, different from what hath been generally received for many ages; which is called by some atomical or corpuscular, by others mechanical." † This learned author traces the theory beyond Epicurus and Plato, up to Democritus and Leucippus. It is, however, much changed and modified on its long way to the modern schools.

TRUE PHILOSOPHY LIMITS HER INQUIRIES AT THIS POINT.

In consequence of not considering our limited capabilities, in respect to the subject before us, many fine minds have wasted their strength in idle speculations. Some have been led to deny the existence of spirit; others, the

* Brown's Philosophy, vol. i. p. 96.
† Intellectual System, vol. i. p. 58.

existence of matter; so that, betwixt both, the entire universe has been annihilated. It was by a similar speculation that some of the ancient Platonists, the Brahmins, and other transcendentalists were led to consider the human mind a portion of the Deity; as if God, instead of creating anew, had divided himself into myriads of parts. "The particular souls of men and animals being but, as it were, so many pieces cut and sliced out of the great mundane soul; so that, according to them, the whole corporeal universe, or mass of body, was one way or other a God."*

Taking the hint from these, others have adopted the absurd notion of the reabsorption of the human soul into the Deity, at death; while others have been led to consider it the result of physical organization, and of course perishable with the body. All such speculations throw no light upon the point at issue; they are strictly unphilosophical. They make none the wiser; they lead the simple astray.

PROPERTIES OF THE HUMAN MIND.

Although ignorant of the *essence* of mind, we have the same knowledge of its *properties* which we have of the properties of matter. In defining matter, we do not attempt to explain its *essence;* we only state its *properties.* We do not tell what it *is*, but what it *does.* It is that which has the property of extension, solidity, gravity, and, under certain modifications, taste, beauty, fragrance. It is that which fills space, resists the touch, &c. So in defining mind. Instead of attempting to explain its essence, our statements are psychological; they respect only its phenomena. The human mind is that which has the properties of thought, volition, affection — that which thinks, desires, wills, loves, hates, enjoys, suffers. Thus mind and matter have each properties peculiar to itself; each has a nature wholly its own.

* Cudworth's Intellectual System. vol. i. p. 112.

IMMATERIALITY OF THE MIND.

We do not, perhaps, know all the powers of matter, nor all its modes of existence. This much, however, we know, that if mind is in any sense material, the matter is different from any with which we are acquainted.* Matter has *extension;* it has length, breadth, and thickness; it has top, bottom, and sides; occupies room, or fills space, so that two portions of it cannot occupy the same space at once. All this is predicable of the smallest portion. But who has ascertained that *mind* has length, breadth, and thickness; that it has top, bottom, and sides; that it occupies space, so that matter is displaced by its presence? We are taught that God, the infinite Mind, fills the universe; yet matter is nowhere displaced by his presence. He may fill the universe with worlds, and yet himself fill the universe as completely as though these worlds did not exist. May he not create minds in his own likeness, to all eternity, and yet space be no more filled than it is now? For aught that appears, all the minds in existence, both human and angelic, might inhabit a place no more capacious than the New Jerusalem described in the Apocalypse; and this, because extension is not a property of mind. It is strictly philosophical to suppose that all the happy spirits in the universe may assemble, at certain periods of joyful worship, within the precincts of the golden city.

Another property of matter is *solidity*,† It resists the touch; we can *feel* it. If matter so ethereal even as *light* touches the eye, the eye instantly feels it. But who ever touched or felt, physically, the presence of a mind? Matter is also *divisible.* But is mind capable of being divided into pieces? Not only the mind itself,

* Dr. Priestley, in his Disquisitions relating to Matter and Spirit, endeavors to show that the substance of mind and of matter is the same; but his argument rests only upon a mere *theory* of matter, the proof of which is beyond human reach. We are, as philosophers, bound to take the position of acknowledged ignorance on this point.

† Dr. Priestley denies this property to matter. To this I reply, the evidence of the property is inductive; the denial of it a mere speculation. See Disquisitions on Matter and Spirit, vol. i. pp. 5–40.

but also its thoughts and affections, are indivisible. Who ever heard of the fifth part of a doubt, the tenth part of a fear, the fifteenth part of a hope, or the twenty-fifth part of a love? If the thoughts and affections are capable of division, they must have length, breadth, and thickness. But how strange to talk of the top of an idea, the south side of a hope, the east side of a fear, the north-west corner of a doubt!

Matter has the secondary properties of *taste* and *smell.* But did ever a person taste or smell of a mind? Has mind ever been ascertained to be either bitter, or sour, or sweet? We apply these predicates, figuratively, to certain mental states, but in no other sense. So, also, matter has *gravity.* But does mind, like matter, gravitate? If the human mind is sometimes said to gravitate towards the earth, or to mount upward to the sky, we all understand this to be the language of figure. We thus see that mind has not a single property in common with matter. Hence, they who assert its materiality assert gratuitously, and of course unphilosophically. Without pretending that there may not be some other kind of matter, of which we are ignorant, which constitutes the essence of mind, it is sufficient to say, that, so far as our knowledge of matter extends, the mind is strictly immaterial.

PERSONAL IDENTITY OF THE HUMAN MIND.

It is said that at fifty a man has not in his body a particle of the matter which he had at five.* The form and

* The reader may be curious to see a specimen of the free thinker's logic on this subject. "Sir John Cutter had a pair of worsted stockings, which his maid darned so often with silk, that they became at last a pair of silk stockings. Now, supposing those stockings of Sir John's endued with some degree of consciousness at every particular darning, they would have been sensible that they were the same individual pair of stockings, both before and after the darning; and this sensation would have continued in them through all the succession of darnings; and yet, after the last of all, there was not, perhaps, one thread left of the first pair of stockings; but they were grown to be silk stockings, as was said before." — *Brown's Philosophy*, vol. i. p. 119.

appearance of his body are also greatly changed. So also the thoughts, emotions, affections, purposes of the mind may be entirely altered. But, through all these corporeal and mental mutations, there is the *same mind still.* There is the same consciousness at fifty as at five — the same which is to continue forever. The man is truly one and the same person, and not another, through all time and forever. "The belief of our mental identity, we may safely conclude, is founded on an essential principle of our constitution; in consequence of which it is *impossible* for us to consider our successive feelings, without regarding them as truly *our* successive feelings, states, or affections of one thinking substance. The belief of our continued identity is universal, immediate, irresistible." * "All mankind," says Reid, "place their personality in something that cannot be divided or consist of parts. A part of a person is a manifest absurdity. When a man loses his estate, his health, his strength, he is still the same person, and has lost nothing of his personality. If he has a leg or an arm cut of, he is the same person he was before. The amputated member is no part of his person, otherwise it would have a right to a part of his estate, and be liable for a part of his engagements. It would be entitled to a share of his merit and demerit, which is manifestly absurd." †

In truth, all the arguments ever raised against our identity are contradicted by the plainest and most peremptory decisions of common sense. It is hardly uncharitable to presume, that even the men who bewilder themselves with speculations subversive of this fact have themselves really no confidence in what they teach. Not long since, a man was condemned and executed for a crime perpetrated twenty years before. But if the mutations of body and mind destroy identity, the law was wrong; the man who was guilty had long since passed away — another man was hung in his place!

* Philosophy of the Human Mind, by Dr. Thomas Brown, vol. i. p. 126.
† Reid's Works, vol. ii. p. 356. Charlestown edition.

QUESTIONS ON CHAPTER IV.

Of how many kinds are inquiries concerning the human mind? What do they respect? With which is true philosophy mostly concerned? Define the mind. Explain. What is said of the creation of the first man? What is meant by the *essence* of mind? What do we know of it? What is said of the question to Marivaux? What do we know of the essence of *matter?* What is said of resolving the essence of mind or of matter into its *properties?* What do those who do this make the mind? What is said of the theory that makes the essence of mind *caloric?* What of the theory of *monads?* What has been the consequence of not duly limiting inquiries on this subject? To what have some been led? To what others? What *do* we know of the mind? How do we define *matter?* How *mind?* What is said of the materiality or immateriality of mind? State the properties of matter, as contrasted with those of mind. What is the *inference?* What is said respecting the personal *identity* of the human mind? By what are all the arguments against our identity contradicted? What is said of a man executed for murder?

CHAPTER V.

IMMORTALITY OF THE HUMAN MIND.

Is the human mind *immortal?* A more interesting inquiry could scarcely engage attention. Whether we are to exist as intelligent beings only during the fleeting moments of this life, or forever, is a question sometimes pressing upon us with resistless force.

Childhood and youth, filled with earthly pleasures and prospects, often think little of the future; but age, sickness, approaching death awaken serious consideration, and send many an anxious thought beyond the grave. Indeed, there are to most persons, quite early in life, seasons of anxious inquiry concerning the future state. It is the design of this chapter to meet persons thus disposed with such considerations as may serve to resolve doubts.

WHY THE MIND'S IMMORTALITY IS DOUBTED.

All virtuous men, in their senses, wish to live forever. Why, then, if our immortality is clearly revealed in the Scriptures, is it so often doubted? The chief cause of doubt probably lies in the difficulty of conceiving *how* we can exist as living and conscious beings after our bodily senses have perished. We are at present so dependent upon them; our seeing, hearing, tasting; our intercourse with friends, and with the world at large; all our intellectual and social enjoyments, — are so related to the sensuous organs, that it is hard to see how the one can continue to exist without the other. At first view, all that pertains to and constitutes the living being seems to perish with the body. But this view is hasty and superficial. A more philosophical and thorough observation leads to a very different conclusion.

NO MAN CAN PROVE THAT THE MIND IS NOT IMMORTAL.

No man has ever proved, nor *can* prove, that the human mind is *not* immortal. Much as man may *doubt* the arguments for its immortality, they must confess that they can bring no *proof to the contrary.* The most they can claim is, that *they know nothing* of what lies beyond this life. But *their ignorance* can have no weight whatever in deciding the question. Ignorance is *negative,* and of course has no weight in a case to be decided only by *evidence.* We may then positively reassert, that no man can show that there is not another and higher mode of being awaiting us hereafter.

EVEN SUPPOSING THE MIND MATERIAL, IT IS NOT NECESSARILY MORTAL.

If matter is eternal, as materialists assert, and if the *mind is material,* then why may not the mind be as enduring as the matter of which it is made? If matter is immortal, and matter makes mind, why may not *mind* be immortal? But it is said that the mind is a result of a peculiar *organization* of matter, and as that organization is destroyed by death, the mind of course perishes. Let us see.

The human mind is either a *material* substance or a *pure spirit.* If a material substance, it has been shown, in the preceding chapter, that the matter must be different from any with which our senses are conversant. It may, then, be matter of so refined and ethereal a character as to be independent of this gross, visible organization. What we know of matter in its more subtile forms proves this. The wonderful operations of light, caloric, attraction, polarization, electricity, galvanism, not only prove that matter *exists* in forms invisible to mortal eyes, but that *the more refined and ethereal the matter, the more mighty are its operations.* What more subtile, more nearly approaching our conceptions of spirit, than caloric or electricity? And what more mighty? If, then, the materialist choose to hold his ground that there can be no existence which has not matter for its basis, we will here meet him on his own ground. In condescension to his habits of thought, grant him that the essence of whatever exists must be matter; still, as has been shown, the essence of mind may be matter so ethereal as that the dissolution of this visible body can have no effect to destroy it. The dissolution of the body may but serve to free it of the grossness which encumbers it, and send it forth on freer wing to higher modes of being. The question of the mind's *immortality* does not, then, necessarily turn on the question of its *immateriality*. Even if man could prove the mind material, he could not prove it to be consequently mortal.

ARGUMENT FROM THE MIND'S IMMATERIALITY.

But if the mind is pure *spirit*, as all facts seem to prove, the dissolution of the body cannot destroy it. The dissolution of the body is only a *physical* change. It is not an *annihilation*, but only a change of *organic combinations*. It does not, of course, touch a purely spiritual existence. The mind being strictly *one* and *indivisible*, — not organic, but spiritual, — its existence is, of course, independent of the body. Dr. Thomas Brown holds on this subject the following argument, which is so much to my purpose, that I quote it entire: "The body, though it may seem to denote a single substance, is but a single word invented by us to express many coexisting substances; every atom of it exists after death as it existed before death; and it would surely be a very strange error in logic, to infer, from the continuance of every thing that existed in the body, the destruction of that which, by its own nature, seemed as little mortal as any of the atoms which have not ceased to exist; and to infer this annihilation of mind, not merely without any direct proof of the annihilation, but without a single proof of the destruction of any thing else since the universe was founded. Death is a process in which every thing corporeal continues to exist; therefore, all that is mortal ceases to exist. It would not be easy to discover a link of any sort that might be supposed to connect the two propositions of so very strange an enthymem. The very decay of the body, then, bears testimony, not to the destruction, but to the continuance of the undying spirit. The mind is a substance distinct from the bodily organs, simple and incapable of addition or subtraction, and nothing which we are capable of observing in the universe has ceased since the universe began. When every thing external fades upon our eye, does the spirit within, that almost gave its own life to every thing external, fade likewise? Or is there not something over which the accidents that injure or destroy our mortal frame have no power — that continues still to subsist, in the dissolution of all our bodily elements, and that would continue to subsist, though not the body only, but the earth, and the sun, and the whole system of external things were to pass into new forms of combination, or to perish, as if they had never been, in the void of the universe? There *is* within us an immortal spirit. We die to those around us, indeed, when the bodily frame, which alone is the instrument of communion with them, ceases to be an instrument, by the absence of the mind which is obeyed. But though the body moulders into earth, the spirit, which is of purer origin, returns to its purer source. What Lucretius said of it is true, in a sense far nobler than that which he intended." *

> "Cedit item retro de terra quod fuit ante,
> In terram; sed quod missum est ex ætheris oris,
> Id, rursus cœli fulgentia templa receptant." †

HOW MUCH THIS ARGUMENT PROVES.

Admitting the strict immateriality and unity of the mind, this argument for its independence of the body is

* Brown's Philosophy, vol. ii. p. 461.
† De Rerum Nat. lib. ii. v. 998–1000.

irresistible. The argument does not prove it absolutely *immortal;* for the same Being who created it has power to annihilate it. It *does* prove that the mere dissolution of the body does not necessarily destroy it. It proves that the conscious mind, *for aught the death of the body can do, may continue to live.* Unless some higher cause than merely the dissolution of the body destroys it, it will live forever. "No substantial entity ever vanisheth of itself into nothing; for if it did, then in length of time all might come to be nothing. But the soul is a substantial entity really distinct from the body, and not the mere modification of it; and therefore, when a man dies, his soul must still remain and continue to have a being somewhere else in the universe."* It is only the man's instrument that perishes; the man himself may still live, with powers to assume another instrument adapted to a higher service.

THE NATURAL IMMORTALITY OF THE MIND.

It is a law of science, that whatever *is* will *continue* to be, unless an adequate cause from without operate to destroy it. On this law philosophy raises an argument for what is called *the mind's natural immortality.* Reduced to a syllogism, it is this: The human mind exists. Whatever exists will not cease to exist, unless some adequate cause destroy it. The dissolution of the body is *not* a cause adequate to destroy the mind: therefore, the mind will continue to exist after the body perishes.

This argument would be conclusive, if there were no higher cause than the dissolution of the body which can annihilate the mind. As it stands, it proves the immortality of brutes, as well as of men — that is, unless we suppose, with some, that brutes have no minds. In the preceding chapter, reasons were given for believing that He who creates the mind or instinct of the brute, annihilates it at death. Other reasons will be furnished in a future place. Let us, at present, confine attention

* Cudworth's Intellectual System, vol. i. p. 95.

to the *human* mind. Having shown that the dissolution of the body does not destroy it, we will show reasons for believing that no other cause ever will.

THE ARGUMENT CONTINUED.

When we are fully convinced that the death of the body does not necessarily destroy the mind, — that we may be as truly living and conscious beings in a future state as in this, — we find no difficulty in believing ourselves immortal. The Rubicon is passed; we are on the other side of death; the king of terrors is vanquished. We then as readily believe that we may *live on*, beyond the grave, as we now believe that we shall live till death overtakes us. But the question, whether we shall *actually* exist as conscious minds *forever*, can be finally settled only by revelation from God. On this subject he has made *two* revelations — one by his WORKS, another by his WORD.

THE FIRST REVELATION OF OUR IMMORTALITY.

The nature of the human mind, its tendencies, aspirations, instincts; its relations, doings, hopes; its distinguishing intellectual and moral powers, — all conspire, harmonizing with the more luminous teachings of the divine word, to teach us that we are immortal beings.

Man is ever throwing his thoughts, his hopes, his imaginings into the *boundless future*. So truly does the human mind live in the future, that, if absolutely cut off from all prospect of continued existence, it could hardly endure the present moment. In the most vigorous and positive impulses of his nature, he is not a mere creature of to-day, but of all coming time. If he fails to live in view of living forever, he acts *unnaturally*. Did the Creator implant this prospectiveness in our nature fo nothing? or only to sport with and disappoint it?

DESIRE FOR POSTHUMOUS REPUTATION.

A desire for *posthumous reputation* is natural to man. Who, that is not in a perverted state of mind, is indifferent respecting the estimation in which he shall be held amongst men after his decease? This desire is founded on an expectation of a continued existence. Were a man annihilated at death, his reputation, so far as he is concerned, might as well be annihilated with him. His reputation lives vainly indeed to *him*, if he no longer lives to possess it. When we think of the reputations of a Nero and of a Washington, sustaining their respective relations to the living minds to whom they belong, they have real importance to their owners. But if their respective owners have ceased to be, the reputation of the one is of no more value to him than that of the other. Why do we instinctively tread so lightly on the ashes of the dead, and count the defaming of them a sacrilege, but that it is in our nature to feel that their reputation is dear to them?

THE POWERS AND GRASPINGS OF THE HUMAN MIND ARGUE ITS IMMORTALITY.

The human mind *expatiates in illimitable space and duration.* The mighty reaches of man's thoughts are out of all proportion to the little time and space in which his body lives. It is but a point of time and space that the body occupies; the mind stretches itself every way into infinity. "The sublime attainments which man has been capable of making in science and the wonders of his own creative art, in that magnificent scene to which he has known how to give new magnificence, have been considered, by many, as themselves proofs of the immortality of a being so richly endowed. When we view him, indeed, comprehending in his single conceptions the history of ages that have preceded him, and, not content with the past, anticipating events that are to begin only in ages as remote in futurity as the origin of the universe is in the past, measuring the distance of the remotest planets, and naming in what year of other centuries the nations that are now gazing with astonishment on some comet are to gaze on it in its return,—it is scarcely possible for us to believe that a mind, which seems equally capacious of what is infinite in space and time, should be only a creature whose brief existence is measurable by a few points of space and a few moments of eternity." *

THE IDEA OF OUR IMMORTALITY UNIVERSAL.

The immortality of the human mind has ever been, in some sense, almost universally admitted. Even the rudest pagan and savage nations have entertained some vague ideas of a kind of shadowy, ghostly, mystical existence hereafter. The metempsychoses of the heathen systems are a part of the same crude speculations. It is, however, a prevailing sentiment in these speculations, that the mind, when separated from the body, is but a feeble, half-conscious existence; that the minds of brutes, as well as of men, are immortal; and that there is, in the progress of ages, an interchange of bodies and states between them. That the existence of the mind absolutely depends upon the bodily organization, is an opinion which has ever been confined to a very few minds. It is due to the wisest of the heathen philosophers to say, that they never entertained so gross an idea.

OPINIONS OF PAGAN PHILOSOPHERS.

Pythagoras, the renowned philosopher of Samos, nearly five hundred years before Christ; Socrates, of Athens, the most celebrated of the ancient philosophers, four hundred years before Christ; Plato, the illustrious founder of the school bearing his name, three hundred and fifty *years before Christ; Aristotle*, the distinguished pupil of Plato, and founder of another school; Cicero, the brightest

* Brown's Philosophy, vol. ii. p. 476.

star in the firmament of Rome, equally brilliant as a statesman and a philosopher, who flourished a century before Christ; Seneca, the wise philosopher, a teacher of Nero,—all these masters in philosophy, and their numerous pupils, favored with uncommonly keen mental vision, and perhaps with some faint adumbrations of revealed light, were enabled to see and teach the spiritual and immortal nature of the human mind. Their conceptions were, however, faint, their thoughts confused, and many of their speculations wild and fanciful. Pythagoras was the first to teach explicitly the doctrine of metempsychosis; and most of the great philosophers succeeding him imbibed more or less of his speculations. They exhibit striking examples of great and vigorous minds groping in twilight. These are among the original thinkers of whom the world has so few.

THE MIND'S ESSENTIAL INDEPENDENCE OF THE BODY.

We shall have occasion to see, hereafter, the mind's constituted dependence on the bodily senses, as instruments for acquiring knowledge. But after knowledge has entered the mind, the mind can operate without these instruments. In the last moments of life, in swoons and trances, when all the senses have been locked up as in death's cold embrace, and every avenue of bodily communication with the mind has been closed, the mind has realized its most intense activity; it has then enjoyed the most splendid visions; it has walked amidst the flowers of paradise; it has gazed upon the splendors, and drank the melodies, of brighter worlds than this. We have abundant testimony to numerous facts of this description, some of which will hereafter be given.

If it be replied that, in the cases supposed, the body was not actually *dead*, that does not affect our inference; for as to all power of communion with things visible and real, as an instrument of the spirit, it *was* dead. That bodily eye did not see, that ear did not hear, that hand did not feel. Yet brilliant visions passed before the mind, unearthly music poured upon it, and the most exquisite and intense joys were realized. The mind saw, but not with the bodily eye; it heard, but not with the bodily ear; it felt, but not with the bodily senses. It is thus evident that the mind can live, and assert all its glorious prerogatives, independently of the body.

PROOF FROM THE SACRED SCRIPTURES.

Having given some of the principal reasons, drawn from the light of nature, for believing the human mind immortal, it comports with our design to refer to the Sacred Scriptures for our final and positive proof. This source of proof is indeed of itself sufficient; but as philosophy is now our study, it is our duty to attend to her teachings. Having attended to these, it is both interesting and useful to observe how they harmonize with the higher and more luminous teachings of the divine word.

THE OLD TESTAMENT.

A state of existence and of everlasting rewards beyond the grave was revealed to the saints of the early ages; and it is expressly recorded, as a monument to their excellence, that they hence deduced their motives of action. "These all died *in faith*, not having received the promises, but having seen them afar off, and were persuaded of them, and embraced them, and confessed that they were strangers and pilgrims on the earth." "They desired a *better* country, even an heavenly; wherefore God was not ashamed to be called their God," — as if he would have been ashamed to own them as his heirs on any other condition than that of their recognizing their immortality, and acting in view of it.

THE NEW TESTAMENT.

Clearest of all is the revelation of our eternal existence, by JESUS CHRIST, "*who hath abolished death, and brought life and immortality to light through the gospel.*" Heathens obscurely dreamed it; philosophers argued it; Socrates, Plato, Cicero made it appear reasonable; Abraham, Moses, Job saw it as through a glass darkly, —but JESUS CHRIST BROUGHT IT TO LIGHT. The last cloud was dispersed, when an invisible hand rolled the stone from the door of the sepulchre, and the Conqueror ascended with triumph into the heavens. It was in the light thus shed upon the grave that the apostles labored and suffered reproach, declaring that for them to live was Christ, and to die, gain; and that they even desired to depart and be with Christ, which was far better than to abide in the flesh. Walking in the same light, all the truly good and noble of the earth, all the heroes and martyrs of the cross, all the friends of truth and righteousness, have ascended the shining path to higher worlds. To adduce isolated proofs from the Scriptures, were quite superfluous; for it is the acknowledged basis of its religion—the golden warp, into which are woven all its doctrines, precepts, motives, hopes. If Christianity be truth, the endless existence of man as a rational being is certain.

THE IMMORTALITY OF THE MIND A CHEERING TRUTH.

This view of the human mind, apart from moral considerations, disarms death of its terrors. We no longer fear that which kills the body, but has no power to kill the soul. We perceive the true dignity, value, and security of our existence; and, if true to our nature, we feel it in our hearts to rise above the caprices and disappointments of earth, and fasten our hopes in the skies. Assured that the dissolution of the body is but the freeing of the spirit from its prison of clay, that death to the righteous is but the passage to a higher and more congenial mode of life, we feel inspired with more than earthly desires, that this imperishable flame, which the breath of the Almighty has kindled, may burn brightly upwards towards the eternal throne, and mingle its incense with that of angelic beings.

How cheering to anticipate a state, in which *the light*

now freely shed by science will break forth into the full splendors of noonday! "While the mind rests, with a pleasing satisfaction, on these great deductions of philosophy, it yet pants for a fuller and higher revelation. If the man of clay has been honored with such magnificent apartments, and fed at such a luxurious table, may not his undying and reasoning soul count upon a spiritual palace, and sigh for that intellectual repast at which the Master of the feast is to disclose his secrets? In its rapid, continued expansion, the mind, conscious of its capacity for a higher sphere, feels even now that it is advancing to a goal more distant and more cheering than the tomb. Its energies increase and multiply under the encumbrance of age; and even when man's heart is turning into bone, and his joints into marble, his mind can soar to its highest flight, and seize with its firmest grasp. Nor do the affections plead less eloquently for a future home. Age is their season of warmth and genial emotion. The objects long and fondly clasped to our bosom have been removed by Him who gives, and who takes what he gives; and lingering in the valley of bleeding and of broken hearts, we yearn for that break of day which is to usher in the eternal morn — for the house of many mansions which is already prepared for us, and for the promised welcome to the threshold of the blest, where we shall meet again the loved and lost, and devote the eternity of our being to the service of its almighty Author." *

THE ETERNAL GROWTH OF THE MIND.

The immortality of the mind is a pledge of its *eternal progression.* All its powers increase in strength and compass by use, and, unless interfered with by bodily infirmity, this process continues to the end of life. The legitimate inference is, that, when no longer subject to interruptions from physical causes, it will steadily *grow forever.* We cannot avoid this inference, at least in regard to virtuous minds. The effect of moral virtue on

* North British Review.

all minds are health, vigor, progression. Shoot the eye, then, down the long track of ages, and behold that mind, now tabernacled in this body, if true to itself, comprehending more knowledge, more capacity for enjoyment, more actual felicity, than the aggregate of all these ever yet possessed by the human race. Let the ever-expanding circles of eternity continue to move round, and we at length reach the point where the attainments of that mind leave those which Gabriel has now made in almost sightless distance. This is what the sacred writers call *glory added to glory* — exceeding and yet exceeding forever — as the fruit of a life true to our immortality; an immortal mind, forever speeding its way on the wings of eternity TOWARDS THE INFINITE PERFECTIONS OF JEHOVAH.

QUESTIONS ON CHAPTER V.

Subject of this chapter? What renders it peculiarly interesting? Design of the chapter? Why do men doubt their immortality? How does it seem at first view? To what does a more philosophical observation lead? What has no man been able to prove? What is said of human ignorance on this subject? Suppose the mind *material* — what then? State the argument. Suppose the mind *pure spirit* — state the argument in this view. Does this prove the mind absolutely immortal? Why not? What *does* it prove? State the argument for the mind's *natural immortality*. Under what circumstances would it be conclusive? What does it prove as it stands? State what is said of us, when convinced that the death of the body does not destroy the mind. How is this question finally settled? How many revelations has God made to us? What is said of the *nature* of the human mind, &c.? What is said of man's ever throwing his thoughts, &c., into the future? What of desire for posthumous reputation? Nero and Washington? In what does the mind expatiate? State the substance of what is said here. State what is said respecting the idea of our immortality being *universal*. State the opinions of *pagan philosophers*. What is said of men in the *last moments* of life — in *swoons*, *trances*, &c.? Suppose it be said that the body, in these states, was not *dead*, what is the answer? State the proof from the OLD TESTAMENT. From the NEW TESTAMENT. Why is the mind's immortality a *cheering* truth? Of what is it a pledge? State the argument and inference.

6

CHAPTER VI.

ORIGIN OF HUMAN KNOWLEDGE.

It is an inquiry of much philosophical interest, how the human mind comes in possession of its *first knowledge.* Is the mind *created* with the elements or germs of knowledge *within it?* or is it created with only the *powers to acquire* knowledge? Are the elements of its earliest knowledge *innate* or *acquired?* This has been the great question of the schools.

Of the advocates for the doctrine of *innate ideas*, Plato among the ancients, and Descartes among the moderns, are eminent. The Kantian philosophy of Germany, and the transcendental speculations generally, are in some form favorable to this theory, and, in fact, more or less dependent upon it. Among the advocates for the theory that all our ideas are *acquired*, Aristotle among the ancients, and Locke among the moderns, are most prominent. Indeed, Locke has the honor to be the first who brought this theory into full symmetrical form, and impressed it on the convictions of a large part of the thinking world. After all the merciless attacks upon this dry philosopher, probably no name is to this day greater in mental science than John Locke.

THE THEORY OF INNATE IDEAS.

The theory of *innate ideas* is this: that the human mind is created with certain ideas or elements of knowledge *inherent in it*, as part of the mind itself, or at least as its concreated furniture. All minds are supposed to have original ideas, since, without some innate capital with which to commence, it is thought the mind could never obtain any knowledge whatever. Comparison is made between a human mind and a seed. The seed is the embryo of the future plant. The plant is but the development and growth of what was concreated with the seed and wrapped up in miniature within it. As the seed, when under the influence of the warm and moist earth, spontaneously germinates and puts forth the embryo plant within it, so the human mind, when subjected to appropriate influences, is supposed spontaneously to germinate and put forth into actual knowledge the ideas inherent in its nature.

ANSWER TO THE ABOVE.

The analogy fails in the *essential point*, and therefore furnishes no evidence. The human mind is an *intelligent spirit;* the plant is mere *animated matter.* Each has a nature unlike the other, and peculiar to itself. The mind is *active,* the plant is *passive.* The mind is a *living intellect,* and has therefore the power to *acquire* knowledge; the seed is *vitalized matter,* without intellect, and can, therefore, only be made to develop itself. To suppose that the mind *germinates* knowledge, instead of *acquiring* it, is to rob it of its distinguishing nature, and *reduce it to a kind of vegetable.*

THE THEORY OF LOCKE.

The theory of Locke is, that the human mind is created *without any ideas whatever;* that in this respect it resembles a sheet of white paper, on which nothing is written, but on which ideas of every description may be imprinted.* He maintains that our first knowledge is obtained in the form of simple ideas, through the senses; that by means of its reflecting powers, in the use of capi-

* Essay concerning Human Understanding, book ii. chap. i. sec. 2, p. 73. New York edition, 1818.

tal thus received and additions continually made through the senses, the mind gradually rises to its highest attainments. His theory is, then, briefly this, *that all our knowledge is obtained by* "SENSATION AND REFLECTION." This theory, with some modifications, is now generally received in Great Britain and America.

WHAT LOCKE MEANS BY "IDEA."

It was supposed by the ancient philosophers, that, as mind is so unlike matter, the former can hold no intercourse with the latter, without something between them acting as a kind of mediator. Hence the notion of an *image* or *species*, intervening between the organ of sense and the percipient mind. The mind was not supposed to perceive the *object itself*, but the *image* of it. This *image* was either innate, and the mind was only excited to notice it, or it was first introduced to the mind through the eye. The former was the theory of Plato; the latter of Locke. Neither pretends to tell us exactly what it *is*, but all agree to make it something resembling its object; as far removed from matter as possible, and yet not exactly spirit; since if it were supposed to be matter on the one hand, or spirit on the other, it might as well be dispensed with. This *something* the ancient schoolmen called a *phantasm*, *notion*, or *species*, and Locke called it an *idea*. "It being that term," he says, "which, I think, serves best to stand for whatsoever is the object of the understanding when a man thinks, I have used it to express whatever is meant by *phantasm*, *notion*, *species*, or whatever it is which the mind can be employed about in thinking." * It hence seems that Locke employed the term in accommodation to the usage of the schools; and whether he meant to indorse the then current speculations respecting an intervening *phantasm*, or only used a term of accommodation, meaning by *idea* what *we* do, is, perhaps, doubtful.†

* Essay concerning Human Understanding, vol. i. p. 28. New York edition, 1818.

† Cousin seems, on this point, to have misapprehended Locke, and done

If any insist that he *did* countenance the notion of a literal image, they still need not reject what is true in the teachings of the great philosopher because associated with a baseless speculation. This speculation he found in the schools; it was not originally his; nor were his inquiries directed to this point. It was the *origin, existence*, and *agency* of the idea, not the *matter* of it, that engaged his attention. That *something*, whatever it be, (and Locke did not undertake to tell what it is,) which we have in our minds when we have what we call an *idea* of an object, is what he undertakes to prove not innate. But the reader may be curious to know something respecting the speculations of the ancients on this subject.

VIEWS OF ARISTOTLE AND OTHERS.

"By Aristotle and the Peripatetics, the images presented to our senses were called *sensible species or forms;* those presented to the memory or imagination were called *phantasms;* and those presented to the intellect were called *intelligible species;* and they thought that there can be no perception, no imagination, no intellection, without species or phantasms. What the ancient philosophers called species, sensible and intelligible, and phantasms, in later times, and especially since the time of Des Cartes, came to be called by the common name of *ideas.*

"The Cartesians divided our ideas into three classes — those of *sensation*, of *imagination*, and of *pure intellection.* Of the objects of sensation and imagination, they thought the images are in the brain; but of objects that are incorporeal, the images are in the understanding, or pure intellect. Locke, taking the word *idea*, in the same sense as Des Cartes had done before him, to signify whatever is meant by phantasm, notion, or species, divides ideas into those of *sensation* and those of *reflec-*

him injustice. Fairly interpreted, Locke may be supposed to attach to the term *idea* essentially the same meaning that philosophers of this day do; hence the formidable artillery of Cousin is aimed at a man of straw. See Cousin's Psychology.

tion; meaning by the first, the ideas of all corporeal objects, whether perceived, remembered, or imagined; by the second, the ideas of the powers and operations of our minds." * It should be observed, that both the Platonists, who held to innate ideas, and the Peripatetics, who held that our ideas are obtained through the organs of sense, agree in this, that material objects act on the mind only through the medium of certain *forms* or *images* representing them.

THE NEXT STEP — MALEBRANCHE.

Father Malebranche seems to have become somewhat more refined and modern in his explanation of the matter. "I suppose," he says, "that every one will grant, that we perceive not external objects immediately and of themselves. We see the sun, the stars, and an infinity of objects without us; and it is not at all likely that, upon such occasions, the soul sallies out of the body, in order to be present to the objects perceived. She sees them not, therefore, by themselves; and the immediate object of the mind is not the thing perceived, but something which is intimately united to the soul; and it is that which I call an idea; so that, by the word *idea*, I understand nothing else but that which is nearest to the mind when we perceive any object. It ought to be carefully observed, that, in order to the mind's perceiving any object, it is absolutely necessary that the idea of that object be actually present to it. Of this it is not possible to doubt. The things which the soul perceives are of two kinds. They are either in the soul, or they are without the soul Those that are in the soul are its own thoughts; that is to say, all its different modifications, [operations.] The soul has no need of ideas for perceiving these things. But with regard to things without the soul, we cannot perceive them but by means of ideas." † Here the notion of intermediate forms, or images, is

* Reed's Works, vol. ii. p. 135. Charlestown edition, 1814.
† *Recherche de la Vérité*, p, 125.

partly relinquished — relinquished as related to inward perceptions; and it is further conceded, that, by the idea of an external object, nothing more is intended than that which is nearest to the mind when an object is perceived. This, it will be seen, is a considerable advance towards the more simple and satisfactory view which obtains at present.

THE PRESENT VIEW — REID.

The theory of an *image*, intervening between the mind and outward objects of perception, is now *wholly discarded.* The mind is believed to be so constituted as to hold direct intercourse with the material world through the senses. That mankind should have been some thousands of years in arriving at a fact so simple and obvious, can be acounted for only by their excessive fondness for explaining every thing, and their not having drawn the line of demarcation around the limits of human knowledge. The writer who has done most to brush away the cobwebs of the ancient metaphysics on this subject is THOMAS REID.* He proposes no theory of perception in place of that which he demolishes; in the spirit of sound philosophy, he leaves the *inexplicable* without attempting to explain it.

There is no need of supposing any *image* or *phantasm* between the mind and the object without. All we know on this subject is, that, when objects are presented to our organs of sense, certain *effects* or *changes* are produced in the mind, whereupon the mind *perceives* them.† Some things affect our senses, which cannot be perceived. There may be sensation without perception. Every true *idea* of an object, then, instead of being an *image* or *phantasm*, by means of which we *perceive* the object, or

* Thomas Brown denies to Reid the honor of originality in this matter; but after considerable examination, I am satisfied that he was the first to set the notion of an intervening image effectually aside. See Brown's Philosophy, vol. i. p. 256. The theory of an intervening image, or idea, was called "The *Ideal System.*"

† See Inquiries concerning the Intellectual Powers, &c., by John Abercrombie. Boston edition, 1845.

what the object is like, is the *result* of perception. The ancient metaphysicians put *effect* for *cause*. A man's *perceiving* an animal gives him a true *idea* of it; it is not his *idea* of it that enables him to *perceive* it. In other words, *perception gives the idea, not idea the perception.* This view sweeps entirely away *the supposed necessity for innate ideas.*

PRESENT STATE OF THE QUESTION RESPECTING THE ORIGIN OF KNOWLEDGE — LOCKE.

The question, whether our knowledge originates through the senses, is now considered of far less importance than it was formerly.* That *all* our knowledge is to be referred to the senses, according to the extreme doctrine of the sensuous philosophy, is a theory maintained by scarcely any of the present day. Locke himself, the great advocate of the sensuous philosophy, did not carry his doctrine to this extreme. His own account of the matter reads thus: "The other fountain, from which experience furnisheth the understanding with ideas, is the perception of the operations of our own minds within us, as they are employed about the ideas they have got; which operations, when the soul comes to reflect on and consider, do furnish the understanding with another set of ideas, which could not be had from things without; and such are perception, thinking, doubting, believing, reasoning, knowing, willing, and all the different actions of our own minds; which we, being conscious of, and observing in ourselves, do from these receive into our understandings as distinct ideas as we do from bodies affecting our senses. This source of ideas every man has wholly in himself; and though it be not sense, as having nothing to do with external objects, yet it is very like it, and might properly enough be termed internal sense. But as I call the other *sensation*, so I call this *reflection*, the ideas it affords being such only as the mind gets by reflecting on its own operations within

* See Stewart's Philosophy, book i. p. 61.

itself. By *reflection*, then, in the following part of this discourse, I would be understood to mean, that notice which the mind takes of its own operations, and the manner of them; by reason whereof there come to be *ideas* of these operations in the understanding. These two, I say, namely, external material things, as the objects of SENSATION, and the operations of our own minds within, as the objects of REFLECTION, are to me the only originals from whence all our *ideas* take their beginnings. The term *operations*, here, I use in a large sense, as comprehending not barely the actions of the mind about its *ideas*, but some sorts of *passions*, arising sometimes from them; such as is the satisfaction or uneasiness arising from any thought." *

OPINIONS OF SUBSEQUENT WRITERS.

The theory of Locke, as thus explained, has been admitted by subsequent philosophers of the Scotch and English schools to this day. THOMAS REID substantially admits it, while he strenuously resists the theory of intermediate images.† DUGALD STEWART, although opposed to the peculiar theory of causation and of ideal images, ascribed by some to Locke, and a decided advocate for spiritual efficiency independently of matter, yet yields the right to Locke on this point. "The amount of the doctrine," he says, "is nothing more than this: that the first occasions on which our various intellectual faculties are exercised, are furnished by the impressions made on our organs of sense, and, consequently, that, without these impressions, it would have been impossible for us to arrive at the knowledge of our faculties. Agreeably to this explanation of the doctrine, it may undoubtedly be said with plausibility, and I am inclined to believe with truth, that the occasions on which all our notions are formed, are furnished, either immediately or ultimately, by sense. But, if I am not much mistaken, this is not the meaning which is commonly annexed to

* Essay, book ii. chap. i. sec. 4, p. 74.
† Reid's Works, vol. ii. pp. 211, 345. Charlestown edition, 1814.

the doctrine, either by its advocates or their opponents. One thing at least is obvious, that, in this sense, it does not lead to those consequences which have interested one party of philosophers in its defence, and another in its refutation." * The "*consequences*" here referred to are its claimed alliance with materialism and tendencies to break down all distinction between men and brutes, excepting such as arises from difference of animal organization.

Thomas Brown, who seems to find pleasure in dealing severely, refusing much of the originality to Locke usually allowed him; denying to Reid all the credit of overthrowing the theory of ideal images; asserting that Des Cartes, Arnauld, Le Clerc, Hobbs, and many others meant and taught much the same as he did on this subject, and claiming to set up a new theory of cause and effect, yet gives his full assent to the doctrine of the sensuous origin of our first knowledge.† To the same intent, Professor Upham says, "Were it not for impressions on the senses, which may be traced to objects external to them, our mental capabilities, whatever they may be, would in all probability have remained folded up, and have never been redeemed from a state of fruitless inaction. Hence, the process which is implied in the perception of external things, or what is commonly termed by Mr. Locke *sensation*, may justly be considered the *occasion* or the introductory step to all our knowledge." ‡

CONCLUSION.

Having thus briefly surveyed the ancient and modern theories, in regard to the origin of human knowledge, the present writer may be allowed to state his own conclusion: The human mind is created *without any innate ideas whatever*. It bears no resemblance to things merely mechanical, chemical, vegetable, or animal; and all analogies drawn from them, to show the necessity of innate ideas, in order to a future development of knowledge, are

* Stewart's Philosophy, book i. pp. 61, 62. Boston edition, 1818.
† See Brown's Philosophy, vol. i. p. 267. Hallowell edition, 1842
‡ Upham's Philosophy, p. 121. New York edition, 1846.

utterly futile. The human mind is an *intellectual being*. A free, active, discerning spirit, it is created without any knowledge or any ideas, but with ample powers and capacities to *acquire* them. Human ideas are not *created* by God; they are the *result of mental activity*. As the mind is created, it has no ideas; the moment it acts, it begins to have them. As it is first addressed through the senses, its *first* ideas are of *sensuous origin*. By the agency of these, those powers *are* awakened by which the mind comes gradually into possession of other and higher ideas not derived from the senses. Beginning with sensuous and accidental ideas, it gradually ascends to the apprehension of spiritual, abstract, absolute, essential truths. It rises from the less to the greater; from the lower to the higher; from facts to principles. Hence, the beginning of all true knowledge is in humility.

But while it is admitted that *our* first ideas reach the mind through the organs of sense, it does not follow that *unembodied* minds may not receive, in other ways, all those ideas which *we* owe to sensation. Let us instance the case of *seeing*. The condition of the mind in the body may be compared to that of a person in a dark prison. Confined in that prison from his birth, he could have no idea of colors. Remove him from the prison, or let in a beam of light, and his mind instantly perceives them. That window which admits the light may be compared to the eye. If the mind were unembodied, the eye would be unnecessary. The same may be true of all ideas received through the organs of sense.* Unembodied spirits, and spirits disembodied before the organs of sense have served, or when they have been wanting, may be so constituted, for aught we know, as to receive all kinds of knowledge in a manner entirely independent of the body.

DIFFERENT KINDS OF IDEAS — COGNITION.

It is obvious that mere *ideas* are not tantamount to *knowledge*. An idea may be inadequate, confused, false,

* "If we could suppose the case of a man who had lived all his life in the

as well as adequate, clear, and true.* There is, indeed, a sense in which *every* idea is real. When a man is conscious of entertaining an idea, he actually *does* entertain that idea. His consciousness does not deceive him. But if the idea is inadequate, — that is, if the type does not correspond to the antitype, — it is properly called a *false* idea. When an idea is liable to be inadequate, or false, it is synonymous with *opinion, notion, conjecture*. When the idea is supposed to be exactly true, it is called *cognition*, or *knowledge*. *Idea* may imply *doubt; cognition* implies *complete conviction*. Hence, *idea* is a more *generic* term than cognition. *Idea* stands for *every* thing in the mind, however doubtful its object; whereas *cognition* is restricted to what is *known*. The reader is particularly requested to notice this distinction, as it will be hereafter referred to in an important connection.

SIMPLE AND COMPLEX IDEAS.

Another division of ideas is into SIMPLE and COMPLEX. *Simple* ideas imply a *single sensation* or *perception*. Thus, the idea of pain, quiet, fatigue; of hardness, softness, roundness; of sweet, sour, bitter; of length, breadth, height, &c., is a *simple* idea. All sensuous ideas, as they first enter the mind, are simple, and the mind is passive in receiving them.† These are *cognitions*. We all agree to rely upon the testimony of our senses; what they teach us, we think we *know*. If the ideas that I get of sweet, sour, bitter, are by *tasting* them; of black, blue, red, are by *seeing* them; of length, breadth, height, are by *feeling* them, &c., those ideas are *cognitions* — they are *actual knowledge*.

When simple ideas are contemplated as *united* in an object, they make a *complex* idea. It is hence obvious

dark, he certainly could not see, but we should not say that the admission of light imparted to him the power of vision; it only furnished the circumstances which gave occasion to the exercise of sight." — *Abercrombie's Inquiries concerning the Intellectual Powers*, p. 38. Boston edition, 1845.

* See Locke's Essay concerning Human Understanding, book ii. pp 261–284. New York edition, 1814.

† Locke's Essay, book ii. p. 113.

that all *abstract* ideas are *simple*, while *concrete* ideas may be either simple or complex, according as the object is viewed only as a unit, or as consisting of its parts or properties. The idea of a *tree*, considered as a *unit*, is a simple idea; but when the tree is contemplated with reference to the various *parts* and *properties*, the idea becomes *complex*. When I look upon a tree, the idea of it first enters my mind as a simple idea; subsequent analysis renders it complex. By analyzing the tree, I get many ideas out of one; I recombine them, and now the idea of the tree enters my mind complex. To the common mind, *water* is a simple idea. The object it denotes was for ages considered an *element*, even by men of science. To the chemist, who has analyzed and recombined its elements, it is now a complex idea. Hence, ideas may be either *absolutely* or *relatively* simple.* The mind not only analyzes relatively simple ideas into those absolutely simple, but it also combines absolutely simple ideas, received at first as such, into complex ones. There are, then, two ways which the mind takes with its simple ideas, received by sensation and reflection: first, the way of *analysis*, by which it resolves its relatively simple ideas into those absolutely simple; secondly, the way of *synthesis*, by which it combines its absolutely simple ideas into complex ones. Some philosophers would make the mind go only *from generals to particulars*; † others would make

* I use the terms *absolutely* and *relatively* merely for convenience. They must not be understood in the severest sense. In the present state of science, we do not always know what *is* really absolute. What one man supposes absolutely simple, another may know to be complex. The point most important here is this: that simple ideas, received by sensation and reflection, are the mind's *first* ideas — that all these are real *cognitions*, and that they are the materials or bases of all our future knowledge. "These simple *ideas*, the materials of all our knowledge, are suggested and furnished to the mind only by those two ways, namely, *sensation* and *reflection*." — *Locke's Essay*, vol. ii. p. 83.

† "It is not true that we begin by simple ideas, and then proceed to complex ideas. On the contrary, we begin with complex ideas, and from them proceed to more simple. The process of the mind, in the acquisition of ideas, is precisely the inverse of that which Locke assigns." — *Cousin*. See his Elements of Psychology, New York edition, 1838, p. 176. If Locke and some of his disciples have gone to one extreme, have not Cousin and his disciples gone to another?

it go only *from particulars to generals.* Both are wrong; for the mind goes *both* ways.

The apology for dwelling so long on a speculative, and, to most, uninteresting question, respecting the origin of our knowledge, is in the fact that it has occupied a very large space in philosophical disquisitions, and that ultra theorists, on each side, have pushed into infidelity. It is of the first moment in philosophy to start right; and, however dry the discussion of a fundamental principle, it is of the highest importance to the superstructure.

QUESTIONS ON CHAPTER VI.

What has been the great question of the schools? Who were the special advocates for the theory of *innate ideas?* Who for the opinion that all our ideas are acquired? State the theory of innate ideas. The comparison here made. Reply to it. The theory of Locke. What was supposed by the ancients? What is said of the *image* to which they held? What does Locke call it? What is said of the views of Aristotle and the Peripatetics? Those of Malebranche? What is now thought of the theory of an intervening image? How is the mind believed to be constituted? What is said of the credit due to Reid? How much do we know on this subject? What is said of the ancient metaphysicians? Remark. What is said of the extreme doctrine of the sensuous philosophy? What other writers, besides Locke, have rejected the theory of innate ideas? In conclusion, how is the human mind supposed to be created? To what does it bear no resemblance? What is said of human ideas? How soon does the mind begin to have ideas? Of what origin are its *first* ideas? To what does it gradually ascend? What is said of *unembodied* minds? Illustration. Are mere *ideas* tantamount to *knowledge*? What may be the character of an idea? In what sense is *every* idea true? When is an idea properly called *false?* When liable to be so, with what is it synonymous? What is an idea called when supposed true? What may *idea* imply? What does cognition imply? Inference. What do *simple* ideas imply? Examples. Why are these cognitions? What is a *complex* idea? What are all *abstract* ideas? When are concrete ideas *complex?* When simple? Illustrate. How many ways does the mind take with its simple ideas? Explain each. What apology for dwelling so long on this question?

PART II.

PRIMARY KNOWLEDGE.

CHAPTER I.

PRIMARY KNOWLEDGE OF TWO KINDS.

By *primary* knowledge, I mean that which we obtain without any reasoning process. It is received in the form of simple and direct cognitions.

This knowledge is of two kinds, *sensuous* and *rational*. Sensuous knowledge is that which we obtain by the *senses;* our primary *rational* knowledge is that which we obtain by direct *intuition* and *consciousness.*

Sensuous knowledge precedes rational. Constituted as we are, but for the agency of the senses we have no evidence that intuition and consciousness would ever teach us any thing. Hence *all* our knowledge may be said to *originate in sensation.*

The distinction between mere *ideas* and *knowledge* has been previously made. This must be kept in mind. We are now treating of the origin of *knowledge*, not mere *ideas.* It is only ideas of a *particular class* that imply *knowledge;* these are the ideas which relate to *entities* — that is, to things known actually to exist. In other words, they are *cognitions.* When I feel a pain, or smell a rose, or see an animal, or when I am conscious of loving, or perceive the truth of an axiom, I not only have *ideas* respecting these things, but I *know* them. The pain, the odor, the animal, the mental affection, the axiom become to me subjects of *actual knowledge.* An opinion, a conjecture, a suggestion is a *mere idea;* it does not amount to knowledge; but all ideas obtained by sensation, and by direct intuition and consciousness, are *actual cognitions,* and constitute our PRIMARY KNOWLEDGE.

THE SENSES.

The *senses* are *mental;* the *organs* of the senses are *corporeal.* The senses are no less truly *mental powers* * than *perception*, *abstraction*, &c., although they operate more directly through the physical organs. They are usually classed as follows: —

I. The Sense of Smell.
II. The Sense of Taste.
III. The Sense of Hearing.
IV. The Sense of Touch.
V. The Sense of Sight.

But there are senses which cannot be consistently classed with either of these. And for reasons which will hereafter appear, the following list is added: —

I. The Sense of Temperature.
II. The Sense of Weariness and Fatigue.
III. The Sense of Pleasure and Pain.
IV. The Sense of Appetite.

Some objects make themselves known to us only by *one* of the senses; hence, if the organ of that sense is wanting, the mind remains in ignorance of those objects. Other objects address us by *two*, *three*, or even *four* senses at once. Generally, those things most important

* Most writers use the terms *power* and *susceptibility* as nearly synonymous; but the *former* has more particular reference to its *consequent*, or *effect;* the *latter*, to its *antecedent*, or *cause*.

to be known address us by the greatest number of senses; so that, in the event of the failure of some of them, others may serve.

I. THE SENSE OF SMELL.

The organ of this sense is what physiologists call the *olfactory nerve*. It is situated in the nostrils and surrounding cells. It is in the place most favorable for the discharge of its office. Lying in cells at the bottom of cavities opening just above the mouth, it not only enables us to enjoy the odor along with the flavor of objects entering the mouth, but acts as a sentinel, to warn off or invite objects suitable or unsuitable to enter. It is an organ spread over considerable surface, and acting with every variety of acuteness and energy in different persons.

THIS SENSE OFTEN DEFECTIVE.

This is, on the whole, the least important of the senses, and perhaps more persons are destitute of it, or have it in an imperfect degree, than any of the others. The reasons why we are not better informed of the numerous instances in which this sense is wanting or defective, are to be found in the reluctance of most persons to expose a defect which it only requires silence to conceal, and in the fact that many, in whom this sense is defective, are not themselves aware of it. The action of this sense is suspended by slighter causes than that of any of the other senses. Even a common *cold* will often so derange it that it cannot discriminate between the most opposite odors.

KNOWLEDGE OF ODORS ONLY BY THE SENSE OF SMELL.

It is only by this sense that we obtain a knowlege of *odors*. From the surface of all bodies there is perpetually emanating minute odoriferous particles. When we inhale through the nose, these are drawn into the nostrils, and deposited on the surface of the olfactory nerve. Instantly thereupon arises the sensation of smell. Odors are of endless varieties; yet both science and common parlance have been very parsimonious in the gift of names to designate them. We apply to them only a few general terms, such as *spicy*, *sweet*, *agreeable*, *delicious*, *sour*, *offensive*, &c. To a man whose olfactory nerve is paralyzed, all objects smell alike; or, rather, they have *no smell at all.*

THE VARIETIES OF ODOR VERY GREAT.

Although the sense of smell is the least important, yet, in common with the other senses, it has a wide field, and is competent to explore it with a wonderful discrimination. A dealer in wines said he had handled more than ten thousand different qualities, each of which had an odor peculiar to itself. A person of very discriminating smell said that he had never found two roses, even on the same bush, that had precisely the same odor. It is often remarked, with some truth, that no two things *look* precisely alike; it is equally true, that no two things *smell* precisely alike. There is more reason for the differences in the latter than in the former case, since the invisible effluvia emanating from bodies may assume greater varieties of combination than the more gross substances which are obvious to the eye. The truth is, the sense of smell is perpetually treating us with an infinitude of odors, which we scarcely pause to notice. Let any person who has always enjoyed this sense be suddenly deprived of it, and he will be convinced that, although it yields the palm to the other senses, in parting with it he has lost an important measure of life's enjoyment.

II. THE SENSE OF TASTE.

The nervous *papillæ*, spread over the surface of the tongue and various parts of the mouth, constitute the *organ of taste*. In order that the sense may act, the body presented must be *moist*, so that the papillæ may absorb a portion of it. For this purpose the mouth is provided with *salivary glands*, which act, when a body is received into it, to furnish it with moisture. The more desirable the object, the more vigorously do these glands act. They commence acting as soon as the object is *anticipated*, to prepare the organs to receive it. Hence it is a common saying, that the thought of things delicious "makes the mouth water."

Other purposes are answered by the saliva, of which this is not the place to speak. So soon as the particles of the sapient body come in contact with the nervous papillæ, we are conscious of the sensation of *taste*. Tastes are *sweet*, *bitter*, *sour*, *pleasant*, *agreeable*, *disagreeable*, &c.

KNOWLEDGE OF FLAVORS OBTAINED ONLY BY THE TASTE.

As the sense of smell is usually considered a modification of that of taste, it has been supposed that by the former alone one may learn, with considerable accuracy, the *flavor* of objects. This supposition is strengthened by the fact that persons can usually tell, merely by smelling of an object, whether it is sweet, sour, bitter, agreeable, or disagreeable to the taste. But a little attention may convince us that this is the effect of association. It is because we have formed the *habit* of associating certain odors with certain flavors that we are often enabled to judge of the one by the other. A person deprived of the sense of taste from his birth could never, by the smell, tell how an object would taste. But having both smelt and tasted the same object, and thus having learned to associate the taste with the smell, the one henceforth suggests the other. A person *never* favored with the sense of taste could not form any idea of the flavor of a rose merely by smelling it.

TERMS HAVE DIFFERENT MEANINGS, AS APPLIED TO SMELL OR TASTE.

A sweet or sour *smell* is very different from a sweet or sour *taste*.

When we speak of a thing as smelling *sour*, we convey the idea of something *disagreeable*, *injured*, *offensive*. But many things that *taste* sour are in the highest state of *perfection and deliciousness*. Many things that *smell sour* are *sweet to the taste;* and many things that *smell sweet* are *sour to the taste*. The same thing may have a sour flavor and a sweet odor. A lemon has a sour flavor, but its odor is highly sweet and delicious.

Nor is this merely because the nostrils receive a greater proportion of the volatile aroma than the mouth. The nervous papillæ of the mouth cannot discriminate the aroma as the pituitary membrane of the nose can; neither can the organ of smell appreciate the acid as the organ of taste can. The fact is, there is something *peculiar* to each sense, by which it receives an idea *wholly its own*.*

THE TERMS APPLIED FIGURATIVELY.

On account of the poverty of language, we apply many of the *same terms* to the ideas communicated by these two senses. Common observation, however, leads us to discriminate in the use of them. The terms *sweet*, *sour*, *bitter*, belong primarily to the *taste*, and are applied to the smell only in a secondary and figurative sense. We seldom speak of a bitter smell; and when we do, we convey the idea of something offensive. But things bitter to the taste are often delicious. Not only the drinker, who loves his "bitters," but the epicure, would hardly

* "What is the generical distinction? Is it only that the nose is the organ of the one and the palate of the other? or, abstracting from the organ, is there not in the sensations themselves something common to smells, and something else common to tastes, whereby the one is distinguished from the other? It seems most probable that the latter is the case." — *Reid's Philosophy*, vol. i. p. 218.

consent to relinquish all bitter tastes. It is hence manifest that the sense of *smell* cannot teach us the *taste* of objects; and if this sense cannot, certainly neither of the others can.

THE SENSE OF TASTE SELDOM WANTING.

Next to the sense of feeling, *none is so seldom wanting as that of taste.* Indeed, it is believed that there never was a human being entirely destitute, from birth to manhood, of this sense. It is possessed in endless degrees and varieties by different persons, but all have it to some extent. This is a striking instance of the Creator's beneficent care; since, without this sense, even the taking of our needful nourishment would not only be attended with no pleasure, but would be through life a most odious and disgusting task. Persons are sometimes in a measure deprived of the use of this sense for a short season, during a fever or some affection of the gustatory organs, which arrests the healthful action of the salivary glands, or spreads a coat over the papillæ: the loss of enjoyment, yea, the positive suffering, resulting from the short interruption of this sense, reminds us how great must be the loss to be forever deprived of it.

NUMEROUS VARIETIES OF FLAVORS.

The amount, as well as importance, of the service performed by this sense is more apparent, if we consider the endless *varieties* of flavors. It is somewhere said of a celebrated cook, who had been in service fifty years, and had prepared on an average fifty dishes a day, that he never made two dishes of precisely the same flavor. We have no reason to doubt the remark. Here are a hundred and twenty-five thousand different flavors, furnished by only one person. What, then, must be the number of flavors furnished by all the cooks that ever lived! and what the number furnished from the great *kingdom of nature*, in all the endless departments of the animal and vegetable creations! If the term *infinite* may ever be applied to what is finite, it surely may be here.

THE TASTE COMPETENT TO ALL THESE VARIETIES.

But it may be said that, although the varieties of flavor are endless, our sense of taste is adequate only to a few of them. How, then, did we ascertain their existence? The fact that we know their existence is proof that our taste *has detected* them; for we could have become acquainted with them in no other way. The Being who made the flavors for the taste has adapted the taste to the flavors. There is no mistake, no blunder of calculation, in his work. No person has ever fully tested the capacities of the sense of taste. "The sensations both of smell and taste do undoubtedly admit of an immense variety of modifications, which no language can express. If a man were to examine five hundred different wines, he would hardly find two of them that had precisely the same taste: the same thing holds in cheese, and in many other things. Yet, of five hundred different tastes in cheese or wine, we can hardly describe twenty, so as to give a distinct notion of them to one who has not tasted them." *

Now, if our sense of taste can detect five hundred varieties in a single kind, what must we say of it as employed upon *all* kinds of things, and all their possible combinations? The truth is, our sense of taste is constantly employed upon myriads of flavors, and yielding us their enjoyment, for which we have no names, and of which we do not pause to think.

III. THE SENSE OF HEARING.

The organ of this sense is the *ear*. There are two apparatuses for the service of this sense, as there are also for the sight and smell, that, in case the one fails, the

* Reid's Philosophy, vol. i. p. 219.

other may serve. The ear, like the other organs of sense, is situated in the place most favorable for discharging its office. Standing, as a watch at his post, on either side of the head, it receives the vibrations of the air from all directions, and conveys them to the auditory nerves. The external ear presents a large hollow surface, leading through gentle windings, carefully adapted to transmit the atmospheric undulations. These at last beat upon the drum or tympanum, at the bottom of the ear. The tympanum is a thin membrane, drawn over the orifice leading inward, after the manner of the skin or head of a drum. On the inside of this is spread out a delicate mesh of nerves, communicating with the sensorium. So soon as the vibrating atmosphere beats upon this drum, there arises in the mind the sensation of hearing.

THE KNOWLEDGE OF SOUNDS WHOLLY DUE TO THIS SENSE.

A person deaf from his birth can have no knowledge of *sounds*. The sense of touch is auxiliary to that of hearing, but cannot specifically supply its place. It has been said above, that sound is produced by certain vibratory motions of the air acting upon the drum of the ear. Musical vibrations, as of the harp, viol, flute, organ, can be recognized by the *hand*. In the case of heavy tones, as of the organ, they can be felt through our feet and our whole frame. A deaf person may thus tell when fine and when coarse vibrations are produced, and even when chords and discords are made.

But this does not amount to a knowledge of the *sounds*. The *vibrations* are one thing, the *sounds* another. A knowledge of the former does not imply a knowledge of the latter. Harmonious and discordant vibrations, as well as fine and coarse ones, produce their appropriate effects on the general sense of *feeling*. They are *felt*, not *heard;* and there is the same difference here as between feeling the raised alphabet and hearing the words spoken.

OBJECTION TO THIS VIEW.

It is objected to this view, that deaf persons not only tell where sounds are made, and discriminate nicely between chords and discords, but they actually receive exquisite pleasure and pain therefrom, which could not be, unless they have some perception of them. The inference is inevitable, if the premise be granted. But it is *not* granted. The deaf persons in question do not discriminate between those *sounds* which we denominate *chords* and *discords*. It is only between the *vibrations*, which, to those who have the sense of hearing, produce chords and discords, that they discriminate, and from *these* that "they actually receive exquisite pleasure and pain."

The sense of feeling is implied in that of hearing, and the one has by some been regarded as a modification of the other. In this view, hearing is a kind of inward feeling. Hence certain vibratory motions — such as produce chords — felt through the frame may give feelings of pleasure; and certain other vibratory motions — such as produce discords — felt through the frame may give feelings of pain — such feelings as are occasioned by accordant and discordant sounds. Hence deaf persons may have exquisite pleasure from those vibrations which produce harmonious sounds, and pain from those which produce discords, and yet have no knowledge of the *sounds themselves*. There is no sense, but that whose organ is located in the drum of the ear, that can convey to the mind a specific knowledge of sound.

THIS VIEW SUSTAINED BY FACTS.

We have evidence sustaining the view here taken, in the case of persons *deaf from their birth*, to whom hearing has been restored. Mention is made in a German medical work of the case of a deaf child twelve years old, to whom hearing was restored by the removal of obstructions in the ear. The lively pleasure and pain which she had felt at the performance of good and bad music, and the nice discriminations she had made between chords and discords, had induced herself and others to suppose that she had the same perception of sounds in common with her more favored friends. Having been well educated, she had written about musical sounds, chords and discords, good and bad musical performances, as things of which she knew as much as others. But when hearing was restored to her, she asserted that she had never before had any thing like a *true idea of sounds.* She had had *an idea* of them, but not a *true* idea — not a *knowledge* of them. Other similar instances are on record.

ONLY KNOWLEDGE OF SOUNDS BY THIS SENSE.

The *only* office which the ear can claim *is that of being a vehicle of sounds.* All other sensuous knowledge comes through one or more of the other senses. It would seem from this that the sense in question is not very important; and indeed it may better be dispensed with than some of the others. Still its office will not appear insignificant, if we consider the great number and variety of sounds of which the ear is the organ, and their vast importance to the improvement and happiness of mankind.

NUMBER AND VARIETY OF SOUNDS.

The following remarks are so much to my purpose, that I am induced to insert them at length: "The ear is capable of perceiving four or five hundred variations of tone in sound, and probably as many different degrees of strength; by combining these, we have above twenty thousand simple sounds, that differ either in tone or strength, supposing every one to be perfect. But it is to be observed, that, to make a perfect tone, a great many undulations of elastic air are required, which must all be of equal duration and extent, and follow one another with perfect regularity; and each undulation must be made up of the advance and recoil of innumerable particles of elastic air, whose motions are all uniform in direction, force, and time. Hence we may easily conceive a prodigious variety on the same tone, arising from irregularities of it, occasioned by the constitution, figure, situation, or manner of striking the sonorous body; from the constitution of the elastic medium, or its being disturbed by other motions; and from the constitution of the ear itself upon which the impression is made.

"A flute, a violin, a hautboy, and a French horn may all sound the same tone, and be easily distinguishable. Nay, if twenty human voices sound the same note, and with equal strength, there will be some difference. The same voice, while it retains its proper distinctions, may yet be varied many ways by sickness or health, youth or age, leanness or fatness, good or bad humor. The same words spoken by foreigners and natives, nay, by persons of different provinces of the same nation, may be distinguished." *

A certain writer on ornithology speaks of a single bird that gives utterance to *more than two hundred distinct modulations.* Now, when we think of the myriad voices filling the air around us, each of which has its own peculiarities and its almost endless varieties of tone, all of which become such to the mind by the sense of hearing, the office of that sense appears no sinecure.

ENDLESS VARIETY OF HUMAN TONES.

Every human being has a tone *peculiar to himself*, as is evident by his being known by his voice. Even though he speak or sing on the same *key* with another, yet his voice is different. Now, if each individual of the eight hundred millions of human beings could only raise the eight notes, we should have sixty-four hundred millions of tones, of all which the ear is competent to take

* Reid's Works, vol. i. p. 220.

cognizance. The varieties of sound * in the human *language*, as read and spoken by mankind, baffle all enumeration.

In some respects, the sense of hearing seems to bring us nearer the spirit world than either of the others. So refined and elevated are the charms of music, that divine inspiration has through it largely symbolized the enjoyments of the heavenly state.

* The terms *sound, tone, modulation*, are of course here used merely to indicate those atmospheric vibrations which, to those who have the sense of hearing, *occasion* or *produce* sound.

QUESTIONS ON CHAPTER I.

What is the distinction between primary and acquired knowledge? How many kinds of primary knowledge? Define each. What is the *origin* of all our knowledge? Repeat the distinction between mere *ideas* and *knowledge*. What are *entities?* Illustrations. What are *cognitions?* To which do the senses pertain, the *mind* or the *body?* Name the senses, as usually classed. What senses are here added? What is said of objects being recognized by one or more senses? What is the *first* sense noticed? Its organ? Describe it. What is said of the frequent defectiveness and relative importance of this sense? What knowledge is obtained only by this sense? What is said of odors? Their varieties? Illustrations? Define the organ of *Taste*. What is necessary in order that the organ may act? What provision for this purpose? What are the qualities of taste? What knowledge is obtained only by taste? What is said on this point? What illustrations of terms having different meanings, as applied to smell or taste? Is the sense of smell often wanting? What is mentioned as a striking instance of the Creator's care? What is said of the *varieties* of flavors? Of the competency of taste to recognize them? Illustrations? What is the organ of *Hearing?* Describe. What knowledge is wholly due to this sense? How is it shown that a knowledge of sounds cannot be obtained by the sense of touch? Objections to this view? How answered? What *facts* sustain it. How many offices does the ear perform? What is said of the number and variety of sounds? Of *human* tones? In what respect does the sense of hearing seem to bring us near the spirit world?

CHAPTER II.

IV. THE SENSE OF TOUCH.

The organ of this sense is extended over the *entire surface of the nervous system.* In this respect, it differs from the senses hitherto noticed, whose organs are restricted to a small compass. It not only spreads over the outer surface of the body, but it is, to some extent, diffused over the internal cavities, particularly those of the mouth, ears, nostrils. But physiologists assign its most special seat to the *hand*, on account of the peculiar adaptation of its form, joints, flexibility, and delicate nerves to the purpose of *touching*. The *fingers* are by far the most discriminating and important organs of touch.

THIS SENSE NOT IDENTICAL WITH THAT OF TEMPERATURE.

It seems to me that the philosophy of Reid and Brown, on this point, is incorrect.* They identify the sense of *touch* with that of *temperature.* Now, is there not as much difference between the *touch* and the temperature of an apple, as between the *taste* and the temperature of it? We do not *touch* heat and cold. We touch bodies which *have* heat and cold; it is only the *bodies* that we *touch;* the heat and cold we *feel.* True, we feel when we touch; and so we feel when we taste. But

* Reid's Works, vol. i. p. 226. Brown's Philosophy, vol. i. p. 212. Professor Upham copies from Reid, and adopts his error.

yet, feeling and tasting are not the same. The way in which Reid came to make the mistake was probably this: When we touch a body, we not only have the sensation of touch, but also that of heat or cold, if the body is in a state to produce it. This led him to refer the latter sensation to touch, especially as in his analysis he had no other sense to which to refer it. Brown seems to have adopted Reid's analysis, without stopping to inquire whether it was correct.

We may with as much propriety speak of *tasting* heat as of *touching* it: our sense of temperature is as specific and marked as our sense of taste, and both are equally distinct from that of touch. The sensation of *feeling* is *generic;* it does not pertain exclusively to any one sense.* We feel, when we taste, when we touch, when we smell, when we see. The sensation of feeling, like life itself, is all-pervading. It of course relates to touch, as well as to the other senses. But we may have the sensation of touch without that of temperature; so also we may have the sensation of temperature without that of touch. These are entirely distinct. I hence infer distinct senses.

RESISTANCE LEARNED BY TOUCH.

The first idea obtained by touch is that of *resistance.* We thus learn that there is really something *without* us. The eye could not of itself teach us this, since it is only as assured by the touch we can be certain that what

* Reid endeavors to clear his way by reference to primary and secondary qualities of matter. This distinction was first held by Democritus, Epicurus, and their followers. Aristotle, and all the pupils of the Peripatetic school, discarded it. It was again revived by Des Cartes, Malebranche, and Locke. The Bishop of Cloyne again abolished it. Reid called it again from its ashes, declaring that it had a foundation in the principles of our nature.

The primary qualities of matter are such as are essential to its existence, such as extension, gravity, &c. The secondary qualities are accidental, such as temperature, taste, &c. It is merely the distinction between the *essential* and the *accidental.* But we have specific senses to teach us the *accidental* as well as the *essential* properties of matter; for instance, those of taste and smell. Hence, to dispense with the sense of temperature because we feel when we touch, and because heat and cold are subjects of feeling, is unphilosophical.

appears to the eye is not illusive. One of the first movements of the infant in pursuit of knowledge is to thrust out his hand to what he sees, to ascertain whether or not it is a material object. The touch satisfies him; he is then no longer in doubt.

Something more than mere contact is necessary to produce the sensation of touch. Sensations of temperature, of taste, of smell, &c., may be produced by mere *contact;* but sensations of *touch* imply *resistance.* Moderate pressure, united with gentle motion, affords the the most accurate sensation of touch.

MAGNITUDE, FORM, DISTANCE, LEARNED BY TOUCH.

Not only does the touch teach us that there *is* an external world,* but also the exact *size*, *form*, and *distance* of its various objects. The eye is pupil to the hand, until the hand has taught it to measure; it then learns with vastly more rapidity, but never with so much accuracy, as its teacher. The sense of touch enables us to correct any misconceptions by sight. After the eye has been taught, it measures the height, length, breadth of an object at a glance; but it is not until the slower process of measurement by the touch has been made that we are sure of its precise accuracy. An object seems to the eye near or distant; but we must ultimately depend on the touch to tell exactly *how* near or distant it is. A blind person can perform all measurements of accessible objects, with perfect accuracy, by the sense of touch; but without this sense, a man with the best of eyes could not do it.†

* It is not meant here that infant children have to experiment with the hand before they know there is an external world. They have proof enough of this by other modes of touch, to which they are subject, before they are able to perform such experiments. What is meant is simply this: it is only as objects without us are actually *touched* by us, in some manner and at some period, that we come to the knowledge of an external world. Yet Reid doubts whether we come by this knowledge thus, because we have it at *so early a period!* We should like to ask him how old the infant is before it *touches* any thing. See Reid's Works, vol. i. p. 243–5.

† Reid (vol. i. p. 241) supposes the case of a blind man, with all his

The same is true of *forms*. The eye *guesses*, the touch *knows*, whether an object is square, angular, round, rough, or smooth.

HARDNESS AND SOFTNESS LEARNED BY TOUCH.

Hardness and softness are *relative terms*, about which philosophers speculate; we are only concerned with their obvious import. Taught by the hand to regard certain objects as soft, the eye may ordinarily decide upon them, but it is sometimes deceived. Induced by the eye to suppose the golden orange mellow, the eager man puts forth his hand to grasp it, when it is proved to be made of stone. As he is walking in the silvery light of the moon, his eye tells him that the smooth surface before him is rock; he plants his foot boldly down, and plunges it in mire. So much for trusting his eye. Had he first *touched*, he would have prevented the disaster.

The pressure and motion being given, the hardness of a body is in *proportion to its resistance*. The greater the resistance, the greater the hardness. We thus learn the precise hardness or softness of all bodies subjected to this sense.

V. THE SENSE OF SIGHT.

The organ of this sense is the *eye*. This is an instrument carefully constructed on the scientific principles of the telescope. Rays of light, coming from a luminous object, enter the eye through a small opening called the

limbs tied, experimented upon by the prick of a pin, then by a blunter instrument, then by the pressure of a larger body, and, finally, by having the edge of something drawn over him, to teach him the extension of bodies, but all in vain. He concludes, therefore, that extension and other primary qualities of bodies are not first learned by the touch.

This is ridiculous, utterly unlike the strong good sense usually exhibited by this writer. Let the blind man have his *tools*. If we tell him to measure the length of a board, or the distance to the market, by the touch, let us not tie up his hands and feet. Assuming the breadth of his hand, or an artificial rule, he by it measures off the length of the board. Here is the touch mechanically applied. It would be quite another affair to have the board drawn over him. Having determined the length of his board, he can by it measure the distance to market.

pupil. They thence proceed through the crystalline and aqueous humors of the ball, which serve as a lens to gather them to a focal point, whence they diverge and present an inverted image of the object upon the *retina.* The retina is a delicate expansion of the optic nerve, covering the entire posterior part of the internal globe of the eye, in the right place to receive the image. The instant the image of the object falls upon the retina, there arises in the mind the sensation of sight. Here is the extent of human knowledge on this subject. We can trace the rays of light to the optic nerve. If that nerve is perfect, and the image of the object is perfectly formed upon it, the mind can see; if either the nerve or the image is wanting, the mind does not see. Here is certainly the relation of antecedent and consequent; but whether the one is really the *cause* of the other, or what the nature of the connection is, man has never known.

Around the pupil is a circular-colored portion of the eye, called the *iris*, because it resembles the rainbow. The color seems especially designed to minister to beauty and expressiveness; but other important purposes are served. The iris is made capable of contracting and enlarging on its interior boundary, so as to diminish or expand the opening it surrounds, according to the intensity of light. When the light is feeble, the iris and pupil expand; as the light becomes intense, they contract; an interesting illustration of divine wisdom and goodness, since, without this arrangement, the transition from feeble to intense light would destroy the delicate organ. For further protection, the pupil and iris are overspread with a firm transparent covering, called the *cornea.*

KNOWLEDGE OF COLORS ONLY BY THE EYE.

A person blind from his birth has no true idea of colors. An amusing proof of this is given by Locke. A blind man flattered himself that he had at last arrived at a knowledge of colors; on being asked to define *red*, he said it was like the *sound of a trumpet.*

It is evident that a person with only four external senses must liken an object, which can be perceived only through the wanting sense, to something perceptible through one of these four. Hence a man without eyes must liken colors to something touched, heard, tasted, or smelled. Now *red* is a *sharp* color. It is not only so to the *eye*, but to the *touch;* so that blind persons have sometimes distinguished it by this sense alone. The delicate touch of the hand, as well as the eye, discriminates between the harshness of red and the softness of blue. So that, in one respect, scarlet *is* like the sound of a trumpet. The blind man was right; still he had no just idea of colors.

KNOWLEDGE OF COLORS ALL THAT THE EYE ORIGINALLY GIVES US.

The sight receives credit, with most people, for giving us knowledge due to the touch and other senses. In strict accuracy, the knowledge of colors is *all* that the eye originally gives us. These colors pertain to light. The eye is an instrument adapted to analyze and separate these colors, and to exhibit them on the retina for the mind's perception. A red body is a body suited to reflect those rays upon the retina, which give the peculiar perception of red. The same is true of bodies of every elementary color and of all possible combinations of colors.

Although the colors are not in the bodies, but in the light, — the medium through which they are seen, — yet, as they *appear* to be in the bodies, popular usage places them there. As to the speculation, whether they are really in the light, or whether certain rays have only the power to *produce certain perceptions* of color, — in other words, whether there is really any such thing as *colors*, except as they exist in our own minds, — it is left for the idealist and the realist to settle as they please. *That something* which we *call* color, whatever it be, it is the *prerogative of the* eye *alone to make known* to us.

FIGURE NOT LEARNED BY SIGHT.

All that the eye gives us is a variety of light and shade, as presented in the different colors. Of this every person has proof, in the numerous deceptions practised upon him. Who that has seen the human form rise under the hand of the painter, that has seen large cities and magnificent landscapes stand in bold relief, in all their endless forms, upon the plane surface of the canvas, can doubt this? By the various combinations of light and shade, a plane surface may be made to exhibit to the eye every possible form of elevations and depressions; of squares, spheres, pyramids, and figures of all descriptions. Hence we cannot obtain our original knowledge of figures by the mere sight.

DISTANCE NOT LEARNED BY SIGHT.

Every man has proof of this, in the mistakes he makes when he trusts his sight alone to teach him distances. It is not until the eye has been *educated*, under the admonition of other senses, that it can convey to the mind any idea whatever of the distance of a perceived object. Every object seems equally near to it, and indeed actually present, until the infant puts forth his hand to correct the mistake. Blind persons, when first restored to sight, have no idea of distance, but regard all objects viewed as in contact with their eyes.

MAGNITUDE NOT LEARNED BY SIGHT.

This follows from what has been said. The apparent magnitude of an object depends upon its distance; if, then, the eye cannot tell its distance, it cannot tell its magnitude. A ball six feet in diameter, upon the spire of a lofty steeple, may seem to the eye only six *inches* in diameter; nor is it until the distance of the object is known, and a calculation made, that a correct judgment of its real size can be formed.

The apparent magnitude of an object depends also upon the *relative size of things around it.* Dr. Abercrombie remarks, that, as he was once passing the door of St. Paul's Cathedral, several persons were standing in it, who "appeared to be very little children; but on approaching them, they were found to be full-grown persons. In the mental process which had taken place, the door had been assumed as the known magnitude, and the other objects judged of by it. Had he attended to the door's being much larger than any door that one is in the habit of seeing, the mind would have made allowance for the apparent size of the persons; and, on the other hand, had these been known to be full-grown persons, a judgment would have been formed of the size of the door." * A man a little below the ordinary stature seems a pygmy, when standing by the side of a very large man; under other circumstances, there is nothing in his stature to attract attention.

All men have noticed that the apparent size of objects is varied, also, by their being *near the horizon*, or *high in the heavens;* (instance the sun and moon;) by their being over land or over water; by the state of the atmosphere; and by other accidental causes sufficiently obvious. It is hence manifest that *the size of objects is not originally determined by the eye.*

EDUCATION OF THIS SENSE.

No one sense is so dependent on the others as that of sight; no other sense requires so much discipline before it learns to tell the truth. And we may add, after it has been well educated, it immeasurably transcends all the others, in the rapidity, magnificence, and glory of its revelations. It is for the eye to take up and rapidly carry out, on a large scale, ideas introduced to the mind by a slower process. A person blind from his birth could

* Abercrombie's Philosophy, p. 45. Boston edition.

have nothing like an adequate conception of the vast heights, distances, and endlessly variegated forms presented to the eye of man by an extended landscape. The gigantic hills and snow-clad mountains, the great rivers and rolling seas, the glorious arch of heaven, the great world of wonders, bursting on the vision at a glance, can never fully enter the mind through the slow and limited sense of touch.

MOST OBJECTS ADDRESS THE MIND THROUGH SEVERAL SENSES.

A benevolent Providence has made the objects most essential to our being and happiness address us by most of the senses. Food, drink, &c., are of this description. Take a peach. It first addresses us through the *eye*. Having admired the beauty of its form and colors, we apply the *touch*, and are pleased with its mellowness. We are next delighted with its agreeable *fragrance*, and sometimes linger long in these preliminary enjoyments, before proceeding to the consummation. We at last apply the *taste*, and thus put in requisition *four* of the external senses, to extract from the little peach the full amount of pleasure which it proffers.

COMPENSATION.

There is a kindly *compensatory office* performed by the senses for each other, which greatly alleviates the affliction resulting from the loss of any one or more of them. The blind man converts into eyes the ends of his fingers. As he cannot *see* the forms of letters, he is enabled to *feel* them. Guided by the touch, he is able to perfect himself in many of the useful and elegant arts where others depend mostly upon the *sight*.

The *ear*, too, becomes a substitute for the eye. A blind man will often tell, by the *tread*, who enters the room, as accurately as the man who sees. If he passes a post, a house, a fence, the change of atmospheric vibrations admonishes him of the object he is passing. It is generally remarked, that, when one of the senses is wanting, the others become more acute. The senses of touch and hearing, in blind persons, are usually very keen. The sight, in deaf mutes, is wont to be remarkably quick and discriminating. They will read a man's language on his lips. The explanation is, that the mind *concentrates* its energies on its remaining instruments, when some of them are removed, and that more care is bestowed upon their education.

QUESTIONS ON CHAPTER II.

Where is the organ of the sense of *Touch* situated? With what do Reid and Brown identify this sense? How does it appear that they are incorrect? What is said in the note of Reid's views? What is the first idea obtained by touch? What do we thus learn? How illustrated? What *other particulars* are learned by touch? To what is the eye pupil? What is said of the eye after being taught by the hand? Of a blind person? Give Reid's supposition in the note and the reply. How do we learn the qualities of *hardness* and *softness?* What is said on this point? What is the organ of *Sight?* Define its nature and operation. The *retina?* How far does our knowledge on this point extend? What relation is here clearly traced? Describe the nature and uses of the *iris.* With what are the pupil and iris covered? What knowledge do we obtain only by the eye? Give the anecdote from Locke, and remarks upon it. In strict accuracy, what is the *only* knowledge that the eye gives us? To what do colors pertain? To what, as an instrument, is the eye adapted? How does it appear that *figure* is not learned by sight? How that *distance* is not? *Magnitude?* What is said of the *education* of this sense? After it has been educated? What arrangement of Providence respecting objects addressing the mind through several senses? Give the example. What is said of compensation? Give the illustrations.

CHAPTER III.

ADDITIONAL SENSES.

I. THE SENSE OF TEMPERATURE.

THAT we have a sense of *temperature*, or, in other words, that there is a *specific provision in our mental constitution for the affections which we denominate sensations of heat and cold*, seems as certain as that we have a sense of *smell*. It is equally as specific and determinate, and the sensations to which it gives rise are subjects of as distinct consciousness. The organ of this sense seems to pervade the entire membranous and nervous system. Without it, the coldest blasts of February and the hottest breath of August would be to us the same. We should experience no other sensations from drinking hot water than from drinking cold, excepting what might result from injuries done to our organs. The burning of a fever and the chill of death, considered as physical phenomena, would be by the mind alike unnoticed.

II. THE SENSE OF WEARINESS AND FATIGUE.

Weariness and fatigue, *being counterparts to each other*, may be considered, like the sensations of heat and cold, as *referable to one and the same sense*. *Weariness* arises from *inaction*, *fatigue* from *labor*. Hence weariness is attended with *desire of action;* fatigue, with *desire of rest*. The organ of this sense, like that of temperature, seems to pervade the entire muscular and nervous system. A sensation of weariness may be realized *through the whole body*, when the whole body has been in a state of inaction; a sensation of fatigue may be more particularly realized *in particular members*, as the arms, feet, legs, eyes, when these members have been particularly overworked.

Men accustomed to labor are most liable to weariness from inaction; men accustomed to inaction are most liable to fatigue from labor. Were it not for this sense, we should be both without the means of judging whether we have reached or passed the due measure of bodily exertion, and without any admonition to prompt us to that measure of exercise and of rest which our well being demands.

If any object to assigning to this sense a specific existence in the mental constitution, I would ask, What shall we do with it? Are we conscious of this class of sensations? Yes. Are they of sufficient importance to deserve notice? Certainly. Do all sensations imply a sense? As truly as any mental act implies a power to that act. To what, then, shall we refer the sensations in question? To the sense of *smell?* We do not *smell* weariness and fatigue. *Taste?* We do not *taste* them. Touch? We do not *touch* them. Sight? We do not *see* them. Hearing? We do not *hear* them. Temperature? They are neither *hot*, *cold*, nor *lukewarm*. We must, then, refer them to a specific sense. The mind is *so constituted*, that, in certain states of the body, sensations of this class are realized, as truly and determinately as, in other states of it, are those of smell or of hearing.

III. THE SENSE OF PLEASURE AND PAIN.

These also, being counterparts, may be referred to the same sense. It may be questioned, whether we have any distinct sense of pleasure and pain, or whether these sensations are not referable to the individual or combined action of the other senses. The former seems the more philosophical supposition. All will admit that the *pleasure* we realize in smelling a rose is a different thing from the *sensation of smell*. The smell is one thing, the pleasure is another; yet both are sensations. The term *sensual pleasure*, as distinguished from purely mental pleasure, conveys a distinct idea to all minds.

The calm and continued pleasure — so constant that we scarcely notice it, except when interrupted — arising from a state of health and the free and full play of all the bodily functions, and the painful uneasiness resulting from a state of debility or disease, are sensations too marked not to be referred to a specific source. Who can reasonably doubt that there is a specific provision in the mental constitution for these sensations?

What has been said of pleasure is equally true of pain. The *smell* of a disagreeable odor is one thing, the *pain* attending that smell another; yet both are real sensations. Both afford us distinct cognitions. "To experience those states of the bodily organs which are adapted to produce pain is one thing, and to experience pain another; the former is continued during certain periods, the latter occasional or remitted. What is generally considered continual pain consists usually of a series of painful sensations, more or less protracted, and separated from each other by longer or shorter intervals of repose or relief from the occurrence of other mental exercises." *

It is the obvious design of pain to admonish us of something wrong in our system, and incite us to correct it, and to avoid its recurrence. In this view, the sense of pain, as well as of pleasure, is a great blessing.

It is perhaps unnecessary to add, that all *kinds* and *degrees* of the sensations of pleasure and of pain, which we receive through the body, are referable to this sense. Whether, then, it is of sufficient importance to deserve a name and a place, let humanity, in the multitude of her pleasures and pains, judge.

* Critical Exposition of Mental Philosophy, by Leicester A. Sawyer. New Haven edition, 1839.

IV. THE SENSE OF APPETITE.

By the sense of *appetite*, I designate that in our constitution which gives rise to *hunger*, *thirst*, and *sexual desire.* For popular convenience, we speak of *thirsting* for water and of *hungering* for food; but both hunger and thirst, as also the other instinctive desires or cravings of nature, now considered, are referable to the same generic sense of appetite. This sense is variously developed at different periods of growth, according to the demand for it.

To those who may object to there being a particular sense of appetite, and who would refer all appetite to ordinary sensations of pain seeking relief, I would say, Is not that uneasiness which occasions desire for food, drink, &c., *unlike any other?* Do not all other uneasy or painful sensations tend to *destroy* this desire? The pain (if so they choose to call that which I call *appetite*) which gives rise to this desire implies a *natural* and *healthy* state; all other pain implies an *unnatural* and *diseased* state. The latter directly *destroys*, the former directly *produces*, the desire in question. The one belongs to man in *innocence* and *soundness;* the other pertains to him in *sinfulness* and *disease.* I infer, therefore, a *specific provision in our constitution* for the sensations in question. In other words, that we have a *sense of appetite*, which is as truly a part of our original constitution as the sense of smell or of taste. The importance of this sense is certainly not inferior to that of any pertaining to our system.

"The ultimate purpose of the sensations connected with the appetites is evidently the voluntary preservation of life, and the continuance and multiplication of the different orders of voluntary beings. They serve as the exciting causes of desires and actions, which are necessary to the attainment of these ends, and are an essential part of the nature of all voluntary beings. Man is not alone in the exercise of them. All the other tribes of voluntary beings which are subject to his dominion, or divide with him the empire of the world, are capable of similar exercises." *

* Sawyer's Mental Philosophy, p. 30.

Before leaving the consideration of the additional senses noticed in this chapter, I would remark, that the various sensations to which they give rise furnish us with a vast fund of primary knowledge; that they minister largely to our enjoyment or our suffering, according as they are rightly used or abused; and that they are the occasions of *numerous desires and aversions*, from which spring those affections and volitions which are the subject matter of moral philosophy. To that department a more extended notice of the nature and uses of appetite must be referred. It would seem that sensations of this class have not hitherto received sufficient notice, owing, probably, to the difficulty of defining and classing them.

QUESTIONS ON CHAPTER III.

What is meant by a sense of *Temperature?* What comparison is made between this and the sense of smell? Where is the organ of this sense located? What would be our experience without it? Why may weariness and fatigue be referred to the same sense? From what does *weariness* arise? From what *fatigue?* With what is weariness attended? With what fatigue? Where is the organ of this sense located? Where and when may a sensation of weariness be realized? A sensation of fatigue? What is said of men accustomed to labor, and the reverse? What would be our condition without this sense? State the substance of the reply to those who object to assigning to it a specific existence in the mental constitution. Why may pleasure and pain be referred to the same sense? What question may be raised here? Which of the two suppositions seems most philosophical? What reasons are given? What is the obvious design of pain? What is meant by the sense of *appetite?* What reasons are given in answer to those who deny that we have a specific sense of appetite? What importance is assigned to the sensations due to the senses here considered?

CHAPTER IV.

SENSATION.

Having considered those mental susceptibilities or owers, together with their organs, which are the sources f sensation, we are prepared to notice the various *sensa-ons themselves* to which they give rise.

SENSATION IS A MENTAL AFFECTION IMMEDIATELY RESULTING FROM A CHANGE IN AN ORGAN OF SENSE.

Mental affections, not originating through organs of ense, such as love, joy, hatred, are sometimes called sen-ations, but not with philosophical accuracy. They are ental feelings, but not sensations. The term *sensation* , by the best authorities, restricted to those mental affec-ons which are *directly due to the organs of sense.* When omething is said to have produced a great *sensation* mong a people, — as the news of a victory or a defeat, · the expression is to be understood as popular and not hilosophical language.

Under the head of *sensations*, I include *all* the mental ffections of which the senses are the direct subjective ause. It is as philosophical to speak of sensations of leasure and pain, of weariness and fatigue, of heat and old, as of smell, or of touch, or of taste. Those who al-ow only five senses are puzzled to know where to place e first class of the above sensations.

THE MIND THE AGENT IN SENSATION.

Sensations are *effects*, in the production of which are *causes without*, exciting the organ, and *the mind*, an intelligent agent, *acting in connection with the organ* at the same time. The united action of *both the organ and the mind* is essential to sensation. The organ, then, is the mutual instrument of mind and matter — the point *at which the two worlds meet.*

Whatever operates upon the organ from without is the *occasional* cause of sensation: the organ is the *instrumental* cause; the mind is both the *agent* and the *subjective* cause of it. If I smell a rose, the odorous effluvia are the occasional cause, the olfactory nerves the instrumental and the mind the agent and subject, of the sensation of smell. It is only by this joint action that birth is given to the phenomenon in question.

HOW SENSATIONS ARE KNOWN.

Sensations are known only by *consciousness.* To know them, we must experience them. Suppose you undertake to explain to one who never experienced it the sensation produced by the prick of a pin. You may labor with explanations a month, and he will be no wiser. Put the point of a pin into his skin, and he knows in a moment. Before, he only *conjectured;* now, he *knows* What volumes of explanation could not explain to him in years, the point of a pin can teach him at once. Who ever learned, from scientific explanations, the precise sensation realized in the extraction of a tooth? The dentist's chair can teach what no books can.

Accordingly, we seize on the most common and prominent sensations, — such as all are presumed to have experienced, — and compare others with them. When a man would describe his sensations in gout, fever, paralysis, or some other affection not common to us, he compares it with the prick of a pin, burning, freezing, or any thing similar to it which we have all experienced. This is to us but an *approximation* to the fact. He alone *exactly* knows the sensation who has *experienced* it.

And here we may notice the folly of those who would maintain the utter impracticability of a mutual interchange of definite and exact thoughts by language. When language represents a common experience, its utterances, as received, are essentially true to fact; human experience, in relation to most things, is the same.

ALL IDEAS BY SENSATION ARE COGNITIONS.

Whatever we directly learn by sensation is *absolute knowledge*. The idea always exactly corresponds with the fact. Our consciousness cannot deceive us. I have an *idea* in regard to the flavor of a peach, by hearing it described; my idea may be true or not — it is a conjecture. When I *taste*, I *know*.

But we must not confound the knowledge of the *sensation* with that of its *cause*. The *sensation* produced by a pinch of snuff, and the *snuff itself*, are distinct things. It is only the *sensation* of which we are *conscious;* the *cause* of the sensation is an object of *perception*. When my hand touches a hot body, a certain change takes place in the organ of touch; whereupon a corresponding change instantly takes effect in my mind, termed a *sensation of heat*. Of this sensation I am conscious. I *know* it. Respecting its *cause*, I may be in ignorance or doubt.

PHYSIOLOGICAL VIEW OF SENSATION.

The seat of sensation is usually termed the *sensorium*. It is by some located in the *brain*, — the supposed seat of the mind, — while the nerves are considered mere messengers, to bear reports thither from all parts of the body. Others regard the nerves as constituting, in connection with the brain, the sensorial organ.

NERVES AND BRAIN.

The *nerve* is a fine, white, fibrous thread, ramifying minutely into all parts of the body, and connecting with the brain. The *brain* is an organized mass, or rather a congeries of organized little masses, of the same substance with the nerve. In the *substance* of the nerve itself, as well as in the substance of the brain, there is no sensibility.* The sensibility resides in the *envelope*, called the *neuralima*. Around every nervous thread, however minute, and around the great mass and all the little portions of the brain, this thin membrane is spread, of extreme delicacy and sensibility. It is of the same general nature with the other membranes of the body, only more refined and sensible. Indeed, it varies its own texture to suit the organ it invests. It is more sensible in the special organs of sense — the eye, ear, mouth, &c. — than in other parts of the body; and more so in some of these organs than in others. It is more delicate in the ends of the fingers than in any other parts of the hand. Along with the nerves, running in every direction, it connects with all the other membranes of the body.†

All the muscles, every little fleshy fibre, as well as the bones, are pervaded with it, and hence instinct with sensibility.

THE SEAT OF SENSIBILITY NOT EXCLUSIVELY IN THE HEAD.

Sensibility, therefore, cannot be regarded as having a seat exclusively in the *head*. Its seat is *all over and*

* See Bichat's Anatomy and Physiology.

† "Our fundamental idea of a nervous system includes a central organ or *ganglion*, essentially composed of *vesicles* or *cells*, with a plexus of capillary vessels distributed amongst these, and a set of trunks and ramifying branches, composed of tubular fibres, and connecting the ganglion with different parts of the fabric. These branches are for the most part distributed, on the one hand, to the sensory surfaces and organs; and, on the other, to the muscles or motor organs." — *Principles of Human Physiology, by William B. Carpenter, M. D., F. R. S., F. G. S., Examiner in Physiology in the University of London*, p. 230. This work comprises a complete view of the most scientific and approved doctrines of physiology down to the present time.

through the body, wherever there is membrane and nerve.* Touch *any* part where these are found, and there we are conscious of feeling. Sensibility, like life itself, is *all-pervading*.

If we must ascribe the seat of sensation to any one part rather than another, both physiology and experience would designate the *stomach*. This is one of the most vascular, tissuous, fibrous organs of the human system. It is a thorough congeries of the very elements which give rise to feeling.

Experience also teaches us that our mental feelings are first realized in the stomach rather than in the head. Sadness, depression, the glow of joy are first felt at the epigastrium. If we hear bad news just as we are about to dine, we feel a depression at the stomach; we cannot eat. Grief destroys digestion; cheerfulness promotes it.†

It may be said that the good or bad news we hear acts on the stomach through the brain, the brain being first affected. That is not to the point. I am now speaking of *sensibility* and of our *consciousness*. The question is, Where are we *conscious* of realizing the feelings in question? While some parts are more sensible than others, sensibility is more or less diffused through the *entire living body*.

* The ganglionic masses at the base of the brain are highly charged with the elements of sensibility, and seem to have a special agency in sensation. Here the membranous and vascular systems predominate. "At the base of the brain in man, concealed by the cerebral hemispheres, but still readily distinguishable from them, we find a series of ganglionic masses, which are in direct connection with the nerves of sensation, and which appear to have functions quite independent of those of the other components of the encephalon." — *Principles of Human Physiology, by William B. Carpenter*, p. 320.

† "It is stated by Bichat, that, in some of his experiments upon the *par vagum*, some hours after section of the nerve on both sides, the surface only of the elementary mass was found to have undergone solution, the remainder of the mass remaining in the condition in which it was at first ingested; and if this statement can be relied upon, it would appear that the movements of the stomach, like those of the heart, *can be readily affected by a strong nervous impression*. It may be partly in this manner, therefore, and not by acting upon the secretions alone, that *strong emotions influence the digestive process, as they are well known to do*." — *Carpenter's Physiology*, p. 491.

AGENCY OF NERVES AND BRAIN.

What, then, is the office of the nerves and brain? I have said that, *apart from their membranous envelope*, they are without sensibility. They are not, then, in themselves, organs of feeling.* If they have any thing to do with the mind, they must be organs of *intelligence* or *knowledge*, as distinguished from *feeling*. Of the latter, the *membranous* system is the organ; of the former, including the brain, the *nervous*. Both are essential to sensation. Neither the nerves and brain alone, nor the membranes alone, can produce it. Without the one, there can be no sensibility; without the other, the excited sensibility is unnoticed.

SENSATION NOT STRICTLY SIMPLE.

Sensation has been considered a *simple* act of mind.† It is, however, when fully analyzed, not strictly so. The change that takes place in the organs of sense rouses the *feelings;* the change in the nerves and brain makes the mind *conscious* of this new state. If it be said that we can have no mental feelings of which we are not conscious, — this has been doubted, but grant it, — does it follow that a mental emotion and a consciousness of that emotion are strictly the same thing? Certainly not. And yet both are esential to sensation. Not only so, we seem to have two distinct sets of organs for this twofold

* The reader will carefully note the distinction between *sensibility* and *sensation*. Sensation is the more comprehensive. It includes both the excited sensibility and the mind's *cognizance* of it. Perhaps an illustration will be better understood. A gentle word may awaken no sensation in my friend, because his mind is absorbed in thought. The sharp voice of a pistol in his ear would probably awaken sensation. If there were no sensibility, the report of a pistol would be no more effectual than the feeblest whisper. Until the excited sensibility of the organ rises to a point to overcome the influence that holds the attention to something else, and call it to what is taking place in this particular organ, there can be no sensation of sound.

† See Upham's Philosophy, p. 24. New York edition, 1847. Also Reid's Works, vol. ii. p. 28.

mental operation. This is not given as a fact, but as a theory based on the best physiological authority. There are other considerations tending to confirm this view, which I shall notice.

HOW OBJECTS ACT ON THE ORGAN OF SENSE.

It is by all admitted, that objects around us produce in us sensations, *by causing some change in the organs of sense.* The precise nature of this change is not always evident, and yet we know something about it. Although the nerves, apart from their envelope, are insensible, yet, as they always have their envelope, we are justified in the popular use of the term *nervous sensibility.* Both common people and men of science know what the term means. Whether the excitement is in the substance of the nerve itself, or in the covering of the nerve, is of no consequence in this connection. All I wish to assert here is, that the first effect produced upon us by external objects is an excitement of what is usually called the nervous sensibility of the organ affected.

THE ORGANS OF SENSE ARE STIMULATED.

The most common effect produced on the organs of sense, by external causes, is that of a *stimulus.* Thus light stimulates or excites the optic nerve. It stimulates all living things. Next to caloric, it is the most important of the agents with which the Almighty operates upon the material universe. The vegetable, when it feels the presence of light, is roused to newness of life.

When rays of light, coming to the eye from an object, are converged within it to a focal point, and thence thrown upon the delicate expansion of optic nerve investing the retina, it operates as a powerful stimulus to that organ. Its sensibilities are thus roused in reference to the object, and sensation immediately follows. Different colors have different degrees of sharpness and mellowness; various forms make their various impressions;

the sensibilities excited, and the sensations produced, vary accordingly.

This is a simple statement of *fact.* *How* the presence of light stimulates the optic nerve, and *how* the excited sensibilities of that organ produce in the mind the sensation of sight, are questions beyond human reach.

In a similar manner, the presence of odors to the olfactory nerve stimulates that organ. The ordinary pleasures resulting from the delicious odors attending our meats and drinks, and from the mellow fragrance of fruits and flowers, not less than the more gross and potent luxury of snuff-taking, depend upon the excitement thus produced. Similar, also, is the excitement of the sensibilities of the gustatory organs, by the presence of food; and of the organs of hearing, by the atmospheric vibrations. In all cases, an immediate sensation attends this nervous excitement.

In the case of touch, some other word than *stimulus* would, perhaps, be more appropriate. And yet it is essentially the same thing. The part touched is excited, moved, stimulated, and thus made sensible of the presence of the cause. If the part is hit severely, or wounded, the excitement becomes violent, and a painful sensation is the result.

Other sensations result from the *want* of due stimulus, or from the reaction of over excitement. Such are sensations of weariness and fatigue.

SENSATIONS ARE LOCAL.

It follows, from what has been said, that the popular mind is not so much mistaken, as has been supposed, in assigning *localities* to sensation. "Sensation is often regarded," says Upham,* "as something having a position, and as taking place in the body, and particularly in the organ of sense. The sensation of touch, as we seem to imagine, is in the hand, which is the organ of touch, and is not truly internal; the hearing is in the ear, and the

* Mental Philosophy, p. 25.

vision in the eye, and not in the soul. But all we can say with truth, and on good ground, is, that the organs of sense are accessory to sensation, and necessary to it; but the sensation or feeling itself is wholly in the mind. How often it is said the eye sees; but the proper language, if we look at the subject philosophically, is, that the soul sees; for the eye is only the organ, instrument, or minister of the soul in visual perceptions."

"A man," says Reid, "cannot see the satellites of Jupiter but by a telescope. Does he conclude from this that it is the telescope that sees those stars? By no means; such a conclusion would be absurd. It is no less absurd to conclude that it is the eye that sees, or the ear that hears. The telescope is an artificial organ of sight; but it sees not. The eye is a natural organ of sight, by which we see; but the natural organ sees as little as the artificial." *

Here is a *fallacy*. Both the telescope and the eye are *instruments*, but the essential difference between them is *not* that the one is natural and the other artificial — that is a point of no consequence; it is, that the one is a *dead* instrument, and the other *instinct with living mind*. But what Reid wished to illustrate is true. In strict philosophy, it is the mind that sees, not the eye. It is the mind that tastes, smells, hears, feels, &c. The mind is the agent; the organ of sense, the instrument. Nobody disputes this. It is the *inference* that I deny. Because it is the mind that feels, does it follow that the feeling may not take place in certain parts of the body — in the hand, head, or foot?

If the entire body is instinct with sensibility, may not the mind be conscious of feeling in *any part* of it? May not the feeling be in the *mind* and in the *organ* of sensation too? Evidently so, if the mind is in the organ of sensation, and in that organ it *must* be, to experience a sensation from it; unless we adopt something like the exploded theory, that the mind stays in the brain, and the nerves act as telegraphic wires, to tell it what is going on in the various organs; or the yet more objectional theory, that the mind is *nowhere*.

* Reid's Works, vol. ii. p. 50.

The inference to which I object seems to be founded on a false notion respecting the connection of the mind with the body. It seems to suppose that the mind is lodged in some quarter, whence it looks forth upon the body, and operates it by a kind of machinery, as we operate a lifeless engine. As it is important that the mind should have a favorable position, most philosophers have concluded to assign it the *head.* To place it in the toe, would be too great a blunder for any philosopher. "Though philosophers have disputed much about the place of the mind," says Reid, "yet none of them ever placed it in the toe." *

But if we have taken the right view, — and it is the view sustained by the most scientific physiology, — then *the mind is confined to no one part.* It is all-pervading. *The whole living body is instinct with mind,* although the nerves and brain are organs of thought, while the membranous systems are organs of feeling. This being so, in a being of soul and body, sensation *must* be "regarded as something having a position, and as taking place in the body, and particularly in the organs of sense."

OBJECTION TO THIS VIEW.

It is objected to this view, that if the mind thus pervades the entire body, and may be said to be in the hands, feet, toes, &c., then we have only to cut off a man's limb to take away a part of his mind; whereas, he has as much mind after the amputation as before. Here, again, there is a confounding of mind with matter. Mind is *pure spirit;* hence its existence is substantially independent of matter in every form and measure. The mind of God pervades the entire universe; yet the annihilation of a world takes away no portion of his mind.

So the mind of man pervades his entire body; yet the removal of a limb removes no part of his mind. The mind *concentrates* its action, so to speak, in what

* Reid's Works, vol. ii. p. 269.

remains. Pluck out one eye, and the same entire mind concentrates its vision in the remaining eye. Go on removing member after member, and, so long as life remains, the *mind* remains, the same one entire being, doing the best it can with its remaining and mutilated instruments, until you destroy life.

CASES CITED BY REID.

"Cases sometimes happen," says Dr. Reid, "which give occasion even to the vulgar to distinguish the painful sensation from the disorder which is the cause of it. A man who has his leg cut off, many years after feels pain in a toe of that leg. The toe has now no existence, and he perceives easily that the toe can neither be the place, nor the subject of the pain which he feels; yet it is the same feeling he used to have from a hurt in the toe; and if he did not know that his leg was cut off, it would give him the same immediate conviction of some hurt or disorder in the toe." *

The distinction between the sensation and the disorder which occasions it is made by the simplest minds. The question is, whether the disorder and the sensation are *in the same place.* I maintain that they are. If the head is disordered, the pain is in the head; if the foot is disordered, the pain is in the foot. Nor are cases of *sympathetic* pains, as they are called, exceptions. A disordered stomach occasions pain in the head, because it occasions pressure of blood or some other derangement in that part.

Such is the connection of the various membranes and organs of the body, that a disorder in one part creates disturbance in another; and, moreover, the sensation may sometimes become most intense in the part indirectly disordered, because the sensibilities of that part are least blunted. But there is real disorder there, and that disorder occasions the sensation in question. To put my meaning in plainest English, if the irregularity in the

* Reid's Works, vol. ii. p. 270.

stomach occasioned no irregularity in the head, there would be no headache.

As to the supposed pain in the toe after the limb was cut off, it is a strong confirmation of this view. It shows that the man's mind had been accustomed to *feeling the pain in that particular part*, until it had become a *mental habit*. If he had not *actually felt* it in the toe while the toe was on, would he have *imagined* it in the toe after the toe was cut off? We all know how easily the imagination recreates what the mind has previously experienced.

PHILOSOPHY AND EXPERIENCE.

Other things equal, that is the soundest philosophy which tallies with common experience and observation. Now, there is no hazard in asserting that ninety-nine hundredths of men without pretensions to science do really suppose that their vision is in their eyes, their taste in their mouths, their smell in their noses, their hearing in their ears, and their feeling wherever they happen to feel.

Why, then, are philosophers so anxious to resist this universal belief? Is it because they are afraid of materializing the mind, or because they covet a philosophy too deep for common people? Is it not, rather, because they have assumed a definition of sensation which compels them to do it? — a *limited* definition, which makes no account of any thing actually realized by the mind in the organ of sense. The latter is the undoubted reason.

When a simple-minded man burns his finger, he speaks of *pain* in it. "Hold," says the philosopher, "there is no pain in your finger; the pain is in the mind."

"But I am certainly conscious of pain in my finger. If my finger were well, my mind would be well enough."

"Now, I can prove to you, philosophically, that all the pain is in the mind, not in the body; for if we take away the *mind from the body*, you may burn the body to cinders, and it will realize no pain."

"Very well. And so, if we take away the *body from the mind*, you may burn the body to cinders, and the *mind* will realize no pain. So I do not see but my simplicity is as good as your philosophy."

At another time, the same untaught man sees a fine-looking apple, but, on tasting, finds it very *bitter*. "This fruit," he says, "is not so good as it looks; it is pleasant to the eye, but very disagreeable to the mouth."

"Stop," says the philosopher, "that will not do. There is no such thing as pleasant to the eye and disagreeable to the mouth. There is no vision in the eye, nor taste in the mouth. You ought to say, 'The apple is pleasant to the mind, when the mind sees it; but disagreeable to the mind, when the mind tastes it.'"

"But in my simplicity, I always supposed," he replies, "that the mind does its seeing in the eye, and its tasting in the mouth. At any rate, it will take something more than your philosophy to convince me that it is not in my mouth that I realize this bitter taste."

Now, if we but consider that the *mind* is the *I*, — that, when I speak of my MIND, I speak of MYSELF, — we see that the simpleton here is wiser than the philosopher. What sense in saying, I have a pain in *myself?* Where else *could* I have it? But there *is* some sense in saying, I have a pain in my *head;* for it might be in some other part.

All agree that sensations are, and of course must be, in the mind; there can be no question of this; and we are disposed to regard them, also, "as something having a position, and as taking place in the body, and particularly in the organ of sense." Asking none to take our judgment, and content to let it pass for what it is worth, we are disposed to say, with our fellow-simpletons, that vision *is* in the eye, that taste *is* in the mouth, that smell *is* in the nose, that hearing *is* in the ear, and that feeling *is* just where something is felt.

QUESTIONS ON CHAPTER IV.

What is *sensation?* What is the difference between sensation and other mental feelings? To what is the term *sensation* restricted? How much is included under the head of sensations? What is said of those who hold to only five senses? What is the *agent* in sensation? How many causes combine to produce sensation? Illustration. How are sensations known? Illustrate. What may we here notice? What are all our ideas obtained by sensation? What is cognition? Answer — Knowledge. Illustrate. With what must we not confound sensation? What is the *seat* of sensation? What is the *nerve?* The *brain?* Where does the *sensibility* of nerve reside? What is said of the *neuralima?* To what conclusion are we brought respecting the seat of sensibility? What is said of seating it in the *stomach?* How widely is sensibility diffused? What is the office of nerves and brain? And what of membrane? Is sensation strictly *simple?* Why not? How do external objects act on the organs of sense? What is their *effect* on these organs? Illustrations — sight, odors, food, &c. Are sensations *local?* What say Upham and Reid? What is the *fallacy* here? Remarks. Is the mind confined to any one part of the body? Inference. What *objection* to this view? Answer? What case is cited by Reid? Reply to it? What is said of the supposed pain in the toe? Other things equal, which is the soundest philosophy? State the substance of the colloquy between the uneducated man and the philosopher. How does it appear that the former is right? Let the reader give his own opinion.

CHAPTER V.

IMPROVEMENT OF OUR SENSATIONS.

As our knowledge originates in sensations, and as they contribute so essentially through life to our entire mental furniture and to our social and moral character, it becomes an interesting inquiry, *How may they be improved to best advantage?* It has been previously said, that sensation always involves an affection of the organ of sense as well as of the mind. As they mutually depend upon each other, we must have an eye to both.

THE ORGANS OF SENSATION SUSCEPTIBLE OF CULTURE.

There is undoubtedly a great difference between men, in the *original* capacities of their organs of sense, and a great difference, in the same person, between the relative capacities of his own; some being often very feeble or entirely wanting, while others are in a high state of perfection. This difference seems to be mostly owing to greater or less original delicacy and integrity of the nerves and membranes composing the organs.

But the difference is owing vastly more to the *manner in which we use them.* Keenness or obtuseness of taste and smell, quickness or dulness of hearing, delicacy or grossness of feeling, dimness or clearness of vision, together with the qualities of all our inward sensations, are ordinarily more the result of our own doing than of constitutional endowment.

HOW THE ORGANS OF SENSATION MAY BE IMPROVED.

All the organs of sensation may be improved by a *judicious use* of them, in connection with *habits of strict temperance.* They may be enfeebled by neglect; they may be injured by over-working; they may be prostrated by habits of licentiousness, gluttony, drunkenness. Hence he who would rise to the highest intellectual attainments should be thoroughly *temperate and virtuous.* The brightest names on the roll of intellectual greatness belong to men of such habits.

The person in question must not only be temperate and virtuous, but *industrious.* All the instruments of sensation must be kept bright with use. Industry is as essential to the health and efficiency of the organs of sensation as to the acquisition of knowledge by the reasoning powers. By habits of indolence and sensual indulgence, the organs of sensation relapse into a condition in which they teach us little more than they do the brute. They then give us only the lowest and most animal ideas.

He who rises late in the morning, lives luxuriously, lounges in indolence, or drags his body about only to make it minister to his pleasure, in respect to the knowledge he obtains by sensation is more an animal than a man. If we would have our sensations entire and true, our perceptions clear, our judgments sound, and all our ideas and thoughts expand and shoot vigorously upward, we must keep our intellectual tools in the best of order.

HOW OUR SENSATIONS MAY BE IMPROVED.

The senses pertain to the mind, and are united to the body in a special relation to the organs of sensation. Hence, while the organ acts as an instrument on the sense, the sense reacts as an agent on the organ. Their influence is reciprocal and intimate. I look upon an object with a view to knowing it. That object makes through the eye an impression on the sense of sight. The impression tends to fix the eye. The fixedness of the eye tends to make the impression more clear and exact. By exerting my will to direct and continue the process to a suitable degree, the physical organ becomes the better adapted, and the sense becomes habituated, to such an effort. Thus the sense is gradually enabled to operate with more ease and efficiency. In this way, all our voluntary sensations have to be educated. Our involuntary sensations are more directly concerned with admonishing us of our physical wants. They do not so much require to be *educated* as carefully *noticed*, in order to furnish those higher ideas which belong to us as rational and moral beings.

Two advantages are secured to the senses by their proper use — *strength* and *habit*. All the mental, as well as bodily powers, are strengthened by exercise. If I lay my hand fixedly upon the table for months, it becomes so feeble that I cannot use it. On the contrary, if I vigorously exercise it in some gymnastic school, I may increase its natural strength fourfold. It is precisely so with all the voluntary senses. God has placed them in subjection to our *will*, as talents which we are bound to improve. The responsibility is upon us, and ours must be the irreparable loss if we fail to discharge it. There is doubtless a limit, beyond which the vigor of the senses cannot be raised by exercise; but it is doubtful whether even the most industrious have ever fully reached it.

The next advantage secured to the senses, by their appropriate use, is that of *habit*. Some may suppose this advantage includes the other. They are intimately related, but not the same. *Strength* may be *natural; habit* is always *acquired*. Acquired strength is the same thing as natural strength, differing only in its origin. Hence the acquired strength and the habit of a given sense are two things. Now, we all know something of the power of habit. It becomes a second nature, and sometimes more than a match for nature herself.

He who has from childhood accustomed himself to neglect all his sensations, excepting those which minister only to animal wants and pleasures, has lost what the gold of California cannot redeem. If such has been his course up to manhood, the die is cast; he may be much of an animal, but he will never be much of a man. On the contrary, he who has trained all his senses to be ever on duty has formed a habit by which knowledge from all points is perpetually flowing into his mind. It becomes natural and easy for him to learn from all sources. Young people should consider this. They should endeavor to form those *habits of careful* and *ever-wakeful observation* which are at the foundation of all mental greatness. The importance of this subject justifies the use of a few moments on each of the voluntary sensations.

IMPROVEMENT OF THE SENSATION OF SMELL.

This sensation, as a source of intellectual furniture, is ordinarily considered of so little importance, that we might be justified in passing it. Excepting the case of persons engaged in some business that makes special demand upon it, and of those deprived of other sensations, we have no means of testing the improvement of which it is susceptible.

Individuals incapable of exercising any sense but that of smell have brought it to such a state of perfection as to rival the sharp-scented spaniel. They have become able, in the use of this sense alone, to distinguish their friends from each other, their acquaintances from strangers, and sometimes to trace the way to the place of their residence. They have distinguished between colors, and have even found stolen articles of dress. We thus see how much valuable knowledge may be gained, even from this humble source, and how great its importance in the absence of others.

Intemperance of all kinds tends to impair the action of this sense. Snuff-taking, and all other unnatural and violent stimulants addressed to the olfactory nerves, while they create a morbid desire, gradually exhaust the sensibility of the organ, and with it the pleasure at first afforded. That there is some pleasure in thus unnaturally stimulating the nose, and through it the nervous system generally, is not denied. But how soon does this pleasure degenerate to a slavish necessity! The keen sense of this organ being blunted, all the sweet odors of balmy spring, all the rich perfumes of the summer landscape, all the mellow fragrance of autumnal fruits, are lost. On the score of mere *pleasure*, therefore, young people should be admonished to avoid all habits deleterious to this sense. But as a source of knowledge, of pure sentiments, of delicate and refined feelings, it is of vastly more importance. Some of the sweetest imagery in the whole range of literature is founded on discriminations of this sense, without which none can enjoy or even understand it.

IMPROVEMENT OF THE SENSATION OF TASTE.

The discriminating power of *the sense of taste* depends also on *strict temperance and careful attention.* When the organ is unduly excited, irritated, inflamed, the sense gradually loses this power. The most discriminating dealer of wines, other things equal, is the most temperate man. Intemperate men sometimes discover much accurate judgment in the choice of liquors, but this is *despite* of their intemperance. The use which *led* to intemperance contributed to educate their taste, but intemperance itself contributes to injure it. Besides, the taste, as applied to intoxicating drinks, is mostly an *acquired* taste, not a natural one. It soon degenerates into a morbid hankering, and all pleasure is lost, except that of allaying the pain thus produced. It ceases to be the *positive pleasure* afforded by the gratification of *taste*, and becomes only the *negative* satisfaction of arresting a morbid *craving*.

On this point, one of our writers * seems to have fallen into an error, by not distinguishing between *taste* and disordered *appetite*. He says that "the sensation of taste acquires an enhanced degree of pleasantness" as the habit of drinking advances. On the contrary, we believe that the drunkenness, which he says, in just and forcible

* Upham's Mental Philosophy, p. 61.

language, "presses him like a coat of iron and galls like fetters of steel," so *injures* his taste, that his enjoyment from it becomes far less vivid than at first; while, at the same time, the craving of his sinking sensibilities, the feverish *appetite*, is so enhanced, that he is compelled to cry out in agony for another dram, even though the dreadful *scowl* upon his face when he drinks it — so unlike the smiling *pleasure* which danced there at first — tells us plainly that it has become to him as wormwood and gall. And this is the most terrific view of intemperance. Such is the irrepealable law of our nature. Every time we pass over the limits of strict virtue, we invade the integrity of our taste, and thus diminish the pleasure attending the use of Heaven's bounties; while, at the same time, we increase the demands of a *perverted appetite*.

The same is true of *all* pleasures, in which the mind is passive, when not under the law of absolute temperance. "Experience diminishes the influence of passive impressions on the mind, but strengthens our active principles. A course of debauchery deadens the sense of pleasure, but increases the desire of gratification. An immoderate use of strong liquors destroys the sensibility of the palate, but strengthens the habit of intemperance." *

The sensation of taste is impaired by habits of *gluttony*. Experienced cooks have a very discriminating taste in regard to dishes; but although perpetually exercising it on a great variety, they are usually quite temperate in the use of them. It is said of one of the kings of England, that after he became a glutton he would not trust his own taste to decide upon the qualities of his dishes, but referred the decision to his cook. He showed his good sense in this, at least, that he would not venture his reputation in attempting to pronounce upon a dish, before his assembled court at feast, without taking counsel of better authority than his own impaired taste.

The inebriate, too, cannot safely trust his own taste to select the wines for his banquet. Even if his discrimination was once good, it is so no longer; he must have recourse to the dealer in wines — a person in whom

* Stewart's Philosophy, b. i. p. 289.

temperance has preserved the naturalness of taste, while careful tasting has rendered it discriminating. A pure, delicate, natural taste is a great and constant source of enjoyment. To him who has it, appetite is healthy, relish is keen, participation satisfies desire, the cup of sensuous pleasure is full. Every morsel of food, however plain, every article of drink, even a glass of cold water, is a luxury — a truer, more enviable luxury than the intemperate ever experience, even at the most sumptuous entertainment.

IMPROVEMENT OF THE SENSATION OF HEARING.

The sense of hearing, like all the others, is improved by appropriate and diligent use, in connection with temperate and virtuous habits. It is indeed astonishing to what a pitch of discrimination this sense may be elevated, by a persevering course of right training.

I was acquainted with a blind man in Boston, now dead, whose sense of hearing had acquired such accuracy and quickness, that he seldom failed to recognize any person by his voice with whom he had at a former time conversed. His ears did actually more for him in this respect than the eyes of most persons do for them. His business was to tune pianos. As he walked the busy streets of the metropolis alone, from house to house, on his business, he knew when he passed a building, a corner, or a post, by the change which they occasioned in the vibratory motions of the air. He could tell by the ear, with as much exactness as most can by the eye, the dimensions and form of any room which he entered, the height of a person with whom he was conversing, and the magnitude and form of buildings which he passed.

Philosophy teaches us that these causes must produce their several effects upon the atmospheric movements, and that these must act upon the drum of the ear; but how few of us ever thought of attending to them. Such examples show what *may* be done in the way of improving this sense.

The blind are notorious for their musical taste and skill,

owing to the great care they bestow upon the sense of hearing. And persons not blind have sometimes rivalled their afflicted brethren in this particular. Men of naturally dull ear have, by a course of training, brought it to an uncommon degree of acuteness. It is somewhere said of a young man, whose ear was so dull that he could not distinguish between Old Hundred and Yankee Doodle, that, by a persevering study and observation of musical sounds, he at length became a very discriminating critic, and a skilful performer of the most elaborate harmonies.

Young persons can scarcely be too much urged to improve to the height of their ability the sense of hearing. It is not partial deafnesss, or the reverse, of which I speak; it is of the *quality* of the hearing, not the *quantity*. Many a person almost deaf has, in the sense I intend, a good ear; while others, whose hearing is perfect, have a very bad ear.* I refer to that quick and nice discrimination which makes the mind sensible to the numerous melodies and harmonies of music, and to the varying tones and inflections of human eloquence, by which the soul of man puts itself forth into the souls of his fellowmen; to the myriad tongues of nature, calling from hills, dales, forests, and skies, to reach and move our hearts; to the repeated words of teachers, laboring at the ear, with incessant toil, to pour the lessons of wisdom into the understanding; in short, to *all* those voices from around and above us, which ought to be heard, to render us wise and happy.

Every teacher of youth has observed how much more easily a pupil learns a language by having the sense of hearing well cultivated. Most people are unapprised how

* The *sense* of hearing is often uncommonly keen in persons almost deaf, owing perhaps to the fixed attention which they are compelled to give. The fault is wholly in the organ. When I speak of a good or bad ear, of the eye seeing, &c., I conform to the popular use of language, indicating by the name of the organ the sense of which it is the instrument. When the workman says his *axe* cuts well, his meaning is that *he* cuts well, in the use of a sharp tool; otherwise the tool, not he, ought to be paid for the service. As the best of workmen do poorly with bad tools, so the brightest mental endowment may be frustrated by the capacity of its organ. This must excuse my frequent reference to the importance of taking the best possible care of the body, if we would have clear and efficient minds.

much depends upon this. Especially in learning a spoken language, almost every thing depends upon it. What the sense of hearing clearly discerns, we easily remember, and learn to utter.

IMPROVEMENT OF THE SENSATION OF TOUCH.

I have spoken of the great delicacy of nervous organization at the ends of the fingers. Proof of this, as well as of the extent to which the sensation of touch may be improved, is furnished in the case of the blind. Let any person, who has not bestowed special culture upon the sense of touch, close his eyes, and undertake to read the blind man's book with the ends of his fingers, and he will be as much confounded as though he were attempting for the first time to read Chinese. By careful training, the blind pupil has so educated the touch, that he can read with it as accurately as others can with the eye.

In the same way he learns even to distinguish *colors.* Some writer mentions the instance of a blind female, who would tell every red from every white or black piece of cloth upon the counter in a shop, by merely *feeling* of it. Such facts seem at first incredible, and we are half inclined to suspect some deception; but they are well authenticated, and after all not incredible. For what is color? It is something in the light — the medium through which objects are seen; and the reason why one object reflects black and another red is, that the *material* upon the surface is different. This material is a subject of touch.

The person above, if always blind, had really no just idea of colors; but when once told that a certain piece of cloth was red, she could ever after, by the touch, identify all cloths of the same peculiar feeling. It is not merely a difference of roughness and smoothness, of regularity and irregularity of surface, that makes the difference of colors, for objects of all colors may have this; there is something peculiar in the *feel* of that which reflects the several *colors*, which none but a highly-educated touch can discriminate.

The same skill and accuracy may be obtained by this sense in reference to all objects. "In the celebrated Dr. Saunders, who lost his sight in very early youth, and remained blind through life, although he occupied the professorship of mathematics in the English University of Cambridge, the touch acquired such acuteness that he could distinguish, by merely letting them pass through his fingers, spurious coins, which were so well executed as to deceive even skilful judges who could see." *

IMPROVEMENT OF THE SENSATION OF SIGHT.

No other of the sensations is susceptible of such a variety and extent of improvement as this. By accustoming the eye to view objects at a distance, the axis of vision may be so elongated as to extend the sight almost indefinitely. Every person who has crossed the ocean has been struck with the fact, that the sailor at a post of observation will discover a ship, an iceberg, or a breaker, in the distance, long before the passengers can discover the least sign of it. It is because he has accustomed his eye especially to this service.

On the other hand, the student, by habitually placing his book near his eyes, contracts a shortness of vision so that he is often unable to recognize his most familiar friend when he passes him in the street.

The artist, by studiously habituating his eye to observe colors, shades, forms, acquires such an accuracy of perception in regard to them as seems to most persons quite incomprehensible. The well-trained inspector of wares discovers a fault where others see only perfection. The eye long practised to examine proof sheets detects errors and defects which escape the notice of all other persons. The architect, the gardener, the engineer, by a faithful education of the eye, acquires a wonderful quickness and accuracy of observation in respect to whatever pertains to his peculiar calling. To adduce particular

* See Upham's Philosophy, p. 64. The fact is taken from Memoirs of the Manchester Philosophical Society, vol. i. p. 164.

examples in proof of these assertions would be superfluous, because numerous facts in point are familiar to all.

SUMMARY.

Before leaving the subject of sensation, let us briefly survey our ground.

1. Sensations are *mental* affections produced by *bodily* affections. They are purely mental, although they take place in the affected parts of the body. The pain of the gout is not in the head,* nor is toothache in the toe; yet both these pains are alike mental.

2. Although sensations may be popularly considered *simple* affections, yet in strict accuracy they imply *two* mental acts — the *change* in the mind, and the *consciousness* of it. There must be a change in the state of the mind, and the mind must take cognizance of that change, or there can be no sensation. The consciousness of pain implies a sensation of pain. We thus separate in *thought* what is inseparable in *fact*. This may seem a needless refining, but it is founded on the distinction which physiology makes between the respective offices of nerve and membrane; the one being an instrument of *feeling*, the other of *knowing*. Cut off the nerve from any organ, and there can be no sensation, because the *knowing* power, the *consciousness*, cannot operate.

3. The mind is a living, sentient *being*, communicating with all parts of the body, but not identical with it or with any of its organs. To ascribe sensations to the organs of sense, or to the brain, as their ultimate agent, is a doctrine of materialism utterly unsupported by evidence. Various causes affect the organs of sense, whereupon the sentient mind as an agent, taking cognizance

* "The appropriate seat of the gout is in the great toe." — *Notes from the Physiological Lectures of Dr. James Jackson, Boston.* If any still object to assigning localities to sensations because they are mental, I would ask, although the mind is the agent in obtaining education, may it not be educated in different *places?* It goes to various institutions to learn the various things which make its education complete. So it learns its various lessons of sensation in the several organs or schools which God has constituted for this purpose.

of that organic change, is itself affected. Thus the organ is the physical cause, and the mind the intelligent agent and subject of sensation. The organs of sense, then, are only the media or instruments of communication between mind and matter.

4. This method of sensation through bodily organs is merely *by divine appointment.* It is a temporary arrangement. For any thing we can see, the same sensations may be produced by other means than bodily organs. But for reasons in the divine mind, all who live in the flesh must realize their *first* sensations in bodily organs. Having taken its first lessons, the mind may repeat and enlarge its sensations after the physical organs have ceased to act. This is proved by facts, of which abundant evidence will be given. Hence the conscious activity of the mind beyond death, and its experience of painful or delightful sensations, is, in a philosophical view as probable as any other future event.

Those who suppose that death divests us of all capacity of experiencing sensations, because it divests us of the organs of sense, should consider that sensations are strictly mental, and that the mind is invested with *powers of retention and repetition*, by which it can realize over and over again, in endless varieties and combinations, sensations received through the bodily organs after those organs have ceased to act. Suspend *all* the organs of sensation, so that the one cannot supersede and counteract the other, and not only the sensation, but the object of it, becomes to the mind a reality. What the mind then perceives becomes a conception, replacing as it were the very object itself.

Such, we are to suppose, is the condition of the mind between death and the resurrection. The sensations then experienced had their origin in this mortal body. The body dies; sensations may live, pleasurable or painful according to the character and relations of the mind The resurrection of the body will invest us with other capacities of a similar but higher nature.

5. Sensations give rise to our *first ideas*, and are thus at the foundation of all our knowledge. They also give rise to our first *desires*, and through them to affections

and volitions. Hence, as intellectual, social, and moral beings, as well as subjects of pleasure and pain, we are ultimately dependent on sensations. As we have these in common with brutes, our superiority is not derived from greater or more numerous capacities of sensation, but from the possession of other and higher attributes, to be considered in their place. Man and the brute start together with sensations, but the brute, having nothing higher than the capacity for these, soon runs his circuit, and passes with his body to the dust: man, having higher attributes, passes from mere animal sensations to a higher mode of being. Such are the teachings of philosophy, as enlightened by Christianity and supported by facts.

QUESTIONS ON CHAPTER V.

What is the opening remark? What does sensation involve? What is said of difference of capacities? To what is it owing? How may all the organs of sensation be improved? How injured? Subjoined remarks. What is said of the reciprocal action of the sense and the organ? Illustration. What two advantages are secured to the senses by their proper use? How illustrated? Remark. What is said of *habit?* What habits should young people endeavor to form? What is said of the sensation of *smell?* What improvements have been made of this sensation? What habits are particularly injurious to it? What is said of it as a source of knowledge? On what does the discrimination of *taste* depend? Illustration. Into what does unduly excited taste degenerate? The consequence. What *error* is here noticed? How replied to? What is Stewart's remark? What is said of gluttony? Of experienced cooks? Anecdote. The inebriate? Concluding remarks on taste. What is improving the sensation of *hearing?* Fact. For what are the blind notorious? What is said of a young man of remarkably dull ear? What constitutes what is called a *good ear?* What has every teacher observed? What example is given of great improvement in the sensation of *touch?* What does some writer mention? Are such things incredible? Why not? Has the person in question any just idea of colors? What is said here? Case of Dr. Saunders? Comparative susceptibility to improvement of the sensation of *sight?* Illustration. The artist? Inspector, &c.? What are sensations?

Where do they take place? What two things do they imply? What two *physical* parts are essential to sensation? Of what is each the instrument? What is the *mind?* May we ascribe sensations to the organs of sense, or to the brain, as their agent? What then is the *organ*, as related to sensation? And what the *mind*, in this relation? To what is this method of sensation referable? What may the mind do, after taking its first lessons in sensation? The inference? What is said respecting sensations after death? To what do sensations give rise? What is said of man and the brute in this connection?

CHAPTER VI.

PERCEPTION.

No subject in intellectual philosophy has occasioned more controversy than this. It has been involved with theories respecting the nature of ideas, the origin of knowledge, the reality of an external world. It was formerly connected with the great dispute respecting nominalism and realism; that is, with the metaphysical question, whether our ideas are mere names, or realities existing in nature. The doctrine of realism, that our ideas are archetypes, according to which all things in the external world are formed, prevailed from the time of Aristotle till that of Roscellinus, in the eleventh century. It was subsequently disputed, and the controversy rose even to bloodshed. Among the more modern nominalists, Reid and Stewart may be named.

It is certainly a question of great interest, under what circumstances, and to what extent, we may trust our perceptions to give us knowledge of the external world? This is the *only question at issue*, of any practical importance. And to this will our principal inquiries be directed. To review all the theories of the schools upon this subject would far transcend our limits, and serve rather to confuse than edify the reader. If some of the following statements shall seem too simple to need to be made, let it be remembered that the points defined have been subjects of endless controversy. The greatest truths in science are often the simplest, and yet the most difficult to state, strange as it may seem, just because they *are* so simple.

PERCEPTION DEFINED.

Perception is the *next mental act after sensation.* It conducts the mind from sensation *itself* to its *cause.* It is a more *purely* mental act, and of a higher order. Thus, I have a painful sensation resulting from the prick of a pin — perception reveals to me the *cause* of it. I taste something bitter — perception discovers to me what that something is. Riding out on a bright spring morning, my sense of smell is regaled with a delicious odor: looking into the fields, I perceive the cause of it in the full-blown orchards. Considered as a *mental attribute*, therefore, perception may be defined THE POWER OF DISCERNING THE CAUSES OF OUR SENSATIONS.

INTUITIVE PERCEPTION.

Perception is also applied, in a less restricted sense, to the mind's notice of *metaphysical* truths, *mathematical* axioms, and the connection and force of *argumentative reasoning*. It is in such cases synonymous with *intuition.* The individual mental acts here are *intuitive perceptions.* We may therefore consider them under the head of intuition. We have the authority of the best classical writers on philosophy for abiding by the restricted definition of perception.

MUTUAL RELATIONS OF SENSATION AND PERCEPTION.

We now restrict our inquiries to PERCEIVING BY THE SENSES, and we ought to notice the mutual relations of sensation and perception. When we realize a sensation, we feel a desire to know the *cause* of it. Perception enables us to *gratify* that desire. Hence sensation is the *prompter* to knowledge — perception is the *obtainer* of it. Sensation sets the mind at work — perception accomplishes the undertaking. Without sensation, we should never *desire* to know any thing of the world around us; and without perception, however much we might desire the knowledge, we could never obtain it.

MORE PARTICULAR DISTINCTIONS BETWEEN SENSATION AND PERCEPTION.

As readers are wont to confound sensation with perception, and writers have often failed duly to distinguish between them, let us more particularly mark the difference. They differ in these two respects: —

1. *Sensations have nothing to do with what is extraneous to our minds.* The organic change is necessary to the sensation, but is not of itself any part of it. Strictly speaking, the sensation begins and ends with the mind itself. Perception carries the mind *quite out of itself to the causes* of its sensations. These causes, or objects of perception, may be found in our own bodies, as well as around us, but never in our minds; for what is in our *minds* is known by *consciousness*, not by perception.

2. All ideas obtained by sensations are *cognitions.* What we *experience*, we *know.* But we cannot be said to experience *causes.* We experience the *effects* of causes; these effects are sensations. But we know *causes* only by *perception*, and perception may deceive us. Hence, while our sensations are subjects of positive knowledge, without a question, our perceptions must be *examined* before what they profess to reveal is positively known. This examination is our present task.

ENTITIES AND NONENTITIES.

The term *entity* is employed to designate *any thing having existence independently of our idea of it.* It will be recollected that one of the questions of the schools was, whether any thing *really exists*, excepting in *idea.* An entity, then, is any thing that has actual existence; so that even an *idea* is itself an entity. The term *entity* is from a Greek and a Latin word, which signifies whatever *is.* Entities include all *abstract* and *necessary* facts, such as time, space, number, on which the exact sciences are built; all *spiritual* existences, *virtues*, *vices*, *mental states*, and *material substances* in all their forms. At present, we have to do mostly with the latter, as these only are objects of perception by the senses. *Nonentity* is a term designating the *opposite* of entity — that which has *no* existence, excepting in idea.

OBJECTIVE AND SUBJECTIVE ENTITIES.

Objective entities are *things themselves; subjective* entities are our *ideas of them.* Of the latter we are conscious; but how do we know the former exist? I answer: First, all ideas of material objects are derived *from the objects themselves.* This has been proved, in showing that a man blind from his birth has no idea of colors, a man deaf from his birth no idea of sounds, &c. To deny the reality of objective entities is, then, to admit an *effect* without a *cause.* If the one exist, — and that it does we are conscious, — the other *must* exist. Secondly, our *combined senses* teach us that there are objective entities, as truly as our consciousness does that we have ideas of them.

I take an orange in my hand, look upon it, feel it, cut it, smell it, taste it, and thus obtain the direct testimony of my senses to its existence and qualities. The *orange itself*, not the *idea* of it, is now the subject of my attention. Afterwards, in the *absence* of the orange, I have only the *idea* of it. I am conscious of having this idea, and know experimentally that, whatever it is, it is not the orange itself. I should, perhaps, be very glad if it were. But is neither round, yellow, fragrant, nor delicious; it has no *form;* I can neither handle, cut, nor eat it. Yet it is *something;* it is a *real idea*, and an *idea of that orange.* We thus see the distinction between *objective* and *subjective* entities, and that both *have actual existence.*

TRUE PERCEPTIONS.

Those perceptions are *true* in which our *ideas* correspond with their *objective entities;* that is, in which we perceive things to be *what they really are.* We must, however, remember that there is no resemblance between our *ideas* of entities and *entities themselves.* A stone is a solid substance; our *idea* of a stone is not a solid substance, nor any thing like it.

What, then, do we mean, when we speak of our ideas corresponding with their objective entities? Simply this — that the difference between entities is represented by *some corresponding difference of ideas;* so that a given idea becomes to us *the exclusive representative of its appropriate object.* Such is our mental constitution, that the same entity, when fairly noticed, always produces in the mind the same representative idea. If this were not so, we could not have that mutual understanding of things around us, which enables us, in their absence, to converse about them.*

Although my idea of fire is not *like* fire, nor my idea of water *like* water, yet, when I have an idea of fire, or an idea of water, I have the same *object* in view which my neighbor has when *he* has an idea of the one or of the other. Why ideas so wholly unlike objects without us should yet become *representatives* of them, is a question of curiosity beyond our reach. We can only say it is so, because God has *made it so to be.* The reason why he has done it, none can fail to see. The world would otherwise have been a Babel.

This is, perhaps, no more strange, after all, than that

* "In all our reflections on absent entities, and our attempts to classify them, our *ideas* of their properties, and not the properties themselves, are the subjects of our attention. We spend our whole life in acquiring mental representatives of different entities in the universe, but can classify these entities only by comparing and arranging the ideas thus obtained." "All men have the same uniform representatives of entities; hence they can converse intelligibly about them. If the same entity afforded to different persons different representatives of itself, men could no more converse intelligibly about it than if they did not understand the same language." — *Schmuker's Psychology*, pp. 38, 65.

words, so unlike the things they represent, should yet be made to represent them. The one is of human education, the other of divine constitution. Nor is the case materially altered, whether we adopt Brown's theory, that ideas are only mental states, or the theory that they are something distinct from the mind.

EXAMPLES OF TRUE PERCEPTION.

I observe what appears to be an animal grazing in the field. It looks to me like a horse; that is, the idea which I am led to form of it is that of a horse. If the animal really *is* a horse, my perception is true. It must be remembered that the perception gives the idea, not the idea the perception. On this point, the schoolmen were exactly wrong. They supposed the idea *innate*,—existing in the mind before the object is seen,—and that it gives rise to the perception.

A friend presents to me a flower, and asks me of what kind it is. I look at it, smell of it, and perceive it to be what is called a *pink*. If my perception is true, the flower really is what I perceive it to be. Thus in all cases, when the *idea* corresponds with the *object*, the perception is *true*. We then have what Locke calls an *adequate* idea. The reader must excuse the apparently unnecessary illustration of what seems so simple. The importance of the subject, and the mystery which has so much enveloped it, is the apology.

FALSE PERCEPTIONS.

Those perceptions are *false* in which our ideas do *not correspond with their entities;* that is, in which we do not perceive things to be *as they really are*. They may arise from *three causes*—a fault of the organ, a fault of the medium, a fault of the mind. First, some defect in the *organ of sense* may occasion false perceptions. When any instrument, as a telescope, is out of order, it often reports falsely. Secondly, the *medium* through which objects are perceived may produce an illusion. Objects seen through a mist, or through imperfect glass, or by reflected rays, may be falsely painted on the retina, and thus deceive us. Thirdly, *hallucinations*, or certain deranged states of intellect, may also give rise to false perceptions.

EXAMPLES OF FALSE PERCEPTIONS.

A person under the influence of a disease which particularly affects the organ of taste was requested by a friend, who wished to experiment upon her discrimination of flavors, to eat some sugar. Not being told what it was, she put it in her mouth, and immediately rejected it, supposing it to be *sand.* The diseased organ of taste was insensible to sweetness, and the sensation being that usually produced by taking dry sand into the mouth, led to a false perception.

A person looking through a pane of uneven glass, perceived, as he supposed, a man murdering a child with an axe. The man was really several feet from the child, splitting wood, and the child was gathering some sticks in his arms.

A man, entering a large hotel, was making rapid strides through its spacious hall, when he suddenly dashed against a mirror. The reflected rays from the mirror had doubled the apparent length of the hall, and thus deceived him.

In all these cases the *mind was true*, being deceived by the *means with which it operated.* Examples in which the mind is in fault will be given under the head *Insanity.*

HOW WE MAY KNOW WHETHER OUR PERCEPTIONS ARE TRUE.

This has been one of the most important and disputed points in mental science. *Is there an external world?* And if there is, *how may we know it?* Some have concluded, with Berkeley, that there *is* none, but that all which passes with us for it exists *merely in idea*. Others have concluded, with Hume, that for aught we can tell there may be one, and may not.

Under the head of *Objective and Subjective Entities*, I have adduced what appears to be *one* conclusive proof of the objectivity of our ideas. But the exact point now is, *How may we know the truth or falseness of any particular perception?* There is a way of testing perceptions; and, when duly tested, the knowledge they afford may be as firmly relied upon as that afforded by our sensations. I may as certainly *know* the reality of an object before me, or in my hands, as that of the pain which I feel in a diseased tooth.

For the present, we will suppose the organs of sense and the mind in a *sound state*. Let the following particulars be noticed.

PHYSICAL ENTITIES ARE KNOWN BY CONTACT.

The influence of physical entities is always exerted by *actual contact with the organ*. Thus, in *smelling*, the olfactory organs are touched by particles emanating from the odorous body. Place that body in a close vessel, and there is no odor from it. In *tasting*, the gustatory organs are touched by the thing tasted. Let those organs be coated, and there is no taste. In *hearing*, the drum of the ear is struck by the atmospheric vibrations. Cut off these vibrations from the ear, or paralyze the auditory nerve, and nothing is heard. In *vision*, the organ of sight is touched by the rays of light coming from the object viewed. Cut off these rays from contact with the eye, and nothing is seen.

Such being the fact, we may at once dismiss all speculations and difficulties respecting the passage of impressions to the mind, by nervous fluids, cerebral vibrations, &c., and also respecting intervening ideas, or images, which might give rise to false perceptions. The naked truth comes to be this. Here is a sense, with its organ. When something actually *touches* that organ, an *impres-*

sion is made, and the attentive mind *knows* it. This is sensation. And now, can the mind take *another* step, and know infallibly what that something *is?* I maintain that it can.

EACH ENTITY IS ORIGINALLY KNOWN BY ITS APPROPRIATE SENSE.

Until our perception is *educated*, so to speak, we must rely, for the absolute accuracy of it, on that sense only which is originally appropriate to the object. A great source of doubt, in regard to our perceptions, has arisen from relying on the wrong sense. Thus, when we rely upon the eye, in a case where any thing but colors is to be perceived, we may be liable to deception. Let the reader, then, refer to what has been said in relation to the specific office of each sense.

The greatest source of false perceptions is the eye. It is so much more easy and rapid an instrument of perception than the hand, that we are led to place ultimate reliance upon it. But all must admit, that if we had no evidence of an external world excepting what the eye affords, we could not know that such a world exists. Every man has had optical illusions enough practised upon him to have learned this. But when the hand is applied, all illusion, if there was any, is dispelled; and the mind *knows* whether the perception is *true*.

ENTITIES MAY ALSO BE KNOWN BY OTHER THAN THEIR APPROPRIATE SENSES.

When one sense has become *accustomed* to take the place of another, we may ordinarily trust its decisions. For instance, although we must originally rely upon the touch for our knowledge of objects around us, yet, when the eye has been trained, we may in most cases depend upon its perceptions. It was obviously *designed* to supply the place of the hand, as a more rapid and convenient instrument; and, when properly taught, it will do it with entire accuracy.

All persons favored with sight from infancy have so disciplined their eye, that in ninety-nine cases out of a hundred it does not deceive them. When they ride in the country, they do not need to descend from the carriage into the fields, and put their hands upon every object they see, to make their perceptions sure. When they look upon a great city, they need not thread the streets, and lay their hands on all parts of all the buildings, to be certain that they are not mere "castles of airy fancy." When they meet their friends, they need not *feel* them, in order to be sure that their perceptions are true, and that there is no risk in tendering to them their welcome. Indeed, the eye has been so accustomed to notice them, that it has become a more certain instrument than the hand.

All *civil courts* rely upon the testimony of the eye. Men are arraigned, tried, condemned, executed, on the mere testimony of the eye, where only that of the hand is our original and ultimate reliance. How idle, then, the speculations of those philosophers who would bring the reality of all we see into doubt.

HOW THE ORGANS OF SENSE ARE TESTED.

I have said that our organs of sense may be in a state to deceive us. How can we know whether they are so? I answer, By comparing our perceptions *with those of mankind in general.* Disorder is the *exception*, not the *rule.* The perceptions of the *great body* of mankind are the *standard.* If, for instance, all objects present to me one color, where others see a variety, I am to infer that my organ of vision is disordered, and must not trust it. If I do, I am liable to take silver for gold. So, also, if my *taste, smell*, &c., are contradicted by the perceptions of mankind in general, I am to infer some organic derangement. Cases of organic defect, like the above, sometimes occur; and they are easily detected.

HOW THE MEDIA OF PERCEPTION ARE TESTED.

Media of perception are tested by *experiment.* A rod with one end under water looks crooked. Take it from the water, and it looks straight. We thus learn that the apparent crookedness of the rod was owing to the medium in which a part of it was seen. A stump, seen through a dense mist, may look like a man; after the mist has gone, it looks like itself. To a person having on green spectacles, all creation looks green; even the dazzling sun is of a sickly hue. Take them off, and creation resumes her natural colors. In this way children amuse themselves; and experiment teaches them, long before they reach manhood, — what philosophers have so often failed to learn, — when they may rely upon their perceptions.

HOW THE SANITY OF THE MIND IS TESTED.

Supposing the organs of sense sound, and the media of perception understood, the *mind* may be in fault; and and how is this to be known? No man may be his own judge. The very fact that a man's intellect is disordered, disqualifies him for this office. Judgment passes from his mind to that of others. When others see him the unhappy victim of false perceptions, which can be referred to no cause but the mind, the case is too painfully clear to justify withholding the merciful appliances due to an insane person.

These, then, are the conditions under which we may know whether our perceptions are true. The question which we have started is answered. If we are sure the right sense is applied, the organ sound, the medium proved, the mind sane, — and sure we may be, — what we *think* we perceive we certainly *do* perceive. Under these circumstances, what we learn by perception is as *certain knowledge* as what we learn by sensation.

PERCEPTION PRESUPPOSES ATTENTION.

There can be no perception without some kind of attention. The mere *presence* of an object to the organ of sense does not make us perceive it. The image of an object upon the retina does not of itself make us see the object. Thousands of pictures of objects are every day impinged on the retina of the eye, of which no notice is taken; myriads of vibrations on the ear, of odorous particles in the organ of smell, of things touching our bodies, are not perceived, for want of attention. As it is the mind that perceives, if its attention is diverted or wanting, there can be no perception.

It has been previously shown, that even sensation supposes, at least, involuntary attention, and there can be no perception without sensation. Other things equal, *the more fixed the attention, the clearer and more accurate will be the perception.*

PROCESS OF PERCEPTION.

Is the full perception of an object strictly *instantaneous*, or is it *gradual?* My opinion favors the theory, that it is to some extent gradual; although so unfortunate in this particular as to differ somewhat from Dugald Stewart, and also from Professor Upham, who quotes him with approbation. As most that Stewart says on this point expresses what I would wish to say, I will quote him entire, and then notice what I judge erroneous. "Suppose the eye," he says, "fixed in a particular position, and the picture of an object to be painted on the retina. Does the mind perceive the complete figure of the object at once, or is this perception the result of the various perceptions we have of the different points in the outline? With respect to this question, the principles already stated lead me to conclude, that the mind does at one and the same time perceive every point in the outline of the object, — provided the whole of it be painted on the retina at the same instant, — for perception, like consciousness, is an involuntary operation.

" As no two points, however, of the outline are in the same direction, every point constitutes just as distinct an object of attention to the mind as if it were separated by an interval of empty space from all the rest. If the doctrine, therefore, formerly stated be just, it is impossible for the mind to attend to more than one of these points at once; and as the perception of the figure of the object implies a knowledge of the relative situation of the different points, with respect to each other, we must conclude, that the perception of figure by the eye is the result of a number of acts of attention. These acts of attention, however, are performed with such rapidity, that the effect, with respect to us, is the same as if the perception were instantaneous.

" In further confirmation of this reasoning, it may be remarked, that if the perception of visible figure were an immediate consequence of the picture on the retina, we should have, at the first glance, as distinct an idea of a figure of a thousand sides as of a triangle or a square. The truth is, that, where the figure is very simple, the process of the mind is so rapid, that the perception seems to be instantaneous; but when the sides are multiplied beyond a certain number, the interval of time necessary for these different acts of attention becomes perceptible.

" It may, perhaps, be asked, what I mean by a *point* in the outline of a figure, and what it is that constitutes this point one object of attention. The answer, I apprehend, is, that this point is the *minimum visibile.* If the point be less, we cannot perceive it; if it be greater, it is not all seen in one direction. If these observations be admitted, it will follow, that, without the faculty of memory, we could have had no perception of visible figure." *

These observations are ingenious, and seem to be in the main sound and instructive. With some exceptions, they are what we should all probably admit on the subject of perception. The exceptions which I would make are these: he supposes *perception* without *attention*, and

* Stewart's Philosophy, vol. i. p 78.

on the ground that "perception is an involuntary operation," concludes that "the mind does at one and the same time perceive every point in the outline of the object, provided the whole of it be painted on the retina at the same instant."

Attention is partly voluntary and partly involuntary.* Involuntary, when something is addressed to the sensibilities so urgently as to *force* attention; voluntary, when the attention is designedly given. Now, the reasons before assigned seem conclusive, that without *some* attention there can be no perception.

My inference is, "that the mind does" *not* "at one and the same time perceive every point in the outline of the object," but that its final perception is the result of several combined perceptions.

The only difference between us is, Stewart supposes that the mind *perceives* "every point in the outline of the object" at once, but does not *attend* to it; whereas, I suppose the mind does *not* perceive the whole at once, for the *want* of the requisite attention. The want of this attention he allows, and therefore, placing attention in the relation of a necessary means of perception, his argument is conclusive in favor of the view which I have maintained.

* This subject has been more fully considered under the head *Attention*, p. 146.

QUESTIONS ON CHAPTER VI.

What is said of controversies on the subject of perception? What is the only important question at issue? What is said of the greatest truths in science? What is perception, considered as a mental *act?* What considered as a mental *attribute?* What is *intuitive* perception? To what are present inquiries restricted? What are the relative offices of sensation and perception? In how many respects do sensation and perception differ? *First? Second?* What is an *entity?* What do entities include? What is a *nonentity? Objective* entities? *Subjective?* How do we know the latter?

How, *first*, do we know the former? How *secondly?* Illustrate. What perceptions are *true?* What must we remember? What do we mean when we speak of ideas corresponding with entities? Illustrate. Why do ideas, so unlike their objects, represent them? Remarks. Give examples of *true* perception. Does perception give the idea, or the idea the perception? What is said of the schoolmen? What are *false* perceptions? From what may they arise? *First* cause? *Second? Third?* Give *examples* of false perception. What has been one of the most important and disputed points? What have Berkeley and others concluded? What Hume and others? What is now the exact point? What is said of testing perceptions? How are *physical* entities known? Illustrations? Inference? By what is each entity originally known? What is the greatest source of *false* perceptions? What must all admit? What may we do after one sense has become accustomed to take the place of another? Examples. What is said of *civil courts?* How may we *test* our organs of sense? Example? How may we test the *media* of perception? Example. How may we test the sanity of the mind? What does perception presuppose? Remarks. Other things equal, on what does clearness and accuracy of attention depend? Is the full perception of an object *instantaneous* or gradual? Let the reader examine what is said, and give his own opinion.

CHAPTER VII.

CONCEPTION.

We have now reached the point where we may suppose the ideas of the external world fairly presented to the mind. It is believed that the way has been pointed out, by which we not only *obtain* our ideas of things around us, but by which we may *certainly know* that those ideas are *correct.* The next subject in course is *conception.* Considered as a mental *faculty*, it is, in the strictest sense, *that power by which we form notions of absent objects of perception and of past sensations.*

This definition will be best understood by an example. A man has visited Niagara Falls, and has *perceived* the sublime object there displayed. After returning home, that object frequently comes up to his mind afresh. While standing upon the banks of the river and looking upon the cataract, he had a *perception* of it; the recurrence of that object to his mind after returning home is a *conception* of it.

The mind first *perceives* its object before *conceiving* it; and it never conceives a physical object but in its absence. Perception is the introduction of a stranger; conception the entertaining of an acquaintance. The first *looks* at a thing; the second *takes it up*, to hold it before the mind as an object of contemplation.

So of a sensation. It is first *experienced*, as a present reality; it afterward recurs to the mind, and is, as it were, *felt over again;* thus the former experience becomes a conception.

CONCEPTION OF SPECULATIVE TRUTHS.

The term *conception* is also applied, in popular language, to *abstract* and *metaphysical* truths. It is thus used with the same latitude assigned to perception. Dugald Stewart says, "In ordinary language, we apply the same word, *perception*, to the knowledge which we have, by our senses, of external objects, and to our knowledge of speculative truths; and yet an author would be justly censured who should treat of these two operations of the mind under the same article of perception. I apprehend there is as wide a difference between the conception of a truth and the conception of an absent object of sense as between the perception of a tree and the perception of a mathematical theorem."

There is, undoubtedly, the same difference in the one case as in the other; the instances are exactly parallel. In the one case it is an intuitive conception, in the other an intuitive perception. The perceptive and conceptive mental acts sustain to each other the same relation, whether applied to internal or external objects.

FURTHER APPLICATION OF THE TERM.

Conception is also applied to the mental act by which we form a *notion of objects described, or in any way represented.* A history, a drama, a play, furnishes materials of perception, from which the mind conceives the objects represented. It is evident, that in all these cases the mental act of conceiving is essentially one and the same.

DISTINCTION BETWEEN CONCEPTION AND MEMORY.

At first view, conception may seem to be the same as memory. But, on examination, it will appear that they differ in essential particulars. They do certain things in common, but each has also its peculiar offices.

Memory goes back to the *time*, *place*, *circumstances* in which objects were perceived. Conception has nothing to do with all these.* It stays at home and takes the objects there, as handed over to it by memory. The latter is servant to the former. Memory *collects* the materials, conception *reforms* them into the semblance of the original structure. "When a painter makes a picture of a friend who is absent or dead, he is commonly said to paint from memory; and the expression is sufficiently correct for common conversation. But in an analysis of mind, there is ground for a distinction. The power of conception enables him to make the features of his friend an object of thought, so as to copy the resemblance; the power of memory recognizes these features as a former object of perception. Every act of memory includes an idea of the past; conception implies no idea of time whatever." †

Moreover, an object is often conceived on *representations*, at the very time they are made.

DISTINCTION BETWEEN CONCEPTION AND IMAGINATION.

The distinction between conception and imagination may not be at first so obvious. These also have some things in common, but they have still distinct offices. Conception takes *all* the materials which memory brings to it, and reforms them into the identical semblance of the original structure. Imagination *selects* such materials as it pleases, and forms them into similar, varied, or quite original structures, to suit the fancy. Hence con-

* Reid usually identifies conception with imagination. On the other hand, owing probably to the common doctrine of ideas, Des Cartes, Gassendi, Locke, Hume, and Berkeley often identify it with *perception*. I am, therefore, led to be what might otherwise seem unnecessarily explicit on these points.

† Stewart's Philosophy, book i. p. 79. Shakspeare calls this power "*the mind's eye*."

"My father! Methinks I see my father."

"*Where, my lord?*"

"In my *mind's eye*, Horatio."

ception is *reformative*, imagination *recreative*. Conception presents an *exact transcript* of the objects of perception. Imagination exhibits them under *every fanciful variety*. A more particular account of memory and imagination will be given under the appropriate heads.

VIVIDNESS OF CONCEPTIONS.

There is a great difference between men, as to the *vividness* of their conceptions, and also, in the same man, between his conceptions of *different objects*. Things which we have *seen* recur to us most readily. The *sight* of an object paints it, as it were, upon the mind, in such vivid form and color as to leave less for conception to do. When once an object has been clearly seen by the natural eye, there is ever after an exact *image* of that object at the service of the mind. That the form or image of an object greatly facilitates our conception of it, is a matter of universal experience. How much more easily does the pupil conceive of the form and movements of the earth by looking upon an artificial globe!

INFLUENCE OF ASSOCIATION ON CONCEPTION.

Another reason why we more easily conceive of objects of sight than of others is found in the *influence of association*. All objects which address the eye are *complex;* they have more or less of *parts*. If, then, only one part or feature of the complex object is recalled, association helps to replace the whole. There is presented, as it were, a variety of points for the mind to lay hold of, in its attempts to recover the object. The same association extends to surrounding objects.

Objects of *taste*, *smell*, *feeling*, *hearing*, present no form or image of themselves. There is nothing that they look like; nothing pictured to the mind to assist in conceiving them. Being also much more simple than objects of sight, they present fewer points of apprehension.

INFLUENCE OF ATTENTION ON CONCEPTION.

In smelling, tasting, &c., the mind is mostly *passive* Comparatively little attention is demanded. It has bee; already observed, that when we look upon an object, as a picture, house, landscape, we do not embrace the whol at the first glance. The mind takes up one point at time, and, by a process of active attention, rapidly com bines them into a whole. Now, it is a known law of mind, that what is acquired with most *effort* is ordinaril the most firmly retained. As the perception of an objec becomes clear and full, the conception of it becomes pro portionally vivid.

An artist looks upon a fine picture. As he gazes point after point falls under his notice, until, after perhap hours or days of attentive study, the picture is unfolde to his perception in something of the minuteness an fulness of its real excellence. He has *mastered* it. A his mind has thus taken firm possession of it, ever afte when memory serves, conception readily reforms it.

But let him merely *smell* or *taste* something, and tl sensation comes and goes in a moment. He is almo wholly *passive* in it; it flits through his mind, and gone. It is, therefore, with difficulty — a difficulty pro portioned to the ease with which it came — that he ca afterwards recall it.

CONCEPTION OF MUSICAL SOUNDS.

Next to visible objects, *sounds* are most readily cor ceived. This may be accounted for, *first*, because the require more *attention* than objects of taste, smell, &c *secondly*, because they excite more deep mental *feeling* and are therefore better remembered; *thirdly*, becaus they are attended with more *association of ideas;* an *fourthly*, because there is more exact *repetition.*

Precisely the same taste, smell, or feeling probabl never recurs; there is of these an endless variety o modifications perpetually recurring, so as to confuse the onception of any one of them. But musical sounds re *distinct*, *unique*, the same note being struck over and ver again. The perception of the sound thus becomes *xact*, and the subsequent conceptions of it proportionably *istinct* and *vivid*.

INFLUENCE OF HABIT ON CONCEPTIONS OF SIGHT.

Our conceptions may be indefinitely *improved.* "A erson accustomed to drawing retains a much more per- ct notion of a building or landscape which he has een than any one who has never practised that art. A ortrait painter traces the form of a human body from nemory, with as little exertion of attention as he em- loys in writing the letters which compose his name." *

I have known several persons whose conceptions were t first so feeble that they could hardly arrange the out- nes of an absent object, by a course of diligent training cceed in such efforts admirably. This was, perhaps, in rt owing to the increase of mechanical skill, but more the increased clearness and vigor of perception.

INFLUENCE OF HABIT ON CONCEPTIONS OF MUSICAL SOUNDS.

Scarcely less marked is the improvement of which con- ptions of *sound* are susceptible. The ear, nearly as uch as the eye, requires to be educated, and this specially in relation to musical sounds. Probably not ne in a thousand has a discriminating perception of elodies and harmonies until experience has taught him; nd until his perceptions of them become distinct, his nceptions must of course be confused.

Through the mind of the inexperienced youth, the rains of the opera float as a confused mass of pleas- g sounds. In process of time, his perceptions become

* Stewart's Philosophy, book i. p. 81.

discriminating; the strains then recur to him on days fol lowing the exhibition, not, as at first, in unmeaning confusion, but in the order and beauty of well-arrange harmonies. Nothing but the knowledge of musical char acters is wanting to reduce them to paper. When thi knowledge is acquired, and the association is establishe between the notes and the sounds, a person may men tally realize the most exquisite music by merely lookin upon the notes. There is music in the *mind*, though no in the *ear*. Beethoven is said to have composed some of his finest pieces of music after he became deaf. Th music in his mind he imprinted on the page, and left i to those favored with hearing to interpret and give audibl utterance to his symbols.

CONCEPTION SUBSERVIENT TO DESCRIPTION.

It is believed, on good grounds, that a person of vivi conception will write a better description of an *absen* than of a *present* object. Conception never replaces *al* the points perceived. It recalls those that made th *deepest impression* — the most *characteristic and impo tant*. And these, seeing all the points of an object car not be described, are the right ones to be presented.

The most successful painter is he who seizes upon th most characteristic features of his subject and exhaust his talents upon them. This was eminently the metho of the distinguished modern artists Peal and Stewar For the same reason, the most successful writer is h who presents vividly the most striking and characteristi particulars of whatever he attempts to describe. Thes are ordinarily the very particulars which his conception furnish.

FACTS IN PROOF.

Thomson, the celebrated author of the Seasons, sper a large part of his earlier years amid rural scenes. H afterwards retired to a garret, in London, and there re wrote those glowing descriptions of country scener which have immortalized his fame. Homer and Milton, the princes of ancient and modern poetry, were blind at the time they wrote, and of course wrote solely from conception and imagination.

Young, Cowper, Scott, Campbell, Gray, were retired from the busy scenes of the world at the time they wrote. Nearly all poetry and other descriptive compositions have been written some time after, and at a distance from, the time and place at which the objects described were seen.

IS CONCEPTION ATTENDED WITH BELIEF?

Some have supposed that every act of conception is attended with a belief of the existence and presence of its *object*. Of this number is Dugald Stewart. "Every exertion of that power," he supposes, "is accompanied with a belief that its object exists before us at the present moment." In illustration of this he says, "When a painter conceives the face and figure of an absent friend, in order to draw his picture, he believes for the moment that his friend is before him." *

That this belief *sometimes* exists, in cases of very vivid conception, I shall endeavor to show; but that this is *ordinarily* the case, most men will be slow to believe. To draw the face and figure of an absent friend is often the work of days; during all the time in which the canvas is receiving the touches of the brush, the conception must be sustained. Does the painter, during all this time, believe that his friend is *actually before him?*

The exertion of the power of conception must attend every touch of the brush; and if this supposes the belief of the actual presence of its object, how many husbands and fathers would wish to learn the blessed art, and spend their lives in painting their departed wives and children! Conception may be sufficiently vivid for purposes of painting and describing, without rising to the point here supposed. Nothing is gained by pushing

* Stewart's Philosophy, book i. p. 84.

philosophy into the marvellous, or pressing a theory beyond the sober dictates of common experience.

CASES OF SUPPOSED BELIEF ACCOUNTED FOR BY ASSOCIATION.

A young man points a gun, in sport, at his sister. She knows her brother would not shoot her for the world; perhaps she even knows that the gun is not loaded. There can then be no *belief*, in any true sense of the term, that her brother is about to shoot her. Still, she screams out with terror. Having always *associated* the aiming of a gun with the work of death, *it has of itself become terrific.*

A law of the nervous system explains this. It is said of a man who had submitted to a very painful operation on his teeth, that, whenever he saw the surgeon's instrument, he felt the pain renewed. This was not because he believed the operation again in progress; it was clearly the effect of *association* on his nervous system.

CASES OF REAL MOMENTARY BELIEF.

But there are other cases which seem to imply *actual belief.* At an exhibition in a country village, some warrior Indians were personified. When the terrific personages leaped upon the stage, with their instruments of death, and approached the front with menacing attitude, several of the spectators near the stage leaped up, screamed with terror, and rushed violently away; others fainted. It became necessary to drop the curtain, to avert more serious consequences. Some of those individuals afterwards said, that, at the moment referred to, they really thought those hideous characters veritable murderous Indians. They thought, as they expressed it, that they "were sent for." As soon as they had time to reflect, they knew better, but, at the moment of excitement, their conceptions got the better of their knowledge.

A little girl who had lost her mother was constantly

reminded of her by a faithful portrait suspended against the wall. Into whatever part of the room the child went, the mother's eyes seemed to follow her. She could indulge in no forbidden acts but those terrible eyes of rebuke were upon her. She at last watched the opportunity when none were present and erased them. She then felt again at liberty. There seems to be no doubt but that this child was troubled with such vivid conceptions, in regard to what was denoted by those pictured eyes, that at times she really believed her mother was looking through them upon her.

At an exhibition of jugglery, one of the feats to be performed was that of cutting off the head of a fowl, and then seeming to restore it to life. All of course knew it to be a farce; but so dexterously was the trick performed, that, at the moment the chicken flew up alive from the juggler's hand, a simple man near by sprang from his seat, exclaiming, "I would as lief have him cut off *my* head as not," and was about advancing to have the experiment tried upon him, when he came to his senses. Here there seems to have been a real illusion, a *momentary belief*.*

VIEWS OF REID.

Dr. Reid professedly rejects the idea of belief attending conceptions, and yet, in his explanations, virtually concedes all that I have claimed. "I knew a man," he says, "who was as much convinced as any man of the folly of the popular belief of apparitions in the dark; yet he could not sleep in the room alone, nor go alone into a room in the dark. Can it be said that his fear did not imply a belief of danger? This is impossible. Yet his philosophy convinced him that he was in no more danger in the dark, when alone, than with company. Here an unreasonable belief, which was merely a prejudice of the

* The above examples belong to the *third* class of conceptions noticed near the beginning of this chapter. All dramatic exhibitions, and others analogous to them, are designed to awaken *vivid conceptions of absent or imagined objects*.

nursery, stuck so fast as to govern his conduct, in opposition to his speculative belief as a philosopher and a man of sense."

This admission can be reconciled with Reid's expressed disavowal of belief attending conceptions only by supposing him to adopt the explanation of some, who say, perhaps not wide of the truth, that they "believe and don't believe at the same time."

CONCEPTION ATTENDED WITH PERMANENT BELIEF.

Not only does the illusion sometimes rise to *momentary* belief, but, in extraordinary instances, the belief has been rendered *permanent.* I am not now speaking of cases of *insanity*, which will fall under another head. Persons of sane intellect have had conceptions so vivid as to assume, in their minds, the *permanent character of realities.*

A well-educated man, of the middle age, was deeply afflicted by the death of a lady whom he was expecting to marry. He stated that one night, as he was lying on his bed, thinking upon the lost object of affection, suddenly the room became light as noonday, and she stood by the side of him in full form, the same as before her death. She was dressed in white. She looked upon him with a smile; said she had come from the happy world to comfort him, and must soon return. She lifted her hands towards him, blessed him, and vanished: the room was again dark as before.

Now, we believe this to have been a mere conception, the object of previous perceptions having been replaced by highly-excited feelings. But, to this hour, the man in question believes it to have been a reality. He as sincerely believes that the room was actually illuminated, and that the form of his friend, attended with her departed spirit, did actually stand before him, as he believes any fact in history. Such cases differ from those of monomanianism, as a momentary *illusion*, resulting in permanent *belief*, differs from a permanent *illusion.*

CONCEPTION GIVING LIFE TO INANIMATE OBJECTS.

When a man strikes his foot against a stone, or comes in painful contact with any object in his way, his first impulse is often a feeling of *resentment* towards the object. Sometimes he turns in rage to beat it. How shall we account for this? By association? But it seems an instantaneous impulse, and is most common in children, whose associations are less formed than those of adults. But if the man is not angry at the offending object, because he associates it with some living creature against which he might be justly angry, must he not at the moment conceive of some *actual blame in the object itself?* The latter solution seems the most reasonable.

Blame supposes, of course, life and capability of punishment. "It seems impossible that there should be resentment against a thing, which, at that very moment, is considered as inanimate, and consequently incapable either of intending harm or of being punished. There must, therefore, I conceive, be some momentary notion or conception that the object of our resentment is capable of punishment." *

FALSE CONCEPTION FROM IMPERFECT PERCEPTION.

A false conception may precede or attend an *imperfect view of its object.* A man walking out on a moonlight evening saw an object moving, as it seemed to him, just over the fence, in the field. He approached the fence, and *conceived* it to be a woman, dressed in white, moving towards him. He was not a believer in ghosts, but, for the moment, his imagination mastered his philosophy. It was certainly a woman, or the ghost of a woman; possibly the latter. He stopped; the woman stopped also. He called; no answer came. Possibly it was a creature in distress, unable to speak; so he summoned resolution to approach her, when he *perceived* the object to be a *white*

* Reid's Philosophy, vol. ii. p. 385.

birch stump. The previous *dimness of perception,* aided by *excited imagination,* gave rise to the false conception.

FALSE CONCEPTION FROM EXCITED ANTICIPATION.

Sometimes, when the anticipation of seeing an object is intensely excited, the presence of almost *any* thing awakens in the mind a conception of the *object expected.* This case differs from the preceding, in the fact, that here the illusion is owing to *excited anticipation;* in the other, to *defect of vision.* The following fact is somewhere stated: A father and son were pursuing a bear in a wood. The son passed round to turn the animal into a path, but not finding it, was on his retreat through that path, when his father shot him dead for the animal. The open path gave the father opportunity for a fair view; but so filled was his mind with anticipations of the bear, that he could see nothing else. Men are often duped by false conceptions, arising from over-ardent anticipations.

PROTRACTED FALSE CONCEPTION.

When dimness of vision is joined with wakeful and expectant imagination, the illusions of conception are still stronger and more lasting. It is then no difficult task to people the world, for hours together, with our own creations of every kind. The eye must needs see *something,* enough to awaken imagination; leaving as much as possible to be conceived. Or, if we wish in a measure to bridle imagination, and confine the conception to a *particular object,* the representation of that *object* should be made as distinctly as possible, and all *attending circumstances should be thrown into obscurity;* since, if what precedes, attends and follows, is kept in view, it will dispel the illusion.

It is on this principle that *scenic* exhibitions are gotten up. The surrounding world is shut out; artificial lights put a new aspect upon things; imagination is roused; music beguiles the soul and leads it captive; well-arranged lights and shades of the painted canvas open to the eye a long distance of fairy scenes; and when the mind has thus been as much as possible cut off from all connection with the actual past and present, a brilliant picture or representation of the object to be conceived is ushered in before it.

At such times, many a grave philosopher has lost his wisdom, and been carried away captive by the illusions of imagination. He has conceived and felt, as actual realities, the scenes of distress, of terror, of breathless anxiety, of gushing joy represented before him. He has wept with sorrow; he has shuddered with fear; he has held his breath with suspense; he has burst into raptures of joy. He has thus given the strongest evidence of a conceived *reality* at work on his soul.

USES OF CONCEPTION.

What has been already said indicates the importance of this faculty in its relations to *descriptive writing*, *poetry*, *history*, *painting*, and *scenic exhibitions*. It also enters into the more profound and grave mental operations. We cannot analyze a subject, we cannot reason upon it, we can exercise no sound judgment upon it, until we have fairly conceived it. The advocate at the bar, the preacher in the pulpit, the statesman on the forum, are all, with the historian and the poet, equally dependent on this faculty.

It is a clear and full conception of the subject, more than perhaps any thing else, that gives brilliancy to description and poetry, force to argument, soundness to judgment, and power to eloquence. As conception is nearly allied to imagination, and by some identified with it, other remarks respecting its importance will be made in connection with the last-mentioned faculty, especially those which respect its relations to Christianity.

QUESTIONS ON CHAPTER VII.

What point have we now reached? What is *conception?* Illustration? To what else is the term *conception* applied? What does Stewart say? To what else is the same term applied? Is there a distinction between conception and memory? Explain it. Also the distinction between conception and *imagination.* What is said of *vividness* of conceptions? Of what things do we have the most vivid conceptions? Illustration? What is said of the influence of *association?* Of objects of *taste, smell,* &c.? What is said of the influence of attention on our conceptions? Illustrations? What is said of musical *sounds?* How is this accounted for, *first, secondly, thirdly, fourthly?* Are our conceptions susceptible of improvement? Examples? What is said of improvement of conceptions of *musical sounds?* What is said of the subserviency of conception to description? Reasons? State the facts in proof. Is conception attended with belief of the existence and presence of its object? State the views of Stewart. State what is said in reply. How are some cases of supposed belief accounted for? Give the illustrations. Are there cases of unquestionable belief? State those given. Give the views of Reid. Are conceptions ever attended with *permanent* belief? Give the example. State the instance of conception giving life to inanimate objects. How is this accounted for? State the example of false conception from imperfect perception. Give the illustration of false conceptions arising from excited anticipation. What is said of *protracted* false conceptions? Of *scenic* exhibitions? Of the uses of conception?

CHAPTER VIII.

PRIMARY RATIONAL KNOWLEDGE.

It has been stated that our primary knowledge is of two kinds, *sensuous* and *rational*. The former we have briefly considered. We began with the former, because our first knowledge is from this source. Man starts at the lowest point; he learns his humblest lessons first. He is put to school in the flesh, through its humble instrumentality to learn the alphabet of that great volume, which is to unfold to him its bright pages, long after the body shall have returned "to the dust as it was."

At what period the mind begins to have any other knowledge than that of a sensuous origin, it is impossible to tell. Sensuous knowledge is certainly the first. Various sensations of touch, of heat and cold, of pleasure and pain, fall early to the infant's lot. How much the mind learns from these and other sensations at this early period, none can tell us.

"One of the first natural sensations it has," subsequent to birth, "upon which sensational phenomena can be predicated, is that of *hunger*. Of this it must be *conscious*. The *sensation* and *consciousness* of it, co-existing, constitute its first *experience*. Whatever may be the diversity in human character, in this, their beginning experience, they are alike. When the child nurses, *combinations* begin with the outward world, and the blending of the mother's milk with the gastric juice produces the first sensation of hunger *gratified;* and this is its second experience. Here children begin to differ from each other, in the ratio of their different digestive sensations, and the diversity of character begins. The child now remains nearly stationary, till repeated experiences, within very narrow limits, of gratified hunger, enable it to *associate;* then mental combinations begin to grow rapidly, and *memory* combines itself with association, and their mutual interaction excites the imagination, and the *will to enjoy* springs into being. The action and interaction of these attributes of sensation upon each other constitute the whole range of the infant's mind." *

Of the early ideas obtained by sensation, it is only by cries, and smiles, and glances of the opening eye that the little stranger can ever speak to us, for as yet he has no other language; as to the future child, all is blotted from the records of memory. We watch, however, in that kindling countenance, and those significant movements, evident tokens of growing intellect; and long before language gives us a free exchange of thought, he is found to have made considerable progress, not only in that knowledge which comes through the senses, but that which *springs directly from the mind.* In respect to the former, however, he is far in advance of what he is in respect to the latter.

OUR INQUIRY CONFINED TO STRICT KNOWLEDGE.

It should be observed, that our inquiry is here restricted to actual *knowledge of facts.* It has been shown, that what we learn directly by the senses is of this description. What we feel, see, hear, taste, &c., we *know.* The sensations which they produce we know by *consciousness;* the things themselves, by direct *perception,* without any process of ratiocination, without any proof whatever, except what our own senses furnish.

Now we have *other* sources of knowledge, as direct and certain as these, not outward in the flesh, but inward in the pure mind. Here, as in the preceding case, no reasoning process is demanded, no proof wanted, but such as is *immediately furnished by the mind itself.* This point should be clearly settled, for many have stumbled here.

* Laws of Causation, pp. 144, 145.

Distinguished intellects, in other respects wise, by laboring to prove what was never designed to be proved, and therefore cannot be proved, — the proof being in itself, — have only "darkened counsel by words without wisdom," rendering obscure what the Creator has made plain.

DIVERSITY OF VIEWS ON THIS POINT.

At no other point in the whole range of mental science have philosophers diverged so widely as at this. Here, as we have seen, is the grand point of difference between the two great schools. Before John Locke wrote his famous Essay on the Human Understanding, the prevailing continental philosophy gave the widest possible range to the internal or rational sources of knowledge, maintaining that the mind is created with a fund of dormant ideas wrapped up in it, which the senses serve only to wake up; that all external nature is but the semblance or counterpart of ideas already in the mind, and therefore incompetent to teach it.

This method of philosophizing, descending from the ancient Platonic school, originated in a lofty desire to exalt spirit over matter, and restore to the soul the dominion and glory to which it is entitled. The design was worthy of the great minds which conceived it; the fault lay only in the means which they took to accomplish it. It was in the infancy of philosophy that such imposing theories were framed; and when imposing theories, sanctioned by great names, have, from an early period, deeply imbedded themselves in modes of thinking, it is the work of ages to root them out.

Moreover, there was something of *truth* in these theories. *Unmixed error cannot long survive.* Great errors are palmed upon the world *by virtue of the truths involved with them;* and when hoary-headed association has identified error with truth, it requires a bold, original mind, with uncommon powers of discrimination, to enter successfully upon the hazardous task of effecting a divorce. There is always, in such cases, danger of going too far, and removing truth with error. Whether Locke actually did so, in reducing the origin of all our knowledge to sensation and reflection, philosophers are not agreed to this day. But one thing is certain — some of his professed disciples have vibrated widely to the opposite extreme of the errors which he assailed, and have pressed his doctrine to the most absurd and dangerous speculations.

MATERIALISM.

Some philosophers, of the French school especially, have carried the sensuous theory into all the extravagant and revolting forms of *materialism*. They have conceived all the interior workings of the mind to be nothing more than "transformed sensations."

"If we consider," says Condillac, "that to remember, to compare, to judge, to distinguish, to imagine, to be astonished, to have abstract ideas of number and duration, to know truths, whether general or particular, are but so many modes of being attentive; that to have passions, to love, to hate, to fear, to will, are but so many different modes of desire; and that attention in the one case, and *desire* in the other, of which all these feeling are modes, are themselves, in their origin, *nothing mor than modes of sensation*, — we cannot but conclude tha sensation involves in itself [envelope] all the faculties of the soul."

Dr. Thomas Brown remarks, "This system, by the universality of transmutation supposed in it, truly deserves the name of intellectual alchemy;" and he justly adds, "The doctrine, then, as exhibited by Condillac and his followers, whatever merit it may have in itself, or however void it may be of merit of any kind, is not the doctrine of him [Locke] from whom it is said to be derived." *

TRANSCENDENTALISM.

In their attempts to rescue the mind from the grasp of a debasing materialism, others have leaned strongly back

* Brown's Philosophy, vol. i. p. 329.

ward towards the Platonic theory, and ascribed to man larger sources of knowledge, independently of the senses, than truth allows. They are of every grade, from the more free pupils of the primitive school to the more cautious disciples of the Kantian system, and the yet more modern and mystical forms of the Coleridgeian philosophy.

Here, then, we have the modern extremes — *materialism* on the one hand, and *transcendentalism* on the other. Which is the more dangerous, we should not be slow to decide: if we must have either, give us the enchanting dreams of transcendentalism, rather than the intellectual alchemy of materialism. But let us seek for *truth, and truth only.*

ACCURACY OF CLASSIFICATION.

We are never to forget that our classifications of mental phenomena are but the application of *names* to cover groups of similar ideas; that these groups may be more or less extended, to suit our convenience; and that, consequently, our classifications are *more or less arbitrary.* This should make us indulgent towards those from whom we are, in this matter, constrained to differ.

Still, it is of great importance in mental science that the terms we employ significantly represent the precise ideas intended. In defining and arranging classes, the severest accuracy should be observed. These remarks are especially applicable to the point before us.

BROWN'S CLASSIFICATION.

Stripped of its gorgeous drapery, the philosophy of Thomas Brown presents the varying phases of the human mind in a light *exceedingly simple.* Indeed, his fondness for simplification seems to have been a passion. He calls Reid, Stewart, and others to account for too much increasing the classes of mental phenomena. "The philosophy of Dr. Reid," he says, "and, in general, of the metaphysicians of this part of the island, has had the opposite tendency — to enlarge, as I conceive, far beyond what was necessary, the number of classes which they considered as too limited before; and in proportion, more regard has perhaps been paid to the differences, or supposed differences, of phenomena, than to their resemblances."

This philosopher carries his simplifying process so far as to refer *all* the intellectual states of the mind to "*two generic susceptibilities* — those of *simple suggestion* and *relative suggestion*." And much of his labor is eloquently employed in tracing connections between the various mental states, usually arranged under separate heads, to these two generic susceptibilities. But the fact, that he is constrained to adopt much of the usual nomenclature, and acknowledges its convenience, is evidence that, after all, the writers whom he arraigns were not so much out of the way. However this may be, subsequent writers have generally maintained nearly the same classification that had obtained before Brown's Philosophy appeared. But his theory of *suggestion* has found some favor, especially as applied to the sources of primary knowledge.

ORIGINAL SUGGESTION.

Adopting a part of Brown's theory of suggestion, Upham says, "Some of the cases of thought and knowledge which the mind becomes possessed of in itself, without the direct aid of the senses, are to be ascribed to suggestion. This word, in its application here, is used merely to express a simple but important fact, viz., that the mind, by its own activity and vigor, gives rise to certain thoughts. Without any mixture of hypothesis, or any qualifying intimation whatever, it gives the fact, and that is all."

The above writer proceeds to refer to this source a large list of ideas — such as ideas of existence, mind personal identity, unity, succession, duration; space power, right and wrong, and many others, of which, he says, "it might not be easy to make a complete enumeration;" but he thinks that, moreover, "we may probably ascribe the ideas of truth, freedom, design, or intelligence, necessity, fitness, or congruity, reality, order, plurality, totality, immensity, possibility, infinity, happiness, reward, punishment, and perhaps many others, to this source." *

OBJECTIONS TO THE ABOVE VIEW.

The writer above is professedly inquiring after "the origin of *knowledge*," and says, that "the soul has *fountains of knowledge within;*" and one of these fountains he makes "ORIGINAL SUGGESTION." † Two questions arise here: first, whether much that he ascribes to *suggestion* is not referable to *other sources*. It is believed the result will show that it is. Letting this pass for the present, a more important question is, whether a *suggestion* is tantamount to *knowledge*.

A *suggestion* is a mere *idea*, and, as Locke says, "our *knowledge* is *narrower* than our *ideas*." The term *suggestion* signifies *hint*, *intimation*, *insinuation;* the *power* of suggestion, then, is the power to hint or intimate something that is or may be. Under certain impulses, the mind may suggest absurdities and falsehoods, and may suppose them to be truths. Although the term be retricted to suggestions purely original, it is still open to this objection.‡

But it is not wise to contend about the meaning of a term. Authors have the right to define their terms; and if they abide by their definitions, we have no right to complain. In the present instance, the term, itself vague, is defined in the vaguest sense. The stern inquirer after the origin of *knowledge*, not of mere *hints* or *conjectures*,

* Upham's Philosophy, p. 130. † Upham's Philosophy, p. 120.

‡ Professor Upham places original suggestion by the side of consciousness, making them equally grounds of the highest kind of belief. "Consciousness," it may be remarked here, "is to be regarded as a ground or law of belief; and the belief attendant on the exercise of it, like that which accompanies the exercise of original suggestion, is of the highest kind."—*Philosophy*, p. 138. According to this, we are to regard what is merely *suggested* to us, by that power which he calls original suggestion, as equally certain with what we learn by *consciousness*—that is, by our actual experience. It is believed that the reasons for dissent from this position are sufficiently obvious.

is unsatisfied. When told that "the mind has fountains of knowledge within," and that "by its own activity and vigor," as the process of furnishing knowledge by suggestion is explained, it gives rise to the ideas of succession, truth, freedom, happiness, punishment, &c., he can see no sufficient reasons why it may not as well be said, "by its own activity and vigor," to give rise to *all* its knowledge.

It must be remembered that I am now speaking of that knowledge which the mind has without any second step. Spontaneous suggestion may give us *ideas*, but they are not *knowledge*. A higher tribunal must be awaited, before what is merely suggested becomes actually known. A second step, another mental act, besides suggestion, must be resorted to, before what is suggested becomes knowledge. I cannot, therefore, place suggestion among the "fountains of knowledge within," or what I term

THE RATIONAL POWERS OF PRIMARY KNOWLEDGE.

I shall speak of those powers by which the mind obtains its primary knowledge, independently of the senses, under two heads — INTUITION and CONSCIOUSNESS. Although writers, entitled to high regard, have placed *suggestion* in this number, for reasons above given, it is here excluded. Although suggestions of all kinds have an important agency here, as elsewhere, in furthering mental acquisitions, yet the mind's suggestive power is not an infallible teacher of knowledge. To allow it a place here, is really opening the door to all the vagaries of German transcendentalism.

How much do we gain towards defining the mental powers and limiting their range, towards restraining their vagaries and holding them to exact truth, by fighting the battles against the doctrine of innate ideas, if, after all, we allow a power of original suggestion, which can give us ideas without number, and those ideas are to be taken for knowledge?

The importance of this point may not at first be

obvious to all, and some may think less might better be said upon it. But looseness here essentially affects all subsequent inquiries in philosophy, and sends its disastrous effects onward to our views in religion. Reliance on *suggestions, or inspirations within*, to the neglect of a *higher authority without*, has ever tended to flood the world with infidelity. None are so obstinate in error, none so disinclined to receive the lessons of wisdom from above, as those who rely most upon the spontaneous suggestions of their own minds.

It is believed that to these two mental powers, *intuition* and *consciousness*, may be referred all the real knowledge now under consideration to which the human mind can lay claim. They will be considered in the next chapter.

QUESTIONS ON CHAPTER VIII.

What is said at the opening of this chapter? Which knowledge do we have first, *sensuous* or *rational*? What is said on this point? Of the early ideas obtained by sensation? What progress is the child found to have made before he can speak to us? To what is the inquiry here restricted? What is said on this point? What of *other* sources of knowledge? Reasons assigned why this point should be clearly understood? What is said of diversity of views on this point? What is said of the prevailing philosophy before Locke? Remarks? Was there any truth in these theories? How does this appear? What is said of some of Locke's disciples? Of the French school? Condillac? Brown's reply? Of transcendentalism? What are the two extremes? Which would the reader prefer, if he must have either? What is said of classification of the mental powers? What of Brown's classification? How far does he carry his simplifying process? What have subsequent writers generally maintained? What is said of Upham's original suggestion? What is the first question that arises here? What is a more important question? Remarks on this subject? What are the rational powers of primary knowledge? What objections to considering the mind's suggestive power an infallible teacher of knowledge? What importance attaches to this point? To what may *all* our primary rational knowledge be referred?

CHAPTER IX.

INTUITION.

Intuition implies *immediate mental perception.* Some things are known without being proved, their proof being in themselves. They only require to be *stated* to be *known.* Intuition is the power of knowing these things. It may therefore be defined, that power *by which the mind infallibly perceives, without any admonition of the senses, and without any process of reasoning.* It suggests nothing; its office is higher, to *know.* It does this, and nothing more. It goes not from home; it never commutes its office, but remains eternally in the same position — the mental eye ever open, piercing, sure. We are therefore justified in considering it *the power of immediately knowing whatever falls within its sphere.*

REASONS FOR USING THE TERM INTUITION.

As the term intuition has been generally used in relation to matters of proof, and especially in connection with mathematical demonstrations, reasons may be demanded for using it here.* The term being generic, it respects knowledge in general. Logicians and mathematicians have made a specific use of it. Still, the term

* Intuition is nearly synonymous with reason, as the latter term is used in the metaphysical school. The distinction made by German philosophers between *reason* and *understanding* is, in many respects, the same as that made by the Scotch and English between *intuition* and *reasoning* or *discursive* faculties. The former allow, however, a much wider field to *reason* than the latter do to *intuition.*

may properly be used in its original and generic sense. It expresses what needs to be here expressed, and what no other term expresses so exactly. Let us see: suppose we take *suggestion*, the term sometimes used to denote mental phenomena, some of which we call intuitions. The mind *suggests* something; that something is *true*, or *false*, or *doubtful*. Suppose it *false*.

It may be said, that to know a falsehood is real knowledge, as well as to know a truth. So be it. But then the mind does not yet know that it *is* a falsehood. The man is conscious of having a *suggestion* or *conjecture* in his mind respecting the thing in question, but no *knowledge*.* Nor, until some other power than that of mere suggestion is brought to bear, can he be said to have any knowledge respecting it. That other power needed is *intuition*. The thing suggested is *intuitively perceived* to be either true or false. If perceived to be *true*, the mind has thus obtained the *knowledge of a truth*; if seen to be *false*, the *knowledge of a falsehood*.

If it be said that a mere conjecture, doubt, query, rising in the mind as such, or a mere suggestion, indicating something not yet certainly known as either true or false, real or unreal, is all that is meant by the knowledge in question, it is only necessary for me to say, that this is not what I understand and intend to designate by *primary knowledge*. The term here is always meant to indicate an *entity known* — known as a truth, a falsehood, an absurdity, a reality, a conjecture, or whatever it is. And for *this knowledge*, in the present case,† we fall back on *intuition*.

As explicitness is very important here, the following particulars should be noticed: —

1. Although the power of intuition, like all others, is gradually developed, yet there are *no degrees of assur-*

* If we adopt the mode of designating mental phenomena favored by Brown, we should say the man is conscious of having his mind in a *state of conjecture*, not in a *state of knowledge*, respecting the thing in question. He considers ideas mere states of mind, and not any thing distinct from the mind itself.

† I say *in the present case*, because, in numerous other cases, suggestion puts the mind on the track to knowledge obtained by a process of reasoning. It is a handmaid to knowledge of *all* kinds.

ance in its decision. The intuitions of the child, so far as they go, are precisely the same as those of the adult. Years of study and thought cannot change or modify them. The child and the adult, the untaught and the philosopher, are herein alike; so far as their intuitions reach, their knowledge is equally certain.

2. All intuitive, as well as all sensuous knowledge, is *acquired.* The mind has no more knowledge of intuitive truths than it has of any others, until intuition has been exercised upon them. There is a susceptibility to them, requiring only that they be suggested, or in some way brought before the mind, to be at once recognized as truths. This is what D'Alembert meant by the remark, that "all intuitive knowledge is but the mind's recognition of what it previously knew." To the same intent, we sometimes hear a person say, when a self-evident truth is suggested to him, "I knew that before, but never before *thought* of it." In strict truth, he did *not* know it before; for a man cannot be said to *know* what was *never in his thoughts;* but he only needed to *think* of it to *know* it. To *know* a thing by only *thinking* of it, is intuition.

3. Intuitive truths *admit of no proof.* They are *above* all proof, their witness *being in themselves.* Any thing that can be proved is not a subject of pure intuition. All attempts to prove intuitive truths are but a begging of the question, or a running round in a circle. Some have supposed, for example, the existence of God an intuitive truth; but if it is demonstrable by a process of reasoning, it ceases to be strictly intuitive. Although the chain of argument have but two or three links, something more than intuition is demanded.

4. The teachings of intuition are *irresistible.* They take the mind by force. Every man *must* believe what it teaches him. Any thing that a man can willingly avoid knowing is not a subject of intuition; for willingly to avoid knowing a thing implies that he has thought of it; and whatever intuitive truth he has *thought* of, he already *knows.* Suppose, for instance, a man undertake to be ignorant of the truth that there is a moral distinction between right and wrong. His undertaking to be igno-

rant of it implies that it is in his thoughts; and its being in his thoughts, makes him already know it. He has only to *think* of it, and he irresistibly *knows* it.

5. Subjects of intuition being facts, which cannot be proved, *philosophy has only to define them*, leaving their proof with every individual. What every man knows by only *thinking* of it, needs only to be *stated*. Volumes have been written, essaying to prove intuitive truths, which have served no other purpose than to show the folly of attempting to do what the Creator has already done for us.

But great care must be exercised on this point, not to admit as intuitive any thing not strictly so. Intuitive knowledge is quite limited, but of the highest importance. Its great value is in the fact that it is one of the essential elements in all mental acquisitions.

I. MATHEMATICAL AXIOMS.

All *mathematical axioms*, strictly so called, are subjects of intuitive knowledge. They cannot be proved, for they are proved already as soon as they are stated. To know them is to prove them.

So soon, for example, as a child is mature enough to understand you, if you say to him, "The whole of any thing is more than any one of its parts," he intuitively perceives it to be so. Or if you say, "The half of any thing is equal to the whole of it," he intuitively perceives it *not* to be so. The falseness of the one statement and the truth of the other require no proof. Could you prove them a thousand times, you could not make them more certain to his mind. But you cannot prove them. In attempting to do so, you must assume as proved what remains to be proved; you must, indeed, beg at every step.

It is only by availing ourselves of the knowledge furnished by intuition that we can demonstrate the simplest proposition; for every result is dependent on a chain of demonstration, more or less extended, every link of which is an intuition. It is intuition that holds the several parts of the demonstration together, by perceiving their fitness and relations.

The number of mathematical axioms may be more or less extended, but a list of them does not belong to this place. The reader is referred to mathematical works.

II. MORAL AXIOMS.

There are self-evident truths in moral science as truly as in mathematical. Moral axioms may not be clearly understood at so early a period as mathematical; but when they *are* understood, the mind embraces them with the same assurance. Coleridge makes this distinction between mathematical and moral axioms, that the former are what *every* mind *must* believe, the latter what every *good* mind *will* believe.

The apparent reason for this distinction is in the fact, that through moral obliquity men are often more ready to do violence to their moral than to their mathematical intuitions. Men may make themselves fools, if they wil' on *every* subject. All our powers of rational, as well a of sensuous knowledge, may be outraged and destroyed When philosophy speaks of the mental powers, she ha respect to their legitimate use.

ILLUSTRATION.

When a mathematical axiom is first clearly appre hended by a person, he knows it to be true. He ma afterwards speculate upon it, and, through a desire to b original or obstinate, finally prevail upon himself to thin otherwise. There is, however, still a conviction at the bottom of his mind that he is not true to himself; in fact he really knows better. But as the motives to such folly in relation to mathematical truths, are comparatively few such instances of folly are proportionably rare, althoug not wholly wanting.

So, when a person first clearly apprehends a *mora* axiom, he instantly knows it to be true. But througl moral obliquity, his feelings, his wishes, may be against it. He may thus be induced to speculate, cavil, resist, and finally prevail with himself to think otherwise. But he is not without conviction of being false to himself. It is not for us to decide how far a man may carry this desperate warfare against his own intuitions; but we can hardly imagine a case where it may not be said, After all, he really *knows better*. If he have come to the strange pass that he really does not perceive any moral distinctions in conduct, that a lie is to him morally the same as a truth, he certainly *did* know better once. However much of a fool he may have made himself, intuition has done its duty.

SOME MORAL AXIOMS SPECIFIED.

A full account of this class of axioms belongs to moral philosophy; but, for the sake of being understood, let us notice a few of them. They may be expressed in such propositions as the following. Let the reader ponder a moment on each, and see if something within does not testify to its truth.

There is a moral distinction between right and wrong.

We ought to love what is good, and hate what is evil.

It is just that they who do good, and they who do evil, be rewarded according to their respective doings.

If God is infinitely good, we ought to love him supremely.

We should endeavor to promote the welfare, and not the ruin, of our fellow-beings.

There is a moral difference between truth and falsehood.

We ought to be grateful for favors.

We might enlarge the list; but these examples will suffice. All effectual moral reasoners *assume* such truths. If men undertake to prove them, they only weaken what is at first strong. In taking into their own hands the work which the Creator has already done, they show by their bungling how much better his work is than theirs. The most convincing and powerful reasoners in morals are they who assume all such facts as admitted, throw them directly upon the understanding and conscience of those addressed, and go straight forth to frame and apply their argument. This shows that such facts *are* admitted, and that no proof of them is needed; in other words, that they are *subjects of intuition.**

METAPHYSICAL AXIOMS.

This is a convenient term to apply to a class of *speculative axioms* which are neither strictly mathematical nor moral. They are such as these: —

It is impossible for the same thing to be, and not to be, at the same time.

Whatever is not eternal must have had a beginning.

Every effect must have a cause.

The same thing cannot be both cause and effect in the same relation, at the same time.

There cannot be a cause without an effect.

An effect can never precede its cause.

A body cannot go from one point to another, without passing through the intermediate space.

The work of creation supposes omnipotent power.

Omnipotence itself cannot do impossibilities — such as, to make a thing to be, and not to be, at the same time; to make three and two equal to ten, &c.

REMARKS ON INTUITIVE PROPOSITIONS.

Such propositions may seem at first puerile and useless. But no sooner does one undertake to reason, than he finds the necessity of having such first truths, universally known and conceded, on which he can fall back

* The disciples of the metaphysical school have often had the advantage of those of the sensuous school, in this respect. The cautious philosophy of the latter, inclining them to *prove* every thing, has not unfrequently led them to attempt the proof of self-evident truths, and thus to induce a spirit of scepticism.

and rest firmly. He cannot prove them, for he has nothing to prove them with. He takes them as already certain, by intuition, for materials with which to prove those things which require proof by argument. They are not ordinarily drawn out into verbal propositions: all minds entertain such truths almost unconsciously, so that they can be reasoned upon without being stated. It is when something is said in *opposition* to them, rather than in reliance upon them, that the mind is roused to think of them. An intuitve truth, like the atmosphere in which the body lives, is seldom noticed except when disturbed.

Although some of the propositions involving intuitive truths are little else than truisms, or statements of the same thing in different words, they yet express a reality, and one for which no other mode of expression can be framed. The simplest things are often the most difficult to define.

It is also due to the reader to say, that some of the generally received axioms have been debated. For instance, the proposition, that every effect must have a cause, has been by some said to be nothing more than the mere statement of the fact, that, so far as human observation extends, certain things have been uniformly preceded by certain other things;* while, again, it is claimed by some that every human mind spontaneously prompts the belief that neither ourselves nor any thing around us could have come into existence without a cause.

In reply to all this, it is not material to decide precisely how much observation and intuition severally do, in furnishing us with the elements of knowledge, so long as we are all equally agreed as to the knowledge itself. Although philosophers are not agreed as to the relation of cause and effect, and one thinks that his knowledge of it came by intuition, and another that his came by observation, yet if they are equally sure that they *have* this knowledge, and reason together soundly upon it, each may safely be left to his own speculations.

Having stated some of the intuitive *propositions* of the

* Brown's Philosophy.

several classes, let us notice some intuitive facts, expressed by a *single term*. Among these may be mentioned, —

1. Existence. That there is something which we call *being* or *existence*, and that himself exists, every man knows by intuition. Existence cannot be proved; for, in order to prove, there must be a mind, and materials for the mind to work with. Unless these be allowed to exist, there can of course be no proving. The man who maintains that there is no existence annihilates the universe, and himself with it. As he no longer exists, he cannot, of course, maintain any thing.

On the other hand, the man who undertakes to prove that there *is* such a thing as existence must beg his position, and assume his existence, before he can prove it. Hence the attempt of Des Cartes and others to *prove* existence could add nothing to the convictions which all mankind had by their own intuition. Had men consented to abandon their ground of belief furnished by intuition, and to depend upon that furnished by argument, most would have probably fallen, with Hume, into universal scepticism.

Some have supposed that existence is made known to us through the *senses*. The senses make known to us certain *effects* of existence; but for the knowledge of existence itself, we are indebted to intuition. These effects are intuitively referred to their cause.

Others have said that our existence is made known to us by *consciousness*.* To this it is by some replied, that our thoughts, feelings, volitions, — the *effects* of our existence, — we know by consciousness, but of our *existence itself* we are not strictly conscious. I am quite willing to leave this point with the reader to settle for himself — whether it is by *intuition* or *consciousness*, or both, that he knows his own existence.

Others refer the knowledge of our existence to *suggestion*. Professor Upham does this, but in his explanation really makes it a matter of intuitive reference of effect to cause. "If we think, then there is something which has

* See Bowen on Metaphysical and Ethical Science.

this capability of thought; if we feel, then there is not only the mere act of feeling, but something also which puts forth the act."* If any say our existence is thus *suggested* to us, it is only necessary to add, intuition does more, it makes us *know* it.

2. Space. The question here is not in respect to the *nature* of space, whether it is material or immaterial, whether it is real substance or the absence of all substance, whether it is independent of God or dependent upon him; the question is, How do we come by the knowledge of that, whatever it be, *which we call space?* All men perceive, at once, that space is so essentially different from body, that our knowledge of it would not naturally be referred to a sensuous origin. Space is *absolute* and *necessary*, body *may* or may *not* exist; space is *illimitable*, all body has *limits;* the idea of space is strictly *rational*, that of body is accompanied with a *sensible representation.*

Respecting the origin of our idea of space, Cousin has the following just remarks: "Here we have carefully distinguished two points of views, which are intimately blended together, but which analysis should separate, namely, the logical order of ideas, and their chronological order. In the logical view, body presupposes space; for what is body? The juxtaposition, the coexistence of resisting points; that is, of solids. But how could this juxtaposition, this coexistence, happen, but in a continuity of space? But while, in the order of reason and of nature, body presupposes space, it is true, on the other hand, that, in the chronological order, there is a contemporaneousness of the idea of body and that of space; we cannot have the idea of body without that of space, nor of space without that of body. And if, in this contemporaneous process, one of these ideas may be distinguished as the antecedent, in the order of time, of the other, it is not the idea of space which is anterior to that of the body; it is the idea of body which is anterior to that of space.

It is not from the idea of space that we start; and if the sensibility, if the touch, did not take the initiative, and

* Mental Philosophy, p. 124.

give us, immediately, the idea of resistance, of solid, of body, we should never have the idea of space. Without doubt, the idea of body could never be found and completed in the mind, if we had not already there the idea of space; but still, the former idea springs up first in time; it precedes in some degree the idea of space, which immediately follows it." *

The amount of it all is, that, while we arrive at the knowledge of *body* by the senses, we *intuitively perceive that body cannot exist without space to exist in.*

3. IDENTITY. Identity implies *sameness of being.* A man of fifty is the same being to-day that he was forty years ago. No man ever doubts this. The belief of identity is universal. It is more than belief; it is *knowledge.* Whence the origin of this knowledge?

In the first place, it cannot evidently be given us directly by the *senses.* These furnish evidence of only present physical facts. Identity respects the past as well as present. Here, then, is work for memory. But memory alone cannot impart the knowledge of identity; it only recalls *past experiences and events.* It is not its office to decide whether it is the same being who experiences certain feelings to-day who experienced certain feelings ten years ago.

Nor, in the second place, can *consciousness* alone give us the knowledge in question. Consciousness is concerned only with *present experiences.* And yet, without memory and consciousness, there can be no knowledge of identity. Here Locke fails to discover his wonted clearness. "Since consciousness," he says, "always accompanies thinking, and it is that which makes every one to be what he calls *self,* and thereby distinguishes himself from all other thinking things, in this alone consists personal identity, i. e., the sameness of a rational being; and as far as this consciousness can be extended backwards to any past action or thought, so far reaches the identity of that *person;* it is the same *self,* now, it was then; and it is by the same *self* with this present one that now reflects on it that that action was done." †

* See Cousin's Psychology, by Dr. Henry, p. 95.
† Essay, vol. ii. chap. 27, p. 229, New York edition, 1818.

Here is a confounding of *consciousness* with *identity*. If consciousness makes identity, then a man loses his identity, is no longer the same man, the moment he ceases to be conscious. Locke could not have meant to say this. If he meant to say that it is by consciousness and memory that we get our *idea* of identity, he still fails to reach the exact point. I may have been conscious of certain emotions ten years ago, and may to-day *remember* that I was then conscious of them; but then the question returns, How do I know that the SELF — the *I* — is the same identical *being* that he was ten years ago? Am I *conscious* of it? But I can be conscious of only *present* experience. Do I *remember* it? But I remember only what is *past*. Here all must see that something *more* is wanting to give the knowledge in question.

I do not first remember certain experiences in past years, and hence *infer* my identity. So changed are my feelings, and so treacherous is my memory, that I might well distrust this evidence. The evidence of identity rests on no such precarious basis. The case rather stands thus: KNOWING myself to be the same being to-day that I have been from the first, *whatever* may have been the changes in my experience, and *however treacherous* my memory, of *this* I am *certain*, that the joys and sufferings which I experienced twenty or forty years ago, and those which I experience now, *belong to one and the same being*.

Thus, while the knowledge of our identity springs into the mind along with consciousness and memory, it comes not in the relation of a dependent effect, but of an absolute and irresistible intuition. There is no reasoning, inferring, judging in the premises; it is, from the first, *knowledge*. Ask the uneducated child how he knows that he is the same being to-day that he was last year, and he is wont to reply, *Because I am;* which with him means much the same as to say that he knows it by *intuition*.

With these specimens of intuitive facts and illustrations of the manner in which they are shown to be such, the reader may easily identify all others. Among these some would place *infinity*, *eternity*, *unity*, *design*, *sub-*

stance, *cause*, &c. Such facts are not subjects of sense, neither can they be demonstrated by any mere reasoning process. But at certain periods of mental development they are *intuitively perceived*, and perceived at once as *absolute facts*, about which no question can be raised. The importance of not admitting as intuitive knowledge what is not strictly so, and of drawing the line distinctly between what are and what are not proper subjects of logical proof, cannot be too deeply impressed upon the mind.

QUESTIONS ON CHAPTER IX.

What is *intuition?* Remarks. What is said in the note? Why do we use the term *intuition* in this connection? What objections to *suggestion?* Remarks? Suppose that a mere conjecture, doubt, query, be considered as *knowledge*, does the reader so consider it? What is here always meant by the term *knowledge?* What is said of intuition as to *degrees of assurance?* Is intuitive knowledge *acquired?* Remarks? Do intuitive truths admit of proof? What is said here? What is the nature of the *teachings* of intuition? Remarks? What has philosophy to do with subjects of intuition? Remarks? What is said of mathematical axioms? Illustration? What are moral axioms? What is said of them? What distinction does Coleridge make? On how many subjects many men make themselves fools? Illustrations of this? State some of the moral axioms. Is the reader convinced of their being strictly intuitive truths? What is the custom of all effectual moral reasoners? What is the effect of mere attempts to *prove* them? What are *metaphysical* axioms? State some. What remarks are made respecting intuitive propositions? What is the apology for propositions involving intuitive truths, which are little else than truisms? Have any of the received axioms been debated? Give an instance. What is the reply? What is the *first* mentioned intuitive *fact?* Can existence be *proved?* Why not? What have some supposed? What have others said? Others still? What is said of *space?* What says Cousin of it? The amount of it all? What is *identity?* Remarks? Is the knowledge of it by the *senses?* Why not? By *memory* alone? Why not? By *consciousness* alone? Views of Locke? Objections and remarks? What must all here see? How stands the case, then? Concluding remarks?

CHAPTER X.

CONSCIOUSNESS.

The second source of our primary rational knowledge is *consciousness.* This is the *power of knowing whatever is passing in one's mind.* We can be strictly conscious of nothing else, unless it be our existence itself. The term implies knowing inwardly, and its etymology is expressive of the exact idea attached to it in mental philosophy. We cannot, therefore, be at the present time conscious of any thing past, of any thing future, nor of any thing pertaining to the material world; of any thing passing in the mind of another; of any thing above, beneath, around us.

Most philosophers suppose that we are not strictly conscious of our own *existence;* that this is a subject of *intuition;* that we can only be conscious of what is *taking place* within us. Our personal mental *phenomena,* not our personal *being,* are supposed to be the precise and only subjects of our consciousness.*

CONSCIOUSNESS REFERS TO ENTITIES.

All the proper subjects of consciousness are actual *entities* or *realities;* and when we become conscious of

* On this point the most accurate thinkers differ. Francis Bowen, author of the excellent work on Metaphysical and Ethical Science, supposes that we know our existence by consciousness. "This *apperception,* as Leibnitz calls it, or direct consciousness of self, seems to me an invariable concomitant of mental action." "Self is an indivisible unit — a monad, in technical phrase, endowed with intelligence and activity; and we are directly conscious of it in itself, and in its passing into thought and act, without

them, they become subjects of absolute knowledge. For instance, a state of *mental anxiety* is an entity, a fact; and a man's being conscious of it makes him *know* it as a fact. It does not remain to be proved; his consciousness of it is a proof of it, of the highest possible kind.

SUBJECTS OF CONSCIOUSNESS SPECIFIED.

Let us here indicate some of the classes of mental phenomena which we know by consciousness.

1. ALL OUR INTELLECTUAL OPERATIONS — such as *thinking*, *reasoning*, *comparing*, *judging*, *multiplying*, *dividing*, *reckoning*, *planning*. It is not contended that men may not, through the power of habit, sometimes do these things without being conscious of them. It is simply maintained, that, whatever men directly know of them, they learn only by consciousness.

2. OUR MENTAL EMOTIONS. Among these are included emotions awakened by whatever is *grand*, *awful*, *terrible*, *beautiful*, *ludicrous*, *disgusting*, *charming*. We know ourselves to be subjects of such emotions only as we are conscious of experiencing them.

3. OUR SOCIAL AND MORAL AFFECTIONS. Our *filial*, *fraternal*, *conjugal*, *paternal* affections; our affections *towards our fellow-beings in general*, and *towards God*, are all made evident to us by personal consciousness.

4. OUR MORAL EMOTIONS. Emotions of *gratitude* towards man and towards God, in view of favors; emotions of *fear*, *reverence*, *humility;* emotions of *anger*, *jealousy*, *envy;* emotions of *hatred* and *revenge*.

5. OUR VOLITIONS AND PURPOSES. We know that we *will*, *choose*, *purpose;* that we designedly *avoid* this, and *incline* to that; that we have *objects* in view, and strive to obtain them; because we are *conscious* of so doing.

6. OUR PAINS AND PLEASURES. Whatever we experience of *suffering*, *anguish*, *joy*, *delight*, — whether we are

being compelled to infer its existence from these manifestations."— p. 55. Whether our existence be considered a subject of consciousness or intuition, or both, is not a very material point.

in a state of *happiness*, or a state of *misery*, or in a state of *both united*, — we know only as our consciousness informs us.

7. Our various Degrees of Belief. We are so constituted, that, prejudice apart, we yield assent in greater or less degrees, according to evidence. Our minds may pass from the state expressed by positive *disbelief* to a state of *suspense;* thence to *presumption, belief, certainty.* We may not, for want of attention to our mental exercises, be conscious of thus moving over from a state of disbelief to a state of assurance, in regard to a point at issue ; but we can hardly fail to be conscious of the new state of mind, after we have reached it.

The judge on the bench is, at first, without any belief whatever that the man at the bar is guilty. In the course of the trial, evidence against him is elicited ; the judge begins to think his guilt probable, then almost certain, and finally *quite* certain. In the course of the trial, he was so much occupied with evidence, that he did not think of the change going on in his own mind ; but when this mental revolution becomes a subject of attention, he cannot fail to be conscious of it.

8. Our Religious Experience. *Repentance, remorse, peace, hope, faith ;* the sweet sense of *forgiveness*, and the *joys of communion with God ;* feelings of *discouragement* and *gloom*, followed with feelings of *animation* and *delight*, or the steady abiding of the soul in the assurance of divine favor and eternal life, — are known only as they are subjects of personal consciousness.

REMARKS ON CONSCIOUSNESS.

1. From what has been said, it must appear that our consciousness *is as important as our being.* Annihilate it, and our being might as well cease. It is directly the ground of the knowledge which most intimately concerns us, and, indirectly, of all we know. All that we are, all we possess, all we experience, derives its value from this attribute.

2. The question is debated, whether consciousness is

ever *actually suspended.* It is maintained, on the one hand, that in cases of fainting, trance, profound sleep, or intoxication, and under the influence of powerful medicines, of ether and chloroform, there is no consciousness whatever of pleasure or pain, and that hours of existence passed in this state are, to the subject, as though he were not. On the other hand, it is claimed that there is consciousness at the moment, but that *memory* does not serve.

Without entering upon a discussion which would be irrelevant here, it will suffice to say, that the amount of the truth seems to be this: In some cases, *memory* is most affected; in others, *consciousness;* and in some extreme cases, both memory and consciousness are utterly at fault together. For wise purposes, men are sometimes for a season cut off, as it were, from themselves; but their return to consciousness is not as the beginning of a new life; it is the continuance of the old one. They begin their conscious life again at the point where they left off. This proves that their consciousness was not *destroyed,* but only *suspended.* There is the same being, the same identity, the same consciousness stil going on.

3. *Consciousness is immortal.* It may be for a tim *suspended,* as we have seen, but it can never be finall *destroyed.* It is a vital element of the soul. The char acter of the soul may change; vice may give place t virtue, sin to holiness; but consciousness remains eve the same. Physical disease or mental derangement ma impair its action, but the moment the pressure is off— the moment the mind is released from the influence o *all disordered action — consciousness resumes its activi* ty, and with all its felt realities moves on from the poin that was left. In a philosophical view, the event of death will have far less to do with interrupting the course of our conscious being than many events which we encounter on our way to the grave. All this is of cours predicated on the fact before proved — the immortalit of the soul itself.

4. *The relation of consciousness to religion.* If th above views are correct, men may know, and ought t

know, their prevailing thoughts, feelings, views, purposes, aims, in relation to the momentous truths set forth in the Christian religion. Whether they believe them or not, love them or not; whether they repent of their sins, and seek the divine favor; whether they love to pray, and to perform the various duties enjoined by Christ; whether they most love and pursue this world, or heaven, — are questions to be settled only by a faithful attention to the teachings of their own consciousness.

Searching our own hearts, to see what manner of men we are, is nothing more nor less than carefully observing what our consciousness tells us, as compared with God's rule of faith and duty. If we are conscious of a prevailing aversion to prayer, for instance, when God especially enjoins it, we cannot innocently fail to know that our hearts are not right.

Not only are we thus indebted to consciousness for the knowledge of our characters, but for the happiness or the misery to be derived from them. Could the wicked man annihilate his consciousness, he would have nothing to fear; on the other hand, were the good man to be sure of losing his consciousness, he would have nothing to hope. The fact that we are to be forever conscious of our characters — conscious of all the thoughts, the emotions, passions that will eternally play in our souls — is among the most glorious and awful of all known realities. It invests our rational and immortal being with a solemnity and importance which language can but feebly express.

QUESTIONS ON CHAPTER X.

What is *consciousness?* What does the term imply? Remarks. What are the proper subjects of consciousness? Instance? What is the *first* mentioned class of subjects? Examples? *Second* class? Examples? *Third* class? Examples? *Fourth* class? Examples? *Fifth* class? *Sixth?* *Seventh?* Remarks? *Eighth?* From what has been said, what must appear? What question is debated? State the argument on each side. What does the truth seem to be? How *enduring* is consciousness? Remarks? What is said respecting the relation of consciousness to religion? What is implied in searching our hearts? What would be the consequences to good and to bad men, were their consciences to be annihilated? What is said of the fact that we are to be forever conscious?

PART III.

SECONDARY KNOWLEDGE.

CHAPTER I.

ATTENTION.

We have hitherto confined our observations to that kind of human knowledge which comes to the mind *directly* through the *senses*, in connection with *intuition* and *consciousness*. It is called *primary*, because we obtain it *first*, and without any *reasoning process*. It constitutes our mental *capital*, or *primary stock of ideas*.

We have other powers of intellect, which take up these primary ideas, combine, separate, recombine, arrange them, and reason upon them, and thus, in various ways, augment our mental riches. These powers are of a *higher order* than the preceding, are held by men in more unequal degrees, and are susceptible of much more cultivation. Some of them we hold in common with brutes; others distinguish the human mind entirely from all brute mind.

We shall begin with those which we have in common with brutes. Brutes have the various *senses*, in common with man; they have also *consciousness*, and something answering their purpose, as well as intuition and forethought do ours, which we call *instinct*. They have also more than these; they have, to some extent, *attention*, *association*, *memory*.

PRIMARY AND SECONDARY IDEAS.

Before proceeding, we must notice another distinction between primary and secondary ideas. *Primary* ideas are all *cognitions; secondary* ideas are *not* all cognitions. So far as there is *demonstration*, or *proof*, in respect to the latter, they become as truly cognitions as the former; otherwise they stand in the doubtful position of *mere ideas — suggestions, suppositions, conjectures, speculations, fictions, fancies.* But whether they respect things real, unreal, or half real, *passing for what they are*, they are valuable as *intellectual furniture;* they serve to enrich and embellish the mind, to augment its power and happiness.

ATTENTION DEFINED.

Attention implies the *power of fixing the mind steadily upon a given subject.* It is partly involuntary, partly voluntary. Sometimes our minds, drawn by feeling or compelled by circumstances, are riveted so firmly to a subject of thought, that we cannot detach them, until exhausted nature or some other cause interposes. But in far the most numerous instances, our attention is more directly under our control. The more we discipline it, the more obedient it becomes to our volition.

ATTENTION IN BRUTES.

It is evident that *brutes* have, to some extent, the *power of attention*, although they have not reason to guide it. Taught by instinct, they attend to the calls of their young, and sometimes fix their attention for a considerable time upon the object in view. Under the admonition of the lash, the horse, the mule, the monkey is trained to attend to his master's will, and becomes very careful not to resist it. Dogs have sometimes been so attentive to objects of trust as to neglect the calls of hunger.

It is recorded as an instance of fidelity in this fine animal, that a man on a journey, having occasion to leave his effects in charge of his dog, expecting to be absent only a few hours, but being detained some days, found on his return his faithful servant dead of starvation. There was food accessible to the animal; but he was so absorbed in attention to the object of his charge, that he neglected to take it. He had the power of *attention*, but wanted *reason.*

NATURE OF THE MENTAL ACT IN ATTENTION.

There seems to have been some question among philosophers respecting the precise nature of the mental effort in attention; whether it implies a special energetic or impulsive *action of the will*, or whether the effort is *purely intellectual.*

It is evident, from consciousness, that both the intellect and the will are put in requisition. But in the best acts of attention there is, perhaps, less forced mental energy than may be supposed. To be most effectual, attention must be natural, easy, composed. A painful effort often divides attention. Of this we are all conscious. Sometimes a pupil nerves up his attention almost to an agony, with a view to committing a lesson, and gives it up in despair. At another time, in a more composed state, he learns the lesson with ease. Our mental, as well as our bodily powers, should be exerted in a natural way.

HOW TO SECURE FIXEDNESS OF ATTENTION.

There are three rules for learning to fix the attention, which every pupil should early reduce to practice.

1. *He must determine to do it.* In all cases where fixed attention is demanded, he must hold himself resolved to render it. Without this he can secure no mental discipline; his intellect will ever be the puny and helpless child of accident. If any thing is to be learned, whether

from books, or a lecture, or conversation, or a walk in the fields, or a visit to a gallery of arts, or from his own reminiscences, he must resolve on giving fixed attention. If any thing diverts it, with jealous vigilance he must instantly call it back to duty.

But as attention cannot be always on special duty without exhaustion, appropriate seasons of relaxation should be allowed. To this end, seasons of recess in schools are well adapted. The pupil who would succeed must make it a point of settled determination, during every moment not appropriated to recess, to give to his studies a fixed and absorbing attention. He should take notice of nothing around him; he should, for the time, not know that there *is* any thing else in existence but the subject of his study.

2. The mind must be *interested in the object.* It is very difficult to fix attention long upon any thing in which no interest is felt. The pupil should therefore first consider the importance of the knowledge to be acquired, so as to nerve his mind to the work. Attention then serves to awaken interest, and interest serves to fix attention. There is a reciprocity of action. When there is little interest at first, the reliance is mainly on the determination, sustained by a consideration of the importance of the object: as the attention becomes steadily directed to the object, the interest in it increases, until at length this alone may be sufficient to hold the mind to it.

Many a person who has at first felt little interest in a subject, excepting what resulted from a mere sense of its importance, has by the study of it become so deeply interested, that effort became needful, not to *attend* to it, but to *divert* his attention. Let not the pupil, therefore, be disheartened, or abandon a study, because he feels at first no interest in it. If the importance of the study demands attention, let that attention be promptly and resolutely rendered, and an interest will rise in the mind, which, by faithful nurture, will steadily grow, and result in complete success.

3. Efforts of attention must be *systematically repeated.* The mind does not grow by fits and starts, but by *systematic training.* *Systematic repetition* has the effect to

form a *habit*, and this renders attention both steady and easy. Even after the interest at first felt in a subject has by long familiarity become diminished, if a *habit* of attention to it has been formed, continued attention costs but little effort. The mechanic, the artist, the professional man may not, after years of devotion to his calling, feel the same enthusiasm in it as at first, but, having become accustomed to it, the requisite attention is easy.

Here we see a wise provision of Providence, in making the power of habit take the place of freshness of interest. And he who *has failed to secure this habit under the impulse of fresh interest* will never realize the blessing of a *well-disciplined intellect.*

RESULT.

When all these conditions are fulfilled, — when there is a firm *purpose*, a deep *interest*, a systematic and persevering *effort*, — the most profound and efficient attention is the result. This is the grand element of success in every study, in every pursuit. With this, Alpine difficulties are surmounted, walls of adamant give way, before the firm and resolute ongoings of the mind. This attainment is within the reach of all; and when made, it renders even the feeblest intellect effective. Let every pupil aspire to it, as of greater and more enduring value than treasures of gold. Let us now notice some of its *particular advantages.*

1. Fulness and Accuracy of Perception. What has been previously said respecting perception must be here noticed.* The mind does not perceive all the points of an object at a glance. It apprehends one point after another, until, by a protracted attention, the entire object is apprehended. The time required for this fulness of perception varies with our previous knowledge of the object, with its extent and complexity, and with the power of attention. For, a measurable time, more or less, — varying from minutes to hours and days, — a fixed and absorbing

* Page 146.

attention is indispensable to a clear and full perception of its object. On this, therefore, depends the *accuracy and extent of our primary knowledge.*

2. Reach and Value of our Associations. Our most *obvious* associations with any object are of course naturally *first in our thoughts.* If the attention is unsteady, bounding from one thing to another, these will be the *only* associations formed. But the more *remote* associations, or, at least, those less obvious at the first glance, are usually the *most valuable.* They are the more scientific. Here runs the line of demarcation between the superficial and the profound thinker.

The man of feeble and fickle attention sees things only in their more obvious, simple, accidental relations; the man of firm and penetrating attention sees them in those far-reaching, complex, all-embracing relations which bind the universe together. The former sees facts only in a fragmentary and disjointed state; the latter sees them in their mutual and wide relations.

Originality of thought, invention, discovery, scientific induction, result from that power of attention which throws the associations out of the beaten track. In this, more than perhaps any thing else, lies the difference between the most ordinary mind and that of a Newton or a Milton.

3. Memory. The memory depends upon attention almost absolutely.* Indeed, without some degree of attention, it is impossible to remember distinctly even for a moment. Speak to a man absorbed in thought; he hears, answers, and in one minute has forgotten all. He paid so little attention, his mind having been otherwise occupied, that there was not impression enough made to be remembered.

The clock strikes; the student takes out his watch, sets and winds it, returns it to the pocket, and in less than a minute has entirely forgotten what he has heard and done. He was of course conscious of all at the

* "C'est l'attention, plus ou moins grande, qui grave, plus ou moins profondement, les objets dans la mémoire." — *Helvetius de l'Esprit.* See Stewart's Philosophy, vol. i. p. 65.

moment, but his attention was too much wanting to fix it in the memory.

What makes the schoolboy forget his father's errand? Because his thoughts are so much occupied with his studies or his play, that he does not sufficiently attend to what his father says.

EXAMPLE.

A remarkable instance of the dependence of memory on attention is furnished by a fact in the life of the late Professor Fisher, of Yale College. On one occasion, he was so absorbed in scientific investigations, that, on the ringing of the bell for dinner, he left his room, went to the dining hall, took his official position, invoked the benediction, presided and ate his meal as usual, and returned to his studies, without having afterwards the least recollection of any thing that had taken place. Towards night he had solved his problem, and bethought himself of dinner. On looking at his watch, he was surprised to find the time for dining had gone by several hours. Alarmed at his official neglect, he went to an adjoining room to inquire who presided in his absence, and was yet more surprised to learn that he had presided himself.

The reasons why memory is so dependent on attention are involved in what has already been said, and what remains to be said, under the head of *Association.*

PROFOUND ATTENTION CHARACTERISTIC OF GREAT MINDS.

It is impossible to make eminent intellectual attainments without an *unusual degree of the power of attention.* Hence truly great minds have ever been eminently characterized by it. It is said of Sir Isaac Newton, that he was often so absorbed in study, that days and nights passed, and with them his customary sleep and meals, without being by him remembered. La Place is said sometimes to have forgotten not only his sleep and his meals, but the presence and attentions of his dearest friends. Leibnitz was so intensely occupied with study for weeks together, as to forget the season of the year and sometimes to mistake winter for summer.

Napoleon, a distinguished mathematician as well as general, when earnestly engaged in his studies, forgot the customary civilities of his station, although at other times one of the most courteous of men. The truth is, the human mind *cannot* give the amount of attention requisite to excel in a great and difficult subject of thought without for the time neglecting every thing else. It must be what Horace calls *totus in illis* — wholly absorbed in its subject.

ABSENT-MINDEDNESS NO MARK OF GREATNESS.

Absent-mindedness sometimes passes for evidence of *profound attention to important subjects.* A man may be absent-minded, because his thoughts are occupied on great subjects; but, ordinarily, it is because he is listless, thoughtless, stupid. Whenever men of deep thought are absent-minded in company, it is their weakness, not their greatness, that makes them so. *There is a time for all things;* and it is a mark of a truly great and well-bred mind, *to be attentive to the things on hand.* Ordinarily, it is the weaker minds, not taught to control attention, which are regardless of the proprieties of time and place. Young people cannot be too careful to form habits of ever-wakeful presence of mind.

DIVIDED ATTENTION.

Some interesting facts connected with this subject seem worthy of notice, especially as philosophers have made them matters of controversy. It is well known that men sometimes attend to two or three subjects at the same time. A violinist will play one part and sing another. When a man has become accustomed to setting types, he will set up page after page with perfect accuracy, and be meanwhile thinking upon another subject.

The late Dr. Dwight sometimes held conversation with his friends, gave directions to others connected with his official duties, and dictated a sermon to his amanuensis, all at the same time. Almost every man is sometimes engaged in writing letters of friendship or business while holding conversation with persons present. The school teacher is frequently engaged in solving a mathematical problem, requiring a long and careful process of calculation, while attending to a recitation in some other branch, and does both with a vigilance that detects the first error.

Now, what is the solution of these facts? Does the mind actually attend to two or three things at one and the same *instant?* or does it pass rapidly *back and forth* from the one to the other? The latter seems to be the most philosophical solution. In this respect, the mind seems like the *eye*. We know that the eye is physically incapable of being directed to but a single point at a time, and yet, by the rapidity of its movements, it takes in many at a glance. It seems, indeed, a contradiction to ay that the mind can point its attention two ways at ,nce.

That we are unconscious of the passing back and 'orth of our volitions, is accounted for by their rapidity, .nd by the fact that our attention is wholly directed to ts several subjects, and not to what is passing within us. ;urely if the eye, a physical instrument, can move with a rapidity defying notice, much more may *the mind 'tself*, whose movements are the very lightning.

HARTLEY'S THEORY.

But there is another question, beyond the above, touching the existence of the *mental act itself.* When a lady has become an accomplished performer on the piano, she will hold conversation, or have her mind otherwise occupied, while going through a long and difficult piece with the utmost accuracy. She is perhaps so much absorbed in thinking upon some interesting matter, as not to recollect what she performed, or even that she performed at all.

The question is, whether every touch of the keys is accompanied with a *mental act* on her part. Dr. Hartley supposes that the intense rapidity of thought, bounding back and forth between the keys and the other subjects of attention, is *inconceivable;* and maintains, that, b repetition, the movement of the fingers has becom purely *mechanical* or *automative.*

"Habit," he says, "differs from instinct, not in its na ture, but its origin; the last being natural, the firs acquired. Both operate without will or intention, with out thought, and therefore may be called mechanica principles. I conceive it to be a part of our constitu tion, that what we have become accustomed to do, w acquire not only a facility, but a proneness to do, on like occasions, so that the doing of it often requires no wil at all. An expert performer will play from notes, o ideas laid up in the memory, and at the same time carry on a quite different train of thoughts in his mind, o even hold conversation with another. Whence we ma conclude that there is no intervention of the idea c state of mind called *will.*" * Cases of this kind he ca "transitions of voluntary or intentional actions in automatic ones."

OBJECTIONS TO THE ABOVE THEORY.

It is, perhaps, a sufficient objection to the above theor in a philosophical view, that it supposes an *unknown e ment* in the human constitution — an element which philosophical analysis has ever been able to find. T theory is, therefore, an admission of an *effect* without *cause.*

That the movement cannot be mechanical or aut matic, seems evident from the fact that there is no ma chinery, no mechanical contrivance, to operate as motive power on the fingers. The movement *mu* therefore be produced by the performer's *volitions,* f there is *no other power.* To say that *habit* does it,

* Hartley's Essays on the Active Powers of Man, p. 128.

saying nothing to the purpose; for the *habit* of it is the *habitual doing* of it.

Moreover, that the performer's thoughts and volitions are engaged in the performance, would seem certain, from the fact that, if any thing happens to disturb it,—a chord falter, a discordant note be struck, or a person playing in concert make a mistake,—she instantly stops. This she could not do, unless her thoughts and volitions controlled her fingers. It seems surprising that even no less a thinker than Thomas Reid should have countenanced the above theory.

HOW PHILOSOPHERS CAME TO ADOPT THIS THEORY.

We come to this conclusion: that philosophers have felt themselves forced into the above theory by not duly considering the amazing rapidity of which human thoughts and volitions are capable, and the comparative ease with which they are directed, when long attention and practice have brought them under perfect control. They may then be made to pass back and forth between two or more subjects, with lightning speed, superintending and directing all; and the subject which at the time most interests the mind is the one best remembered, perhaps the only one remembered at all.

This, again, shows how much memory depends upon the *feeling* or *passion* with which a subject is contemplated, and how little upon the mere thought and volition. It is a *feeling of awakened interest* that secures the measure of attention to any one subject, when brought into competition with others, requisite to secure for it a place in the memory.

The lady supposed above was passionately interested in a special subject of thought; while the piano performance had become an old affair, that awakened no feeling excepting when something went wrong. Into the latter she carried only thought and volition, and therefore instantly forgot what she played, and perhaps forgot even that she played at all; into the former she carried her *passion*, along with her thoughts and volitions, and therefore retained a lively remembrance of it.

RELATION OF ATTENTION TO RELIGION.

The importance of a well-formed habit of attention to mental growth and the acquisition of knowledge has been already shown. It is equally effective and still more important, as related to the momentous verities of Christianity. It is this, more than perhaps any other natural cause, that contributes to the securing of that "faith" which "is the substance of things hoped for the evidence of things not seen."

Why do so many walk in darkness, even amid the splendors of heaven's most glorious beams? Why do so many live and die as though there were no God to serve, no Savior to trust, no soul to save, no heaven to gain? A sufficient reason would be assigned, were it only replied, Because they have never given that ATTENTION to Christianity which it justly claims. The Creator implanted the power of attention in their minds for great purposes,— of which this is the greatest,— but they have failed to improve it.

Let all pupils early commence, not only a thorough and systematic training of the power of attention, but its faithful application to the teachings of Christianity let them give, at all appropriate seasons, a full and absorbing attention to its stupendous facts, its high demands, its solemn sanctions; let them thus habitually bring their minds in close and earnest contact with those gracious developments which solve the enigma of life, unbind the fetters of sin, lift up the gates of the tomb, and pour the radiance of heaven over eternity; and the laws of mind and of God's government assure us that we have every reason to believe eternal life will be theirs.

QUESTIONS ON CHAPTER I.

To what have we hitherto confined our observations? Why is this called *primary* knowledge? What does it constitute? What is said of *other* mental powers? With which shall we begin? What powers have *brutes?* What *other* distinction is noticed between primary and secondary ideas? Considered as a mental attribute, what does *attention* imply? Is it voluntary? Have *brutes* the power of attention? Examples? What question among philosophers? What seems evident from consciousness? Which are the *best* acts of attention? Illustrate. How many rules for fixing attention? *First* rule? Remarks? *Second* rule? Remarks? What encouragement is given to the pupil? *Third* rule? Remarks? What the *result?* *First* particular advantage? How explained? *Second?* How explained? What results from that power of attention which throws the associations out of the beaten track? *Third.* How *much* does memory depend on attention? How shown? State the *example.* Of what is profound attention the characteristic? What is here said to be impossible? What cases are cited? Is absent-mindedness a mark of greatness? What is said of it? What is meant by *divided* attention? Cases in illustration? What questions in solution of these facts? What view is here given? What was Hartley's theory, as illustrated by a musical performance? State the objection to this theory. How does it appear that the movement cannot be mechanical? Suppose we refer it to *habit?* How does it appear *certain* that the performer's *thoughts* are engaged? Why have philosophers held the above theory? Remarks? How is the above case explained? What is said of the relation of attention to religion?

CHAPTER II.

ASSOCIATION.

Our thoughts do not flow on at *random*. There is a mental power which binds them together. That power is called *Association*. One thought never lives and dies alone. Long before it dies, it brings another, another, a family of thoughts, to take its place; and when it dies, it dies to live again, by the magic touch of memory, in connection with the vast progeny of thoughts to which it gave birth. We may therefore define association, *that power which, when we think of one thing, induces us to think of others sustaining to it some relation.*

ASSOCIATION AND SUGGESTION.

Thomas Brown merges Association in Suggestion, and returns only the latter term. But the advantage is on the side of the established nomenclature. Used in its largest sense, the former term includes all that is expressed by the latter, while it has the advantage of more exactly defining the laws of mental operation. The mind is not moved to suggest, excepting as it is *caused* to do so; and that cause is referable to some form of association.*

* "A man, while awake, is conscious of a continued train of perceptions and ideas passing in his mind. It requires no activity on his part to carry on the train, nor can he at will add any idea to the train. For how could this be done? What idea is it that we are to add? If we can specify the idea, that idea is already in the mind, and there is no occasion for any act of the will. If we cannot specify any idea, I next demand, How can a person will, or to what purpose, if there be nothing in view? We cannot

The falling of an apple suggested to Sir Isaac Newton the theory of universal gravitation. The existence of evil in a perfect moral government suggests the hypothesis that it was unavoidable. A trifling incident suggested to Mr. Whitney the problem, whose solution resulted in the invaluable cotton gin. The disastrous effects of intemperance suggests the inquiry, whether total abstinence is not best.

In all these cases, we see some form of association giving rise to the suggestions. We see the working of that mental power, by which one idea suggests or becomes in thought associated with another. We shall therefore proceed, including whatever might be referred to suggestion under the generic term *association.*

ASSOCIATION IN BRUTES.

That brutes have association, must be obvious to all who notice their *movements.* The horse associates the *manger* with *food,* the *carriage* with *movement,* the *lash* with *pain.* When we drive a hungry horse along the road, if he sees a shed with a manger by the way, he inclines to go to it. He evidently thinks of his *provender.* When harnessed and placed upon the way, he is impatient to move; and when the lash is raised, he leaps through fear, although no blow is inflicted.

All domestic animals learn to associate certain *sounds* with certain *acts:* the ox, for instance, turns to the right, to the left, halts, quickens his pace, or stops, as the sound indicates. The fox, the squirrel, the rat learns to associate the *trap* with *danger.*

In most animals, *day* is associated with *activity, night* with *repose.* Nor can it be said that this is owing merely to *fatigue* at night, inviting rest; for in case of an *eclipse,* early in the day, cattle low as at nightfall, and fowls go

form a conception of such a thing. If this argument need confirmation, I urge experience: whoever makes a trial will find that ideas are linked together in the mind, forming a connected chain, and that we have not the command of any idea independent of the chain." — *Kaims's Elements,* p. 19, with note. New York edition, 1845.

to roost. Other periods of time have with them their associations, as is evidenced by the periodical crowing of the cock, the singing of the nightingale, &c. But association in brute mind is very limited, involving no reach of thought, being connected with no rational powers.

LAWS OF ASSOCIATION.

Association is not a *blind* power, but is regulated by *exact laws.* To a certain extent, it is affected by causes without us; and to a certain extent, it is under our own control. The point where causes without us and our own agency meets is so nicely adjusted as to secure our accountable moral agency, and make us responsible subjects of government. Let us first notice those causes without which act upon and move our power of association.

1. Place. When we look upon a battle field, we think of carnage, fallen heroes, victory, defeat. When we look upon the former residence of a poet, statesman, philosopher, philanthropist, the illustrious dead who once lived there is in our thoughts. When we survey the ruins of Rome, Greece, Egypt, the great men and great events once moving there are moving in our own minds.

We associate the home of our childhood with our childish sports; and ever, to visit the place of our youth, instruction, marriage, and earlier years of service recalls the events once realized there, and revives something of the feelings they once inspired.

Topical association feeds the poet's inspiration; it consecrates and renders classic the places of distinguished men and signal events; it gives to the mountains, groves, rivers, plains, the moss-grown mounds and tumbling walls of certain countries in the old world, a present and ever-growing importance.

2. Time. To the American, the *fourth of July* is associated with *independence.* We associate the twenty-fifth of December with the birth of Christ and with the wonted benedictions and festivities of the occasion. The New Englander associates Thanksgiving day with his noble ancestors who instituted it and with the customary

domestic festivities of that occasion. Association has filled our almanacs and chronological tables with an almost endless list of interesting days. Hence periodical association is of great service in perpetuating both the facts and the interest of history.

3. Resemblance. When we see a person resembling some dear friend, his presence brings that friend to our thoughts. When in a strange land we pass a house, or other objects resembling those with which we have been familiar in our own country, we think of home; and if the resemblance is striking, we almost imagine ourselves there.

Certain sounds make us think of the sounds of instruments or of the human voice which they resemble. A picture reminds us of the person whom it represents. The art of the painter and of the sculptor is founded on this law of association. Classification is also mostly dependent upon it.

4. Contrast. We are inclined to associate in our thoughts things *opposed* to each other scarcely less than those which are *alike*. When shivering with cold upon a bleak, wintry road, we think of the warm comforts of the fireside. Never does the storm-beaten mariner think more intensely of sweet home than when in circumstances the most unlike it. The mind loves contrast. There is an excitement — a thrill of pleasure — in dashing from one extreme to another.

Hence the mind passes in thought from the pygmy to the giant, from sorrow to joy, from despair to hope, from pain to ease, from the cradle to the grave, from life to death, from time to eternity. The mind delights to bring together opposite colors, opposite tastes, opposite causes, opposite characters. The figure called *Antithesis* is founded on this law of association — a figure in which bold and dashing writers abound.

5. Symbols. The picture of an eye does not *resemble* God, but it *symbolizes* him as the All-Seeing. A pair of scales does not resemble justice, nor does a ring resemble eternity; but they are appropriate symbols of the things they severally suggest. The ant is not like industry; yet the picture of so industrious an animal naturally

suggests that virtue. On this principle, the entire alphabet of symbols is constructed. So strongly do religious symbols become associated with what is symbolized, that they sometimes become *themselves* objects of religious homage. Hence idol worship.

6. Cause and Effect. When we contemplate a *cause*, its *effect* is suggested; and in like manner the effect suggests the cause. The thunderbolt ringing in our ears makes us think of the work of destruction; and the rifted oak directs our thoughts to the lightning that rent it. A raging pestilence reminds us of death; and as the dead are borne by our windows in rapid succession to the grave, we think of the raging pestilence. When we read an interesting book, we think of its author; and when we see the author, we are reminded of the book. This principle of association has a very wide and important range, inciting the mind to various philosophical inquiries.

7. Resemblance of Effects. We are wont to associate things which produce *effects* bearing to each other a resemblance, however dissimilar may be the *things themselves*. Thus things that exhilarate or depress us, strengthen or weaken, encourage or discourage, we group together in thought, although the one is a physical and the other a spiritual cause. The presence of a *friend* in trouble we associate with a *cordial*, because in some sense both *refresh* us. Whatever afflicts us we associate with wormwood, because both are *unpleasant*.

On this principle, by an abridged metaphor we directly substitute the one cause for the other, thus rendering description sprightly and elegant. We thus speak of smiling skies, frowning cliffs, angry seas, treacherous winds This is the foundation of some of the finest poetical allusions; and unless the sensibilities of the reader are in accordance with those of the poet, he can neither appreciate nor enjoy them.

8. Accidental Relations. A *present* is associated with the person who *gave* it; a *dress*, with the person who *wore* it; a *house*, with the distinguished man who once *lived* in it. When relations of this sort become permanent, however arbitrary, they are as suggestive as

any that can be formed. The relation is thus established between musical characters and musical sounds; between certain words and the sounds they denote, and between sounds and the ideas they represent; between language and thought. Hence the entire machinery and power of language depend on this principle of association.

Such are the principal causes tending to excite the mental power now under consideration. We at once perceive that without this power in exercise our thoughts would be isolated, scattered, floating at random in every direction. Each fact entering the mind through the senses would be an individuality, standing apart from every other fact on the great sea of observation, without either meaning or value. Each idea must come alone, introduced by a special act of attention, — a stranger and sojourner, — to be taken care of, but to do nothing towards introducing and taking care of others. Association lifts her potent sceptre; the marshalled hosts obey, and gather before the mind's eye in beauteous order, to go forth to service with ever-growing numbers. The relations of this power to *memory* will be considered in connection with that subject.

HOW WE MAY CONTROL OUR ASSOCIATIONS.

Although we cannot stop the current of ideas produced by association, we may *direct* it. It is in every man's power to render his association of ideas either good or bad. He may hold an idea suggestive of evil long in his mind, until it has put his associations upon an evil track; or he may at once dismiss that idea in favor of another tending to good.

"Of the powers which the mind possesses over the train of its thoughts," says Stewart, "the most obvious is its power of singling out any one of them at pleasure, of detaining it, and of making it a particular object of attention. By doing so, we not only stop the succession that would otherwise take place, but, in consequence of our bringing to view the less obvious relations among our ideas, we frequently direct the current of our thoughts into a new channel." *

Lord Kaims holds the following language to the same purpose: "Though we cannot add to the train an unconnected idea, yet, in a measure, we can attend to some ideas, and dismiss others. There are few things but what are connected with many others; and when a thing thus connected becomes a subject of thought, it commonly suggests many of its connections. Among these a *choice* is afforded; we can insist upon one, rejecting others; and sometimes we insist on what is commonly held the slighter connection." †

Association, then, is so placed under our control, as to lay on every man the full responsibility of the consequences to which it leads him.

CIRCUMSTANCES AFFECTING ASSOCIATION.

Constitutional difference and difference of *pursuit* have much influence in modifying our associations. Every man's associations gather with peculiar force around the things connected with his *particular calling*. Those connected with scenes of classic interest, for example, are stronger and more numerous with the student than with the man of business.

Let a clergyman, a machinist, and a money-getting man visit a manufacturing establishment together, and, with precisely the same objects before them, the thoughts of the first will be employed upon the moral and religious aspect of things; those of the second, upon the perfection, ingenuity, or defects of the machinery; those of the third, upon the value of investments there and prospects of gain. Entirely different trains of association will be started in these several minds, and each will probably think the others remarkably stupid.

"In consequence of these associations, every man appears to his neighbor to pursue the object of his wishes with a zeal disproportioned to its intrinsic value; and

* Stewart's Philosophy, vol. i. p. 167.
† Kaims's Elements of Criticism, p. 20.

the philosopher, whose principal enjoyment arises from speculation, is frequently apt to smile at the ardor with which the active part of mankind pursue what appear to him to be mere shadows." *

INFLUENCE OF ASSOCIATION ON SCIENCE AND THE ARTS.

The principal reason why some men are more inventive than others is, that they so control their associations that they conduct them out of the beaten track to things unnoticed by others. A variety of things may be so related to the same object, that either of them may be more or less brought into view. Most men let their thoughts light upon the more obvious relations, and then pass along. The man of genius pauses, thinks, looks after things rare and valuable rather than those first in his associations, and thus strikes out an original track.

Most men, sitting in an orchard, and seeing apples fall from the trees, would be led to think of the ripeness and desirableness of the fruit, of its scarcity or abundance, of its market value, &c. A man of genius thought, perhaps, of these things; but he did not dismiss the matter here; he thought of more. The falling of that apple is like the falling of other bodies. What makes them fall? Does not the same law regulate the falling of all bodies? Their velocity increases as they approach the earth. How is this? May it not be that *all* bodies tend towards each other in obedience to one and the same law?

Thus suggestion keeps extending the operation of the associating principle, until the falling of that apple becomes connected with the rolling of suns and planets in the heavens. In the same way does this principle become subservient to all the inventions and improvements in the various arts that bless and adorn humanity.

The pressure of *necessity* sometimes contributes to *force* the mind out of its wonted channel to objects more remote, and thus to make a dull genius inventive. Many of the inventions most important to mankind have come

* Stewart's Philosophy, vol. i. p. 219.

to pass in this way. Hence the common remark, "*Necessity is the mother of invention.*"

INFLUENCE OF ASSOCIATION ON SPECULATIVE JUDGMENT.

When truth is dug from the mine, it seldom comes free of alloy. The pure and the base being thus associated in our minds, it becomes the work of original thought to separate them. Some of the errors incorporated with early systems of philosophy, we have, to this day, hardly consented to abandon; and false philosophies, ingrafted with religious truths, often become so sanctified by association, that the most vigorous originality of thought, at the hazard of incurring public odium, can scarcely avail to disunite them. This results from the fact that the two subjects of thought, the truth and the error, have become so closely united in the mind, that it requires a peculiar effort to consider them apart. and conduct a process of reasoning which relates exclusively to either.

INFLUENCE OF ASSOCIATION ON LOVE OF MONEY.

The untaught child places no value on a bundle of old bank notes. A picture, worth only a penny, is to him more valued than thousands of dollars. The value which he subsequently learns to attach to these little bits of rusty paper is the work of *association*. He connects them with independence, luxury, importance, distinction. A man witnessing for the first time the burning of a large bundle of old bank notes, as is done at banks when new are to be substituted, fetched a sigh, and said, "*That goes to my heart.*"

The same is true of the origin of our love of all property. If the affection passes over from the objects which money *represents* to the *money itself*, it constitutes not only a worldling, but a *miser;* not only a miserable man, as the term denotes, but one of earth's most eminent fools.

INFLUENCE OF ASSOCIATION ON FASHION.

The prevailing fashions of any place or period are regulated almost wholly by association. Convenience, comfort, economy, health, education, even life itself, are all more or less under its stern control. This proves the dominancy of this attribute in the mental constitution. Let a particular dress, custom, style of living become associated with high life, and it is soon adopted by all classes as fashionable. When the lower orders have adopted it, it becomes vulgar with the higher, and they hasten to reject it for another. Thus fashion runs an eternal round, laying the bands of an iron slavery on all who have not enough of good sense or philosophy to control their association of ideas.

INFLUENCE OF ASSOCIATION ON TASTE AND GENERAL CHARACTER.

Every day, every hour, is furnishing materials around which our future thoughts are to cluster. Every idea now cherished will become a nucleus to others; every mental act parent to a future progeny of mental acts. Thus the poetry that tells us the child is the father of the man becomes sober and earnest prose. While the mental associations are young and partially formed, they are easily directed; but when they have become mature and full, they are as the great river formed of many streams. If reformation is attempted, success is partial; all future life is a struggle to break the chain of early associations.

Even in a mere *literary* view, the subject is important. Let two youths of equal talent enter upon literary pursuits, the one previously of grovelling, and the other of elevated habits of thought and conduct; although equally industrious in their pursuits, the one will be ever pure, dignified, refined, in his thoughts, words, figures; such will be the natural current of his mind; while the other will frequently offend taste with the vulgarity of his allusions and the coarseness of his expressions. His writings will present a strange medley of refinement and grossness, of splendor and vulgarity. The man of pure taste and true refinement has been so formed from childhood by the influence of right associations.

INFLUENCE OF ASSOCIATION ON MORALS.

Many a youth has been led into immorality, vice, and ultimate ruin, by false associations. Let him once learn to associate idleness, extravagance, profanity, licentiousness, with high life and fashion; let him associate austerity, gloom, bigotry, with strict morals, and the high way to ruin is already paved. Nothing short of a complete mental revolution can save him.

In his Theory of Moral Sentiments, Adam Smith remarks, "In the reign of Charles II., a degree of licentiousness was deemed the characteristic of a liberal education. It was connected, according to the notions of those times, with generosity, sincerity, magnanimity, loyalty; and proved that the person who acted in this manner was a gentleman, and not a Puritan. Severity of manners and regularity of conduct, on the other hand, were altogether unfashionable, and were connected, in the imagination of that age, with cant, cunning, hypocrisy, and low manners.

"To superficial minds, the vices of the great seem at all times agreeable. They connect them not only with the splendor of fortune, but with many superior virtues which they ascribe to their superiors; with the spirit of freedom and independence; with frankness, generosity, humanity, and politeness. The virtues of the inferior ranks of people, on the contrary, their parsimonious frugality, their painful industry, and rigid adherence to rules, seem to them mean and disagreeable. They connect them both with the meanness of the station to which these stations commonly belong, and with many great vices which they suppose usually accompany them — such as an abject, cowardly, ill-natured, lying, pilfering disposition." *

* Smith's Theory of Moral Sentiment, quoted by Dugald Stewart, vol. i. p. 216.

The truth and importance of the above remarks cannot fail to commend themselves to every mind. To all youth, and to those who have the charge of their education, they read a lesson of duty which cannot be mistaken.

INFLUENCE OF ASSOCIATION ON RELIGION.

The power of association, partially applied, has contributed largely to create a fatal prejudice in multitudes against Christianity. From the earliest ages, the Christian religion has been eminently the poor man's friend, and vast numbers from the humbler walks have lived and died rejoicing in its blessings. "*To the poor the gospel is preached*," said Christ; and the sacred writer informs us, that "the *common people heard him gladly*." This circumstance gives to Christianity, in many minds, the aspect of vulgarity.

Thoughtless minds, looking upon Lazarus in rags and Dives in splendor, associating the one with irreligion and the other with Christianity, would hardly fail to consider Christianity a mean and beggarly affair. But is it so? or has the Creator given us this mental power to mislead us? Far otherwise; the fault lies in the *perverted use* of it. Let the Christian be contemplated in *all* his relations — to God, to angels, to heaven, to eternity, as well as to time; let Lazarus be seen in Abraham's bosom, amid the riches and splendors of heaven's court, and Dives infinitely more abject and poor than Lazarus ever was; let the despised exile in Patmos be viewed, not as a condemned criminal, but an honored servant of God, encircled with bright spirits, and held in special honor by heaven's nobility; let all those early Christians who toiled in poverty and reproach be contemplated in the light of the benign work they accomplished, the mighty wave of blessings which rolled out from under their hands, and which continues to sweep downward, with ever-swelling volumes, through all ages, while the worldly and the gay, who rolled in wealth and splendor over them, have long since passed to utter oblivion ; and if faith can look on ward to the final judgment, and to the scenes that lie beyond, let impiety and irreligion be there seen in the relations assigned them by Christianity ; *then* let it be determined *to which side Association gives her aid.*

This power, like all others, was given us to be *used;* and like all others, when used aright, will not fail to do its part towards elevating us to the dignity and glory for which we were made.

Here is an important particular in which man differs from the brute. The associations of the brute can extend only to what is *seen* and *temporal;* those of man can penetrate that vast kingdom of *moral* interests and relations, whose centre is GOD, and whose throne is ETERNITY. Let every pupil, who would aspire to a thorough education, throw his associations far upward and onward, and shape his course for an ETERNAL LIFE.

QUESTIONS ON CHAPTER II.

What is said of our thoughts ? How may we define *association?* Into what does Brown merge association ? What is said of his view ? Instances of association ? Have *brutes* association ? Give examples. What causes operate to control our associations ? The *first* cause without us ? *Illustrations ?* The *second ?* Illustrations ? *Third ?* Illustrations ? *Fourth ?* Illustrations ? *Fifth ?* Illustrations ? *Sixth ?* Illustrations ? *Seventh ?* Illustrations ? *Eighth ?* Illustrations ? What do we hence perceive ? Can we control our associations ? How ? Remark of Stewart ? Kaims ? What circumstances affect association ? Around what do every man's associations gather with pecular force ? Illustrations ? The principal reason why some are more inventive than others ? Illustrations ? What is said of the influence of association on speculative judgment ? On love of money ? On fashion ? On taste and general character ? In a *literary* view ? Of the influence of association on *morals ?* Remark of Adam Smith ? On *religion ?* Remarks on this subject ? What must every pupil do, who would aspire to a thorough education ?

CHAPTER III.

MEMORY.

We were not made to live merely in the *present.* Indeed, strictly speaking, all our experiences and observations relate to *past* time, the present being but a point.

Memory may be briefly defined *the power of recalling the past.* It is by virtue of this that we, as it were, live over and over the lives of our former days and former years. Memory has been supposed to denote *two* faculties — the capacity of *retaining* knowledge, and the power of *recalling* it; * the term *memory* being applied to the former, and *recollection* to the latter. In this view, we are said to commit to memory a poem, and keep it for use whenever we wish to call it up. Hence the poem may be said to be permanently in our memory, but not in our recollection, excepting when we choose to think of it.

But, strictly speaking, the mind does not carry the thing remembered around with it, as in a vessel; it is simply placed in such relation to it, or made so well acquainted with it, as to be *able to recall it at pleasure.* Capacity is a figure, implying a vessel which holds what we put in it. As memory is an active principle, we are in less danger of being misled by divesting the definition of all figure borrowed from physical ideas, and considering it simply the power by which we recall the past.

* "This faculty implies two things — a capacity of retaining knowledge, and a power of recalling it to our thoughts when we have occasion to apply it to use." — *Stewart's Philosophy*, vol. i. p. 224.

IS MEMORY AN ULTIMATE POWER?

Some philosophers have not considered memory an ultimate power in the mental constitution, but a compound of conception and perception. Thus every act of memory is supposed to be a conception of some object or event, attended with a perception of its relation to past time. Such is the view of Dugald Stewart, and it has been adopted by others.*

Now Stewart maintains that "every act of conception is accompanied with a belief that its object *exists before us at the present moment.*" Here is a *contradiction*, inasmuch as the very idea of memory implies the *absence* of its object. The following is his solution: "The only way that occurs to me of removing this difficulty is, by supposing that the remembrance of a past event is not a simple act of the mind; but that the mind first forms a conception of the event, then judges from circumstances of the period of time to which it is to be referred." †

Memory may operate in this way *sometimes;* but does she *always?* How often, running back the track of time, *with a view* to recalling an event, does she light upon it *as* an event of the past? — so that the event could not enter the mind, that is, be thought of *as* a *present*, but only as a *past* event. Memory is a free and active power; she will not brook the trammels of a rigid philosophy.‡

* "Our remembrances are nothing more than conceptions, united with the notion of a certain relation to time." — *Brown's Philosophy*, vol. i. p. 412. "Memory is that power or susceptibility of the mind by which those conceptions are originated, which are modified by a perception of the relation of past time." — *Upham's Philosophy*, p. 167.

† Philosophy, vol. i. p. 225.

‡ "Conception," says Stewart, "implies no idea of time whatever." — Vol. i. p. 79. If, then, memory is made up of conception and perception, there remains no other theory of solution than the one given by him. Now I agree that conception alone implies no idea of time; but I consider memory an *ultimate mental power*, which, by the aid of conception and other powers, directly recalls past events as such.

REASONS FOR CONSIDERING MEMORY AN ULTIMATE POWER.

1. Although conception and perception are in the service of memory, so also are attention, association, and other powers. All the mental powers are brought by the mind, more or less, into mutual service. The mind is itself a *unit;* its ultimate powers are powers of one and the same unit, to do, in various ways, certain classes of things. Memory is no more dependent on the other mental powers than the others are on memory; and as the services performed by memory are as characteristic and important as those which we ascribe to the other mental powers, it seems to claim a rank with them.

2. The *operations* of memory are *too multiform* to be brought within the range of the restricted definition to which I object. That we first put into operation *one* mental power and *conceive* of a past event, and then put on duty *another* power and determine its relation to the *past*, and that this is the *uniform* and *only* mode in which memory operates, is a theory too narrow to tally with human experience. The theory originated among the early writers, as part of a system, and appears to have been handed along down to us, without having been seriously disputed.

3. Stewart's method of defending this theory *does not meet the difficulty.* He explains it by the rapidity of our mental operations, placing them beyond our observation. But rapidity cannot change the *order* of things, although it may place them beyond our immediate notice. When a man in the country sets down to relate to his family the incidents of the *fourth of July* which he witnessed the *day before* in the city, all minds *first* go back to the *past day; past time* is thought of; and it is thought of, not as a *present*, but as a *past* day. He begins and recalls incident after incident, every one of which is *directly thought of* as an *incident of the past day.* That he *first* thinks of those incidents as *present* realities, and then by a *second* act refers them to the *day* on which they happened, is reversing the real order. Instead of its being first the *incidents* and then the *day*, it is first the *day* and then

the *incidents.* It may be *either* way, and *every* way, according as the mind sets itself to work. As I have intimated, memory is a very free power; she is limited to no one method of operation.

Perhaps the above strictures may seem unimportant. They have not been made without feelings of reluctance at differing from such eminent authorities; but it has appeared to me that so important a power as memory ought to be restored to its rank among the elemental faculties of the soul. Too many are inclined to think it a secondary and comparatively unimportant faculty. But it is one on which, preëminently, all the mental functions depend. Without it, we could live only in the present point; all the past would lie eternally under the dark blot of oblivion. Mental life would be but a series of perceptions and intuitions, flitting through and passing away, without leaving a trace of themselves behind. Letters written by the finger upon water would be as enduring as impressions made upon the human mind. Of course, all the mental powers would be at a stand, and man would be the mere creature and sport of the present moment.

MEMORY IN BRUTES.

So important is this power, even to *life itself*, that it is bestowed on the brute creation in common with man It is certain that brutes *remember*, although it might be difficult to show that they *first conceive* of a past event as a present reality, and *then perceive* its relation to past time. Bereaved kine remember their offspring, and often mourn for weeks on being bereaved of them. If they did not remember, they would cease to mourn. The dog remembers his master; years of absence do not avail to sunder the chords which bind this faithful servant to the man who reared and caressed him. The horse remembers his keeper, the place where he was fed, where he fell, where he was frightened.

Some have attempted to resolve all these into mere *recognitions.* On this theory the absent object is not thought of, but only recognized when returned. But this does not account for the signs of bereavement and sorrow. If the absent object were not thought of, it could not produce these effects. Moreover, the trained animal remembers the smart of the lash, and hence takes precaution to *avoid* its return. If it were a mere recognition, he could not be trained; since fear, in this case, implies memory. It is on the power of memory that we rely, in the training of all our domestic animals.

MEMORY UNIVERSAL.

The existence of memory is clearly marked in every human being from the dawn of intellect. It is also possessed in more equal measure than is usually supposed. Mankind generally do or may remember all that is essential to their well being. The events of former days, months, years; the course of their past lives; the histories of men and nations of other times, which they have read, are all rememered with great accuracy. Probably every individual of the thousands who served in the revolutionary war could relate, at any subsequent period of a long life, all the campaigns, battles, victories, and various important incidents of which he was witness.

Scarcely less perfect is our recollection of events of which we have *read*, provided we were *interested* in them. Who that has read the history of Napoleon's expedition into Russia has ever forgotten it? It is a quarter of a century since I read that eventful tragedy, and its thrilling incidents are nearly as vivid in my recollection now as at the first month after the book was read. And this is the common experience. Not one in a thousand who ever read that history will ever forget it. Memory is, then, a faculty possessed in almost equal measure by all men. Its inequalities are like those of the earth's surface, which, though they seem great to the superficial observer, are small compared with the entire depth of the globe.

CIRCUMSTANCES AFFECTING MEMORY.

Still there are *inequalities* of memory. Some men remember better than others. The difference, however, is more in *kind* than *degree*. One man's memory is *quick*, another's is *slow*. The memory of one is *general*, that of another *minute*. One man is famous for remembering *names*, *dates*, *localities*. Another scarcely remembers these at all, but remembers all the important *facts* connected with them.

Every man's memory varies with the *periods of his life* and *states of his physical system*. Causes affecting memory may be included in the following particulars: —

1. CONSTITUTIONAL TEMPERAMENT. Some are *constitutionally quick in all things*. They attend, perceive, associate, compare, and judge quickly. Their eyes flash like the electric fire, and are the index of their thoughts. Both their physical and mental movements are full of nerve; they step quick, they think quick. Their memory is of course in keeping. Others are, in all these particulars, constitutionally *slow*. But although their memories, like their other powers, are slower in operating than those of the other class, they are no less comprehensive, exact, retentive. They only require *more time*.

2. HABITS OF ATTENTION. One person, on returning from church, can repeat the *heads*, *arguments*, *inferences*, and *most striking thoughts* of the sermon which he heard; while another remembers little else than the preacher's *manner*, *voice*, *gestures*. Without adverting here to other causes, it is sufficient to say that the *attention* of the one was directed to the *manner;* that of the other to the *matter*. It is by a fixed attention that the mind obtains a firm and enduring embrace of its subject. What was said under the head of *Perception* must here again be called to mind. As the mind does not embrace all the points of an object at once, it is only by a *fixed attention* that sufficient fulness of perception is obtained to secure to the memory a permanent hold.

Two men ride out together on a summer's morning, to enjoy a country scene. On returning, the one is able to recall the features of that scene: every hill, dale, grove, cottage; the frowning rock, the deep ravine; the meandering stream, and the waving corn in the valleys; the cattle grazing on the slopes, and the men gathering the harvest; the gardens, orchards, fruits, flowers,—are all so imprinted on his memory, that he needs only a painter's hand to picture them exactly on canvas. His companion has only the general recollection of an agreeable ride through a very pleasant country. The one *attended*, the other did *not* attend, to what was passing before their eyes as they rode along.

3. Habits of Philosophic Arrangement. When a mind has formed the habit of associating things together in the relations of *cause and effect*, *genus and species*, the *whole and its parts*, the *container and the contained*, memory is far more comprehensive and retentive than when she deals in mere details. This is called *philosophical memory*. Apply it, for example, to the study of geography. The object is so to learn as to *remember* the most important facts.

Suppose the learner first ascertains the natural productions of a given temperature, and the temperature embraced between given latitudes. He has then only to learn the *latitude* of a country in order to know with considerable exactness all its varieties of animals, birds, insects; all its numerous grains and vegetables; its probable exports and imports; he is much assisted in determining the general character and habits of the people, the prevalent diseases of the country, &c. Having ascertained that elevation affects climate like higher degrees of latitude, he perceives that Mexico, and other mountainous countries of the tropics, must furnish the productions of both warm and cold climates.

With such helps, it is easy to remember. The truth is, there is little left for *memory to do*. The mind is furnished with *à priori* knowledge. The work is in a great measure taken from memory and given to the associations and deductions of philosophical thinking. The same method of assisting memory may be extended to nearly or quite all studies, and every wise teacher will encourage it.

4. Habits of Detail. Whether there is really so

much difference between this kind of memory and the preceding as is generally supposed, may be doubted. All men are philosophers, in their way. The chief difference between them is, that while some associate by the set rules of *science*, others, not conversant with these rules, associate things and remember by rules *of their own devising*.

Men of the merest detail have their associations of ideas by which they are enabled to remember. But their associations being more obvious and less comprehensive than those of philosophical minds, their memories are of course more conversant with details than with *classes* of facts. These are called *circumstantial* memories. The term is very expressive of the thing meant. Circumstantial denotes the things or events that *stand around*. Memory is here dependent on what happens to stand directly around what is remembered, rather than by any scientific arrangement of ideas.

I knew a stage-coach driver, who had for many years done errands in Boston for people living on his route through the country. The fidelity with which he uniformly executed his commissions had procured him a extensive business. After discharging his passengers a' the hotel, he would drive around into various parts of the city, thread numerous alleys and by-ways, attend to some twenty or thirty commissions at as many places, and then return to the hotel, having with great exactness performed all that was assigned him. Yet he used no paper, and kept no visible record of any kind.

Curious to know how this was done, the common privilege of our country was indulged. He replied, that when he began he had but one or two errands. As his business increased, his power of memory increased; so that he could now as easily remember thirty errands as at first he could five. He had formed the habit of so associating every errand, and whatever was peculiar in it, with the name of the family, the name and number of the street to which it belonged, and he so strung them all together in his mind, that he knew the precise route to take. The doing of the first errand suggested the next, and that the next, and so on until the whole was completed. This is *circumstantial* memory, resulting from careful *habits of detail.* It has its value. In some callings, success depends almost absolutely upon it.

5. VOCATION. Every person best remembers things *onnected with his own vocation.* This is because he is best *acquainted* with them, and most *interested* in them. Those things in which we are most interested fix our attention most, and are therefore best remembered. When a student visits a foreign library, he ever afterwards remembers various books there, which the ordinary visitor scarcely remembers beyond the threshold of the building.

A lady conversant with the fashionable toilet remembers all the particulars of a distinguished belle's dress at a ball; while most of the gentlemen present, with memories not inferior to hers, recollect very little about it. The memory of an epicure is very retentive of the various wines and dishes of an entertainment; while the man of literary or philosophical pursuits remembers only the interesting topics of conversation connected with his studies.* This may be called *professional* memory — that is, memory as modified by a man's *pursuits.*

6. AGE. All have observed the failure of memory with the advance of old age. Ordinarily, it begins to serve less faithfully near the age of fifty, and becomes gradually impaired as years pass over. There is also a difference as to the *things* remembered. In youth, memory is more *casual*, clinging most tenaciously to incidents which happen to interest, however unimportant. At a later period, it becomes more *judicious*, selecting the more important things, and being more methodical.

The failure of memory, as age advances, is owing mostly to *physical causes.* Passion, the handmaid of memory, is enfeebled through loss of the sap of life; hence, things being regarded with less feeling, they are more readily forgotten.

Some philosophers have supposed, as a cause of the failing of memory, a derangement or partial loss of the

* "A person who has not been accustomed to attend particularly to horses or cattle, may study for a considerable time the appearance of a horse or of a bullock, without being able, a few days afterwards, to pronounce on his identity; while a horse dealer or a grazier recollects many hundreds of that class of animals with which he is conversant, as perfectly as he does the faces of his acquaintances." — *Stewart's Philosophy*, vol. i. p. 227.

power of *association*. But this is a gratuitous supposition, since the fact is sufficiently accounted for by the single cause above noticed. Moreover, the fact that very aged people remember so minutely the events of childhood, is evidence that their association is still vigorous.

7. DISEASE. The effects of *disease* upon memory are very marked, sometimes extraordinary. The most curious fact is, that the same disease sometimes *quickens* and sometimes *suspends* its functions. This is doubtless owing to the different effects of congestion, withdrawing the vital force from the organs more especially concerned with memory, or concentrating it upon them. So that, although it may be technically the same disease in both cases, it differs in degree and in respect to the point of concentration. A *certain degree* of congestion may *quicken* memory; *another* degree may *suspend* its functions; just as a certain quantity of alcohol *exhilarates*, and that quantity *increased* produces *torpor* and even *death*.

On arising from severe sickness, men have frequently been alarmed at the failure of their memories. Students have forgotten their languages, their mathematics, their history; men of business have forgotten the details of their affairs, and have scarcely known how to proceed or where to begin. The same persons, while the exhilaration of the fever was on, betrayed symptoms of extraordinary memory in all these particulars. The lessons of boyhood, long neglected, were revived and repeated with extraordinary fluency and exactness.

By a natural law of reaction, when the undue excitement is over, a proportionate torpor succeeds. As much as the powers of memory were before *above* their natural level, so much are they now *below* it. Gradually, however, as health and strength return, does memory rise to her true position and resume her appropriate functions.

CHARACTERISTICS OF A GOOD MEMORY.

As men have ordinarily memory enough, a *good* memory is rather a term of *quality* than of *quantity*. Many have the unenviable habit of remembering much that ought to be forgotten, and of forgetting much that ought to be remembered. The memory should be trained to sever the wheat from the chaff, and to store up healthful food for the future nourishment of the mind. He who is at no pains to direct the memory, but allows it to run at large, remembers as *much*, perhaps, as he who carefully trains it; but the one grows up a simpleton, the other a wise man. The memory of the one stores the mind with treasures of valuable knowledge; that of the other fills it with a world of nonsense. The conditions of a good memory, then, are, to be *susceptible* to what ought to be remembered, to be *retentive* of it, and to have it at *ready command.*

QUESTIONS ON CHAPTER III.

What is *memory?* What has it been supposed? What is strictly true? What have some considered memory? What does Stewart maintain? Reply? What is his solution? Does memory *always* operate thus? Remark? Are not other powers, besides conception and perception, in the service of memory? Remarks? What is said, *secondly*, of the *operations* of memory? How does Stewart attempt to explain the difficulties of his theory? What is said in reply? Illustration? Apology for the above strictures? Have *brutes* memory? What might be difficult to show? Examples of brute memory? Into what have some attempted to resolve all these? Reply? What is said of the *universality* of memory? Remarks? What is said of events of which we have *read?* Are there *inequalities* of memory? In what do they mainly consist? Illustrate. *First* cause affecting memory? Remarks? *Second* cause? Give examples. What is said of *attention?* Illustration? *Third* source? What is called *philosophical* memory? Give the example. Advantage of such helps? *Fourth* source? What is said of all men? What is the chief difference between them? What are *circumstantial* memories? What is said of the term? Give the example. *Fifth* source? How explained? Examples? *Sixth* source? What have all observed? Difference as to the *things* remembered? To what is the failure of memory in old age owing? What have some philosophers supposed? Reply? *Seventh* source? Remarks? What is said of the characteristics of a *good* memory?

CHAPTER IV.

MEMORY CONTINUED.

CULTURE OF MEMORY.

SPECIAL and direct efforts to strength the memory are of little value. Like all the other mental powers, it is strengthened by being *appropriately exercised upon its appropriate objects.* All artificial rules, all machinery, all exercises of memory, for the express purpose of strengthening it, are rather injurious than beneficial. They place the mind in a *false position. If we suitably apply our mental powers to their appropriate objects, they will grow with sufficient rapidity and in due proportion.*

EARLY CULTURE OF MEMORY.

The first object in childhood is to direct the attention to things which *ought to be remembered* — things of *future value.* Childhood is the age to learn spelling and reading — to learn to associate letters and words with the sounds they represent. Not only are the organs of speech then most flexible, but the mind is best qualified to operate in that small and circumstantial way by which letter after letter and word after word becomes forever associated with its sound.

At the same age, much that is of prospective value may be committed to memory, although the mind is not yet capable of fully understanding it. Some dispute this, and contend that children should learn nothing but what they understand. But the laws of mental progress are against this theory, and facts condemn it. Memory is developed before the reasoning power, that she may lay up materials for it to work upon when it comes into service.

Those early lessons, those grammatical rules, those portions of the Sacred Scriptures, those hymns, those maxims of wisdom, those details of geography, chronology, arithmetic, committed to memory before we were able fully to understand their meaning, we find of great and ever-growing value as we advance in life. The attention of childhood should also be called to the *most important facts in nature.* Some of the first lessons in natural history, botany, geology, ornithology, serve to form a taste for these studies, and to lay the foundation for future success in them. If childhood does not learn *these* things, it will learn *something else.* Memory *will work,* to store the mind with *something,* either valuable or *useless.*

SUBSEQUENT CULTURE OF MEMORY.

As the mind matures, memory should take a more systematic and philosophical course. Nature suggests this; for now the reasoning powers come into alliance with memory, to guide her associations and direct her course. She has hitherto dealt mostly with *details;* she is now to remember in *groups* and *classes,* and by more remote associations. If she could once better recall the numerous pretty flowers seen in a ramble, she can now better recall the several genera and species to which they belong, and their scientific relation to the great family of which they are members.

Hitherto memory has been mostly conversant with *words* and *signs;* she has now to do with *realities.* If she could once more easily learn to repeat a chapter, she can now more easily learn to recall its meaning. She is perpetually working her way beneath the surface, and in every direction, whither philosophical associations conduct her.

Such is the course where memory is rightly cultivated; and this makes the difference between being always a child and ascending from that state to intellectual manhood. Thus the mind not only advances broadly in knowledge, instead of bounding over a single track, but she puts all her knowledge on duty, to trace out new relations and to discover for it new uses. The growth of the mind in valuable knowledge depends not so much on the number of new individual facts acquired and remembered, as on the number, extent, and value of their perceived relations.*

The failure of memory in regard to details, as age advances, may, on the whole, be regarded as a blessing. It harmonizes with the laws of mental growth, and seems a necessary condition of those more philosophic and comprehensive modes of thinking which characterize maturity of intellect.

CONFIRMING THE MEMORY.

Still a vast store of details, as well as of classes of facts, must be at command through life, or the judgment will suffer, since a sound judgment is exercised *in view of facts.* But if childhood and youth have taken the course above indicated, little difficulty will be realized in permanently securing whatever needs to be remembered. The lessons that childhood has imprinted a thousand times will never be fully effaced. What is subsequently acquired would be more easily forgotten, but for those habits of philosophical arrangement to which we have adverted. At the same time, frequent *recalling* at this age should take the place of frequent *repeating* in childhood.

The rules here to be observed are, first, give the closest possible *attention* to what you would remember;

* Maclaurin justly remarks, "New knowledge does not consist so much in our having access to a new object, as in comparing it with others already known, observing its relations to them, or discerning what it has in common with them, and wherein their disparity consists; and therefore our knowledge is vastly greater than the sum of what all its objects separately could afford; and when a new object comes within our reach, the addition to our knowledge is greater, the more we already know; so that it increases, not as the new objects increase, but in a much higher proportion." — *Conclusion of "Views of Newton's Discoveries."* See also Stewart's Philosophy, vol. i. p. 240.

secondly, reduce it to *system*, and fasten it in the mind by as many *philosophical associations* as possible; thirdly, frequently *recall* it, and *reflect* upon it. What is *thus* learned will never be forgotten. Whether it be history, language, science, law, theology, or any thing else, the mind will be able to recall and use it, so long as reason is on the throne. By this means, the judge on the bench, at the age of sixty-five, may give as sound judgment in view of the facts in law studied at an early age as at any previous period.

The importance of reducing to *system* and of accurately *classifying* what we learn, cannot be too much urged. This, well done, saves the necessity of much recalling. The mind can hardly help remembering what is thus framed into it, and is made, as it were, part and parcel of its own being. The mechanic who has always been accustomed to *have a place for every thing, and every thing in its place*, will always find his tools at command. So the student in every calling and profession, by systematic arrangement of his materials of thought, will be able at any time to call them into service.

COMMITTING TO PAPER.

He who would have both a ready and retentive memory, should *rely as little as possible upon the pen.* Memory *loves to be trusted*, and will pay large interest on what she receives. The practice of taking notes on the spot can hardly fail to weaken her powers. It is taking her work out of her hands. But there is a limit, beyond which she cannot go without assistance. At this limit, the pen may come to aid her. Notes of a sermon, for instance, should not be taken at church; but after returning home, it is well to write down the heads and most important thoughts in connection with them. This will serve to imprint them more deeply on the mind.

So in studying *history.* After reading and reflecting upon the contents of a volume, it is well to write out, from memory, a synopsis of its contents. This synopsis may be subsequently used to assist the mind in recalling the historic facts.*

There are other cases in which the pen must be used, or the memory will be over-tasked. In an interview with the late Noah Webster, the distinguished lexicographer, I asked him how much reliance he placed upon his memory in regard to the origin and the etymological and current import of words. He replied, "None at all; I rely wholly on the pen." In a case where so many particulars must be noted with exactness, entire reliance on memory is demanding of her too much. Dr. Webster complained, however, that he had a bad memory. The reader will perceive that this is accounted for by what has been said above. His necessary reliance on the pen, as a lexicographer, for a long series of years, would unavoidably render it difficult to retain any thing without that aid.

ARTIFICIAL MEMORY.

Artificial memory is secured by combining things easily remembered with those not easily remembered. In this way, we recall the latter by the aid of the former. Suppose we wish to remember a man's name. Standing apart from all associations, it is not easily retained. But if it happen to be the name of some person, place, or object with which we are acquainted, association enables us to remember it with ease. Or suppose we wish to remember a *date*. If we can associate it with some other date, or with some name familiar to us, if the association holds firm, the date is remembered. These, however, are the simple artifices, and do not differ much from the ordinary associations.

Systems of more artificial memory, involving considerable machinery, have been invented by Mr. Gray, of Europe, and Mr. Johnson, of this country. They are called *Memoria Technica*, and have found considerable

* The writer went through Rollin's Ancient History in this way, during a college vacation, and no portion of his reading in history has been more accurately remembered. The same course was subsequently taken with Hume's History of England, and is recommended to all students.

favor. Several distinguished men have used them, as they inform us, to advantage.* But whether the effect upon the mind, of training it to such strange and artificial associations, is on the whole beneficial, is with some reason doubted. Some minds have a *propensity* to strange, unnatural, ridiculous combinations. It is questionable how far this should be indulged.

It has been remarked above, that system and order aid memory. Sometimes the very *opposite*, by its extreme *oddity*, has the same effect. Whatever strikes the mind *forcibly*, even though it be the novelty of confusion itself, may help us to remember.

In illustration of the importance of order to aid the memory, Professor Upham states the following fact: "A person was one day boasting in the presence of Foote, the comedian, of the wonderful facility with which he could commit any thing to memory, when the modern Aristophanes said he would write down a dozen lines in prose, which he could not commit to memory in as many minutes. The man of great memory accepted the challenge; a wager was laid, and Foote produced the following: 'So she went into the garden, to cut a cabbage leaf to make an apple pie; and at the same time a great she-bear coming up the street, pops its head into the shop. What, no soap? So he died, and she very imprudently married the barber; and there were present the Picininnies, and the Joblillies, and the Gargulies, and the grand Panjandrum himself, with the little round button at the top; and they all fell to playing catch as catch can, till the gunpowder ran out of the heels of their boots.'" Upham remarks, "The story adds, that Foote won the wager. And it is very evident that statements of this description, utterly disregarding the order of nature and events, must defy, if carried to any great length, the strongest memory."†

To test this, I put some of the young ladies of my school on trial, and, in less than *ten* minutes, two of them

* Mr. Johnson exercised a class in his system, in a school of young ladies in Boston under my charge, and the examination, in the judgment of competent gentlemen, demonstrated the success of his system.

† Upham's Philosophy, p. 179.

repeated the whole, *verbatim;* thus beating "the man of great memory" himself, and proving the truth of the saying, that there are points where extremes meet.

RELATION OF MEMORY TO RELIGION.

The relation of memory to the Christian religion, although of the highest importance, is too obvious to require much notice. It was by virtue of this that Christianity itself was handed down to us; it is by virtue of this that all our past observation and experience of its benign influences are now available; it will, in eternity, be by virtue of the same that the deeds of the present life will send down their record through those ceaseless ages.

Memory is a *ground of belief*, not less imperative than the absolute knowledge of present realities. Indeed, in the strictest sense, all knowledge depends upon it; for the present is but a point, and all behind it depends on memory. Nor, if the memory be good, does it matter whether the remembered event took place a week, a year, or five years before. Criminals are condemned and executed on testimony running back ten, and even twenty years, provided the case is clear. And when we consider that the sacred historians wrote of things in which they were deeply interested, and under the influence of an inspiration which was vouchsafed to "bring all things to their remembrance," we ought to repose the same confidence in their narrations, provided they were honest and competent men, as in the subjects of our personal knowledge.

It is memory, also, that brings to us our own history, as individual subjects of this gracious religion. Our past sins, conflicts, victories, hopes, repentings, joys, promises — all that renders the past a means of guidance and impulse in our future course towards the "prize of our high calling," depends on memory. "Thou shalt *remember* all the way in which the Lord thy God led thee these forty years in the wilderness, to prove what is in thy heart, whether thou wilt keep his commandments."

Memory, also, will connect time with eternity; being one of the constitutional powers of the soul, any question of its eternal duration cannot be philosophically raised. The immortality of the soul *implies the immortality of its essential attributes.* Take away memory, and the soul is no longer a rational being. If memory is made up of perception and conception, as some think, then, so long as the soul can perceive and conceive, she can remember; if it be an ultimate constitutional power, as I think it is, it holds a place *with the other constitutional powers of the soul*, and will perish only with them and with the soul itself.

If the question be, How *long* shall we remember? the answer naturally is, So long as we have the *power;* which brings us to the same point. If the question be, How *much* shall we remember? there may be ground of doubt. It does not seem to be the province of philosophy to settle this point.

In the light of Christianity, we are led to conclude that we shall in eternity remember *all the deeds and events of this life having a moral bearing.* The fact that we seem now to have forgotten many of our right or wrong actions, does not militate against this conclusion; for there is a mighty power in pressing emergencies, especially in moments of alarm, to lift the veil of oblivion and bring up long-forgotten deeds. At such moments, events of by-gone years have rushed with lightning wing upon the mind. In this view, past forgotten deeds have been compared to letters written with sympathetic ink upon a sheet of white paper; they are not seen until the paper is held to the fire, and that potent agent brings the colors out.

We have reason to believe that the awful scenes of the judgment day will not fail to put memory on duty, and bid her call up *the entire record of our moral doings in this life.* "SON, REMEMBER," are words once addressed to a spirit from this world in eternity. Thus philosophy and Christianity combine to admonish us *to do nothing which we could wish to forget, and to fill up life with as many as possible of those deeds* WHICH IT WILL BE OUR ETERNAL JOY TO REMEMBER.

QUESTIONS ON CHAPTER IV.

What is said of the *culture* of memory? What is the first object in childhood? Remarks? What is said of committing to memory things of *prospective* value? What do some contend? Reply? Particulars? What should memory do as the mind matures? Remarks? What is the course of the mind when rightly cultivated? What is said of the failure of memory in regard to details? Remarks on *confirming* the memory? *First* rule? *Second? Third?* What is said of the importance of *system*, &c.? Of committing to *paper?* Instance? Studying *history?* Noah Webster? What is said of *artificial* memory? What of the *opposite* of order? Instance? What is said of the relation of memory to religion? Of memory as a ground of belief? Illustrate. Of memory as related to our own history? As connecting time with eternity? In the light of Christianity, what are we led to conclude? Remarks? What have we reason to believe? What do philosophy and Christianity combine to admonish us?

PART IV.

DISTINGUISHING POWERS OF THE HUMAN INTELLECT.

CHAPTER I.

GENERAL VIEWS OF MAN'S SUPERIORITY.

Among the pretending illuminators of mankind, is a class of speculating philosophers, referred to in preceding pages, who tell us there is no difference in kind between the intellect of man and that of a brute. They maintain that the difference is merely in *degree*, not in *kind;* and in the way of illustration, they inform us that the disparity is greater between the intellect of a lobster and that of a horse than between the intellect of a horse and that of a man.

How they have been enabled to take the precise gauge and dimensions of the lobster's intellect, and to demonstrate the points of distinction between it and that of the horse, they have not told us; but by denying all difference in *kind*, and maintaining only a chain of *degrees*, running from the lowest order of sentient creatures up to man, they have not wanted zeal in attempting to show that man is not the fallen image of God, but the exalted image of a *lobster*.

CHAIN OF DEGREES.

There is, indeed, a chain of degrees. Nature seems to avoid, so far as possible, violent transitions. The passages from the mineral to the vegetable, from the vegetable to the animal, from the animal to the rational,* are made as gently as the case admits. But then the passages are really made. The vegetable is more than the mineral, the animal is more than the vegetable, and a rational mind is more than an animal.

Nor, in the regular course of nature, are there any intervening *nondescripts* between the great kingdoms and classes of being. Where any thing like these occurs, it is the result of some violation of nature's laws; an accident, which soon vanishes. Such apparent caprices are no more to be cited as illustrations of the steady and undeviating course of nature, than the accidental ripples on the surface of a river of the course of the stream. The speculations of philosophers, drawn from supposed examples of hybridous life, are thoroughly unphilosophical, and betray as much ignorance of physiology as of the true principles of inductive logic.†

* "The simplest combination of animal life, where sensation first manifests itself in matter, is found in mines, where, 'unmolested by winds, or changing temperature, *infusoria* or *moulds* cover the damp wall.' The proper element of infusoria, or mould, is albumen, which they receive from the mineral body to which they adhere; the mineral being the matrice of the mould. Its delicate tissue is composed chiefly of nitre, eighty-five per cent. of which is oxygen; it has a feeble circulation, with little or no sensation." "Sensation, circulation, and voluntary motion are the second simplest combination of sensation with matter." — *Sensational Physiology; Laws of Causation*, p. 102.

† "Experiments have rendered it certain that *hybridity* in animals results from the *absence* of a proper degree of sensible heat. The mule that has hitherto been regarded as a hybrid, is so only from accidental circumstances. Prevost and Dumas, in repeating the experiments of Lewenhoeck, have discovered the hybridity of mules in northern climates to be caused by the absence of spermatic animalcules; while these being present in the mules of hot climates, explain the phenomena of reproduction. In this example, the law defines its degrees so clearly as to give us all the particulars, namely, that, in northern climates, sensation is unfelt in the spermatic vessels by the hybrid, and reproduction is impossible; whereas a hot climate, in establishing the necessary degree of heat, produces the necessary supply of circulating fluid, whereby sensation in the spermatic vessels of the hybrid

WHEREIN MEN AND BRUTES ARE ALIKE.

In respect to animal life, man commences, in many respects, as low as the brute, and even lower. No brute animals at birth, and for months after, are as helpless as human infancy, or certainly not more so. Man steps *below* brutes at his origin, as if to take a position for the great leap with which he is to pass them.

We have followed man with the brute through the various *sensations* which they hold in common, and have also indicated those powers of which the brute seems, in some degree, to participate. We have seen, however, that these powers are in man associated with others, lifting them into a sphere of activity immeasurably higher than ever falls to the range of brute intellect. We are in subsequent pages to contemplate those other, those distinguishing powers.

Our knowledge of brute mind is mostly *negative*. I propose to show that there are certain powers of the human intellect, demonstrable by experience and observation, of which we have not a shadow of evidence that they pertain to brute intellect, and that they differ from every development of brute mind, not only in *degree*, but in *kind*.

DOMINION OF MAN.

There was science as well as poetry in what the royal minstrel flung from his harp, when he sung of man: "Thou hast made him a little lower than the angels, and hast crowned him with glory and honor; thou hast made him to have dominion over all the works of thy hands; thou hast put all things under him." The Septuagint reads, "Thou hast made him a little lower than Elohem;" that is, a little lower than God, or as God in miniature.

And how like his Creator is man, in his dominion

is developed, and the animal resumes its place in the laws of causation, by becoming reproductive. Thus I have bridged over the chasm that has hitherto been leaped, and connected mineral, vegetable, and animal life by the chain of causation."—*Ibid.* p. 104.

over the world! Over all these vast mineral, vegetable, animal kingdoms, he holds lordly dominion; over them all he has such power and control, that there is no imaginable form of strength, utility, or beauty, to which he cannot subdue the mountain rocks; no quality or condition grateful to the taste, nutritious to the body, or pleasing to the eye, to which he cannot bring the wild vegetable creation; and no purpose of convenience, labor, or recreation to which he cannot make the animal tribes subservient.

IN WHAT MAN'S POWER OF DOMINION CONSISTS.

The power of man over the lower creation results partly from his superior physical organization, particularly that of his *hand*, — his most distinctive physical characteristic, — but more especially from the superior endowments of his *mind*. It is not the want of *speech* that holds the brute creation in relative abjectness; for brutes have language, as well as men, and that adequate to express all they know. That it is neither the cunning of the hand, nor the peculiar organs of speech, that distinguish man from the brute, as some affirm, is evident from the fact that a human being without hands, and dumb from his birth, has developed all the distinguishing properties of the human intellect.

If we speak of *physical strength*, what is the power of man compared with those vast mountains of rock which sink to plains before him, compared with those huge structures and massive columns of architecture which tower under his little hands to the skies? What is the puny arm of man compared with the mighty forests, the wildernesses of stately cedars and majestic oaks, which recede from his presence, and by his magic touch give place to smiling and verdant fields? What but a feeble speck is man on the great ocean, whose proud, swelling waves, angry billows, and furious tempests he fearlessly encounters? What is the strength of man compared with that of the ox, the horse, the elephant, which he so readily subjects to the yoke of his dominion?

How, then, is man enabled to maintain this dominion over the world? The only philosophical answer is, By the superior powers of his *mind*. It is because he *knows how*. By virtue of *superior intellectual endowments*, he is enabled to apprehend means of appropriating all the laws and powers of nature to his use, thus making them to become, as it were, his own sinews and muscles, guided by his wisdom, and obedient to his will.

LIKENESS OF THE HUMAN TO THE DIVINE INTELLECT.

Let us notice, in this respect, the striking resemblance of the human mind to THAT in whose image* it was created. When we look upon the four great kingdoms of nature, — the mineral, the vegetable, the animal, the mental, — upon the globe itself which we inhabit, and the shining worlds around us; upon the boundless varieties of created beauty in the plants, the flowers, the trees of the forest; upon the numberless surpassing wonders of animal organization; upon the more wonderful creation and endowments of human intellect; and finally, upon the most sublime and glorious of all objects in creation — the *moral* government divinely established and maintained over the universe; and then, when we consider that all this was conceived, planned, perfected *by the mind of God*, we are compelled to exclaim, *How amazing the powers of that mind!*

And in addition to the inherent powers of his personal mind, he employs all his *works* as instruments of his will. He makes certain things means of accomplishing others, and these again means to others; the number ever rising in an infinite progression. Thus all matter, all created beings, all the laws and operations of nature, from motes to worlds, and from worlds to systems of

* "And God said, Let us make man in our image, after our likeness; and let them have dominion over the fish of the sea, and over the fowl of the air, and over the cattle, and over all the earth, and over every creeping thing that creepeth upon the earth. So God created man in his own image, in the image of God created he him; male and female created he them." — *Genesis* i. 26, 27.

worlds, become as it were his own bones and sinews, by which he executes the lofty and all-embracing purposes of his mind. Hence they are variously termed his instruments, his vehicles, his ministering agents. In the bold and beautiful figure of the sacred writers, he makes the forked lightnings his arrows, the clouds his chariots, and the winds his angels.

Now all this is similar to what *man* does on a *smaller scale.* When we look upon the various fabrics of strength and beauty which clothe our persons; when we see the dark and gloomy desert giving place to cultivated fields, laughing with golden harvest; when we behold the magnificent houses, temples, cities which man has reared; when our enchanted eyes glance at the fire-sped car, thundering on its iron track as with lighting wing; when we behold a highway for nations thrown across the oceans, and proud ships of merchandise and war riding fearlessly forth to all the ports and continents of the globe; when we see how much *science* has done, in discovering the amplitude, laws, and operations of nature; when we see knowledge reduced to language, language to written letters and words, and these to books, by which man makes his thoughts travel the world over, and live and speak through all ages; when we look upon the vast libraries which have been made to give utterance to human thoughts; when we see civil governments, founded on principles of equal justice, established over great nations; and when we consider that all this is the work of the *human intellect*, can we avoid exclaiming, How *unlike* that of the *brute*, how *like* to HIS in whose image it is declared to have been made, is the intellect of man!

The most important of those intellectual powers which distinguish man from the brute may be comprehended under the following heads — ABSTRACTION, CLASSIFICATION, INDUCTION, REASON, JUDGMENT, IMAGINATION. Brute mind cannot be shown to possess these powers in any proper sense; and it will be seen, as we proceed, that it is by the use of these that man, availing himself of the materials furnished by his lower faculties, rises from the mere animal to the rank of a rational and immortal being.

QUESTIONS ON CHAPTER I.

What is said of a class of speculating philosophers? Their illustration? Remarks. What of a chain of *degrees?* What of apparent caprices? Wherein are men and animals alike? With what are the human powers, in distinction from those of the brute, *associated?* What is our knowledge of brute mind? What is proposed? What is said of the dominion of man? In what consists man's power of dominion? What is said of the want of *speech* in brutes? Of man's *physical strength?* How, then, can he maintain his dominion? The operations of the divine Mind in the four kingdoms of nature? In making part of his works means of accomplishing others? To what is all this similar? Illustrations? Under what heads may be comprehended the most important of those powers which distinguish man from the brute?

CHAPTER II.

ABSTRACTION.

Abstraction implies *the power of considering any part or property of an object by itself.* Thus, if we take an apple in our hands, we may think of its magnitude, or of its smoothness, or of its mellowness, or of its odor, or of its color, or, if we taste it, of its flavor. Considering any one of these *properties* apart from the *apple itself* is called *abstraction.*

Some have confounded abstraction with *analysis;* but there is some difference between them. Abstraction is the considering of *one part* or property of an object by itself; analysis is the resolving of the *whole object* into its elements. Analysis implies *more* than abstraction. We abstract when we analyze, but we do not always analyze when we abstract. The chemist *analyzes* when he decomposes water, air, marble, &c., into their simple elements; he literally *abstracts* when he withdraws some *one* element from the object to which it belongs.

But we may separate in *thought* when we do not in *fact;* the former is commonly called abstraction, the latter analysis. Hence abstraction belongs more properly to *mental* science, analysis to *physical.* We can in *thought* separate the length, breadth, thickness, hardness, &c., of a marble slab from the *slab itself;* this is *abstraction.**

* It was a theory of the ancient schools, down to the eleventh century, that there were certain universal realities, or "forms of things from eternity immersed in matter," to which abstract names are given. "Such," says Stewart, "appears to have been the prevailing opinion concerning the nature of universals till the eleventh century, when a new doctrine, or, as some authors think, a doctrine borrowed from the school of Zeno, was proposed by Roscellinus, and soon after very widely propagated over Europe by the

We can, in *fact*, separate the *elements* of that slab — the lime, carbonic acid, &c. — from *each other ;* this is *analysis.* The latter term is, however, applied figuratively to mere *mental* action.

IMPORTANCE OF ABSTRACTION.

Abstraction is at the foundation of all *classification*, and some merge them into one ; but as they are really distinct, their offices are sufficiently marked and important to justify contemplating them apart. Abstraction is as essential to our reasoning powers, both in morals and mathematics, as to our classification. The direct office of this power is, to enable the mind to derive a multitude of ideas from a single object ; ideas applicable not only to other objects of the same kind or species, but to those of every description. Here we begin to see the broad line of distinction between the human and brute intellect.*

ILLUSTRATION.

When the brute looks upon an object, he seems to regard it only as a *whole ;* he derives from it, as it were,

abilities and eloquence of one of his scholars, the celebrated Peter Abelard. According to these philosophers, there are no existences in nature corresponding to general terms, and the objects of our attention in all our general speculations are not ideas, but words.

"In consequence of this new docrine, the schoolmen gradually formed themselves into two sects ; one of which attached itself to the opinions of Roscellinus and Abelard, while the other adhered to the principles of Aristotle. Of these sects, the former are known in literary history by the name of Nominalists, the latter by the name of Realists. It is with the doctrine of the Nominalists that my own opinion on this subject coincides." — *Stewart's Philosophy*, vol. i. p. 98.

* " This power of considering certain qualities or attributes of an object apart from the rest, or, as I would rather choose to call it, the power which the understanding has of separating the combinations which are present to it, is distinguished by logicians by the name of *abstraction*. It had been supposed by some philosophers (with what probability I shall not now inquire) to form the characteristic attribute of a rational nature. That it is one of the most important of all our faculties, and very intimately connected with the exercise of our reasoning powers, is beyond dispute." — *Ibid.* vol. i. p. 90.

but a *single idea.* But man regards it also in its numerous *properties* and *elements.* Thus, when he looks upon a stone, a tree, or a flower, he not only receives the one idea of that object as the brute does, but he also gathers from it the *abstract* ideas of length, breadth, thickness, solidity, color, &c. These abstract ideas, by the aid of other faculties, he can employ in forming *conceptions of unseen and distant objects.*

When he hears an object *described*, having properties similar to those with which he has thus become familiar, he as readily conceives it, although thousands of miles distant, as though it had just lain directly before his eyes. By examining the properties of the few objects about him, his mind obtains the means of becoming acquainted with the universe at large. Histories, descriptions, paintings of distant places and objects present them to him with scarcely less exactness than their actual presence. A description of St. Paul's Church, in London, or of Mount Vesuvius, or of the Egyptian Pyramids, enables the distant artist to draw a picture nearly or quite as true to the original as though his eyes had actually seen them.

Thus, while brute intellect is confined to the little spot or the particular objects on which the animal gazes, the human intellect, like that of Him in whose likeness it was made, overleaps the boundaries of physical vision, expatiates abroad, accumulating treasures of ever-growing wealth in all parts of creation.

While the student's body is living only in one small spot, his mind may be living in distant continents — now exploring the busy streets of London, or gazing upon some of the objects of special interest in that great metropolis; now looking with admiration upon the stupendous structure of St. Peter's, in Rome; now casting a glance of solemn awe upon the Pyramids of Egypt; now indulging its taste with fine relics of Grecian architecture; and now again, with bolder adventure, travelling amidst the wonders of India and China, or, perhaps, exploring the coral beds of the ocean; or ascending the towering mountains of the land of the sun into regions of everlasting winter and storm.

Thus has the human intellect power to appropriate to itself all the works of creation, far and near; it can know, possess, enjoy them; while, for aught that appears, the intellect of the brute has no part nor lot in any thing, except what lies within the little circle of his *bodily vision.*

RELATION OF ABSTRACTION TO MATHEMATICS.

The whole science of mathematics is one of abstract numbers and relations. Hence it is eminently dependent on that mental power which we are now considering. Other powers are also called into exercise, more or less, but all depend on these.

We learn most things first in the *concrete.* The child has his marbles, his blocks, &c. From these, or any thing else which he happens to play with, he begins to get the notion of length, breadth, thickness, of roundness, squareness, &c. He also learns to consider his toys as one, two, three; as few or many. All these ideas he abstracts from the toys themselves, and employs them as *elements of abstract or mathematical science.* These abstract ideas are called *general,* because they apply to *all* subjects. When a person has once learned to *compute* and *measure,* he may apply his computations and measurements to objects of every description. But the science of mathematics stands aloof from these objects; considered in itself, it is a science of *pure abstractions.*

RELATION OF ABSTRACTION TO THE PRACTICAL ARTS.

It is in the exercise of this power that the machinist, the architect, the mason, the carpenter is enabled to adjust his materials to the relations for which they are severally designed. An abstraction, a measurement of what is wanted, is first obtained; by this the material is wrought and adjusted to its design, so that when the several parts of the machinery, the house, the ship, or whatever it be, are brought together, although from various and distant places, they are found to fit each other precisely. Many a complicated machine, many a splendid edifice, has been thus erected of materials wrought in different parts of the world.

The Temple of Solomon is said to have been built of materials wrought in the distant mountains, with such an exact application of the abstract principles, that, at its erection, the sound of the hammer did not break the sacred silence of the holy place. It is truly a beautiful illustration of the mental power we are considering, to behold a vast edifice rising under the workman's hands, every joint, every pin, every mortice moving into its exact place, as though it had been there before. Indeed, by the application of abstract principles, a more perfect "fit" can often be obtained than by the actual application of the objects themselves.

RIGHT USE OF THIS POWER.

On this point, Stewart has well remarked, "In a perfect system of education, care should be taken to guard against both extremes, and to unite habits of abstraction with habits of business in such a manner as to enable men to consider things, either in general or in detail, as the occasion may require. Whichever of these habits may happen to gain an undue ascendant over the mind it will necessarily produce a character limited in its powers, and fitted only for particular exertions. Hence some of the apparent inconsistencies which we may frequently remark in the intellectual capacities of the same person.

"One man, from an early indulgence in abstract speculation, possesses a knowledge of general principles, and a talent for general reasoning, united with a fluency and eloquence in the use of general terms, which seem to the vulgar to announce abilities fitted for any given situation in life; while, in the conduct of the simplest affairs, he exhibits every mark of irresolution and incapacity. Another not only acts with propriety and skill in circumstances which require a minute attention to details, but possesses an acuteness of reasoning and a facility of expression on all subjects in which nothing but what is particular is involved; while, on general topics, he is perfectly unable either to reason or to judge." *

A perfect combination of the two habits — that of dealing in abstract and general principles and that of dealing in details — makes the most perfect education. It bridges the gulf between the learned and the uneducated. "Expert men," says Lord Bacon, "can execute and judge of particulars one by one; but the general counsels, and the plots, and the marshalling of affairs come best from those that are learned."

RELATION OF ABSTRACTION TO RELIGION.

This distinguishing prerogative allies man to that invisible empire of objects revealed in Christianity. It furnishes his conception and imagination with the materials for embracing other beings, other modes of existence, other and higher interests than this world affords. He is thus placed in relation to the Christian religion. He becomes acquainted with distant objects, not only of the present age, but also of ages preceding and ages coming. He becomes both a chronicler of the past and a prophet of the future.

The same intellectual power acquaints him with the abstract properties and qualities of *mind.* When a man contemplates the mental character of a fellow-being, he considers not merely that one character as a *whole;* he also gathers from it the *abstract* properties of *reason*, *judgment*, *memory;* the various qualities of *virtue*, *truth*, *justice;* of *vice*, *falsehood*, *dishonesty;* of *love*, *hatred*, *revenge.*

By means of these abstractions, so combined as to answer to descriptions of character, he is enabled to form just conceptions of thousands of men on record whom he has not seen. He thus becomes, as it were, personally acquainted with Adam, Abraham, Noah, Job, Daniel; with Cyrus, Alexander, Cæsar, Hannibal; with Plato,

* Stewart's Philosophy, vol. i. p. 131.

Demosthenes, Cicero, Virgil; and with all the illustrious dead whose histories have reached us.

In the same way he becomes acquainted with that wonderful personage, JESUS CHRIST. He has never seen him, but he has abstracted, from various sources, something like the mental and moral qualities predicated of him, and, by the aid of imagination, so combines them as to conceive of a being answering to the historic description of him. Thus does Jesus Christ, although never seen by his bodily eye, stand as it were in living form before his mind, the object of his admiration and gratitude.

In the same way he becomes, as it were, acquainted with the angelic beings mentioned in the Sacred Scriptures, and finally with GOD himself. His mind thus gradually ascends, as on the patriarch's ladder, from the cold, hard earth on which his body rests, into the warm and glorious realms of heaven. All this is wholly without the range of brute mind. It evidently places man *apart* from all creatures upon the earth, *in relation to other and higher worlds than this.*

QUESTIONS ON CHAPTER II.

What is *abstraction?* Illustration? With what have some confounded abstraction? State the distinction? Illustrate. What is said of doing in thought what is not done in fact? What is abstraction at the foundation of? What is its direct office? Illustrations? State the disparity between the human and brute mind in this particular. Relation of abstraction to *mathematics?* How do we first learn things? Illustration? Relation of abstraction to the *practical arts?* Temple of Solomon? Stewart's remarks on the right use of this power. To what does this distinguishing prerogative ally man? Remarks? With what does the same intellectual power acquaint him? Remarks? The several illustrations? Where, then, does this power evidently place man?

CHAPTER III.

CLASSIFICATION.

Classification implies the *power of arranging things into genera and species.* Suppose a promiscuous heap of fruit which it is proposed to classify. We remove all that is of a particular shape and appearance, and place it by itself; to this heap we give the name *apple.* We do the same in reference to all the fruit of another shape and appearance, and call it *pear;* the same in reference to that of another, and call it *peach;* in reference to that of another, and call it *plum;* to that of another, and call it *cherry.* We have now arranged the fruit into *genera.* We have the genus apple, the genus pear, the genus peach, &c.

SUBDIVISION OF GENERA INTO SPECIES.

But, on examining the apples further, we find that some are sweet and others sour. We divide again, placing the sweet by themselves, and the sour by themselves. Under the genus apple, the sweet and the sour are species. We examine more minutely, and find that the sour apples have various flavors. We select those characterized by peculiar flavors, and place all of like flavors together in separate heaps; we do the same with the sweet apples.

If, now, we consider the sour apples a genus, these subdivisions of them are species; so also, if the sweet apples be considered a genus, the different sorts of sweet apples under this genus are species. As we descend from the general to the specific, species become genera; and as we ascend from the specific to the general, genera become species. We go through a similar process with all the other fruits.

We have now performed a scientific classification of the previously confused heap. Having done this in reference to the heap before us, we have virtually done it in reference to all such fruits in the world. Hereafter, whenever we see or hear of any such fruits, we know *what they are, and where to place them.* From these few facts, our minds have learned a lesson wide as the world. But classification does not necessarily include the *actual* separation and arrangement of the several genera and species: as an abstraction, we often do mentally what cannot be done actually; and it is only the mental process with which we are now concerned.

CLASSIFICATION AN ORIGINAL PRINCIPLE.

That the power of classification is an original and essential attribute of humanity, is evident from the fact that all men give evidence of possessing it, and that *children manifest it prior to instruction.** The rudest savage tribes classify the trees, plants, and animals with which they are conversant; and if we give to the little child a heap of variously-shaped and colored beads, we find it

* "Un enfant appelle du nom d'Arbre le premier arbre que nous lui montrons. Un second arbre qu'il voit ensuite lui rapelle la même idée il lui donne le même nom; de même à un troisième, à un quatrième, et voila le mot d'Arbre donné d'abord à un individu, qui devient pour lui un nom de classe ou de genre, une idée abstraite qui comprend tous les arbres en général." — *Abbé de Condillac.*

"The particular cave, whose covering sheltered the savage from the weather; the particular tree, whose fruit relieved his hunger; the particular fountain, whose water allayed his thirst, would first be denominated by the words cave, tree, fountain, or by whatever other appellation he might think proper, in that primitive jargon, to mark them. Afterwards, when the more enlarged experience of this savage had led him to observe, and his necessary occasion obliged him to make mention of other caves, and other trees, and other fountains, he would naturally bestow upon each of these new objects the same name by which he had been accustomed to express the similar object he was first acquainted with. And thus, those words which were originally the proper names of individuals would each of them insensibly become the common name of a multitude." — *Smith's Origin of Language.* See Stewart's Philosophy, vol. i. p. 89.

immediately engaged in assorting them according to their forms and colors. We see here, as indeed every where else, an adaptation of the human mind to the lessons to be learned. The mind has the constitutional power and propensity to classify; and classes in nature actually exist. Creation is not a confused jumble. Although no two of any genus or species are exactly alike, yet all of each genus and of each species have the *distinctive characteristics which determine its family.* The lines are drawn with a breadth and clearness which can never be mistaken.

Horses, for instance, are of all imaginable varieties; yet no horse partakes of the genus elephant, or tiger, or any other animal but a horse. The same is true, in the strictest sense, of all the classes in the mineral, vegetable, animal, and rational kingdoms. The principle of a severe and exact classification runs through them all, indicating the existence of that attribute in the mind of their Creator which he has implanted in the minds of those he has made to study his works.

INCORRECT CLASSIFICATION.

Although the propensity to classify is early and universally developed, like all the other mental faculties, it *needs instruction.* The classifications of untaught minds are sometimes exceedingly erroneous. The error usually consists in classing things together whose points of resemblance are deceptive and casual, instead of being real and permanent. Thus a child would be likely to arrange glass, crystal, diamond, in one class, being deceived by appearance. Gold, brass, and all modifications of metals of a yellow color would for the same reason be grouped together. When the education of a person is quite limited, in his attempts to bring every new object within the classes which he has formed, he sometimes places it in very strange company.

Dugald Stewart refers to a fact illustrative of this, mentioned by Captain Cook, in his account of a small island called Wateeoo, which he visited in sailing from

New Zea.and to the Friendly Islands. "The inhabitants," says he, "were afraid to come near our cows and horses, nor did they form the least conception of their nature. But the sheep and goats did not surpass the limits of their ideas; for they gave us to understand that they knew them to be birds. It will appear," he adds, "rather incredible that human ignorance could ever make so strange a mistake, there not being the most distant similitude between a sheep or a goat and any winged animal. But these people seemed to know nothing of the existence of any other land animals besides hogs, dogs, and birds. Our sheep and goats, they could see, were very different creatures from the first two, and therefore they inferred that they must belong to the latter class, in which they knew that there is a considerable variety of species."*

CLASSIFICATION A DISTINGUISHING ATTRIBUTE.

Brute mind regards objects only as *individual things*, whereas the human mind contemplates them as *representatives of vast kingdoms of objects like themselves.* Thus, while brute intellect rests upon the single object seen, the human intellect bounds from it to the great *class* of objects to which it belongs. So soon as the human mind becomes acquainted with one oak, it is virtually acquainted with all the oaks of that kind upon the face of the earth. The same is true of it in regard to all plants, flowers, grains; minerals and metals; beasts, birds, reptiles, fishes. In the same way, it classess the shining hosts of the firmament; also all the works of human art, fabrics, cities, kingdoms. It thus educes order from confusion; and the universe, to brute mind little else than a mere blank, becomes to the human intellect a lesson easy and delightful to read.†

* Stewart's Philosophy, vol. i. p. 90.

† The reader should here guard against two extremes — that of supposing absolute classes, independently of real existences, on the one hand; and that of supposing classification a mere grouping of individuals for the sake of convenience, on the other. There are *real classes in nature*, — classes in the concrete, — although classification should proceed on the strict inductive plan. Dugald Stewart, referring to some of the ancient philosophers,

It must here be noticed, that while I maintain the necessity of an examination of *particular objects*, as the *foundation* of all human knowledge, I at the same time claim that our knowledge is not restricted to our individual experience, but extends infinitely beyond it; and this is predicated of *man*, in distinction from the *brute*. The brute knows one thing at a time, and that one thing goes from his mind as it comes — a solitary, uninstructive fact. But man, in learning that one thing, learns all things of the same genus in the universe, and all these, too, in their relations to other genera and to the universal system.

PROGRESS OF NATURAL SCIENCE DEPENDS ON CLASSIFICATION.

The progress of individuals in knowledge has been seen to depend on the power of classification. It is the same that enables the *human race*, as such, to bear onward the cause of science, *in a course of steady progress, from age to age*. The following interesting paragraph from Condorcet, *Sur l'Instruction Publique*, is too much to our purpose here to be omitted: —

"To such of my readers as may be slow in admitting the possibility of this progressive improvement in the human race, allow me to state, as an example, the history of that science in which the advances of discovery are the most certain, and in which they may be measured with the greatest precision. Those elementary truths of

says, "Forgetting that *genera* and *species* are mere arbitrary creations which the human mind forms, by withdrawing the attention from the distinguishing qualities of objects, and giving a common name to their resembling qualities, they conceived universals to be real existences, or (as they expressed it) to be the essences of individuals; and flattered themselves with the belief that, by directing their attention to these essences in the first instance, they might be enabled to penetrate the secrets of the universe, without submitting to the study of nature in detail." —*Stewart's Philosophy*, vol. i. p. 123. Both this philosopher and the ancient philosophers whom he rebukes fail to hit the true mark. "Genera and species are" *not* "mere arbitrary creations." *They exist in nature.* But we arrive at the true knowledge of them, not as the Platonists and the Peripatetics supposed, by directing attention to imagined abstract essences, but by studying nature in the detail.

geometry and of astronomy, which, in India and Egypt, formed an occult science, upon which an ambitious priesthood founded its influence, were become, in the times of Archimedes and Hipparchus, the subjects of common education in the public schools of Greece. In the last century, a few years of study were sufficient for comprehending all that Archimedes and Hipparchus knew; and, at present, two years employed under an able teacher carry the student beyond those conclusions which limited the inquiries of Leibnitz and of Newton.

"Let any person reflect on these facts; let him follow the immense chain which connects the inquiries of Euler with those of a priest of Memphis; let him observe, at each epoch, how genius outstrips the present age, and how it is overtaken by mediocrity in the next; he will perceive that nature has furnished us with the means of abridging and facilitating our intellectual labor, and that there is no reason for apprehending that such simplification can ever have an end. He will perceive that, at the moment when a multitude of particular solutions and of insulated facts begin to distract the attention and to overcharge the memory, the former gradually lose themselves in one general method, and the latter unite in one general law; and that these generalizations, continually succeeding one to another, like the successive multiplications of a number by itself, have no other limit than that infinity which the human faculties are unable to comprehend."*

MENTAL AND MORAL SCIENCE DEPEND ON CLASSIFICATION.

It is evident that, without the power of classification, we could never take the first step in *mental and moral science* If any mental act were to be regarded as an individual by itself, unlike every other mental act, we could come to no understanding of each other's mental phenomena — we could not even interpret our own. But there are real classes of mental acts which we all have in common. For instance, what we call acts of *memory* and what we

* See Stewart's Philosophy, vol. i. p. 126.

call acts of *perception* have each a character so marked, so peculiar, that we find no difficulty in mutually understanding the same name, as applied to all the myriads of the one or of the other, both in ourselves and in all other beings.

The same is true of our *moral affections.* Those affections, for instance, to which we give the name *love*, and those to which we give the name *hatred*, are each so marked and so peculiar to themselves, that we can easily class them. The term designating all the affections of one of these classes, whether in human or superhuman beings, conveys to our minds a perfectly clear and exact idea. The same may be said of all the moral powers and affections. Hence we are enabled to come to a knowledge of each other's minds; to systematize our mental operations, and to give and receive instruction.

Teaching is addressed to certain *classes* of mental properties and actions, generically the same in all; so that the teaching adapted to *one* mind is essentially adapted to *all* minds in the same stage of progress. It is on this principle that text books are provided for *classes* of children, embracing thousands, and that a book of truly profound and original thought, like Butler's Analogy, adapted to command the homage of the thinking classes of any *one* age, is adapted to do the same in *all* ages.

THE LEARNED PROFESSIONS DEPEND ON CLASSIFICATION.

The profession of the *teacher* is involved in what has been already said. It is evident that the *medical* profession is also wholly dependent on classification. Unless *diseases* and their *remedies* could be classified, the whole science of medicine would be reduced to mere empiricism; not a book could be written, not a single rule of practice instituted, not an examination or an experiment made of the least practical value. In every individual case, the practitioner must needs begin anew, untaught by science, unadmonished by experience.*

* "Without such a classification, it would be impossible for us to fix our attention amidst the multiplicity of particulars which the subject presents

The *legal* and the *clerical* professions would be involved in the same chaos. Unless the characters and actions of men were classified and compared with appropriate rules of duty, the bar could neither advocate nor defend; the bench could neither acquit nor condemn; the pulpit could administer neither instruction, rebuke, nor encouragement. All these points are too manifest to require elucidation.

RELATION OF CLASSIFICATION TO RELIGION.

The relation of this subject to religion becomes thus very evident. A single man, or the men of any one age representing the men of all ages, a book of instruction from God to any individual, or to the individuals of any one age, is adapted to all men of all ages. Hence the Bible, although given to man at different periods, and many generations since, is as perfectly adapted to us of this generation as it was to the ancients. We all belong to the same genus; we all have the same classes of mental and moral attributes. "As in water face answereth to face, so the heart of man to man." Taking advantage of this fact, God makes *one* book of revelation answer for *all men;* and he makes it our duty to recognize the same fact, and receive that revelation as addressed to each one of us.

The human race being thus regarded as a genus, susceptible of one and the same revelation from God, the several *characters* developed under this revelation are also resolvable into distinct classes. There is a *class* of moral dispositions which we denominate *vicious* or *wicked;* there is another class which we denominate *virtuous* or *holy;* and, according as the one or the other has the dominion in men, we call them *bad* or *good* men. We thus

us, or to arrive at any general principles which might serve to guide our inquiries in comparing different institutions together. It is for a similar reason that the speculative farmer reduces the infinite variety of soils to a few general descriptions; the physician, the infinite variety of bodily constitutions to a few temperaments; and the moralist, the infinite variety of human characters to a few of the ruling principles of action." — *Stewart's Philosophy*, vol. i. p. 128.

classify the human race in respect to *character.* We recognize good or bad children, good or bad husbands and wives, good or bad parents, good or bad citizens, good or bad magistrates, and treat them according to their respective characters.

There are *degrees* in good and evil; still, good is good, and evil is evil; and we find little difficulty in assigning men to their appropriate places in the scale of character. All human governments, from the parental upward, proceed on this principle of classification. It is on the same principle that the MORAL RULER of the universe divides the human race into the generic classes, — the *righteous* and the *wicked,* — and assigns to each appropriate rewards. *Christianity is a system of classification;* it came not only to call sinners to repentance, but to make us "discern between *the righteous and the wicked, between him that serveth God and him that serveth him not.*"

SUMMARY.

We thus arrive at the conclusion that the practical arts of life, the progress of the human race in knowledge, all the learned professions, all human governments, are dependent on this principle of classification; and not only these, but also the great and sublime science of moral government. The Creator and Ruler of all has enabled man to unite with himself in classing virtues and vices, in separating good men from bad, as the refiner separates the gold from the dross. As brute intellect has not this power, it is incapable of moral science, and therefore incapable of religion.

QUESTIONS ON CHAPTER III.

What does *classification* imply? Illustration? The subdivision of *genera* into *species?* How does it appear that classification is an *original* principle? Examples? What is said of classes in nature? Illustrations? Incorrect classifications? Examples in children? Fact by Stewart? How does *brute* mind regard objects? How the *human?* Illustrations? What caution in the note? Stewart's remarks in the note on the ancient philosophers, and the subjoined strictures on both him and them? What will here be noticed? How does the brute learn? How man? What is said of the progress of natural science? Remarks of Condorcet? What could we never do without the power of classification? Remarks? Illustrations of the same truth in regard to *moral* affections? What of *teaching* and *books?* The several *professions?* Relation to *religion?* How does God take advantage of our all having the same classes of mental and moral attributes? What are the classes of moral dispositions? What, in this view, is the mission of Christianity? At what conclusion do we arrive?

CHAPTER IV.

INDUCTION.

It is by the power of induction that we *infer general laws from individual facts.* By the term *law*, however, I designate only an *established order of sequence.* Applied to natural science, the term is figurative. When, for instance, we speak of the law of falling bodies, we mean only to say, that, as a matter of fact, bodies actually *do*, under given circumstances, always fall thus and so. Beyond the ultimate fact science cannot go, for all true science is founded on facts. In this view, induction is nearly the same with generalization. It differs from classification in this: classification respects *similarity of properties;* induction, an established *order of sequence.*

Stewart and some other philosophers consider abstraction, classification, generalization, and induction, all under one head. The propriety of considering them under three distinct heads will hardly be questioned. Abstraction separates, classification combines and groups, induction establishes, the order of events. In the last two, generalization is of course involved, referring us to general classes and general laws.

ORIGIN OF OUR BELIEF IN AN ESTABLISHED ORDER OF EVENTS.

How do we come to believe that events do and will succeed each other *in an established order?* Our faith in the constancy of nature's course, all admit, is of infinite importance to us, being essential to our very existence.

But respecting its origin, two opinions have been maintained. The opinion of the German school is, that it is *natural* to us; that it is a connate and essential element of our minds. The opinion of the British school is, that it is wholly the fruit of *experience;* that we *acquire* it, as we do all our knowledge, by a *repeated dealing with facts.**

The real truth seems to be this: we have a *susceptibility* of mind to the faith in question; but the faith itself is the fruit of repeated observation and experience. The first time the child, prior to instruction, sees gunpowder explode, on the application of a spark, he is inclined to *expect* that the same cause will again produce the same effect; but he does not feel *sure* of it. He is disposed to make a *second trial.* The second trial greatly *strengthens* his expectation; a few repetitions dispel all doubt, and he finally settles it in his mind as an established order of sequence.†

Whether there is any inherent *power* in the spark to explode the powder, or whether the application of the spark is the mere *occasion* on which a *higher* efficiency is exerted, is a question of speculation which he is not here called to settle; all he is concerned with is the mere *fact* that such is the established order.

THE POWER OF INDUCTION A DISTINGUISHING ATTRIBUTE.

The brute has memory, by which he is reminded of th place where he fell, or was frightened, or was fed; he ha

* Dr. Thomas Brown, however, favors the first theory. He says, "By an *original principle of our constitution,* we are led, from the mere observation of change, to believe that, when similar circumstances recur, the changes which we observed will also recur in the same order."—*Philosophy,* vol. i. p. 65.

† "Induction is founded on the belief that the course of nature is governed by uniform laws, and that things will happen in future as we have observed them to happen in time past. We can have no proof of a permanent connection between any events, or between any two qualities either of body or mind. The only reason for supposing such a connection in any instance is, that we have *invariably* found certain things to have been conjoined in fact; and this experience, in many cases, produces a conviction equal to that of demonstration."—*Elements of Logic, by Levi Hedge,* p. 76

also a large endowment of *instinct*, by which he protects himself from danger and provides for his young; but when he sees an effect, he has no power to recognize the general law by which it occurred. When the human intellect, on the other hand, perceives an effect, it has the power to refer it to a cause, and thence to a general sequence or law of events.

ILLUSTRATION.

When Sir Isaac Newton saw an apple fall from a tree, he inferred that there was some cause operating to produce that effect, and inquired whether the same cause, operating in similar circumstances, would not *always* produce the same effects. He thus came to a knowledge of the general laws by which all the atoms of our globe, all the substances in the atmosphere, the whole solar system, all the stars of heaven, and, so far as we know, the whole material universe, are governed.

What a distinguishing prerogative, what a stupendous power, is that by which the human intellect, from observing only the falling of an apple, could ascend to the knowledge of that law by which planets, worlds, suns, and systems are borne up in space and wheeled through the heavens!

VARIOUS PURPOSES OF INDUCTION.

It appears that this power has as wide a range and as important a use as classification. Without this, the laws of gravity, of mechanical forces, of hydrostatics and pneumatics; of sound, light, vision, colors; electricity and magnetism, and all the valuable arts founded upon them, must have been entirely excluded from us.

By virtue of induction, we learn that fire will always burn, and are thus admonished to use it discreetly; that water will always run down an inclined plane, and so we construct expensive mills, trusting the law of gravitation to insure their operation; that light will always move in straight lines, reflected and refracted in a way to cause angles of incidence equal to angles of reflection, and so we make our windows, our glasses, all our optical instruments, as the law of light demands; that dry gunpowder, when touched with a spark, will uniformly explode, and so we construct firearms, go forth to hunt game, venture our lives in the face of wild beasts and assassins, and even march to the battle field, trusting the unfailing operation of this universal law.

By the same means we learn that wood, formed into certain structures, will always float upon water, and so we construct ships, and launch our property and our lives upon the ocean; that metals, heated to certain degrees, will invariably fuse, and so we build expensive furnaces, and provide other customary means of securing the desired effect; that a propitious season and fertile soil, with appropriate tilling, will produce a harvest, and so we labor in hope for this object.

RELATION OF INDUCTION TO RELIGION.

As it is by induction that we learn the general laws of the natural world, and are enabled wisely to regulate our conduct in relation to them, so it is by virtue of the same that we learn the general laws of God's *moral government*, and are guided in the path of wisdom and duty. We hence learn that the character which pleased or displeased Jehovah — which procured his blessing or his frown — in Palestine, Babylon, or Egypt, four thousand years ago, is followed by similar results still, and always will be.

Hence all history becomes admonitory to us, and the sacred writings especially, having the seal of God upon them, pour a flood of light on our pathway to eternity. Induction assures us, as positively as it does the astronomer the course of the planets, and the agriculturist the course of the seasons, that if repentance of sin, faith in the Savior, devotion of heart and life to God, secured an unspeakable and eternal blessing to apostles and other primitive Christians, they will do the same for us.

INDUCTION FURNISHES THE TEST OF WISDOM.

That conduct is truly wise which is based upon the known laws of the natural and moral universe. Here, then, we readily trace the distinction between *wisdom* and *fanaticism*. Are those men fanatical, who, having carefully examined the laws of nature, bestow years of labor and sacrifice upon a great and worthy physical object, — as, for instance, the construction of an extensive manufacturing establishment, or a railroad, — trusting the known laws of nature to secure to them the proposed good? Were there any serious cause for doubting whether water would *continue* to flow downward, or machinery to obey its impulse, or whether steam would *continue* to perform the office of propelling an engine, such a vast outlay might seem to border on fanaticism. But so long as our confidence in the steadfastness of nature's course remains unshaken, it is wisdom to adapt our plans to it.

Are those men, then, fanatical, who bestow years of labor and sacrifice upon a great *moral* and *Christian* object, trusting the known laws of the moral universe to secure to them the expected good in due time? Viewed only in the light of *philosophy*, there is sound wisdom in the apostolic injunction, "*Be not weary in well doing; for in due season we shall reap, if we faint not.*" For it is as true in the moral as in the natural world, that "*whatsoever a man soweth, that shall he also reap.*"

We have only to study the laws of mind and of the moral universe to be assured that it was the highest wisdom in Moses to prefer to suffer affliction with the people of God, rather than enjoy the pleasures of sin for a season; because he had respect to the recompense of reward — a recompense none the less *sure* for being in the *distance*. Duty and happiness, although they may seem distant, are yet bound together by an indissoluble chain; and it is just as certain that wickedness, however triumphant at present, will encounter ultimate defeat, and that righteousness, however oppressed, will eventually triumph, as that the laws of the moral universe cannot fail.

A further consideration of this interesting topic would carry us into the department of *moral* philosophy, which it is not proposed to enter, in the present work. What has been said may suffice to indicate the distinguishing nature of this attribute, and its relation to the Christian religion.

IMPROVEMENT OF THE POWER OF INDUCTION.

This power is possessed by men in very unequal degrees, and it is this, certainly not less than any other, that distinguishes the philosopher from the man of mere details. It imparts a breadth and a penetration of vision, which render man, in one sense, almost omnipresent and prophetic. Hence, as it is susceptible of indefinite improvement, it should have a prominent consideration in the education of all youth.

Respecting the great importance of properly cultivating our inductive faculty, Dr. Brown makes the following judicious remarks: "It is important for us to know *what* antecedents truly precede *what* consequents; since we can thus provide for that future, which we are hence enabled to foresee, and can in a great measure modify; and almost create the future to ourselves, by arranging the objects over which we have command, in such a manner as to form with them the antecedents, which we know to be invariably followed by the consequents desired by us. It is thus we are able to exercise that command over nature, which HE, who is its only real Sovereign, has designed, in the magnificence of his bounty, to confer on us, together with the still greater privilege of knowing that Omnipotence to which all our delegated empire is so humbly subordinate. It is a command which can be exercised by us only as beings, who, according to one of the definitions that have been given of man, look both *before* and *behind;* or, in the words of Cicero, who join and connect the future with the present, seeing things not in their progress merely, but in the circumstances that precede them and the circumstances that follow them, and being thus enabled to provide and arrange whatever is necessary for that life, of which the whole course lies open before us." *

IMPROVEMENT OF THE INDUCTIVE FACULTY.

Most of the particular directions for improving the inductive faculty will be given under the head of *Reasoning*. Indeed, logicians generally include induction with the general subject of reasoning, but, in an analysis of the mental faculties, they should be to some extent considered apart.

All the directions which I would here give on this point may be included under *three heads:* —

First, the minds of youth should be deeply impressed with the *importance* of being trained to habits of sound philosophical induction. One of the greatest of men, Lord Bacon, has assigned to it the very highest rank, both as an instrument for obtaining the knowledge of general truths, and also the rules and maxims for regulating the common business of life. And the illustrious evidence of its value, which he has given to the world, should deeply impress it on all young minds aspiring to eminence.

Secondly, the propensity should be early encouraged, of tracing all facts and events both *backward to their antecedents, and forward to their consequents.* This propensity early indulged, affords one of the brightest indications of future intellectual eminence. It was this that led Bacon, Newton, La Place, and others like them, to discover so many of the great laws on which the course of nature proceeds. Children should be early trained to look at things, not merely in *themselves*, but in their *causes* and *effects;* and not merely in their *proximate* causes and effects, but those more and more remote;

* Brown's Philosophy, vol. i. p. 68. The passage referred to in Cicero is the following: "Homo autem, quod rationis est particeps, per quam consequentia cernit, causas rerum videt, carumque progressus et quasi antecessiones non ignorat, similitudines comparat, et rebus præsentibus adjungit atque annectit futuras, facile totius vitæ cursum videt, ad eamque degendam præparat res necessarias."—*Cicero de Officiis*, lib. i. chap. iv.

and thus, finally, in the light of those *great laws of sequence by which the steady course of nature moves on.*

Let the child begin with the simplest thing. He sees the green grass shooting up in the spring. What, under God, are the causes? As he observes, he perceives three things — the soil, the warmth, the moisture. Remove either of these, and the grass does not grow. Combine these, as in the spring, and the seed or root always shoots upward into the green blade. He observes the same next year, the year following, and thus arrives at the knowledge of a *general law* — a law *running through all time.* He is now a *chronicler of the past;* he can tell what *has been* going on, in this particular, in ages past; he is also a *prophet of the future* — he can tell what *will be* going on in ages coming. Thousands of years hence, as spring sends its warmth and its showers upon the earth, grass will clothe hills and valleys with its living green. From this simple illustration, the student of nature may easily extend his observations and inductions to things more complicated.

Thirdly, early care should be taken to distinguish *real causes*, or *permanent antecedents*, from mere *accidental circumstances.* This marks the distinction between sound and false induction. Some minds are slow to make the distinction; others make it readily.

The following is a good illustration of false induction: "Let us suppose that a savage, who in a particular instance had found himself relieved of some bodily indisposition by a draught of cold water, is a second time afflicted with a similar disorder, and is desirous to repeat the same remedy. With the limited degree of experience which we have here supposed him to possess, it would be impossible for the acutest philosopher, in his situation, to determine whether the cure was owing to the water which was drank, to the cup in which it was contained, to the fountain from which it was taken, to the particular day of the month, or to the particular age of the moon. In order, therefore, to insure the success of the remedy, he will very naturally and very wisely copy, so far as he can recollect, every circumstance which accompanied the first application of it. He will make use of the same cup, draw the water from the same fountain, hold his body in the same posture, and turn his face in the same direction; and thus all the accidental circumstances in which the first experiment was made will come to be associated equally in his mind with the effect produced." *

The remedy for such false inductions is to be found in *careful and repeated observation;* in separating, one after another, those antecedents whose loss does not prevent the effect; and in bringing a general and gradually enlarging experience to bear upon the subject.

QUESTIONS ON CHAPTER IV.

For what are we indebted to the power of *induction?* What do we mean by *law?* Illustrate. How far can science go? On what is science founded? Stewart's classification, and remarks upon it? What is said of our faith in the constancy of nature's course? The two opinions of its origin? What seems to be the real truth? How illustrated? How is induction shown to be a *distinguishing* attribute? Illustration? Some of the various *uses* of induction? Illustrate its relation to *religion.* The distinction between *wisdom* and *fanaticism?* How shown? Moses? What is said of *duty* and *happiness?* Of the relative value of induction as distinguishing the philosopher? Brown's remarks? *First* direction for improving the inductive faculty? Remarks? *Second?* Remarks? The training of the child? *Third?* Remark? Case supposed? The remedy for false inductions?

* Stewart's Philosophy, vol. i. p. 199.

CHAPTER V.

REASON.

ALL philosophers agree that reason is the most *distinguishing and important* of the intellectual faculties; and yet they are much divided in regard to its *nature and office*. Philosophers of the German school make it in part synonymous with what I have called *intuition.* In common discourse, it denotes essentially *the power of distinguishing between truth and falsehood, and of appropriating means to ends.* Hence it has been usually considered the *guide* of man, in distinction from all other faculties.

The Kantian philosophy makes a generic distinction between *reason* and *reasoning*, considering the former as *fixed*, the latter as *discursive*. *Reason* is transcendent, above and independent of the senses; while *reasoning*, in its search for truth, must needs call the senses into service. Regarded as the fixed and permanent eye of the mind, so long as its vision is strictly limited to self-evident truths, it is mere *intuition;* when it is presumed to see more, it transcends our philosophy.

DEFINITION OF REASON.

According to the earlier writers of the British school, reason may be defined *the power of deducing one proposition from another.** Thus, if the proposition be laid

* The propositions involving facts or events are brought together in the mind, and their relation determined. Hence Dr. Abercrombie remarks, "Reason, in the language of intellectual science, appears to be that process

down, God is just, reason deduces from it, Then he will punish the wicked. From the proposition, God is merciful, reason deduces, Then he will forgive the penitent. To the declaration, The plague is raging in the city, reason responds, It is then unsafe to go thither. In all cases in which we thus deduce one proposition from another, we *reason.*

Dr. Beattie gives the following definition, cited in a note by Stewart, which is substantially in accordance with the above: "Reason is used, by those who are most accurate in distinguishing, to signify that power of the human mind by which we draw inferences, or by which we are convinced that a relation belongs to two ideas, on account of our having found that these ideas bear certain relations to other ideas. In a word, it is that faculty which enables us, from relations or ideas that are known, to investigate such as are unknown, and without which we never could proceed in the discovery of truth a single step beyond first principles or intuitive axioms." *

But it should be remarked, that more modern writers of this school have adopted a metaphysical distinction between reason and reasoning. "In opposition to the high authorities of Dr. Johnson and Dr. Beattie," says Dugald Stewart, "I must add, that, for many years past, *reason* has been very seldom used by philosophical writers, or, indeed, by correct writers of any description, as synonymous with the power of reasoning. *To appeal to the light of human reason from the reasonings of the schools,* is surely an expression to which no good objection can be made on the score either of vagueness or of novelty. Nor has the etymological affinity between these two words the slightest tendency to throw any obscurity on the foregoing expression."

Stewart even concedes that we might, perhaps, on

by which we judge correctly of the true and uniform relations of facts or events, and give to each circumstance its due influence in the deductions." *Intellectual Philosophy*, p. 138. "Reasoning is a process by which unknown truths are inferred from those which are already known and admitted." — *Hedge's Logic*, p. 70.

* Beattie's Essay on Truth, part i. chap. i. See also Stewart's Philosophy, vol. ii. p. 43.

some occasions, do well to substitute the word *reason* for *intuition*, in its modern enlarged acceptation.* With all deference to his opinion, there still seem to be conclusive objections to confounding the old distinction of terms; some, perhaps, which had not fully transpired at the time he wrote. Let us now pass from this point to some remarks upon *reasoning*.

PROPOSITIONS.

In *reasoning*, we proceed from *propositions* to *conclusions*.† Propositions are usually divided into *simple*, *complex*, and *modal*. A *simple* proposition consists of *three single parts*, like the following: *God is just.* Here we perceive three parts, of one word each — the *subject*, or that of which something is *affirmed;* the *predicate*, or that which *is affirmed of the subject;* and the *copula*, or that which *unites the two parts of the proposition together*.

A *complex* proposition is one in which the parts consist of *several* words; as, An honest judge will give a just decision. Here the subject is made up of the words, *an honest judge;* the predicate of the words, *a just decision;* and the copula of the words, *will give*. The proposition would be complex, if the copula had but one word; as the difference made by two is only in tense.

A *modal* proposition is one in which the copula indicates some *doubt* or *contingency;* as, Men of wealth *may* do much good. This kind of proposition is indicated by the subjunctive or potential mode.

Propositions are the materials of all processes of reasoning. They are not always *stated in form*, but all sentences in which there is reasoning may be easily resolved into them. They have been compared to the

* "It may be fairly questioned whether the word *reason* would not, on some occasions, be the best substitute which our language affords for *intuition*, in that enlarged acceptation which has been given to it of late." — *Stewart's Philosophy*, vol. ii. p. 43.

† "This process, however, which is commonly called the discursive faculty, is to be distinguished from the simple exercise of reason. It ought to be guided by reason; that is, by a full view of the real relations of the facts about which it is exercised." — *Abercrombie's Philosophy*, p. 138.

blocks of stone, and reasoning to the process of putting them together.

HYPOTHETICAL AND DECLARATIVE PROPOSITIONS.

Propositions may be either *hypotheses*, or *declarations of facts*. This is not essential to the validity of the reasoning. Even if the *propositions* be *false*, the *reasoning* may be *sound;* since the reasoning is not responsible for the soundness of the materials, but only for the manner of putting them together. Hence the saying of logicians, What is true in *reasoning* may be false in *fact*. If the premises, or propositions assumed, be false, the *results* of the reasoning must of course be *false*, but the *reasoning itself* may be *sound*. If the premises are indisputable, and the reasoning from them strictly logical, the result is known and infallible truth, as much so as an axiom.

PROPOSITIONS NEED NOT BE FORMALLY STATED.

But it is not necessary that all the propositions in reasoning be *formally stated;* indeed, the less of form, ordinarily, the better. The old Aristotelian logic has given place to a more free and natural method. Men often reason soundly and forcibly, who never studied any logical rules, and who scarcely know that they *are* reasoning. Ask them to define their propositions, and they do not, perhaps, know that they have any.

I once witnessed a striking proof of this. An uneducated man had addressed a forcible argument to an assembly, on the subject of temperance. Being in some doubt respecting one or two of his positions, I subsequently requested him to restate to me the proposition on which his main argument depended. He was not aware that there was any proposition in the case. I told him my question had no reference to the soundness of his reasoning, but to his premises. He did not comprehend the import of the term. Although he had no definite idea of what is meant by a proposition or a premise, he was yet a sound and forcible reasoner.

This is no argument against the study of philosophy and logic; for the same man, on other occasions, made such ridiculous blunders in his reasoning as to defeat his object. It simply proves, that while the reasoner ought, for personal conviction, to understand the nature of propositions, and to know how to put them logically together, he need not make a formal array of them.

Those propositions which involve intuitive truths, or are so obvious as to be universally conceded, need not be stated at all. They already exist, essentially, in the hearer's and reader's mind. To be perpetually attempting to prove what nobody doubts, setting forth formal propositions of self-evident truths, and thus essaying to reason profoundly upon the very surface, is a disgusting exhibition of weakness and pedantry.

ORDER OF PROPOSITIONS.

Still, all reasoning, as we have said, is really made up of propositions more or less formal; and it is evident, from the remarks just made, that their order should be dictated by association and a natural sense of fitness, rather than by any set rules of logic. Such rules help us more to criticize than to reason; they alone never made an eloquent and forcible reasoner. The general rule, however, should be always observed in reasoning, to begin with the most simple and obvious propositions, and gradually rise from them, by a natural process, to the more involved. This is important to the reasoner himself, as well as to carry conviction to the minds of others. In mathematics, there is no other *possible* way; in moral reasoning, there is no other *good* way.

It must never be forgotten, that the object in reasoning is, from something assumed as known, to find out what is unknown. Unless, therefore, we start with what is clearly apprehended and granted, we shall grope in darkness all the way, and arrive at only doubt and uncertainty at last.

"In applying our reason to the investigation of truth," says Abercrombie, "*in any department of knowledge,* we are, in the first place, to keep in mind that there are certain intuitive articles of belief which lie at the foundation of all reasoning. For, in every process of reasoning, we proceed by founding one step upon another which has gone before it; and when we trace such a process backwards, we must arrive at certain truths which are recognized as fundamental, requiring no proof, and admitting of none. These are usually called FIRST TRUTHS. They are not the result of any process of reasoning, but force themselves with a conviction of infallible certainty upon every sound understanding, without regard to its logical habits or powers of induction. The force of them is accordingly felt in an equal degree by all classes of men; and they are acted upon with absolute confidence in the daily transactions of life." *

DIFFERENT KINDS OF REASONING.

Reasoning may be generically divided into two kinds, *mathematical* and *moral*. Several earnest philosophers have supposed these ultimately resolvable into one and the same. They imagine that the apparent difference results only from the present imperfect state of language. With this view, Leibnitz proposed to frame a language, which would be to *moral* reasoning what the mathematical symbols are to *mathematical* reasoning; but he died, as some think fortunately for science and for his own reputation, before he accomplished his purpose.

Without stopping to discuss this point, it is sufficient to say, that, in the present state of philosophy, the division here made is natural and convenient. Moral reasoning may be subdivided into *metaphysical*, or that which is confined to strictly metaphysical truths; and *moral*, more exactly so called, or that which is concerned with strictly moral truths. But as these more or less involve each other, and proceed upon the same general plan, they may be properly considered under the same head.

* Intellectual Philosophy, p. 145.

MATHEMATICAL REASONING.

1. Mathematical reasoning is founded on *abstract* quantities and relations. These being absolute and universal truths, they afford no possible ground of variation or error. The relation which three bears to ten, for example, is absolute and universal. It must forever be precisely the same. But the relation of three actual substances or events to ten other actual substances or events may vary.

2. Mathematical reasoning places *no reliance on testimony* or *authority*. There is no weighing of probabilities, and nothing is taken on the opinion of others. Every reasoner starts from the foundation, and builds with his own intuitions to the summit of his conclusions.

3. In mathematical reasoning, all the terms are exactly *defined and limited*. There is no possible ground of misapprehension. This is one of the particular points at which Leibnitz aimed, in his design to institute an exact vocabulary of moral definitions answering to the mathematical.

4. Mathematical reasoning admits no *degrees* of evidence. A point is absolutely proved beyond all possible question, or it is not proved at all. No possible room can be left for a doubt. The result of a mathematical demonstration is what every man in his senses *must* believe, without a question.

5. In mathematical demonstration, we never need to examine but *one side*. Whatever proposition is proved to be true, its opposite is known to be false, without examination. The alternative is so presented, that the truth or fallacy of the one proposition necessarily involves the fallacy or truth of the other.

6. Mathematical reasoning proceeds in a *single chain of demonstration*. This chain, every link of which is an intuition, may be indefinitely extended; and the final result is as certain as the first, and even as certain as the axiom or definition itself from which it proceeds. The length of the chain does not reduce its strength. If the

operation be accurate, the result of a problem requiring a *million* of figures is as certain as that of one requiring but *two*.

Such are the most distinguishing characteristics of mathematical reasoning. It leaves little room for the exercise of judgment, except in planning the work. It proceeds, mainly, by direct *positive intuitions*. Admirable as a mental exercise to train the intellect to severe and exact habits, yet, prosecuted *exclusively*, it may tend to disqualify the mind for those processes of reasoning in which large demands are made upon the judgment, in weighing probabilities and estimating evidences which fall below positive certainty. Exclusive mathematicians would be likely to prove very indifferent moral reasoners.

But it may be well to add, that most pupils are in little danger of injuring their reasoning powers by too much study of mathematics; the danger is, rather, that they will suffer for the *want* of that severe discipline which these studies afford.

QUESTIONS ON CHAPTER V.

Opening remark? The Kantian philosophers? Remark? Definition of reason? Illustrations? What have modern writers of the empirical school adopted? Stewart's observations? How do we proceed in *reasoning?* How are propositions divided? Illustrations of *simple?* Complex? Modal? Of what are propositions the materials? Hypothetical and declarative propositions? How may propositions be false and the reasoning from them be sound? Must all propositions be formally stated? Remark and illustration? What is said of propositions involving intuitive truths? What is said respecting order of propositions? Object in reasoning? Into how many *kinds* is reasoning divided? What is said of Leibnitz? On what is *mathematical* reasoning founded? Explain. *Second* peculiarity of mathematical reasoning? Explain. *Third?* Remark? *Fourth?* Explain. *Fifth?* *Sixth?* Remarks. What is said of mathematical reasoning in conclusion?

CHAPTER VI.

MORAL REASONING.

Let us now briefly notice the distinguishing characteristics of *moral* reasoning.

1. Moral reasoning has, like mathematical, its axioms and definitions, but they cannot ordinarily be so *exactly stated.* Instead of shutting us up to an *absolute necessity*, they leave some play for the exercise of our *moral* nature. Let the reader refer to any of the moral axioms laid down under the head of *Intuition*, and he will readily see the truth of this remark.

2. Moral reasoning is not concerned with abstractions, but with *things in the concrete.* Its proof has respect to matters and events as they *actually are* or *have been*, instead of those *abstract* ideas and relations assumed in mathematics. Hence the subjects of moral reasoning are, in their nature, *variable* and *contingent.*

3. In moral reasoning, we are compelled to place more or less *reliance on testimony and authority.* The due consideration of these makes large demands on our *judgment* and our *moral dispositions.* For the proof respecting the life and work of Jesus Christ, for example, we must depend on testimony — testimony which a perverse judgment and an evil disposition may reject.

4. Moral reasoning *admits of degrees.* Evidence in proof may rise through every stage, from the lowest probability to the highest certainty. Any person may find ample illustration of this in our courts of justice. As this kind of reasoning admits of degrees, it becomes expedient, and often necessary, to examine both sides, in

order to obtain a satisfactory result. This principle is recognized in all courts of justice.

5. Moral reasoning does not proceed in a single chain, but is made up of *many arguments combined.* These arguments may sustain some mutual relation, or they may be entirely independent of each other. "Each possesses some weight, and bestows on the conclusion a certain degree of probability; of all which, accumulated, the credibility of the fact is compounded. Thus the proof that *the Romans once possessed Great Britain* is made up of a variety of independent arguments; as, immemorial tradition; the testimony of historians; the ruins of Roman buildings, camps, and walls; Roman coins, inscriptions, and the like. These are independent arguments, but they all conspire to establish the fact." *

6. The *difficulties* attending a course of moral reasoning are entirely different from those attending a mathematical demonstration. "Those which impede our progress in demonstration arise from the large number of intermediate steps and the difficulty of finding suitable media of proof. In moral reasoning, the processes are usually short, and the chief obstacles by which we are retarded arise from the want of exact definitions to our words, the difficulty of keeping steadily in view the various circumstances on which our judgment should be formed, and from the prejudices arising from early impressions and associations." † Other difficulties still more serious, connected with the investigation of moral and religious subjects, result from aversion to truth which conflicts with perverse inclinations. Mathematical reasoning encounters no difficulties here; moral reasoning often encounters them at every step.

RESULTS OF MORAL REASONING MAY BE CERTAIN.

Logicians have frequently applied the epithet *demonstrative* to mathematical reasoning; and *probable*, to moral reasoning. The distinction is not happy. A

* Hedge's Logic, p. 73. † Ibid. p. 75.

mathematical demonstration is as truly a reasoning process as a moral; and a process of moral reasoning may be as convincingly demonstrative as a mathematical. It is by a process of moral reasoning that we are led to the conviction that Cyrus besieged and took Babylon; that Hannibal crossed the Alps with his army; that Julius Cæsar invaded Gaul; that Columbus discovered America; and yet no enlightened mind would hesitate to place its assent to these facts by the side of that which it yields to the simplest mathematical demonstration. Precisely in the same light we must regard the leading historical facts of Christianity

WHAT CONSTITUTES A GOOD REASONER.

There is a vast difference between men in respect to their reasoning powers; and it may be advantageous to notice more particularly what constitutes a good reasoner.

1. *An accurate perception of the relations of things.* When we reason, we bring the several propositions under consideration into comparison with each other; and unless we have a just perception of their relations, our reasoning will, of course, be unsound.

Suppose, for instance, we take the two propositions — Men become intemperate by the use of intoxicating drinks; Peter uses intoxicating drinks. Now, the proposition which reason will deduce from these two must depend on the view taken of the relation of the latter to the former. If it be supposed to sustain to it the relation of a minor to a major, the inference is, Peter will become intemperate.

This is what logicians call a *non sequitur* — an unwarrantable inference. The reasoning is false, because the true relation of the propositions to each other was not perceived. The proposition, that men become intemperate by the use of intoxicating drinks, is not the same as saying that the use of intoxicating drinks *always* leads to intemperance. Hence a comparison of the first two propositions does not warrant the third. Peter may be an exception.

Such inaccuracies tend to destroy confidence in a man's reasoning, and render even his sound arguments futile. The relations of things must, then, be carefully noticed by all who aspire to become sound and convincing reasoners.

2. *A habit of fixed and patient attention.* This is necessary, in order to examine the nature of the propositions, to see clearly their relations, and to determine what inferences may be logically deduced. Every step in this process demands careful attention. We cannot arrive at truth by reasoning, as by intuition, with a single flash of the eye; it can be done only by a protracted and steady direction of the mind to the several points involved. As an encouragement to this effort, it may be said, that practice will soon render it comparatively easy, and that the habit is one of the very highest and most valuable of mental attainments.

3. *A mind well stored with knowledge.* Especially whatever has material bearing on the subject at issue should be at command. "Knowledge is power." This is emphatically true in reasoning. A man might as well undertake to build a house without materials, as to frame convincing arguments without knowledge. "Only fools can be convinced by fools" is an old proverb, none the less true for its age or roughness. "All reasoning implies a comparison of ideas; or, more properly, a comparison of propositions, or of facts stated in propositions. Of course, where there is no knowledge on any given subject, where there is no accumulation of facts, there can be no possibility of reasoning; and where the knowledge is much limited, the plausibility and power of the argument will be proportionally diminished." *

4. *An honest love of truth.* The habit of arguing on all sides of questions against our convictions, as well as with them, for the sake of showing skill, or appearing singular, or gaining the dangerous reputation of originality, is ultimately destructive of sound reasoning. Many a pupil of fine promise has thus fatally perverted his

* Upham's Philosophy, p. 197.

reasoning powers. He who argues in defence of infidelity for the sake of displaying his tact, is very liable to become a victim to his own snares; and the lawyer who is ready to espouse every desperate and wicked cause, either for gold or glory, will in the event become a splendid demagogue and a skilful tactician, but a false and dangerous reasoner. No man can form the habit, or at least long retain it, of reasoning soundly on moral subjects, without honesty of purpose, without an eye single to the truth.

5. *A careful exclusion of weak or doubtful arguments.* Many persons spoil their reasoning by accumulating all the arguments which they can collect, whether good, indifferent, or doubtful. The adversary, and even the friend, upon a laudable watch for errors, will almost inevitably detect the weak points, and make them the occasion of rejecting the whole. On a careful revision, the reasoner should exclude every argument that is liable to be overthrown, and let those which are unanswerable stand in their solitary and massive strength.

6. *A modest self-estimation.* Due confidence in one's self is an essential element of success in all undertakings; but the danger usually lies in its excess. This is especially true in the matter of reasoning. In nothing are minds of a certain cast more prone to pride themselves than in their *reasoning* powers; and in nothing are they so sure to fail. Having, perhaps, a richly-endowed imagination, a bold temperament, a poetic inspiration, a passion for originality, so long as they confine themselves within the limits of their reasoning powers, and rely upon their appropriate strength, they pass for what they truly are — distinguished men, in their way. Nobody questions their ability to reason, for they have never exposed it out of the beaten paths; while the boldness and originality of their imagery and manner render the truth powerful in their hands.

But no sooner does success betray them into an undue self-estimation, than they are emboldened to adventure their reasoning powers upon points to which they are incompetent, and then they fall even below their just level. Such men would be very safe and eminently successful reasoners, did a just estimation of themselves keep them within just limits. However bold and original men may be in the outbursts of their poetry and in the splendors of their style and manner, in respect to those adventures of reasoning whose object is to *settle great principles of truth, faith, and duty*, only the most patient inquiry, the widest search, the most cautious prudence, and the most reluctant consent can safely deviate from the paths on which the maturest wisdom of ages has trodden.

MATHEMATICAL REASONING AS DISTINGUISHING MEN FROM BRUTES.

The human mind, unlike that of brutes, can conceive of objects as divided into hundreds, thousands, millions of parts, as indefinitely multiplied and extended. Hence the noble science of mathematics. With only ten little characters, man can reckon, calculate, measure, adjust all the affairs of the great social, political, mercantile, and physical world. This he does by simply applying the abstract numbers, increased, diminished, multiplied, involved and evolved, to the various objects in question.

To facilitate his progress in the higher calculations, he uses letters and other characters to represent numerical figures, as in algebra and fluxions ; proceeding thus, he is enabled to measure the ocean, to weigh the mountains, to scale the heights of those dizzy summits on which the human foot never trod ; to belt the globe we inhabit, and determine its relative position and movements in the solar system ; ascending the heavens, he places the sun and all the planetary orbs that surround it in his scale, handling them as very little things, and telling all their courses, distances, revolutions, conjunctions, eclipses, for ages past and ages coming. What a stupendous reach of intellect! Well may that living and thinking something, which we call the human mind, consider the universe its home, and immortality its birthright, although doomed for a season to honor this perishing clay with its presence.

MORAL REASONING AS DISTINGUISHING MEN FROM BRUTES.

Brute intellect is wholly occupied with *physical* objects. It seems to have no knowledge of any thing but what is addressed to the bodily senses. The human mind takes a higher and more spiritual range. It performs its humblest task when it operates only upon matter. From the vast and glorious kingdom of metaphysical truths, historical facts, and moral sentiments, in which the human mind expatiates, and from which it enjoys its richest repast, the intellect of the brute is utterly excluded.

The brute is also incapable of appreciating the *evidence* of facts, as furnished by history and other means. A present or a remembered object is made sure to him by the present or former testimony of his senses; beyond this, he is without evidence of the existence of any object or fact whatever. Thus excluded from all knowledge of the beings and events of another world, he is, of course, incapable of religion. The truths and motives of religion cannot reach him.

Man, on the contrary, can so appreciate the evidence of distant things, as to be as well assured of them as of the place in which he resides. He may be as fully convinced that there are such places as Mexico, London, and Calcutta, as though he had actually seen them. He may feel as well assured that Lisbon was destroyed by an earthquake, that Brutus slew Cæsar, that the Jews crucified Jesus Christ, that Bonaparte was defeated at Waterloo, as if his own eyes had witnessed the events. He is thus enabled to act rationally upon the principle of *faith* in the verities of Christianity. If his evidence of such facts is not of the same *kind* with that furnished by his physical senses, which he shares with the brute, it is equally as good, and as binding on his practical regard.

The power of logical argumentation, and of reasoning to sound conclusions respecting what has taken place and what will take place, as the result of existing and forthcoming causes, is, perhaps, the most lofty and distinguishing prerogative of the human intellect. By this we are enabled to form a sound judgment, and to act wisely respecting the future interests of both the present life and the life to come.

THE HUMAN MIND PROGRESSIVE.

Brute intellect *stands still.* Had man been destitute of *reason*, the world would have been now just what it was at the beginning. It would have been only a great wilderness of forests and waters: the very lowest condition of the most savage tribes is immeasurably superior to what would have been the condition of our entire race. The brute creation, so far as appears, has no more knowledge now than it had four thousand years ago; whereas the human mind is constantly *advancing*. It was at first circumscribed within very narrow limits. Its eye embraced only the surface of a few miles of surrounding earth and of the concave firmament. All beyond was in the deep, dark chambers of mystery.

In almost nothing did the human differ from brute mind, save in its inborn *powers of acquisition.* These were the germs of its immortality and pledges of its everlasting growth. Awaking to the consciousness of these, it commenced its career. It has now penetrated many of the profound mysteries of nature, analyzed its own deathless powers and relations, established governments, founded empires, subdued the world by its inventions, explored sciences, soared among the stars; and was never speeding its way into distant regions of discovery with more rapid wing than at the present moment.

How well do these facts harmonize with the revelations of Christianity! As a universe of wonders lies before the human mind, so that mind has a boundless existence in which to explore them. It can grow in knowledge forever, and yet never exhaust its treasures. If true to itself, such is its high destiny. It will brighten and ascend forever; its splendors will eclipse the sun.

These considerations should serve to awaken in us just convictions of the value of our minds, impress us with the magnitude and solemnity of our responsibilities, and induce us to conduct like MEN, and not like the *irrational brute*, that was made only for this world. True to our nature, we should rise to the joy and glory of an endless life.

QUESTIONS ON CHAPTER VI.

What is the *first* distinguishing characteristic of *moral* reasoning? *Second? Third? Fourth? Fifth?* Illustrate. *Sixth?* State the more serious difficulties. May moral reasoning be as conclusive as mathematical? Give examples? The *first* quality of a good reasoner? Remarks? Illustration? *Second* quality? Why is this necessary? Remarks? *Third* quality? Remarks? *Fourth* quality? Remarks? *Fifth* quality? How shown? *Sixth* quality? Observations on this point? What is said of mathematical reasoning, as distinguishing men from brutes? As applied to religion? Of *moral* reasoning, as distinguishing men from brutes? What is the most distinguishing prerogative of the human intellect? Comparison of men and brutes as to *progress?* What has the human mind done? With what do these facts harmonize? What should these facts serve to awaken?

CHAPTER VII.

JUDGMENT.

SOME writers confound *judgment* with *reason.* They consider it that faculty by which we compare facts or propositions with each other, and our mental impressions with external objects.* An act of judgment, of course, implies reason; we cannot judge without reason, neither can we reason without judgment. But this does not prove them one and the same thing.

All our mental powers coexist in fact; they are essential elements of one and the same mind; and many of our mental *exercises* necessarily imply and involve each other. Still they are distinct exercises, and of course imply the existence of the mental powers adequate to produce them. The only question is, whether that mental act which we call *judgment* is sufficiently *peculiar* and *important* to deserve a *distinct notice.*

JUDGMENT DISTINGUISHED FROM REASON.

Considering reason as an *intuitive* † faculty, to identify judgment ‡ with reason, is to confound it with intuition. Now intuition is *always true;* judgment *may be false;* intuition is *certain;* judgment may be *uncertain.* It is

* Abercrombie's Intellectual Philosophy, p. 138.

† See page 173.

‡ The term is sometimes qualified by applying the adjective *intuitive.* Hence some writers speak of *intuitive judgments,* as connecting the several links in a chain of mathematical demonstration. We might as well speak of round squares. The links of a chain of mathematical demonstration are connected in our minds by pure *intuition.* We do not *judge;* we *know.*

proper to speak of good and bad judgment; but to speak of good and bad intuition, is a solecism. Intuition *knows;* judgment is a *substitute* for knowledge.

The judge upon the bench has no intuitive knowledge respecting the innocence or guilt of the man under trial he merely *judges* him innocent or guilty in view of evidence. Had he the knowledge which *intuition* gives, he would not need to *judge.* Hence his judgment is a *substitute* * for such knowledge. And even if we suppose both to exist in the same mind, in reference to the same things, they are yet distinct, both in their nature and relations.†

FURTHER REASONS FOR THE DISTINCTION.

Considering reason as *discursive*, by substituting the participle and giving the definition usually attached to reason*ing*, we find objections to confounding the terms in question no less serious. Reasoning is a *process;* judgment is a *decision.* Reasoning *prepares the way* for a result; judgment is the *result itself.* There are indeed separate judgments, pronounced on the several facts or evidences, in the course of an investigation, until the final issue becomes a general judgment embracing the whole.

Such are the judgments of the civil magistrate on the

* "The faculty which God has given man to *supply the want* of clear and certain knowledge, in cases where that cannot be had, is *judgment*, whereby the mind takes its ideas to agree or disagree; or, which is the same, any proposition to be true or false, without perceiving any demonstrative evidence in the proofs. The mind sometimes exercises this *judgment* out of necessity, when demonstrative proofs and certain knowledge are not to be had. *Judgment* is the *presuming* things to be so, without *perceiving* it." *Locke's Essay*, book iv. ch. xiv. § iv.

† "To *understanding*, we apply the epithets strong, vigorous, comprehensive, profound. To *judgment*, those of correct, cool, unprejudiced, impartial, solid. It was in this sense that the word seems to have been understood by Pope, in the following couplet: —

> 'Tis with our judgments as our watches; none
> Go just alike, yet each believes his own.'"
>
> *Stewart's Philosophy*, vol. ii. p. 17.

All well; but how absurd to speak of a correct, cool, unprejudiced, impartial, solid *intuition!* or of our intuitions varying with our watches!

bench. The judge cannot ordinarily compass the whole question at issue with a single decisive act; he compares and decides, reasons and judges, at the various stages of the investigation. The character of the witnesses, and the evidences they furnish; the arguments of the respective advocates; the different circumstances bearing directly and indirectly upon the case, are all severally considered, brought into relation to the law, and decided upon, as preparatory to the final judgment that is to embrace the whole.

DEFINITION OF JUDGMENT.

Considered as a mental attribute, judgment may therefore be defined *the power of forming a decision in view of facts and evidences.* We may conceive of a mind in which this element might be wholly wanting. It might attend to all the facts and evidences in a given case, compare them with a standard, and yet have no power of judgment — no ability to come to any decision whatever in respect to them. Judgment is, then, a distinct faculty. It is that which, when all the circumstances are brought to bear upon a question at issue, enables us to *decide,* in view of them, what the truth is, and what ought to be done.

This is the real meaning of judgment, as understood and applied by the mass of mankind. Nor does it essentially differ from the meaning attached to it by most philosophers and logicians, excepting when they confound it with reason or intuition. "In treatises of logic," says Stewart, "*judgment* is commonly defined to be an act of the mind, by which one thing is affirmed or denied of another; a definition which, though not unexceptionable, is, perhaps, less so than most that have been given on similar occasions. Its defect, as Reid has remarked,*

* "The definition commonly given of judgment, by the more ancient writers in logic, was, that it is an act of the mind, whereby one thing is affirmed or denied of another. I believe this is as good a definition of it as can be given." — *Reid's Philosophy,* vol. iii. p. 74. But this excellent author immediately admits that the affirmation or denial is not essential

consists in this: that although it be by affirmation or denial that we express our judgments to others, yet judgment is a solitary act of the mind, to which this affirmation or denial is not essential; and, therefore, if the definition be admitted, it must be understood of mental affirmation or denial only; in which case, we do no more than substitute, instead of the thing defined, another mode of speaking perfectly synonymous. The definition has, however, notwithstanding this imperfection, the merit of a conciseness and perspicuity not often to be found in the attempts of logicians to explain our intellectual operations." *

VIEWS OF LOCKE AND COUSIN.

It has been remarked that some writers confound judgment with other mental faculties. This is doubtless owing to the influence of the German school, in which REASON figures very largely, embracing nearly all that we understand by intuition and judgment. Locke stands, in this respect, on high, independent ground. Cousin complains of him in the following language: "Locke founds knowledge and judgment upon the perception of a relation between two ideas, that is to say, upon comparison; while in many cases, these relations and the ideas of relation, so far from being the foundation of our judgments and of our cognitions, are, on the contrary, the results of primitive cognitions and judgments referable to the natural power of the mind, which judges and knows in its own proper virtue, basing itself frequently upon a single term, and consequently without comparing two together in order to deduce the ideas of relation." †

Here Cousin places in the same category cognitions and judgments which Locke is careful to distinguish.

to judgment; that "there may be judgment which is not expressed;" that "affirmation and denial are very often the expression of testimony, which is a different act of the mind, and ought to be distinguished from judgment." — *Ibid.* This brings us back to our definition above.

* Philosophy, vol. ii. p. 18.

† Elements of Psychology, by Victor Cousin, by Rev. C. S. Henry, D. D., p. 342.

Cognitions do *not* necessarily involve any comparing. All intuitions are cognitions, and are referable to a "natural power of the mind, which knows in its own proper virtue." But judgments, with Locke, are quite another thing. They "supply the *want* of clear and certain knowledge," or cognitions.*

VIEWS OF REID.

Reid's view of judgment agrees mainly with our definition. He says, "As a judge, after taking the proper evidence, passes sentence in a cause, and that sentence is called his judgment, so the mind, with regard to whatever is true or false, passes sentence, or determines according to the evidence that appears. Some kinds of evidence leave no room for doubt. Sentence is passed immediately, without seeking or hearing any contrary evidence, because the thing is certain and notorious.† In the other cases, there is room for weighing evidences on both sides before sentence is passed. The analogy between a tribunal of justice and this inward tribunal of the mind is too obvious to escape the notice of any man who ever appeared before a judge." ‡

Yet this writer unfortunately extends the sphere of judgment to intuitions, and, to justify it, calls such mental acts "judgments of things necessary." "That three times three are nine, that the whole is greater than a part, are judgments about things necessary. Our assent to such necessary propositions is not grounded upon any operations of sense, of memory, or of consciousness, nor does it require their concurrence; it is unaccompanied by any other operation but that of conception, which must accompany all judgment; we may, therefore, call this judgment of things necessary pure judgment." § This

* Locke's Essays, book iv. ch. xiv. sec. iv.

† It should be observed that the *certainty* here is not that of *intuition*, but of irresistible *evidence*. The mind of the judge may be forced to a certain conviction of the prisoner's guilt, not because he has an intuitive perception of his crime, but irresistible evidence of it.

‡ Essays, vol. iii. p. 76.

§ Essays, vol. iii. p. 78.

"pure judgment" is what Leibnitz and Kant call "pure reason," and what we have called *intuition.* Reid, as we have seen, assigns *another* office to judgment; why not, then, let *intuition* have its *own?*

VIEWS OF STEWART.

But Stewart not only admits the more enlarged sense of the term, but argues for it. After stating the primitive and appropriate sense of the term, he adds, "When we give our assent to a mathematical axiom; or when, after perusing the demonstration of a theorem, we assent to the conclusion; or, in general, when we pronounce concerning the truth or falsity of any proposition, or the probability or improbability of any event, the power by which we are enabled to perceive what is true or is false, probable or improbable, is called by logicians the faculty of *judgment.*

"Considered as a technical or scientific term of logic, the practice of our purest and most correct writers sufficiently sanctions the more enlarged sense in which I have explained it; and if I do not much deceive myself, this use of it will be found more favorable to philosophical distinctness than Mr. Locke's language, which leads to an unnecessary multiplication of our intellectual powers. What good reason can be given for assigning one name to the faculty which perceives truths that are *certain,* and another name to the faculty which perceives truths that are probable? Would it not be equally proper to distinguish by different names the power by which we perceive one proposition to be true and another false?" *

REMARKS ON THE ABOVE.

The cases supposed above are not parallel. The perception of a truth implies precisely the same assured mental state as the perception of a falsehood. The

* Philosophy, vol. ii. p. 18.

difference between the two cases is not in the *mind;* it is in the object of perception. But the state of mind in which we perceive a truth as *certain* is essentially different from that in which we perceive it as *probable.* Here the difference is in the mind, not in the object perceived; or if it be in the object perceived, it is in the mind also.

The one state implies a *question* to be settled; the other does not. The one holds the mind in a position for the exercise of *judgment;* the other excludes all judgment, by shutting out all possible question, and fixing the mind at once to a *perceived certainty.* The difference of mental states, and of course the difference of mental powers, exercised in these two cases, may be clearly defined, and is very important.

As to the "purest and most correct writers" to whom this philosopher refers, as sanctioning his "more enlarged sense" of judgment, I have been unable to find any of the English language whose authority often transcends that of Stewart himself. If reference be had to *continental* writers, their nomenclature and classifications are so widely different from ours, that the unqualified adoption of any of their definitions would mislead us, unless we should make an entire revolution of our system. The attempt to incorporate fragments of German philosophy with the philosophy of Great Britain must necessarily prove a failure. But Stewart wrote when the Kantian speculations were in the height of their glory, and it is no reflection on his intellectual eminence that he was sometimes overawed by their splendors.

VIEWS OF BROWN.

With his usual passion for simplification, Brown, of course, annihilates judgment. "Those who ascribe judgment to man," he says, "ascribe to him also another faculty, which they distinguish by the name of *reason* — though reasoning *itself* is found, when analyzed, to be nothing more than a *series of judgments.* The whole is thus represented as something different from all the parts which compose it." *

* Philosophy, vol. ii. p. 522.

Is it, then, strange that a *house* should be something different from all the *bricks* and *boards* and *nails* which compose it? We are in the habit of supposing a house a different thing from the materials of which it is built. Whatever we may call these materials, we cannot properly call them a house. In like manner, whatever may be the elements or means of a judgment, they are not the judgment itself.

Now this same writer tells us that "reasoning is nothing more than a series of relative suggestions."* Judgments, then, turn out to be *relative suggestions.* That suggestions are more or less concerned in bringing the mind to a state of judgment, is undoubted; but mere *suggestion* is not *judgment.* The term judgment, whether as applied to the decisions of a tribunal, or to matters of taste, or to the ordinary affairs of life, is *not* represented by the idea usually attached to suggestion; and if applied to mathematical and other self-evident truths, it is equally in fault. A suggestion may imply doubt, and start inquiry; but in self-evident truths, there is no room for doubt.

My apology for saying so much on this point is in the fact, that differing from such high authorities seems to imply an obligation to state their views, together with the reasons for dissent.

ADDITIONAL REMARKS.

In aiming to simplify, men sometimes render plain things obscure. In nothing is this more true than in attempts to simplify the mental faculties. To call intuition judgment, for the sake of simplification, when there is another well-defined sphere of judgment to which all men give their practical assent, renders complex and obscure what was previously simple and plain. Elucidation is not in the fewness of definitions, but in their accuracy.

In his attempts to simplify the mental faculties, Brown has multiplied words, explanations, ingenious specula-

* Philosophy, vol. ii. p. 523.

tions, all to the effect of involving rather than unfolding the essential laws of mind. In an analysis of the mental phenomena, the most instructive method is, to relinquish all theory and speculation, take the facts as we find them, and give to their several classes the names sanctioned by common usage. In this view, considering JUDGMENT sufficiently distinct and important to have a name and a place, I have endeavored to give it its due.

IMPORTANCE OF A SOUND JUDGMENT.

This is one of the highest attributes of humanity. It is not only one of those which distinguish man from the brute, but, more than perhaps any other, it distinguishes man from man. Indeed, the proportion of men who possess a thoroughly sound judgment is very small. The term is nearly a synonyme for that *wisdom* whose price is said to be above rubies. The man who *judges* rightly, and acts as he judges, has indeed the priceless treasure.

The importance of this attribute is felt in all departments of life. In the economic, social, civil, political, moral and religious world, it holds the balance of destiny, and interests of both temporal and eternal moment are suspended upon it. It is indeed a crowning attribute of the SUPREME BEING, divested of the single element of uncertainty incidental to it in man, and on it are suspended the amazing destinies of the final day.

Although a man have all other mental endowments in highest measure, although he have the reasoning powers of a Butler, the imagination of a Dante, the eloquence of a Cicero, without judgment, they will profit him little. Whereas a sound judgment, even in the absence of superiority in all other qualities, will not only conduct a man well through life, and render him a blessing to others, but will eventually cause even mediocrity itself to excel.

CHARACTERISTICS OF A SOUND JUDGMENT.

That this endowment is possessed by men naturally, in very unequal degrees, there can be no question; and yet the difference made by personal education and habits is probably greater. The following are the principal elements of a sound judgment; every person has it in his power to cultivate them to an almost indefinite extent:—

1. Impartiality. The person who would have soundness of judgment must form the habit of excluding from his mind all prejudice, all prepossession, all passion; and of holding it in a balanced position, equally ready to decide in the one or the other direction, as evidence shall preponderate. If he have any interest in the case, he must be careful to keep it out of the scale. He who cannot hold the scales of a severe and unbending impartiality, is unfit to judge.

2. Patience. This balanced state of mind must be patiently retained, till evidences are fully furnished, facts fully disclosed, and brought in relation to the standard of judgment. A sound judgment is not, ordinarily, the work of a *moment.* An intuition, a suggestion, a single perception demands *no patience.* It is as the flash of an eye. But a sound judgment is the fruit of time and patience. No man is fit to be a judge, in any important matter, who has not learned to "let patience have her perfect work."

3. Memory. As judgment is exercised in view of *facts*, memory is essential. The moment memory falters, so that facts bearing on the question slip from the mind, the judgment suffers. Hence civil judges, at the advanced age when memory fails, are considered incompetent. The only remedy for this is a careful noting down of facts, and a repeated recurrence to their bearings and relations.

The failure of memory is usually the first step towards a faltering judgment. All the other elements of a sound judgment usually survive this. The disastrous mistakes often made by men of business, in advanced periods of life, the strange errors of judgment, so unlike their earlier doings, arise from their not remembering all that is material to the business in hand. Hence men should distrust their judgment, and let caution predominate as memory fails.

4. Firmness. Until a man can *face consequences*, and nerve his mind to a straightforward course, *whatever may be the result*, his judgment is not to be trusted. If he

flinches, in view of a painful result, — if facts cease to have their weight, because they lead to an undesirable issue, — he is not a sound judge. There must be a stability, a steadiness, a resolution of mind, which will follow evidence wherever it may lead.

5. Sincere and ardent Love of Truth and Justice. Patience must never degenerate to *pusillanimity*, nor impartiality to *indifference*. No man can wisely judge a matter in which he feels little or no interest. We often hear of great *coolness* of mind as a mark of sound judgment. But the mind may have too much coolness as well as too little. There must ever be an ardent love of truth and justice, and in every specific case there should be a felt emotion proportioned to its importance. It is with the *heart* that man judges aright, as well as with the *head*.

He who brings his mind to a decision in a case of life and death with as little emotion as is due to a cause involving a few dollars, has not in his soul all the proper elements of a judge. Those qualities which should *control* and *guide* his feelings have been mentioned above; the feelings themselves should never be wanting. A *just* judge is always a *feeling* judge. These last remarks have more special reference to judicial tribunals, and to the various higher exercises of judgment; but they apply, to some extent, to its more humble and less important decisions.

The relation of judgment to religion is involved in what has been said under the head of *Reason*.

QUESTIONS ON CHAPTER VII.

With what do some writers confound judgment? Remarks? Considering reason as the synonyme for *induction*, what then? Illustration? Considering reason as *discursive*, &c., what then? Illustrate. Definition of judgment? Explain. Remarks of Stewart and Reid? Why have writers confounded judgment with other mental faculties? What say Cousin and Locke? Strictures on Cousin? Views of Reid? Remark in the note? To what does Reid unfortunately extend the sphere of judgment? and how defend his so doing? What is said of him in reply? Views of Stewart on this point? State the argument in reply to Stewart. What is said of the nomenclature of *continental* writers? Views of Brown? Reply to them? Apology for saying thus much on this point, and remarks? What is said of aiming to simplify? In what does elucidation consist? What is said of Brown? In an analysis of the mental phenomena, what is the most instructive method? What is said of the *importance* of judgment? For what is the term nearly a synonyme? Where is its importance felt? Remarks? *First* characteristic of a sound judgment? Explain. *Second?* Remarks? *Third?* Remarks? *Fourth?* Remarks? *Fifth?* Remarks?

CHAPTER VIII.

IMAGINATION.

IMAGINATION may be defined *the power of forming ideal or fancied objects.* It is believed that this definition will be found sufficiently explicit, while it has the advantage of most others in point of simplicity. Reid confounds imagination with conception.* But there is an obvious and important distinction between them. Conception replaces in the mind an exact transcript of whatever has been perceived or felt; while imagination *selects* from it whatever is preferred, and from this forms a new and fancied object.†

Hence imagined objects may bear *resemblance* to objects which we have perceived, or they may be wholly *unlike* them. Creations of imagination do not imply any *new elementary* conceptions, but only new and fanciful combinations of those previously in the mind.

IMAGINATION AN ULTIMATE FACULTY.

Most persons are somewhat surprised and disappointed when told by philosophers that imagination is not an

* "Conceiving, imagining, apprehending, understanding, having a notion of a thing, are common words, used to express that operation of the understanding which the logicians call *simple apprehension.* Logicians define simple apprehension to be the bare conception of a thing, without any judgment or belief about it." — *Reid's Works*, vol. ii. p. 138.

† "The business of conception, according to the account I have given of it, is to present us with an exact transcript of what we have felt or perceived. But we have, moreover, a power of modifying our conceptions, by combining the parts of different ones together, so as to form new wholes of our own creation. I shall employ the word *imagination* to express this power." — *Stewart's Philosophy*, vol. i. p. 80.

ultimate faculty of our mental constitution, but that what we call acts of imagination are only the joint operation of other faculties. Thus Stewart, for instance, says, "Imagination is formed by a combination of various faculties;" "it includes conception, abstraction, judgment, taste, or fancy." Again he says, "What we call the power of imagination is not the gift of nature, but the result of acquired habits, aided by favorable circumstances. It is not an original endowment of mind, but an accomplishment formed by experience and situation."

According to this, all the difference between any ordinary genius and a Raphael or a Milton is not due to "the gift of nature," but "is the result of acquired habits, aided by favorable circumstances."* I am confident that most readers will agree with me in dissenting from this view.

Whether we have an ultimate principle in our mental constitution which we call *imagination*, or whether what we call *imagining* is only the combined action of several *other* faculties, is a question of sufficient interest to claim some examination.

STEWART'S ILLUSTRATION.

To illustrate his view, Stewart says, "Let us consider the steps by which Milton must have proceeded in creating his imaginary garden of Eden. When he first proposed to himself that subject of description, it is reasonable to suppose that a variety of the most striking scenes which he had seen crowded into his mind. The association of ideas suggested them, and the power of conception placed each of them before him with all its beauties and imperfections. In every natural scene, if we destine it for any particular purpose, there are defects and redundancies, which art may sometimes, but cannot always, correct. But the power of imagination is unlimited. She can create and annihilate, and dispose at pleasure, her woods, her rocks, and her rivers. Milton,

* Philosophy, vol. i. p. 269; also p. 315.

accordingly, would not copy his Eden from any one scene, but would select from each the features which were most eminently beautiful. The power of abstraction enabled him to make the separation, and taste directed him in the selection." "From what has been said, it is sufficiently evident that imagination is not a simple power of the mind, like attention, conception, or abstraction, but that it is formed by a combination of various faculties." *

REMARKS ON THE ABOVE.

1. This work of Milton was one engaging *all* his mental powers; we scarcely know which most. Imagination figures conspicuously amongst them, but they are so involved that they cannot be easily distinguished. In order fairly to test the question, whether or not a given power is an ultimate or simple attribute of the mind, we must take some of its ultimate or simplest acts.

2. The *other* mental powers, attention, conception, abstraction, *according to the above illustration*, are *also complex*. For, in the view of this writer, conception implies something previously perceived or felt; and this, of course, implies attention. But if we suppose the *materials prepared* for the exercise of a given power, so that nothing is wanting but the exercise of *that power itself*, we may regard attention, conception, abstraction, as simple attributes; nor does it appear in this view that imagination is not entitled to the same rank. For I must add, —

3. In the above illustration, the *essential thing* is still wanting; that is, the *archetype* or *model*. Conception places before the mind the vast world of objects which it has perceived; abstraction selects from them; judgment or taste is concerned in directing the selection and combination; but where is the *pattern* — the *form* or *image* — according to which these elements are to be shaped? *Here is the specific work of imagination.*

We cannot indeed *imagine* without the *materials* fur-

* Intellectual Philosophy, vol. i. p. 269.

nished by other mental powers; neither can we, without the same, *attend*, *conceive*, *abstract*. If the mind be *duly furnished*, merely to *imagine* something seems to be as simple and direct an act as, when thus furnished, to *attend* to something, or to *conceive* or *abstract* something.

Under the glow of excitement, the mind imagines in a twinkling of the eye; a thousand fancied forms flit before it; according to the nature of the excitement, images of terror, of beauty, of joy, dance along; and the mind's imaginings seem to outrun all its other acts. Hence this power or proneness to *imagine* or *fancy* seems as primitive and natural to the mind as its power or proneness to *attend*, *conceive*, or *abstract*.

SIMPLE ACTS OF IMAGINATION.

When a person imagines a *sound*, a *taste*, a *smell*, he does not necessarily *abstract* that from all other things; that may be the *only* subject of thought. Abstracting, of course, implies the presence to the mind of two or more objects. *Abstracting* is *selecting;* and evidently we cannot *select*, unless two or more things are in our thoughts from which the selection is made. The simplest act of imagination — and I do not see why it is not as simple as any other mental act — is that in which an *individual thing* is imagined. To call that act abstraction, conception, conjecture, or any thing but imagination, is contrary to the most accredited use of language.

If it be asked *why* the mind thus imagines, the answer is, Because it was *made* to do so. It is its *nature* to do it, as much as it is to *perceive*, *abstract*, *reason*. If it be asked why a person imagines one thing rather than another, the answer is, Because his *susceptibility* to the one is more *lively* than to the other. Constitutional temperament, education, or other circumstances may occasion a *special susceptibility to particular objects*. The lover has *his* peculiar imaginings; the miser has *his;* the hungry man imagines *food;* the thirsty, *drink;* all men imagine as susceptibility prompts.

IMAGINATION NOT CONFINED TO OBJECTS OF SENSE.

Reid, Addison, and some others have limited the province of imagination to objects of sight. Stewart and other writers extend its province not only to all objects of *sense*, but to all the objects of human *knowledge*.*

The word *image*, as understood by the early writers, did not import any thing exactly *physical*, but a sort of *ghostly* existence. Hence *imagination* and *fancy*, as used in the schools, are nearly synonymous. The *phantom*, from which comes the word *fancy*, was a mere airy thing, with which the senses had nothing to do. Giving this latitude to imagination, she takes wings and soars into the heights of the supersensuous; she ranges the spirit world, as well as this.

A man imagines an *angel* in his room: must he needs give that angel a *material form?* He simply imagines, we will suppose, the *presence* and *design* of the spirit; he has nothing to do with its *form*. It is, perhaps, the spirit of some departed friend that he imagines present with him. If any man assert that the mental act is not imagination, unless the spirit is clothed with a form, the common sentiment and usage of mankind, both learned and ignorant, is against him.

Identifying *ghost* with *spectre* naturally leads to the idea of something *visible* when a ghost is imagined. *Ghost* is a Saxon word, denoting a *spirit*. *Spectre* is of Latin origin, denoting something *made visible*, the *appearance* of a ghost. Now a man may imagine not only a *spectre*, — a spirit made visible, — but the *spirit itself*, without the visibility.

* "The sensible world, it must be remembered, is not the only field where imagination exerts her powers. All the objects of human knowledge supply materials to her forming hand, diversifying, infinitely, the works she produces, while the mode of her operation remains essentially uniform." — *Stewart's Philosophy*, vol. i. p. 206. This is no doubt *true;* but it is inconsistent with what the same writer had previously maintained. He confined *perceptions* to objects of *sense; conceptions*, to what we have *perceived* or *felt;* and *imaginations* to *conceptions*. His *theory*, therefore, restricts imagination to things seen and felt; but when that is forgotten, he virtually falls on the precise view of imagination which I have maintained. His foundation was too narrow for his superstructure.

IMAGINATION MAY BE WHOLLY CREATIVE.

When we hear of something interesting in a place, even if we never heard of the place before, and have no knowledge of it by description, we are yet apt to form a *picture* of it in our minds. What we imagine may be wholly unlike the place, and no reason can be given why one picture rather than another is formed, except that the feelings and associations of the mind at the time are such as naturally give rise to it. The picture springs up spontaneously out of materials in the mind, as passion or circumstances prompt.*

In the mind of him who has a highly creative imagination, thousands of fancies thus involuntarily come and go. If, then, he bring his will to bear, store his mind with knowledge, call his other powers into service, to select, combine, arrange, and perfect his imaginings, the result may be some great original work, like that of Homer, Milton, or Dante.

IMAGINATION MAY BE CREATIVE ONLY IN PART.

Every child who studies geography forms some picture of London, Constantinople, Rome. He never saw these places, nor, we will suppose, any picture of them. But they have been *described* to him. His imagination is thus sustained and guided by the description. It is creative only in part. He imagines how Rome looks, but the *accuracy*, not to say beauty of the picture in his mind, depends more upon the accuracy of the description and his power of apprehension than upon the fertility of his imagination. Hence persons of the most poetic imagination do not always form the most accurate ideas

* A child bred in the country, on reading the account of Christ's interview with the woman at the well, would be apt to imagine a well situated in a yard, much like his father's, wanting the pole and bucket. A child bred in the city, and having no knowledge of the country well, would probably imagine something like a deep cistern or reservoir, wanting the pump or hydrant. From those materials, whatever they be, which previous perceptions have furnished, imagination forms her picture.

concerning places of which they read. Yet, without some imagination, they could form no idea of them whatever.

DESCRIPTIVE IMAGINATION.

In the case above, a man imagines how a place looks which he *never saw;* in this case, imagination helps him to *describe* a place which he *has seen.* Conception, memory, and imagination seem to be so closely allied here, that Reid and some others make them all one. But the distinction should not be lost. A man may have an excellent memory, and yet, for want of imagination, describe badly. As only a small part of the things constituting the object to be described can be noticed, imagination assists in selecting and arranging them, and throws over the whole the embellishments of fancy, so as to produce the most happy effect.

We are thus enabled to understand how imagination contributes to poetry and eloquence, to the fine arts, to science, morals, and religion. In all these she is a handmaid of true and effective genius.

IMAGINATION SUBSERVIENT TO POETRY.

Imagination is most creative and original in *poetry.* Some kinds of descriptive and historic poetry, whose design is to detail facts somewhat enlivened with imagination, do not admit of her boldest flights. The same may be said of most didactic poetry. But in poetry where the very *facts* are, as it were, created by the mind of the writer, like those of Dante and Milton, imagination performs her most characteristic and glorious achievements. Compelled to walk in paths hitherto untrodden, divested of all encumbrances, restricted only by taste and judgment, she takes wings and soars at large through the realms of heaven, earth, and hell. From these three worlds, and all others which she can create or explore, she gathers treasures to enrich her verse.

As she plunges into the mysterious depths, or ascends the giddy heights, the novelty of her position kindles yet more her fires; the powers of creativeness are thus stimulated to the utmost; strange and yet stranger fancies rise; the wonderful, the beautiful, the grand, the awful come rushing in, to reward the adventurer with those original and bold conceptions that glow upon his pages. It must be a sturdy mind that can read poetry thus produced, and not feel itself kindle with something of its delicious inspiration. This is *poetry*, — real poetry, — *and the highest style of imagination.*

IMAGINATION SUBSERVIENT TO OTHER KINDS OF ELEGANT COMPOSITION.

In other kinds of elegant composition, imagination often figures scarcely less — not so sustained, not so adventurous, but equally beautiful and sublime. There are passages in the prose writings of English, German, French, and American authors, as truly the work of creative imagination as any thing found in Dante or Milton. They are the brilliant flashes, the glowing and startling pictures, which rouse our feelings, awaken our admiration, relieve the tedium of sober facts and dull commonplaces, and make us love to go on with the author.

But where there is a *redundancy* of such passages, or they are evidently *forced in*, or ambitiously studied, as the writer's chief dependence, they become as offensive as under other circumstances they are pleasing. Hence only persons of creative and lively imagination should attempt this style of writing. There are other kinds in which they may excel, equally honorable and important

IMAGINATION SUBSERVIENT TO ELOQUENCE.

No man can be *truly eloquent* without imagination of a high order. Knowledge, logic, reasoning powers, however important, cannot alone make a man eloquent. Let there be two men of precisely the same logical powers, the one of a high order of imagination, the other possessing almost none, and while an audience will sleep under the demonstrations of the latter, they will be electrified and swayed by the eloquence of the former. Even the sturdy juryman and the wary judge are unnerved and taken captive by the persuasive charms of imagination. Men who have little of it themselves are yet delighted with it in others.

There is something in every human mind which makes it delight in the brilliant creations of fancy; and when the mind is thus pleased, it is in a favorable state to be convinced and swayed by him who has thus gratified it. We throw ourselves, almost unconsciously, into the hands of those who please us. And then, again, the *respect* we feel for the *talent* which can at will call up such splendid creations of imagery, has no small influence in gaining our confidence. The man who thus pleases us, and secures our respect and admiration for his talents, needs but little logic to bring us to his views. It is, indeed, almost surprising to observe with what slender arguments a man of brilliant imagination will carry his points.

Thus the pulpit, the forum, the bar owe much of their power to this noble faculty. There is a fascination in her embellishments, an eloquence in her appeals, which make way through the sternest philosophy, and gain the most stubborn will. If learned infidels went scores of miles to hang with raptures upon the lips of Whitefield, it was not less because he wielded the power of a burning imagination than of a devout enthusiasm. Without it, the piety of a martyr, joined with the logic of a Butler, cannot make a man truly eloquent. Although an accurate logician, a sound reasoner, a faithful expounder of facts, unless he can throw something of the creations of his own fancy into his work, he will be dull and tedious. It was when enthusiasm kindled in the eye, and imagination, like lightning in the cloud, flashed forth with the thunder of eloquence, that Demosthenes, and Chatham, and Patrick Henry carried all hearts with them.

THE RELATION OF IMAGINATION TO THE FINE ARTS.

When the painter is a mere *copyist*, there is little demand on imagination. There is, perhaps, more in painting from nature than in repeating a picture already made; but when the object to be copied is before him, whether it be the picture or the original, the work in hand is more a trial of accuracy of observation, judgment, and mechanical skill, than of imagination. Persons of dull imagination are sometimes excellent copyists. The same is mostly true of sculpture; although this art is, perhaps, more imaginative. But when painting and sculpture have reference to original creations of fancy, the case is quite different.*

RELATION OF IMAGINATION TO SCIENCE.

As we arrive at results in natural science by a severe induction of facts, it might seem to afford little play to imagination. But her assistance is of the greatest utility in framing those theories which guide our inquiries, and in creating in anticipation those beautiful structures after which the inductions of science are striving. Thus the mind is guided, cheered, sustained, on its way to the imagined goal. The man in search of some new truth or law in science is like the adventurer ploughing through tedious and perilous seas, to reach some happy country, seen as yet only by his imagination. Had Columbus been without imagination, he would not have discovered America. Had Archimedes, Newton, La Place, Harvey, and Davy been destitute of this noble quality, they would never have made those splendid achievements in science. Imagination, fearless and winged, goes before, to open and guide the way.

* "As far as the painter aims at copying exactly what he sees, he may be guided mechanically by general rules; and he requires no aid from that creative genius which is characteristic of the poet. When the history or the landscape painter indulges his genius in forming new combinations of his own, he vies with the poet in the noblest exertions of the poetical art." — *Stewart's Philosophy*, vol. i. p. 271.

The more steady and exact steps of induction must needs follow to chastise her wanderings and rectify her mistakes, but she has done an invaluable service in leading forth induction to this work. Accordingly, men distinguished in scientific discoveries have usually been men of vigorous and original imagination. But the converse is not always true. Men may have intense imagination, but lack the patience of detail and soundness of judgment requisite to success in scientific pursuits.

Even in the *abstract* science of *mathematics*, imagination has more to do than some suppose; for as diagrams and other visible signs assist to carry forward processes of demonstration, so imagination, by creating forms to abstract truths, gives them a kind of visible reality, by which the mind can the better apprehend and reason upon them. It is a great mistake to suppose that mathematics and imagination are at variance. *All the mental powers harmonize together and assist each other.*

QUESTIONS ON CHAPTER VIII.

What is *imagination?* Remarks? Have all writers considered it an ultimate faculty? What is said of Stewart's view? State his illustration. *First* remark upon it? *Second? Third?* What is necessary in order to imagine? Is the same necessary in order to conceive, abstract, &c.? What does merely to *imagine* something seem to be? Remarks? What is said of *simple* acts of imagination? What does *abstraction* imply? Is this necessarily involved in *imagining?* What is the simplest act of imagination? *Why* does the mind imagine thus? Why does a person imagine one thing rather than another? Illustrations? How have Reid, Addison, and others limited imagination? Stewart and others? Substance of the note? What is said of *image*, &c.? Imagining a *spirit?* Ghost and spectre? May imagination be wholly creative? Illustrations? What is said of him who has a highly creative imagination? Instances in which imagination is creative only in part? What is said of *descriptive* imagination? Its subserviency to poetry? To other *kinds* of elegant composition? To *eloquence?* To the fine arts? To natural *science?* To the abstract science of mathematics?

CHAPTER IX.

IMAGINATION AS RELATED TO MORALS AND RELIGION.

Probably none of the mental faculties has a more direct and powerful influence upon the moral and religious character than the imagination. Rightly used, it purifies, elevates, ennobles; perverted, it defiles, debases, ruins. Few consider at how many points it touches and moves the hidden springs of character. It is early developed, and it begins to produce its effects at the very dawn of intellect. Children no sooner begin to perceive and to think than they begin to imagine. Let us, then, briefly notice the influence of imagination as concerned, first, in the formation of an *irreligious* and *vicious* character; and, secondly, in the formation of a *Christian* character.

IMAGINATION PERVERTED.

There is a powerful *reciprocity* of action between the imagination and the moral feelings and purposes. They mutually purify or corrupt each other. Those things with which one suffers his imagination to be conversant are perpetually imparting, as it were, their own character to his mind, and gaining an ascendency over him. Thus the man devoted to sensual pleasure sends abroad his imagination in pursuit of materials to gratify his grovelling desires. Whenever he is relieved from the pressure of care, this busy agent renews her service, and paints to him, on living canvas, every variety of scenes and objects adapted to please and to move his sensual passions.

His passions, thus excited, beget a purpose to gratify them.

This purpose, itself vicious, occasions many other vicious purposes and many false deeds, on the way to the final accomplishment of its object. Thus does the unhappy victim of crime become more and more involved in guilt, until it becomes too late to retrieve his folly.

INORDINATE LOVE OF WEALTH.

The inordinate love of *wealth* is often greatly due to the influence of a perverted imagination. This faculty is employed in picturing scenes of worldly distinction, fashion, gayety, abundance, apparent ease and importance, until the heart is stirred with an ardent desire for these things. The person supposed sees only the outside, and that at a distance. Imagination paints to him only the brilliant and fascinating part of the picture. He cannot look within upon the real wretchedness that frequently inhabits the dwellings of ill-gotten and misused abundance, for it is the world's policy to expose only the bright and gay side. Hence these imposing objects gradually assume, in his mind, a paramount importance. His thoughts, desires, purposes, incline more and more to centre upon them. The hours of business, the hours appointed for sleep, the hours due to domestic enjoyment, yes, even the hours of the holy Sabbath become at last alike desecrated to the all-absorbing pursuit of gain.

Thus does the man by degrees become a *miser*. The objects for which he at first desired wealth are lost sight of; he leaves one, another, and another of them behind, in his ardent pursuit of wealth itself. The means become the end. At first, he desired wealth for the ease, luxuries, refinements, and social enjoyments to which it ministers; but as he rises in wealth, and reaches the amount to which he at first aspired, his imagination, more rapid than his gains, holds before him other and higher ends to be obtained. Some person has yet more than he; and the glory of being highest in wealth is a prize too tempting for a perverse imagination to overlook, in her cunning work of enslaving the soul.

THE LOVE OF POWER AND FAME.

Not only do the licentious, the envious, the covetous kindle the flame of their passion by the aid of imagination, but the lust of power and fame is, in a great measure, indebted to the same means. It is in no small measure through the influence of a perverted imagination, mocking them with phantoms of expected glory, that the Alexanders, the Cæsars, the Napoleons, and others of like spirit, have been incited to rise, tread down the nations, and spill human blood like water. Would the renowned son of Philip, or would Cæsar, have done as he did, had he not been led by the illusion of a perverted imagination? It is by the same illusion that the less renowned, but perhaps not less wicked, spirit of the highway robber and of the midnight assassin is moved and emboldened to its horrid deeds.

YOUTH IN CITIES.

A perverted imagination ruins many of the youth in those towns and cities in which character is peculiarly exposed by temptations to vice. The imagination first lingers, perhaps, amid the fascinations of the theatre, until it enkindles a desire, and gives rise to a purpose, to attend it; other scenes of pleasure are there opened; the youth indulges first his eye, then his appetite. Passion is thus inflamed, and rendered too violent for reason to control. Next the company of the riotous is sought; of course means must be obtained to meet his expenses, and he is thus tempted to wrong his employer.

The foundations of character are at length subverted; moral integrity has gone; complete recklessness and abandonment to vice follow, and, perhaps, an untimely grave hides a curse from the world. Such is the brief, sad history of not a few youth — youth of fair promise, ardent temperament, lively susceptibilities; some of them, perhaps, of the finest natural genius and most ingenuous dispositions, who have been ruined by yielding to the allurements of depraved imagination.

VICIOUS LITERATURE.

Many can bear witness to the almost fatal ascendency which a perverted imagination, in love with ficticious writings of a corrupting nature, has at some periods obtained over them. At those periods in life when reason was most feeble, if susceptible to the fascinations of imagination wrought into the forms of fictitious tales, corrupt and bewitching romance has led them quite astray from the truthful world; it has beguiled them of the substantial treasures of intellectual and moral wealth for which the rational mind was made, and amused them with the gay dreams and pictures of fancy, until they were nearly unfitted for the sober realities and pure enjoyments of life.

IMAGINATION RIGHTLY EMPLOYED.

No sooner does a regenerate imagination, having broken away from her corrupting associations, become associated with objects of moral purity, than she begins to act as powerfully on the mind to elevate it as she previously did to debase it.

It is by her aid, coöperating with that of memory, that the Christian expatiates in thought over the past and prospective glories of the Redeemer's kingdom, and thus enjoys his richest repast of devout meditations; that he converses with the good and great of other ages, sympathizes with their conflicts and triumphs, and imbibes something of their spirit; that he becomes a member of the illustrious family, which alone of all the families of the earth was counted worthy to survive the flood, and participates of their faith, fidelity and reward; that he becomes a brother and companion of all those noble men whose names form so bright a roll on the sacred pages of antiquity; and, more than all, that he lives in his thoughts and feelings with the conflicts and victories of HIM who, after an earthly life of more than earthly wisdom, passed through the grave unharmed to a throne of immortality in the heavens. Thus do his affections, his purposes, his hopes become more and more pure, elevated, ennobling.

It is by the aid of the same imagination that he lives, in anticipation, amidst the happy scenes of future days — the regained beauties of paradise blooming over all lands; and perhaps he seldom bows the knee in homage to his Maker, or approaches the sacramental board, but imagination carries him even beyond the scenes of the present world, connecting the duty in which he engages with its consequences in eternity.

It is thus evident that the relation of imagination to morals and religion is exceedingly extensive and important. In all the ways above specified, and in numerous others, it serves to enliven the feelings, purify the affections, elevate the purposes, and enrich the whole soul. Persons of vivid imagination, when it is duly disciplined and rightly applied, have thus a great advantage over those whose imagination is dull.

DISCIPLINE OF THE IMAGINATION.

From what has been said, it is obvious that no faculty needs to be placed under a more vigilant discipline than this. Like that mighty element, fire, — with which it is often compared, — it is a useful servant, but a dangerous master. Few conditions are more perilous than that of the youth over whom imagination has gained ascendency. He is like a ship in a gale without a helm. The greatest caution should therefore be exercised in the development and growth of this faculty.

WORKS OF IMAGINATION.

Works of imagination should never be read without due regard to their character and to the condition of the mind.

An indiscriminate reading of fictitious tales, in every stage of mental growth, can hardly fail to be ruinous. Yet the imagination, no less than the other faculties, ought to be cultivated; and for this purpose, specimens of chaste literature, of the highest imaginative cast, should at suitable times be carefully studied. They should be taken up, not merely to pass an idle hour, but to engage the freshest energies of the mind.

The great error is, that imagination is usually made a mere plaything. Those hours only are devoted to it which are good for nothing else. It was not by so doing that Milton and Shakspeare became what they were. The name of Homer could never have been made immortal by a mere passive indulgence of that noble power which is so vividly impressed on the pages of the Iliad. Generally speaking, imagination *indulged* enfeebles and vitiates the mind; imagination *disciplined* strengthens and exalts it.

HOW WORKS OF IMAGINATION SHOULD BE STUDIED.

At the proper stage of education, select portions from the most brilliant works of imagination should not only be read, but *studied* — studied, not with a primary view to philosophical analysis, but to imbibe the spirit of the writer, enter into a vivid sympathy with his conceptions and feelings, and, on the wings of his imagination, to soar and exult with him. The student should seek to *feel* and *possess* the writer's power before he curiously pries into the secret of it. Writers of the most brilliant imagination sometimes know very little of analysis; and the reader invigorates and enriches his own mind by generously feasting it upon the luxuries proffered by another's, before inquiring into their nature and origin.

There are two ways of studying and admiring the beauties of a rose: the one, that of picking it into pieces and examining its several parts; the other, that of gazing upon it with steadfast eye as a whole, and of smelling its delicious odors; that of dwelling upon its wonderful structure, its blended beauties, its admirable adaptation to its end, until the mind realizes, if I may say so, a sympathy with the Being who made it. The latter method illustrates the way in which the student who would derive most advantage should first study an author.

But this is not the act of an idle hour. The potent stimulus of highly imaginative works will indeed suffice to excite the mind in its more sluggish moods; (and here is the reason why they are, in such moods, so often resorted to;) but this is all, in such passive mental states, that they can do. Like the influence of stimulating drinks upon the man who needs the very opposite stimulus, — that of active exercise, — they leave their subject weaker rather than stronger.

Only those books which were *written* in an idle hour can be suitably *read* in an idle hour. It is only when those sublime passages which intensely taxed the writer's genius are met by the reader with a corresponding mental activity that his soul is truly raised, enlarged, enriched, and made permanently to possess something of its teacher's power.

A careful analysis, both of the mental and rhetorical qualities of the writer, should be subsequently made by the student, if he would realize the highest advantage, especially if he contemplate authorship himself.

Imagination thus cultivated sustains to morals and religion a relation scarcely less important than that of the highest developments of reason itself. Those moralists and preachers whose imaginations have been thus trained and furnished, other things equal, have ever wielded the most powerful influence over the consciences, the affections, and the wills of their fellow-men. Not only have they exerted a benign influence over their own generation, but in their essays, their allegories, their songs, their discourses, they continue to live through all time, regenerating the affections and moulding the characters of men.

CONCLUDING REMARKS.

If what has been said be true, the imagination holds a rank scarcely second to any in the mental constitution. To give it early development and a right direction is, then, of the highest importance. Being an original element of the mind, it is of course possessed by all men in a normal state, although, like other powers, in an unequal degree. After all, the inequality may be less due to nature than to culture. Thousands of men of the most brilliant natural genius have lived and died unknown. Others, who have become distinguished, would have lived and died equally unknown, but for some incident which early called forth their powers and enkindled their enthusiasm. Among the means most favorable to the development and right direction of imagination are the following: —

1. Early Attention to Natural Scenery. Let the child be particularly induced to notice whatever is beautiful, grand, and sublime in nature. Let him be taught to gaze admiringly upon the glories of the setting sun, as it sinks to rest, curtained with its gorgeous drapery of gilded clouds; let him often turn his eyes upward to the splendors of the evening sky, study the mysterious face of that moon, and hold high converse with the stars; let him look off upon the wide ocean, listen to the roar of its billows, and watch its majestic movements; let him be taught to notice the sublime and the beautiful in lofty mountains, majestic rivers, and pleasing landscapes; in a word, let his attention be so directed to whatever is great, sublime, awful, mysterious, delightful, as to excite his admiration, call up his sense of the marvellous, and enkindle his enthusiasm. Let all these things be so associated with their Maker as to lead the enraptured mind "from nature up to nature's God," and whatever of imagination there is will hardly fail to develop itself and to take a religious direction.

2. Reading Books highly imaginative. This has been anticipated. Abraham Cowley, a writer scarcely inferior to any that Great Britain has ever produced, for

beauty and brilliancy of imagination, thus describes the manner in which he came to be what he was: "I remember when I began to read, and take some pleasure in it, there was wont to lie in my mother's parlor — I know not by what accident, for she herself never in her life read any other book but of devotion — but there was wont to lie Spenser's works; this I happened to fall upon, and was infinitely delighted with the stories of the knights, and giants, and monsters, and brave houses which I found every where there, (though my understanding had little to do with all this,) and, by degrees, with the tinkling of the rhyme and dance of the numbers; so that I think I had read him all over before I was twelve years old. With these affections of mind, and my heart wholly set upon letters, I went to the university."*

Similar effects are often produced upon the young mind by reading Bunyan's Pilgrim's Progress. In the lives of Dante, Milton, Shakspeare, Scott, and other men of remarkable genius, we find that the early reading of books vividly impressed with the author's imagination had much to do with developing and directing their own.

3. Hearing and telling good Stories. Imagination early excites a love of stories; this love should not be rebuked on the one hand, nor suffered to run wild on the other. It should be both encouraged and guided. It is a pity that the delicate task of shaping the imagination of children should be so often committed to ignorant and unprincipled nurses. The stories which children hear and are allowed to tell should be conceived by minds of the highest order of imagination, — chaste, refined, sparkling, — they should be in the main true to nature, should have completeness and finish, should tend to invigorate all the mental powers, and should always have a good moral. Such stories can hardly fail to assist in developing and rightly directing the youthful imagination.

Some object to all story telling; but this is an untenable position. What they object to meets a want in the mental constitution. Unless children are allowed to hear and repeat good stories, they will hear and repeat bad ones. Objecting to good stories, as a means of intel-

* Compend of English Literature, by C. D. Cleveland, p. 228.

lectual and moral culture, is at variance with the usage of the Bible and with the laws of mind.

4. SOLITARY MUSING. Imagination is usually most active when we are alone. Youth in the country have, in this respect, some advantage over those in the bustle of large cities. They are more alone with nature. Their attention is less engrossed with the mere passing fashion and parade of life. Rambling alone in the fields and groves, sitting in solitude under the big elm or by the side of the stream, eyeing the ever-changing phases of the earth and the heavens, without a human being present to interrupt the thoughts, can hardly fail to set the imagination at work.

Not that it is well to be *always* alone with nature. This would ultimately tend to mental derangement. It would exalt the imaginative at the expense of the social; it would tend to misanthropy. In his true state, man yearns for some friend to participate of his wonder and joy. Yet solitary musings, frequently practised, are of the greatest advantage. They are almost as essential to the growth of eminent literary genius as to the growth of rich spiritual piety. Without them, we as rarely find the one as the other.

5. FREQUENTLY PRACTISING IMAGINATIVE COMPOSITION. The effort to embody our conceptions, and give them a permanent form, puts the mind in a state of prolonged tension, by which it rises to yet higher and fuller conceptions. When we think we have a full conception of an object or event, we often find, on attempting to describe it, that our conception of it is very imperfect. Writing helps the mind to fill up and perfect what it had begun to imagine.

Milton could never have drawn the full picture which he did, even in his own mind, without the aid of the pen. Mental conceptions soon vanish away, frequently leaving the mind much as they found it, unless reduced by the pen to a permanent form. They then become, as it were, the author's fixed capital, on which he can fall back, and of which he can take advantage, in making further acquisitions. It was thus that Bunyan went on, step after step, in that wonderful work which has rendered his fame immortal. He did not dream, when he began to write, how much he was going to accomplish; but as he wrote, the dream went on. Sustained and animated by what he had done, his imagination wrought more and more, until at last the production surprised both himself and all his readers.

Let the pupil be put to writing descriptions, allegories, stories such as will task his invention to the utmost and keep his imagination on steady and prolonged duty; let him not be discouraged at failure, but be thereby only nerved to a firmer resolution to succeed; and he will at length have the satisfaction to find, not only that he can *call* the spirits from their mighty deep, but that they will *come* when he calls them! The most arduous and discouraging effort will result in the most triumphant and cheering success.

Let the imagination be at an early age thus called up and directed; let it be continuously nurtured and trained with the same diligence which we bestow upon the reasoning powers, and it will be redeemed from the inglorious rank so often assigned it; it will wholly cease to be what it now too often is — a means of debasing and vitiating the soul; and it will become eminently subservient, not only to literary and professional eminence, but to the most important of all interests — the interests of sound morality and pure religion.

QUESTIONS ON CHAPTER IX.

Opening remarks? Illustrations of reciprocity of action? How does perverted imagination produce inordinate love of *wealth?* Love of *power* and *fame?* What is said of youth in cities? Vicious literature? Remarks on imagination rightly employed? How does it aid the Christian? What is said about *discipline* of the imagination? What is the great error? How should works of imagination be studied? Illustrate the two ways of studying and admiring works of imagination. Remarks? What is said of early attention to natural scenery? Of reading imaginative books? Of hearing and telling stories? Of solitary musing? Of practising imaginative composition? Final remarks?

CHAPTER X.

DREAMING.

Dreaming is a *state of mind in which a part of its functions are suspended.* Sleep composes the mind to rest. But this rest is not always *perfect.* The more restive of the mental faculties sometimes continue awake after the others are composed. In absolutely profound sleep, — that is, a state in which *all* the mental faculties are entirely at rest, — there is, of course, no dreaming.

The involuntary functions of the body, in sleep, continue their course much the same as when we are awake. The heart beats, the blood flows, the lungs play, the organs of digestion operate, all the involuntary functions go on, as at other times, although with somewhat relaxed energy. With these some of the mental faculties are more closely allied than with others, and hence they are less easily suspended by sleep.

MENTAL ACTIVITY MAY BE ENTIRELY SUSPENDED.

Some suppose our mental activity is *never* entirely suspended, and that only *memory* is wanting, on waking from the profoundest sleep, to assure us that we have still been dreaming. But this supposition seems to be gratuitous. Our minds, in the present state, *need* repose, — the more perfect the better, — nor does it appear that all our mental powers do not more or less participate in it. Indeed, the relative time in which we dream is probably much less than is usually supposed. Our dreams, when in health, are mostly confined to a few moments after retiring, or, more frequently, to a few moments in the morning, thus preceding or following the hours of profound sleep.

WHAT FACULTIES ARE MOST ACTIVE IN DREAMING.

The faculties most active in dreaming are imagination and the passions, the more grave faculties of reason and judgment being usually suspended. Hence the trains of thought in sleeping are irregular and confused, like the movements of a mutilated or disturbed machine. To vary the illustration, the mind, in dreaming, is like a ship at sea without a helm. Imagination spreads the sails, passion fills them, but reason is wanting at the helm to guide. Dreams are thus mostly made up of strange and confused imaginings.*

THE LAWS OF ASSOCIATION CONTINUE TO OPERATE IN DREAMS.

So far as we can judge, the succession of our thoughts, in dreams, is regulated by the same laws of association as when we are awake. The objects which most interest us when awake are those of which we are wont to dream. The miser by day is the miser by night; his dreams are of money gained and money lost. The dreams of the student, whose thoughts when awake are with books and men of learning, take their direction and character from these objects. The dreams of the melancholy man are tinged with his peculiar temperament; whereas the man of cheerful disposition, if in good health, has ordinarily pleasant dreams. The shipmaster, after passing through perilous storms, and the general, after engaging in bloody battles, dream of new perils and fresh encounters.

" After having made a narrow escape from any alarming danger, we are apt to awake in the course of our sleep

* *Reverie* is a kind of dreaming state in which the rational will is not entirely suspended, but yields itself up to the pleasing illusions of imagination. It is thus an approach towards dreaming.

with sudden startings, imagining that we are drowning, or on the brink of a precipice. A severe misfortune, which has affected the mind deeply, influences our dreams in a similar way, and suggests to us a variety of adventures, analogous, in some measure, to that event from which our distress arises. Such, according to Virgil, were the dreams of the forsaken Dido." *

"Agit ipse furentem,
In somnis ferus Æneas; semperque relinqui,
Sola sibi; semper longam incomitata videtur,
Ire viam, et Tyrios deserta quærere terra."

SUSPENSION OF WILL IN DREAMING.

The most marked distinction between the succession of our thoughts in dreaming and when awake is in the fact that, when awake, our associations are under the control of the rational will; but when dreaming, this power of will is suspended.† This is the explanation of the extravagance and incoherence of our thoughts and conceptions. The suspension of the will suspends, of course, the voluntary exercises of reason, judgment, recollection, &c., thus leaving the associations to run on unrestrained. We hence bound in thought from one place to another, from one scene to another, and often confound objects and events of very remote realms and periods. Our associating power is as active as ever, but the rational will is wanting to control it.

REASONING IN SLEEP.

It is true that we sometimes reason in sleep, ‡ but this is accounted for on the *ground of association.* Processes

* Abercrombie's Intellectual Philosophy, p. 205.

† *Somnambulism* differs from ordinary sleep mainly in this, that the will retains its control over the bodily members. The man not only *imagines* himself walking, but actually *walks.* He labors under the same illusions as in ordinary dreaming, but the sleep has not so much composed the voluntary action of the body.

‡ "Dreaming persons sometimes reason better than they do when they

28

of reasoning to which we have become accustomed when awake will often go on spontaneously when we are dreaming. The man who never reasons when awake never reasons when asleep. Mathematicians have sometimes solved problems in dreaming which puzzled them when awake. The explanation is, that having accustomed their minds to such solutions, in the freedom from distraction secured by sleep, their associations spontaneously suggest the solution in question. This is done without any effort of the reasoning powers; it is a pure spontaneity.*

I am acquainted with a preacher of the gospel who was commencing to write a sermon, when, under the influence of headache, he dropped upon his bed and fell to dreaming about the subject of his study. He audibly named his text and went through his sermon. His wife being present, took it down in short hand. The sermon was subsequently written out and preached to his congregation, and was considered one of his most eloquent and effective discourses. It was doubtless a train of thought with which he had previously made his mind familiar, and in the composed state secured by sleep, his association naturally called it up, with perhaps more clearness and concentration than could have been secured amidst the distractions of his wakeful hours by the exercise of his rational will.

" The following anecdote has been preserved in a family of rank in Scotland, the descendants of a distinguished lawyer of the last age. This eminent person had been consulted respecting a case of great importance and

are awake. When we would reflect deeply upon any subject, we escape from the noise of the world and external impressions by covering our eyes with the hands; and putting a great number of organs to rest, we endeavor to concentrate all vital power in one or in several. In dreaming and in somnambulism this naturally happens; the functions of the active organs are then often more perfect and more energetic, the sensations more lively, and the reflections deeper than in the state of watching."—*Phrenology, by J. G. Spurzheim, M. D.* Boston edition, 1834.

* When in college, I was once laboring upon a very difficult problem in the higher mathematics, and not being able at the time to solve it, threw myself down in anxious study upon a couch, and fell into a dreamy state. In that state the solution occurred to me, and I awoke and readily solved the problem.

much difficulty, and he had been studying it with intense anxiety and attention. After several days had been occupied in this manner, he was observed by his wife to rise from his bed in the night and go to a writing desk which stood in the bed room. He then sat down and wrote a long paper, which he put carefully by in the desk, and returned to bed. The following morning he told his wife that he had a most interesting dream; that he had dreamed of delivering a clear and luminous opinion respecting a case which had exceedingly perplexed him; and that he would give any thing to recover the train of thought which had passed before him in his dream. She then directed him to the writing desk, where he found the opinion clearly and fully written out, and which was afterwards found to be perfectly correct." *

DREAMS APPEAR TO BE REALITIES.

Owing to the suspension of our rational and perceptive faculties, our dreams seem to be *realities*. Reason is not in action to teach us otherwise; neither does perception disabuse the mind of its errors by placing before it the realities of the external world. Hence dreaming places one in a very interesting predicament. The admonitions of the external world withdrawn, imagination turned loose, the mind is abandoned to the wildest suggestions of a headlong association; and whatever is thus dreamed has all the importance of reality. The most ridiculous forms, the most absurd anachronisms, the most contradictory conceits are not too extravagant to pass with the wisest philosopher for sober verities.

Such strange work does dreaming make with the mind. It places the learned and the ignorant, the wise and the simple, the rich and the poor upon the same level. They may feast together at the king's table, or expatiate together amid the glories of creation, or pine together in dungeons; and to all are these dreams alike realities.

* Abercrombie's Philosophy, p. 216.

IMPERFECT ESTIMATE OF TIME AND SPACE IN DREAMING

That our estimate of time and space in dreaming is so imperfect, is owing to the same cause to which we have referred in the above phenomena. Imagination, unguided by reason, being hurried from scene to scene by the mere impulses of a blind association, confounds times, places, events widely separated, and often condenses into a few moments the events of years. Something like this is realized in scenic exhibitions, where imagination takes the reins, and the sober calculations of reason are set aside. It is not strange, therefore, that, in such a state of mind as we have defined dreaming, this should be realized to perfection. The events of weeks and months are crowded into moments. We cross seas, explore distant continents, and return to our homes, all within the few moments of time that precede our rising from the morning pillow, after the profound slumbers of the night are ended.

"Dr. Gregory mentions a gentleman, who, after sleeping in a damp place, was for a long time liable to a feeling of suffocation whenever he slept in a lying posture; and this was always accompanied by a dream of a skeleton, which grasped him violently by the throat. He could sleep in a sitting posture without any uneasy feeling; and after trying various expedients, he at last had a sentinel placed beside him, with orders to awake him whenever he sunk down. On one occasion he was attacked by the skeleton, and a severe and long struggle ensued before he awoke. On finding fault with his attendant for allowing him to lie so long in such a state of suffering, he was assured that he had not lain an instant, but had been awakened the moment he began to sink.

"A friend of mine dreamed that he crossed the Atlantic and spent a fortnight in America. In embarking, on his return, he fell into the sea; and, having awoke with the fright, discovered that he had not been asleep above ten minutes." *

* Abercrombie's Philosophy, p. 202.

DREAMS RECALL THINGS FORGOTTEN.

Every person has observed that he sometimes dreams of things long since gone from his mind. This also is accounted for by the same cause as above. We remember mostly by means of association. When the reasoning powers are at rest, our association flies, unguided, from one thing to another, influenced only by those feelings of interest which may have been at any period awakened. Hence a certain mental predisposition may at any time lead to a recognition of things long since forgotten, merely by the *coincidence* between the *present* state of the mind and the *feelings which they inspired at the time of their occurrence.* Thus the wrecked and storm-beaten mariner dreams of forgotten incidents of childhood, in connection with his mother — his *mother*, to whom he was once accustomed to fly in trouble — trouble exciting feelings like the present.

Our associations operate by *contrast*, as well as resemblance, no less in dreaming than when awake; hence the man pining with hunger, in a desert, dreams of feasting again at a table at which he had eaten long before, and which he had ceased to remember. Old people often dream of incidents in their childhood of which they had not thought for many years.

DREAMS FROM BODILY SENSATION.

Most men have experienced the effects of certain *bodily sensations* upon dreams. An empty stomach occasions dreams of food, and of eating or attempting to eat; while recent or undigested food in the stomach, causing a sensation of oppression, leads to various unpleasant dreams, as of being confined under a weight, struggling to escape from danger, or laboring ineffectually to accomplish some work.*

* *Incubus*, or *nightmare*, is usually occasioned by indigestible food in the stomach, or by a sluggish circulation. It is characterized by a consciousness of an entire want of power over our bodily members, and is generally

In Abercrombie's Philosophy are furnished the following illustrations of this law: "Dr. Gregory mentions that, having on one occasion gone to bed with a vessel of hot water at his feet, he dreamed of walking up the crater of Mount Etna, and of feeling the ground warm under him. He had at an early period of his life visited Mount Vesuvius, and actually felt a strong sensation of warmth in his feet when walking up the side of the crater; but it was remarkable that the dream was not of Vesuvius, but of Etna, of which he had only read Brydon's description. This was probably from the latter impression being the most recent. On another occasion he dreamed of spending a winter at Hudson's Bay, and of suffering much distress from the intense frost. He found that he had thrown off the bedclothes in his sleep; and, a few days before, he had been reading a very particular account of the state of the colonies in that country during winter. Again, when suffering from toothache, he dreamed of undergoing the operation of tooth-drawing, with the additional circumstance that the operator drew a sound tooth, leaving the aching one in its place.

"But the most striking anecdote in this interesting document is one in which similar dreams were produced in a gentleman and his wife, at the same time, and by the same cause. It happened at the period when there was an alarm of French invasion, and almost every man in Edinburgh was a soldier. All things had been arranged in expectation of the landing of an enemy, the first notice of which was to be given by a gun from the castle, and this was to be followed by a chain of signals calculated to alarm the country in all directions. Further, there had been recently in Edinburgh a splendid military spectacle, in which five thousand men had been drawn up in Prince's Street, fronting the castle. The gentleman to whom the dream occurred, and who had

in connection with some unfavorable posture. I knew an aged gentleman who was in the habit of occasionally indulging, just before retiring, an appetite for a certain preparation of *cheese*. This seldom failed to produce *incubus*, in which he was found lying upon his back in the greatest distress, without the power of moving a finger.

been a most zealous volunteer, was in bed between two and three o'clock in the morning, when he dreamed of hearing a signal gun. He was immediately at the castle, witnessed the proceedings for displaying the signals, and saw and heard a great bustle over the town from troops and artillery assembling, especially in Prince's Street. At this time he was roused by his wife, who awoke in a fright in consequence of a similar dream, connected with much noise and the landing of an enemy, and concluding with the death of a particular friend of her husband's, who had served with him as a volunteer during the late war. The origin of this remarkable concurrence was ascertained, in the morning, to be the noise produced in the room above by the fall of a pair of tongs, which had been left in some very awkward position in support of a clothes screen.

"Dr. Reid relates of himself, that the dressing applied after a blister on his head having become ruffled so as to produce considerable uneasiness, he dreamed of falling into the hands of savages and being scalped by them."*

Such cases are easily accounted for on the same principle as those above. The absence of reason and judgment leaves imagination to all the natural workings of its spontaneity suggested by these bodily sensations. If only imagination is to decide, the dressing of a blister on the head might as naturally be referred to the operation of a scalping knife as to its true cause. Some incident in history, or some conversation, perhaps forgotten, revived in dreaming, would *turn the associations in that direction.*

The case of coincident dreaming of the man and his wife is clearly this: Their sympathies, thoughts, associations *were all enlisted in the same direction*, and their imaginations excited by the same external cause. There was precisely the same difference in their dreams which we should expect — the husband going forth to the action; the wife remaining at home, and being afflicted with the death of a friend.

* Abercrombie's Philosophy, p. 200.

ARE DREAMS EVER PROPHETIC?

That dreams have sometimes been made prophetic by God, when giving special revelations to man, is admitted by all who believe in the divine authority of the Bible. But the question respects the *present* time. I suppose that those dreams which are so fulfilled as to have a prophetic aspect, may be accounted for on *natural principles.*

In the first place, there may be a casual *coincidence* between the dream and the event, without any divine interposition. In the second place, the *causes* which led to the dream may conspire to produce the event. A man dreams of committing murder some time before he perpetrates the crime, because the elements of murder are already at work in his mind. A man dreams of meeting friends and of enjoying a delightful interview with them long before the event is actually realized, because the event is in anticipation.

A man, prostrate with rheumatism and under the influence of severe pains, dreamed that his servant cut a quantity of hemlock boughs, steeped them in water, and applied them hot to the diseased parts, and thus effected a cure. The next day he employed his servant to perform this service, with entire faith in the result, and the result was a cure, as he dreamed. He had doubtless heard of the efficacy of this article in cases of rheumatism; this led to the dream, and the dream suggested the steps towards its fulfilment, which faith contributed to the result. In all such cases, the thoughts and emotions which lead to the dream arise from the causes, and are themselves among the causes, conspiring to their fulfilment.

The following fact is mentioned by Dr. Abercrombie, and his explanation of it seems sound and rational: "A clergyman had come to this city (Edinburgh) from a short distance in the country, and was stopping at an inn, when he dreamed of seeing a fire, and one of his children in the midst of it. He awoke with the impression, and instantly left town on his return home. When he arrived within sight of his house, he found it on fire, and got there in time to assist in saving one of his children, who, in the alarm and confusion, had been left in a situation of danger. Without calling in question the possibility of supernatural communication in such cases, this striking occurrence, of which I believe there is little reason to doubt the truth, may perhaps be accounted for on simple and rational principles. Let us suppose that the gentleman had a servant who had shown great carelessness in regard to fire, and had often given rise in his mind to a strong apprehension that she might set fire to his house. His anxiety might be increased by being from home, and the same circumstance might make the servant still more careless. Let us further suppose that the gentleman, before going to bed, had, in addition to this anxiety, suddenly recollected that there was on that day, in the neighborhood of his house, some fair or periodical merry-making, from which the servant was very likely to return home in a state of intoxication. It was most natural that these impressions should be embodied into a dream of his house being on fire, and that the same circumstances might lead to the dream being fulfilled."

NO NEW SIMPLE IDEAS IN DREAMS.

It seems to be a well-settled fact, that, however complicated and novel the combinations of ideas in dreams, there are yet no other elemental or simple ideas than those obtained when awake by conversation and reflection. A man dreams of seeing a glass mountain; he has never actually seen that object, when awake, but he has seen glass, and he has seen a mountain. His imagination in dreaming combines these, and thus creates a glass mountain. He dreams of strange animals, and of various frightful or splendid scenes, such as his wakeful moments never even conceived; but on examination they are found to be *made up of elemental ideas*, obtained in the natural way when awake.

As dreams thus depend upon our perceptions, and our perceptions of *visible things* are the most *vivid*, our dreams are mostly conversant with *objects of sight.* We seldom hear, taste, smell, in dreaming, unless something is at the time addressed to the senses. If a man in dreaming hears thunder, or the report of a gun, or cries of distress, or sweet music, it is usually in connection with some noise within or near the house. If he dreams of tasting unsavory or delicious food, it is because of some disagreeable or agreeable taste actually in his mouth. If he dreams of sweet or unpleasant odors, there is usually something about him to occasion this sensation.

One of the most pleasing circumstances connected with *serenades* is, that, as the music breaks upon our ears while we are asleep, we often enjoy its effects in producing a kind of brilliant dream, before entire wakefulness dispels the illusion.

CONCLUDING REMARKS ON DREAMING.

I conclude that all the phenomena of dreaming are referable to the *same general cause — the suspension of some of the mental faculties.* According as the faculties are more or less suspended, and their action modified by incidental circumstances, dreams will vary. There seems to be no more mystery connected with our dreaming than with our wakeful hours. We clearly trace in each the workings of the same mind, according to the same laws of mental operation.

But dreams are, on the whole, undesirable. They imply an imperfect state of rest. Pleasant dreams are less exhausting than unpleasant ones; but even such were better dispensed with. We do others no good by our dreams, neither do we ordinarily benefit ourselves. It is the perfect rest of dreamless sleep from which we awake most refreshed. Every person should therefore endeavor to avoid dreaming. The habit of dreaming may be usually corrected by observing the following rules: —

1. Retire to rest *at suitable and uniform periods after eating*, so that there may be neither the sensation of hunger nor of oppression at the stomach. Very many

dreams are occasioned by taking food too near the time of retiring.

2. On going to bed, *throw off all care*, and compose the mind to sleep as soon as possible. To lie awake, anxiously thinking, will almost certainly lead to dreaming.

3. *Promptly rise in the morning at the first wakening.* Dreams occur mostly in the morning, after nature has obtained her needed rest. The sleep then obtained is forced and unsound, tending to exhaust the nervous system, and produce dreams on the following night.

4. *Avoid telling your dreams.* The more you make of them, the more troublesome they will become. Neglect them, and they will neglect you. The man who tells his dreams on awaking in the morning will scarcely fail to dream again on the following nights.

By taking appropriate food and exercise, retiring and rising at suitable hours, maintaining a cheerful temper, and never paying any attention to what is dreamed, the habit of dreaming may be usually corrected, and that perfect soundness of sleep secured which is so conducive to health and long life.

QUESTIONS ON CHAPTER X.

What is dreaming? What functions continue their course? Remarks? What do some suppose as to the suspension of our mental activity? What reply to this? What faculties most active in dreaming? Explain. Do the laws of association continue to operate in dreams? How shown? What is the most marked distinction between the succession of our thoughts in dreaming and when awake? Of what is this the explanation? Do we reason in sleep? How accounted for? Illustrate. What is said of a preacher? Anecdote from a family in Scotland? Do dreams seem to be realities? Why? What strange work does dreaming make with the mind? What is said of our estimate of *time* and *space* in dreaming? Illustrations? Dr. Gregory's fact? Do dreams recall things forgotten? How explained? What is said of *contrast?* Illustrate. Of dreams from bodily sensations? Instances cited from Dr. Gregory? Reid's personal fact? Explain these cases. Are dreams prophetic? What is said of apparently prophetic dreams in the *first* place? In the *second* place? Illustrations? Case of the man prostrate with rheumatism? Fact and explanation by Abercrombie? Have we any new simple ideas in dreams? Explain. With what objects are our dreams most conversant? Illustrate. What is one of the most pleasing circumstances connected with *serenades?* Concluding remarks? What is said of the *undesirableness* of dreams? *First* rule for avoiding them? *Second? Third? Fourth?* State the whole together, with concluding remark.

PART V.

ABNORMAL MENTAL STATES.

CHAPTER I.

INSANITY.

Having examined the intellectual powers in those developments which may be considered *normal* or *regular*, let us devote some time to those phenomena which may be considered *abnormal* or *irregular*. They are mental acts more or less extraordinary, being the result of disease, or of peculiar occasional causes from without. They may be considered under the following heads: *Insanity*, *Mesmeric States*, *Apparent Death*, and *Trance*. We will begin with the first of these.

Insanity always implies a DISEASED STATE OF MIND. Diseases of the mind, as well as of the body, belong most properly to medical treatises, and, for obvious reasons, it is inexpedient to portray, at length, causes of mental derangement for the indiscriminate perusal of the young. I shall therefore be brief upon this subject.

WHEREIN DREAMING AND INSANITY ARE ALIKE.

Dreaming and insanity are analogous in these two respects: in both, the mind's imaginings are mistaken for realities; and in both, the thoughts succeed each other as suggested by associations, uncontrolled by the rational will. Thus Dr. Abercrombie, whose authority is very good on this subject, remarks, "It appears, then, that there is a remarkable analogy between the mental phenomena in insanity and in dreaming, and that the leading peculiarities of both these conditions are referable to two heads:—

"1. The impressions which arise in the mind are believed to be real and present existences, and this belief is not corrected by comparing the conception with the actual state of things in the external world.

"2. The chains of ideas or images which arise follow one another according to certain associations over which the individual has no control; he cannot, as in a healthy state, vary the series, or stop it at his will." *

WHEREIN DREAMING AND INSANITY DIFFER.

Dreaming and insanity are essentially *different* in the following respects:—

1. In *dreaming*, a part of the mental faculties is in a state of *rest;* in *insanity*, they are in a state of *diseased action.* Hence the former is *transient*, the latter *permanent.* As the former results from only a *dormant* state of some of the faculties of a *sound* mind, we only need to arouse them to service, to restore the balance of mental action; but as the latter implies a *diseased* state, the rousing up of the faculties no more restores sane action to the mind than the waking up of a sick man restores health to his body.

2. In *dreaming*, we are ordinarily *insensible to the objects around us.* The eyes are usually closed, and all the other organs of perception are composed to rest. But in cases of insanity, there is ordinarily a *high degree of sensibility* in relation to surrounding objects and events. Indeed, the perceptions of insane persons are often remarkably keen. All who have been conversant with

* Intellectual Philosophy, p. 226.

them must have noticed how quick a word, a look, an action, even a cautious whisper, is by them perceived and interpreted.

Some have supposed that in the higher states of disease the subject becomes insensible, as in dreaming, to external objects. Thus Dr. Abercrombie says, "In the higher states, or what we call perfect mania, we see them exemplified in the same complete manner as in dreaming. The maniac fancies himself a king possessed of boundless power, and surrounded by every form of earthly splendor; and with all his bodily senses in their perfect exercise, this hallucination is in no degree corrected by the sight of his bed of straw and all the horrors of his cell." *

But there is still this difference: in dreaming, the subject takes no notice of surrounding objects; in the mania supposed, the subject *notices* the bed of straw and the cell, but his disordered imagination transforms them to a throne and a palace. The idea that maniacs are insensible to surrounding objects has often led to a neglect of their external condition. The "bed of straw and all the horrors of his cell" is what *no maniac should be subjected to:* an imagination transforming them into circumstances of power and splendor is the rare portion of the few triumphantly intent on making the best of their wretchedness.

MONOMANIA.

One of the most common forms of insanity is that in which the mind is diseased in reference to *one particular subject*, and sound in reference to all others. This is what the name imports—*monomania.* It is no uncommon thing for men to become highly nervous or excitable on one subject only. It is, perhaps, one on which their feelings have been much tried, or in which they have a special interest.

Disappointed *lovers; misers* who have met with severe losses; ardent *philanthropists* who have been thwarted

* Intellectual Philosophy, p. 226.

in their prospects of reform; men severely tried in their *religious* experiencc; persons under deep *affliction*, — are all very liable to this disordered mental action. Where the excitement becomes *intense* and *absorbing*, so that the one impression controls the mind, despite of reason, it is *monomania*. The proper balance of mind, in reference to a particular subject, is lost. The line between that *eccentricity*, or *oneideaism*, as some have termed it, which merely magnifies a subject above its relative importance and real monomania, is not distinctly drawn; the one gradually merges into the other.

In cases of decided monomania, the victim of the disease usually continues to be morbidly excited upon one and the same subject, and sane upon all others, until the restoration of health or the close of life. But sometimes the hallucination changes from one subject to another. A man mentioned by some medical authority was haunted several years with the idea of being poisoned; his hallucination became suddenly changed; he imagined himself lord of the world, and enjoyed the pleasing illusion until death. This seems to be accounted for on the principle of reaction. When the mind has been long pressed to an extreme point in one direction, it sometimes vibrates and passes to an opposite extreme.

ORIGIN AND PROGRESS OF INSANITY.

Insanity usually first discovers itself by *some slight deviations from the ordinary mental action*. The subject of it is unusually *depressed*, *light minded*, *absent*, or *irritable*. He begins, perhaps, to labor under some illusion. He imagines that some person has attempted to poison him, or to injure his character or property. He becomes exceedingly jealous and suspicious, and sometimes revengeful. At other times his imagination presents a pleasing picture: he fancies himself about to be promoted to distinction and wealth, and embarks in visionary projects. His friends notice these things with surprise, and begin to blame and rebuke him, not as yet suspecting the true cause. The disorder goes gradually on, until at length it develops itself in actions so decidedly irrational as to unmask the disease.

The fact that insanity usually advances slowly is very important, as serving to assist in detecting both the incipient *stages* of the disease, and also *pretensions* to it. When a person exhibits symptoms of insanity immediately after being detected in some crime, without having previously exhibited the same, or something approaching them, his case is very suspicious.

There may be sudden derangements of mind from a fall or fright, the death of a friend, or a fever: these are not usually chronic, are clearly traced to their cause, and therefore form no serious exception to the above remark.

PECULIAR CHARACTER OF INSANITY.

"The peculiar character of insanity," says Dr. Abercrombie, "in all its modifications, appears to be, that a certain impression has fixed itself upon the mind in such a manner as to exclude others; or to exclude them from that influence which they ought to have on the mind, in its estimate of the relations of things. This impression may be entirely visionary and unfounded; or it may be in itself true, but distorted in the application which the unsound mind makes of it, and the consequences which are deduced from it. Thus a man of wealth fancies himself a beggar, and in danger of dying of hunger. Another takes up the same impression, who has, in fact, sustained some considerable loss. In the one, the impression is entirely visionary, like that which might occur in a dream; in the other, it is a real and true impression, carried to consequences which it does not warrant." *

Insanity is also, perhaps, always characterized by an unusual stupor, or a greatly increased activity of mind, or more commonly by the alternations of both. The former is an approach to idiocy; the latter, to something superhuman. The latter is by far the more common. Imagination becomes exceedingly fertile, memory quick

* Intellectual Philosophy, p. 250.

and exact, conception rapid, and comparisons are made and inferences drawn, right or wrong, with wonderful readiness. Persons of ordinary parts have, in such paroxysms of insanity, surprised their friends by the exhibition of genius.

But such mental fervors are at the expense of permanent intellectual vigor, and even of life. Persons liable to periodical attacks of insanity have sometimes even anticipated them with impatience, on account of the pleasure afforded by the preternatural excitement. But in most cases the pain immeasurably surpasses the pleasure; and in all cases there is a rapid wearing down of the mental energies, and hastening towards the destruction of all that renders life desirable. In every view, we must consider insanity amongst the greatest of all earthly calamities; and instead of filling our pages with its painful and startling pictures, I may, perhaps, more profitably conclude the chapter with some account of its *causes* and *preventives*. I shall notice them together.

Among the causes of insanity, the following are most prominent: —

1. Hereditary Tendency. A predisposition to this disease seems to follow some families through several generations. This has been especially noticed among families who have long been in the habit of intermarrying. Where the children of brothers or sisters, or others nearly related by blood, intermarry, evil tendencies on each side, instead of being counteracted, as in cross marrying, are *perpetuated and increased*. Consumption, sterility, idiocy, and insanity are all more or less inclined to follow these unnatural affiances.

The *prevention*, therefore, in this case, is obvious. But where persons have themselves actually *inherited* the predisposition in question, it may be much counteracted and resisted by observing the directions that will be given subsequently.

2. Vice. All kinds of vice tend to derange the mental functions; but those most directly tending to insanity are *intemperance* and *licentiousness*. The statistics of insane hospitals prove that a very large proportion of

their inmates have become such by one or both of these vices. By irritating and exhausting the nervous system, producing chronic inflammation of the brain, prostrating the digestive functions, and impairing the mental energies, they lead to the utter dethronement of reason.

Here, again, the *prevention* is at hand; let every youth, as he would be safe from this terrible disease, be ever strictly *temperate* and *virtuous*. Many a youth has destroyed himself by *secret* vices, long before his parents or guardians suspected them. It should be remembered that the *effect* in question does not follow the vice *immediately*, but often after succeeding months and years.

3. NOVEL READING. Many imaginative youth, particularly of the more delicate sex, have brought upon themselves a nervousness, resulting in insanity, by an *indiscreet and absorbing devotion to fictitious tales.* By exalting the imagination to a region of exciting fiction, in which the realities of life are neglected, the proper mental balance is finally lost. Fancies, dreams, illusions, all the maniac forms of hallucination, naturally follow.

One of the most interesting and accomplished young ladies of a certain place not distant became excessively devoted to novels. Without the knowledge of her parents, she was in the habit of sitting up in her chamber, and poring over them, long after the family had retired. She first manifested some flightiness of mind at breakfast. The next morning it was repeated, with other eccentricities. The father, who was a physician, mistrusted something wrong, and on inquiry, learned the course his daughter had been pursuing. But it was too late. She soon became a confirmed maniac, and has been for several years in an insane hospital, without the least prospect of being ever removed from it but by death. Several somewhat similar instances have fallen under the limited observation of the writer.

Here, again, the prevention is plain. The reading of fiction should be restricted within narrow and cautious limits; and where there is the least tendency to insanity, the mind should be kept as familiar as possible with the sober but cheerful *realities* and *duties* of life, and as *much removed as possible from whatever unduly excites the imagination.*

4. Overworking the Brain. Students, professional men, inventors, merchants in times of financial pressure, and all men intensely and anxiously employing their minds upon any subject of study, are liable to exhaust the intellectual nerve, and bring on permanent mental derangement. The first scholar in the writer's class in college became insane from too severe application to study. He has since died in a lunatic asylum. Cases of insanity among gentlemen of the several professions, particularly those of law and divinity, resulting from overtaxing the brain, are familiar to all.

There is also a class of persons highly ingenious, whose minds are intensely occupied with inventions of machinery, who are particularly liable to insanity. The perpetual and absorbing study of profound and intricate problems gradually exhausts the brain. It has also appeared from the statistics of our asylums, that, after seasons of great financial trouble and disaster, not a few of their unhappy inmates have been furnished from gentlemen in mercantile business.

In all these cases, to know the *cause* is to know the *prevention.* All men whose pursuits lead to great mental effort should advance cautiously. There is scarcely a limit to the power of mental action, provided it be approached gradually. The mind gathers firmness and strength as it advances; but unduly pressed, especially in its earlier stages, it may lose its balance forever.

5. Religious Melancholy. When the mind is for a long time in a state of deep anxiety and gloom in respect to religion, it is very liable to become permanently deranged. Some decided cases of this description have fallen under my observation.

The wife of a distinguished lawyer, devoted to gayety and fashion, became depressed and gloomy in consequence of many of her gay friends becoming religious. At length she quite withdrew from society, and for several weeks remained at home in a state of deep despondency. One night she took the keys of the several closets and other apartments of her house, and after putting things in order, locked them up, and delivered the keys to the servant, with the declared intention of going on a journey the next day. The next morning she awoke with decided symptoms of insanity. She was under a course of treatment for that disease about two years, at her own dwelling. One morning, on awaking, she arose and dressed herself, went to the room of her servant, and demanded the keys. She imagined that she had just returned from her intended journey. From that moment her symptoms of insanity disappeared; she became perfectly well, and lived many years a consistent Christian.

Another lady, after a long period of deep religious gloom, fell a victim to the illusion that she had committed the unpardonable sin. On this point her mind became perfectly insane. No reasoning could convince her, no light from heaven could irradiate the dark chamber of her mind. She *knew* that she was to be lost, and it was in vain to do any thing for her. She described the horrors of perdition with a boldness and power of imagery seldom equalled, and concluded by saying, "This is all to be my portion."

A course of judicious medical treatment, with subsequent journeying and change of scenery and employment, dispelled the illusion and restored the mental balance. She is still living, a very devoted and useful Christian.

There is now, in one of our asylums, a man suffering under the idea that his soul is in perdition. Some years since he resisted very strong religious convictions, and at length became gloomy, and at last insane. Converse with him on most other subjects, and he appears much as men do in sound mind; but the moment any allusion is made to his spiritual condition, he is in the greatest *conceivable distress, declaring that the miseries* of perdition have taken hold of him.

The prevention of such unhappy cases is to be found, not in putting religion aside, — for the religious wants of man will rebel against this, and take occasion from it to induce the deeper gloom, — but to bring Christianity to bear *fully* upon the mind, *with all her healing and gracious power.* If the mind is actually diseased, other remedies should not be wanting. But the testimony of our most distinguished physicians, conversant with this subject, is decisive to the point, that such are the moral wants of the soul, that Christianity, contemplated *in its true character and bearings, is among the most important of all means*, both for the prevention and cure of insanity. Hence the reading of the Scriptures and a system of chaplaincy are becoming a part of the curative system of our lunatic asylums.

Other causes of insanity, such as gambling, frequent theatre-going, dissipating amusements continued late at night, jealousies and disappointments in matters of love, are familiar to most, and their prevention is obvious. In general, *the saneness of our intellect is mostly at our own disposal;* and a wise regard to the preventives of insanity might save thousands from that dreadful calamity into which they are rushing.

QUESTIONS ON CHAPTER I.

What is insanity? Wherein are dreaming and insanity *alike?* Remarks of Dr. Abercrombie? *First* particular in which dreaming and insanity *differ?* *Second?* What have some supposed respecting the higher states of the disease? What says Abercrombie? Answer to him? What is monomania? Examples? What is said of cases of decided monomania? How does insanity usually first discover itself? Explain. What importance to the fact that insanity advances slowly? Any exceptions to the fact? What is the peculiar character of insanity? What is said of insanity being characterized by *stupor* or increased *activity* of mind? Remarks? *First* mentioned cause of insanity? In what families is it especially noticed? Remarks? *Second* cause? Remarks? Prevention? *Third* cause? How explained? Instance cited? Prevention? *Fourth* cause? Illustrations? What is said of highly ingenious minds? What has appeared from the statistics of asylums? *Fifth* cause? Example? Instance of another lady? Another instance? The *prevention?* To what point is the best medical testimony? Concluding remark?

CHAPTER II.

MESMERIC STATES.

In a recent distinguished work on Human Physiology, the learned author says, "It appears that the time has now come, when a tolerably definite opinion may be formed regarding a large number of the phenomena commonly included in the term *mesmerism*. Notwithstanding the exposures of various pretenders which have taken place from time to time, there remains a considerable mass of phenomena which cannot be so readily disposed of, and which appears to have as just a title to the attention of scientific physiologists as that which is possessed by any other class of well-ascertained facts." *

OPINIONS OF SCIENTIFIC MEN.

The most that is usually admitted on this subject by the more cautious men of science is, that a state of *coma*, more or less profound and peculiar, may be produced by *titillation*. That the gentle passage of one's hands over another's head, or any agreeable and soothing action upon the person, tends to compose the nervous system, and induce sleep, is within the experience of all. And it is observed that some are much more subject to such influ-

* Principles of Human Physiology, by William B. Carpenter, M. D., F. R. S., F. G. S., Examiner in Physiology in the University of London, &c., &c., p. 731. This is the most recent and comprehensive work on physiology, comprising the best authorities and most important discoveries down to the present time.

ences than others. While persons of iron nerve can be scarcely affected in this way, persons of feeble nerve can sometimes be put to sleep with ease.

But even among persons the most sensitive, there is a wide difference; some being morbidly wakeful, others morbidly disposed to coma. This influence may be sometimes exerted without contact. By a gentle movement of the fingers, at a little distance from the head and arms of the patient, a kind of magnetic influence is made to pass from the operator upon him.

WHAT MESMERISM CLAIMS TO DO.

But modern mesmerism claims to do *more.* How much was actually done or claimed by him whose name it bears is a matter of some question, not important here. As advocated at the present time, it claims that mesmerizers acquire such power over some mesmerized persons, that the minds of the latter become, in their operations, identified with those of the former, so as to think, imagine, desire, love, hate, suffer, enjoy, choose only as the former *will;* and more than this, that the mesmerized subject may be put into what is called a *clairvoyant* state — a state in which he not only thinks and feels as he is willed to do, but actually *sees* and *reveals* distant objects and events, at the will of the mesmerizer. These are certainly very high claims; whether the foundation is broad enough to sustain them, must be left to the reader's judgment.

CONDITIONS OF PRODUCING THE MESMERIZED STATE.

It is claimed that one person may be put into the mesmerized state by another, under the following conditions: —

1. The operator must sustain to the patient the relation of a *positive* to a *negative;* the *potentiality* pertaining to the former, the *susceptibility* to the latter.
2. The operator must *concentrate his thoughts and*

feelings, so as firmly to WILL the result, with the *full expectation of securing it.*

3. There must be an entire *agreement* between the parties, the will of the patient being entirely resigned to that of the operator.

4. The result may be *facilitated* by the gentle passage of the operator's hand over the head of the patient; but this is not essential, as the act is considered mostly mental.

5. No *disturbing* cause must be allowed to interrupt the process, but the free and full action of mind over mind must be allowed to take effect.

6. The *first* operation usually requires *more time and effort* to produce the result than is needed on subsequent occasions. The connection once established facilitates future results.

EFFECTS PRODUCED ON THE PATIENT.

The substance of most that I shall say under this head is taken from the Physiology of Dr. Carpenter, to whom, of course, belongs whatever of responsibility or of credit it may demand. The principal phenomena, which he regards as "having been veritably presented in a sufficient number of instances to entitle them to be considered as genuine and regular manifestations of the peculiar bodily and mental condition under discussion," are the following: —

1. "A state of complete *coma*, or perfect insensibility, analogous in its mode of access and departure to that which is known as the hysteric coma, and, like it, usually distinguishable from the coma of cerebral oppression by a constant twinkling movement of the eyelids. In this condition, severe surgical operations may be performed without any consciousness on the part of the patient; and it is not unfrequently found that the state of torpor extends from the cerebrum and sensoria ganglia to the medulla oblongata, so that the respiratory movements become seriously interfered with, and a state of partial asphyxia supervenes."* These phenomena have been

* Physiology, p. 732.

frequently witnessed among us. I have often seen surgical operations of the most painful kind performed upon patients in this state, without producing in them the least sensation.

2. A state of *somnambulism*. In this state the patient exhibits all the varieties of phenomena pertaining to natural sleep walking;* from a very limited activity of the mental powers, to a state of complete *double consciousness*, in which he manifests all the ordinary powers of his mind; but, after the spell is broken, remembers nothing of what has passed. In this state, the thoughts of the patient are usually much under the direction of the operator, being guided by the principle of suggestion, without any correction from the teachings of common experience.

The emotional powers are more excited than the purely intellectual, and the attention may be so completely fixed upon one object as to produce an entire insensibility to all impressions not connected with it. There is, in this respect, a correspondence with the phenomena of ordinary somnambulism; but there is this difference, that the mind is more subject to external influence, and may, therefore, be more readily played upon by the operator. Insensibility to pain may be produced in this state nearly as complete as that which occurs in the comatose state mentioned above, by causing the mind to be exclusively directed towards another object.†

* "The state of [natural] somnambulism appears to be nearer to that of wakeful activity of the whole mind than is that of dreaming. In the latter condition, the individual is unconscious of external objects; for, if they produce an effect upon him, it is in modifying the current of ideas, frequently in some extraordinary manner; and he does not form any true perception or idea of their nature. But in somnambulism, his senses are partly awake, so that impressions made upon them may be properly represented to the mind, and excite there the ideas with which they are connected; moreover, the cerebellum is also awake, so that the movements which the individual performs are perfectly adapted to their object. Indeed, it has frequently occurred that the power of balancing the body has been so remarkably exercised in this condition, that sleep walkers have traversed narrow and difficult paths, on which they could not have passed in open day, when conscious of their danger." — *Carpenter's Physiology*, p. 373.

† The "*double consciousness*" referred to above has its parallel in natural phenomena induced by disease or over-sleeping. Dr. Spurzheim says, "It is not true that consciousness is always single, either in reference to external

3. *An extraordinary exaltation of one or more of the senses.* In this state, the patient becomes susceptible of influences which, in his natural condition, would be unnoticed. In speaking of the senses, I had occasion to mention instances in which some of them, even in their

senses or to the internal faculties. There are diseased persons who see all objects double. Numbers of madmen hear angels singing, or devils roaring, only on one side. One of Gaul's friends, a physician, often complained that he could not think in the left side of his head; the right side was one inch higher than his left.

"There are other sorts of remarkable cases, which prove that consciousness is not always single. Mr. Combe (System of Phrenology, p. 108) quotes from the Medical Repository the case of a Miss R. in the United States, who naturally possessed a very good constitution, and arrived at adult age without having it impaired by disease. Without any forewarning, she fell into a profound sleep, which continued several hours beyond the ordinary time. On waking, she was discovered to have lost every trait of acquired knowledge. Her memory was *tabula rasa.* All vestiges both of words and things were obliterated and gone. It was found necessary for her to learn every thing again. She even acquired, by new efforts, the art of spelling, reading, writing, and calculating, and gradually became acquainted with the persons and objects around, like a being for the first time brought into the world. In these exercises she made considerable proficiency.

"But after a few months, another fit of somnolency invaded her. On rousing from it, she found herself restored to the state she was before the first paroxysm, but was wholly ignorant of every event and occurrence that had befallen her afterwards. The former condition of her existence she called the old state, and the latter the new state; and she was as unconscious of her double character as two distinct persons are of their respective natures. During four years and upwards, she had undergone periodical transitions from one of these states to another. The alterations were always consequent upon a long and sound sleep. In her old state, she possessed all her original knowledge; in her new state, only what she acquired since. If a gentleman or lady be introduced to her in the old state, or *vice versa*, and so of all other matters, to know them satisfactorily, she must learn them in both states. In the old state, she possesses fine powers of penmanship; while in the new, writes a poor, awkward hand, not having had time or means to become expert. In January, 1816, both the lady and her family were able to conduct affairs without embarassment. By quickly knowing whether she is in the old state or the new, they regulate their intercourse, and govern themselves accordingly. The Rev. Timothy Alden, of Meadville, has drawn up a history of this curious case." — *Spurzheim's Phrenology*, vol. i. pp. 76, 77.

After citing other cases, the author adds, "The same phenomena present themselves when in a state of somnambulism produced by animal magnetism. It has been repeatedly observed that some magnetized persons acquire a new consciousness and memory during their magnetic sleep. When this state has subsided, all that passed in it is obliterated, and the recollection of the ordinary state is restored. If the magnetic sleep is recalled again, the memory and the circumstances which occurred in that state are restored, so that the individuals may be said to live in a state of double consciousness." — *Ibid.*

natural state, manifested very uncommon powers. It is not incredible, therefore, that, under the influence of disease, or some other powerfully exciting cause, they should sometimes give symptoms of extraordinary exaltation.

Dr. Carpenter gives an account of a lad in a state of natural somnambulism, who had his sense of smell so remarkably heightened as to be able to assign, without the least hesitation, a glove placed in his hand to its right owner, in the midst of about thirty persons, the boy himself being blindfolded.*

But the sense whose powers are more particularly exalted, and to which most importance is attached, is that of *sight*. In states of natural somnambulism, this sense has been frequently so heightened as to discern objects in the dark, and through various media which ordinarily quite obstruct vision. The same is claimed for it in those states of artificial somnambulism which are produced by mesmeric influences.

Not long since, I witnessed the following phenomenon: A woman, with her eyes shut and eyelids held firmly together by another person, saw distinctly, and named, every object which was held before her. There was no possible chance for any trick or illusion. But when a solid, opaque substance was interposed between her eyes and the object presented, she could not see it. Her eyelids may have been uncommonly thin and translucent, and her sense of sight in a state of extraordinary exaltation.

It is not incredible that the mind should be made so to concentrate its energies in a certain organ, and that the action of this organ should be so increased, as to require only a tenth or a hundredth part of the usual cause from without to produce sensation and perception. That amount of light which ordinarily seems to the eye almost darkness may suffice, under this extraordinary exaltation of the sense, to enable the patient to see clearly. But this is by no means tantamount to seeing without *any* light. Somnambulists may see to read through bandages and with closed eyelids; but when a plate of

* Physiology, p. 399.

solid metal is interposed, they cannot discern a letter. Whatever is absolutely impervious to light is fatal to sensuous vision.

4. The *muscular* system may be excited to action *in unusual modes and with unusual energy.*

"Notwithstanding the fallacy of many of the cases of cataleptic rigidity which have been publicly exhibited," says Dr. Carpenter, "the author is satisfied, from investigations privately made, of the possibility of artificially inducing this condition. A slight irritation of the muscles themselves, or of the skin which covers them, — as by drawing the points of the fingers over them, or even wafting currents of air over the surface, — is sufficient to excite the tonic muscular contraction, which may continue in sufficient force to suspend a considerable weight for a longer period than it could be kept up by any conceivable effort of voluntary power.

"Further, by directing the attention exclusively to any set of muscles, and by impressing the mind of the somnambulist with the facility of the action to be performed, a very extraordinary degree of muscular power may be called forth, even in very feeble individuals. Thus the author has seen a man of extremely low muscular development and small stature not only lift up a twenty-eight pound weight upon his little finger, but even swing it round his head with the greatest apparent facility, having been previously assured that it was as light as a feather. Upon taking up the same weight upon their own little fingers, the author and his friends were very glad to lay it down after raising it a foot from the ground; and the subject of this experiment (a respectable, middle-aged man, who was not an 'exhibiter,' and upon whom no suspicion of any kind rested) declined, when in his waking state, even attempting to lift the weight, on the ground that it would strain him too much." *

* There seems to be a resemblance between the states produced by mesmerism and cases of *electro-biology*, although in some respects they differ. The abnormal mental states are quite as extraordinary in the latter case as in the former, while those of the body are perhaps still stranger. I have recently witnessed some striking illustrations of electro-biology in a private circle of some dozen persons. A gentleman experimented upon a young man about twenty-two years old. The character of the parties forbids all

"These are the principal phenomena of artificial somnambulism," continues the learned doctor, "in regard to which the author finds his mind made up. He does not see why any discredit should be attached to them, since they correspond, in all essential particulars, with those of states which naturally or spontaneously occur in many individuals, and which he has had opportunity of personally observing in cases in which the well-known characters of the parties placed them above suspicion.

"When the facility with which the mind of the somnambulist is played on by suggestions, conveyed either in

suspicion of any trick or deception; moreover, the young man operated upon had never read nor attended any lectures upon this subject, and knew nothing about it.

Having practised the appropriate movements upon the patient, the operator closed the patient's eyes, and then told him to open them if he could. He could not open them. After straining in vain for some time, he was told that he might open them; he then instantly opened them with the usual ease. In like manner, without touching the patient's person, the operator stopped him while walking, so that he stood like a post, unable to move in any direction; he told him to lay his hands on his head, and when laid there he could not remove them; he told him to extend them in front and bring them together, and when so brought together he could not separate them; he told him to sit down, and when seated he could not rise; in a word, in whatever position the operator placed him, in that position he was compelled to remain, with muscles as firm as iron, until he was permitted to move.

The operator told him that he had come into company strangely dressed; that he had on a green coat, yellow vest, white pantaloons, and red boots; finally, that he was a *negro;* he believed it all, until the illusion was removed by the operator. He placed a staff in his hands, compelled him to hold it, and while he was holding it, made him think it was a snake bending up its head to bite him. The poor young man writhed in agony, and tried to throw the monster from his hands, but could not until told that he might. The operator made him think that he had cut off his right hand, and he realized all the pain, the bleeding, the anxiety of such a calamity. The operator made him mistake cold water for water boiling hot, for vinegar, for wormwood, &c., and to experience all the effects from handling and tasting it which these agents severally produce. He made him think that he threw a rope over the moon, drew it down to him, and found it to be a large green cheese. He seemed much amused, but not surprised.

The operator had such entire control over the patient's *mind*, as well as *muscles*, that whatever *impression* he made upon it continued upon it, and had all the force of a reality, until he removed it. In whatever position or motion he put the body, and whatever impression he made upon the mind, the same continued until he changed it; and he changed it without touching the patient, by only speaking to him. During the whole time, the patient was perfectly conscious of what was said and done, and recollected all his impressions and feelings after the spell was over. In this respect, as well as some others, cases of electro-biology differ from ordinary mesmeric states Yet they seem to be essentially the same in their general character.

language or by other sensations which excite associated ideas, and the absence of the corrective power ordinarily supplied by past experience, are duly kept in view, many of the supposed 'higher phenomena' of mesmerism may be accounted for, without regarding the patient, on the one hand, as possessed of extraordinary powers of divination, or, on the other, as practising deception. Thus bearing in mind that somnambulism is an acted dream, the course of which is governed by external impressions, it is easy to understand how the subject of it may be directed, by leading questions, to enter buildings which he has never seen, and to describe scenes which he has never witnessed, without any intentional deceit.

"The love of the marvellous, so strongly possessed by many of the witnesses of such exhibitions, prompts them to grasp at and to exaggerate the coincidences in all such performances, and to neglect the failures; and hence reports are given to the public which, when the real truth of them is known, prove to have been the results of a series of guesses, the correctness of which is in direct relation to the amount of guidance afforded by the questions themselves.

"In like manner, the manifestations of the excitement of 'phrenological organs' seem to depend upon the conveyance of a suggestion to the patient, either through his knowledge of their supposed seat, or through the anticipations expressed by the bystanders. Many instances are recorded in which the intention has been stated of exciting one organ whilst the finger has been placed upon or pointed at another, and the resulting manifestation has always been that which would flow from the former. It does not hence follow that intentional deception is practised by the somnambulist, since the condition of mind already referred to causes it to respond to the suggestion which is most strongly conveyed to it.

"Many of the emotional states are readily excitable by placing the muscles in the condition which naturally expresses them: thus the combative tendency may be called forth by gently flexing the fingers so as to double the fist; a cheerful, hilarious mood may be induced by drawing outwards the corners of the mouth, as in laughter; and this may be exchanged for the reverse state of gloom and ill temper, by drawing the eyebrows downwards and towards each other, as in frowning. In like manner, on putting the hand upon the vertex, the somnambulist draws himself up, and shows the manifestations of self-esteem; whilst the depression of the head into the position of humility calls for the corresponding emotion.

"Those who have carefully observed the habits of infants and young children, must perceive the accordance of these phenomena with those which continually present themselves at that early period of life when the condition of the mind is so completely under the government of suggestions received from without.

"In regard to the alleged powers, which are said to be possessed by many somnambulists, of reading with the eyes completely covered, or of discerning words enclosed in opaque boxes, the author need only here express his complete conviction that no case of this description has ever stood the test of a searching investigation." *

METHOD OF INDUCING SOMNAMBULISM.

The somnambulic state is frequently induced by the ordinary process of mesmerism. But there are other methods of inducing it. "The modes in which the artificial somnambulism may be induced," says Dr. Carpenter, "are extremely various. The experiments of Mr. Braid have shown that one of the most essential is the continued convergence of the eyes upon a bright object, held at a small distance above and in front of them, and gradually approximated towards them. The more steady direction of the eyes towards a distant object, in persons who have often practised the former method, frequently serves to induce this state.

"All the phenomena described in the preceding paragraphs have been witnessed by the author in individuals thus 'hypnotized;' and he considers that this curious class of observations cannot be better prosecuted than by

* Carpenter's Physiology, pp. 732, 733.

the employment of that method. He is not yet satisfied that, in the ordinary mesmeric process, any other influence than this is really exerted; but the patient is sent to sleep with the dominant idea that some influence is exercised by the mesmerizer, and this idea affects all the subsequent phenomena — producing, for example, in some cases, insensibility to every thing but what is said by the mesmerizer, or by an individual placed by him *en rapport* with the somnambulist.

"It will generally be found, that the degree of this supposed connection depends upon the notions of it previously formed by the individual mesmerized. In the hypnotic state, there is an entire absence of any such peculiar influence, the somnambulist being equally conscious of what is said or done by every bystander." *

CONCLUSION.

If the above views are correct, the line of demarcation between the *terra cognita* and the *terra incognita*, in relation to this subject, is pretty distinctly defined. A state of artificial coma, somnambulism, exaltation of the senses, increased muscular energy, in connection with the effect of the operator's mind guiding that of the patient by suggestions, is fully conceded as the result of mesmeric influence; and to this we may undoubtedly add whatever of charm, fascination, and other pleasing and painful excitements would naturally attend such extraordinary states.

Thus far science clearly conducts us; all beyond seems somewhat involved in uncertainty. Yet we ought to hold ourselves ever subject to the teachings of experience and of well-ascertained facts; it is impossible to foretell to what scientific conclusions they may yet bring us. The history of the past is too replete with instruction to allow prejudice or pride of opinion to stand against any doctrine sustained by a severe induction of facts. Facts are at once both the pioneers and the rear-guards of science.

* Carpenter's Physiology, p. 735.

THEORIES OF CLAIRVOYANCE.

There are three ways in which men undertake to explain the alleged facts of clairvoyance: —

First, by accidental *coincidence.* They assert that the cases of failure are so numerous, that the instances of correct guessing are accounted for on the natural ground of chance.

Secondly, by *suggestion.* They suppose that the suggestions of the operator, enforced by the previous expectation and habitual training of the patient, will naturally conduct to as many true answers as are ordinarily obtained. This seems to have been Dr. Carpenter's theory. Still there are some cases which it is very difficult to solve in either of these ways.

The *third* method or theory of solution admits more of the extraordinary, and more fully recognizes all the alleged facts. It is as follows: Every man's will is the natural agent to move his own mind and body; but the nerves of some persons are less isolated than those of others. They have less individuality; are more susceptible to being influenced. Hence a person of great positiveness may, by mesmeric influence, obtain such control over a person of great passivity, as to subject the passive will entirely to his own. His mind enters, as it were, into the nervous system of the patient; and the patient's mind either retires and sleeps, or acts, as the master mind prompts it. If the master mind wills to go abroad in imagination, the subject mind goes with it, obedient to its volitions.

Such is the substance of the theory; of its value I have nothing to say. Whether there are facts for which the first two methods of explanation do not provide, or whether the third method explains all, if admitted, or whether we must as yet acknowledge some unexplained facts, it would be premature at present to decide. But we can scarcely avoid the conviction, — a conviction from which nothing but the irresistible demonstration of facts should drive us, — that all pretensions to seeing through solid walls; to discovering distant and concealed objects; to revealing secrets of the past and the future; in short, to any thing like that OMNISCIENCE which JEHOVAH claims as his sole prerogative, — seem at variance alike with the sobriety of science and the sacredness of religion.

Yet we ought not to impeach the *motives*, nor question the sincerity, of those who admit these pretensions, even if we were certain that they are not well founded. A too voracious credulity may be their only sin; and even this sin may not be of so enormous dimensions as some would imagine. When we consider how few have learned to separate facts from pretensions, to institute processes of severe inductive examination, to place knowledge and conjecture in the scales of a true judgment, and when we consider, further, how the love of the marvellous, the element of romance, the reaching towards the supernatural, enter into the constitution of the human mind, we cease to wonder that even the wise and good are sometimes deceived.

QUESTIONS ON CHAPTER II.

What is said in a recent work on physiology? Opinions of the more cautious? Remarks? Claims of mesmerism? *First* condition of producing the mesmerized state? *Second*? *Third*? *Fourth*? *Fifth*? *Sixth*? *Seventh*? *First* effect on the patient? Explain. *Second*? Explain. *Third*? Explain. *Fourth*? Explain. Remarks of Dr. Carpenter? Method of inducing somnambulism? Conclusion? How much does true science admit? What reject? What is said of the motives, &c., of those who admit the higher pretensions of mesmerism? How may we reconcile them with sincerity and goodness of intention? The design of this chapter? Remark?

CHAPTER III.

SUSPENDED ANIMATION.

In most cases of suspended animation, either memory does not serve, or the mind is unconscious. But in some instances both consciousness and memory are active, and the subject subsequently reports, with great precision, the entire course of his thoughts during this interesting period.

That the mind is sometimes active, and at others apparently unconscious, during this peculiar state of the body, can be explained only on the general principle, that the mind, as well as the body, has its laws of action, and that, while their intimate connection makes them ordinarily sympathize with each other's states, they are yet so essentially distinct, that causes affecting the one do not always necessarily affect the other in like manner.

That which puts the body to sleep — so to speak — may sometimes put the mind to sleep along with it; under other circumstances, that which puts the body to sleep may rouse the mind to unusual activity. So, also, that which at one time suspends the animal functions may seem to suspend also those of the mind; while, under a change of circumstances, a cause suspending the functions of the body may leave those of the mind in a state of usual, or more than usual, activity.

Passing by the more ordinary cases of suspended animation, I shall devote a few moments to those of a more important character, in this connection, in which the subject is, for a time, supposed to be *actually dead.*

APPARENT DEATH.

Instances in which persons are supposed to have expired, and are even buried alive, sometimes occur. They are less frequent than some have imagined; a single instance of the kind, brought into public notice, sufficing to fill the imaginations of a whole generation. Many live in bondage all their days, through fear of being buried alive, when the chances of such an event could hardly be expressed by a fraction.*

* Due caution may effectually prevent all chances of a premature burial. There are unequivocal methods of distinguishing between mere suspended animation and actual death. This is a little aside from my main subject; but it is of so much interest and importance, that a few words upon it in a note may be excused.

Physiologists make two stages of death — *somatic* and *molecular*. The former arrests the circulation. "The permanent and complete cessation of the circulating current is that which essentially constitutes *somatic* death." — *Carpenter's Physiology*, p. 603. This may result from a failure in the propulsive power of the heart, constituting *syncope;* or from an obstruction in the capillaries of the lungs, occasioning *asphyxia;* or from a disordered state of the blood, interrupting the changes in the general capillary system essential to vitality, producing *necræmia;* or from the direct agency of excessive cold, overpowering the vital forces and producing universal stagnation.

Molecular death implies more than all this. It is not only that state in which the vital *current* has entirely ceased to flow, but the very *vital principle itself* has departed, and left the molecules, or ultimate atoms of the system, under a new law of action — the law of chemical agencies. It implies, in fact, the incipient stage of *mortification*. It is the commencement of the chemical process of dissolution.

From the constant dependence of all those functional operations, in which vital action consists, upon the due supply of the circulating fluid, it results that *molecular* death, in most cases, immediately follows *somatic* death. But it does not *always* thus follow. "As a general rule," says Carpenter, "we find that the more active the changes which normally take place in any tissue during life, the more speedy is its complete loss of activity or death, when the requisite conditions of its vital action are no longer supplied to it." Hence in children and youth molecular death more speedily follows somatic death than in aged people.

"The rapidity with which molecular death follows the cessation of the general circulation will be influenced by a variety of causes, but especially by the degree in which the condition of the solids and fluids of the body has been impaired by the mode of death. Thus in necræmia, and in death by gradual cooling, molecular and somatic death may be said to be simultaneous; and the same appears to be true of death by sudden and violent impressions of the nervous system. But in many cases of death by causes which suddenly operate in producing syncope or asphyxia, the tissues and blood having been previously in a healthy condition, molecular death may

On recovering from this state of apparent death, the subject has ordinarily no recollection of experiencing any thing during its continuance; but sometimes his mind is highly active and conscious throughout, and he remembers his experience with great exactness. An instance of this kind I have concluded, after some hesitation, to introduce.

A CASE OF APPARENT DEATH.

The following facts are from a lady of the highest respectability and of the most unquestionable veracity. She is still living to testify to them. The facts were stated to me by her in the hearing of members of her family, including her husband, all of whom were present when the events occurred. The statements may therefore be relied upon with the utmost assurance.

In the absence of her husband on duty, who was then serving as an officer in the army, she was taken ill, and, after several days of severe sickness, apparently died. Her body was laid out, according to the usual custom, and, after a suitable time, arrangements were made for the funeral. Friends were assembled by appointment, the usual funeral services were performed, and they were about proceeding to the burial.

be long postponed. We cannot be quite certain that it has supervened, until signs of actual decomposition present themselves." — *Carpenter's Physiology*, p. 604.

The rule of safety, then, in all doubtful cases, and especially in all cases of asphyxia and of syncope, is to wait for the definite signs of *molecular death.* In instances of mere *soma*, some warmth remains in the vital organs, which, on close examination, may ordinarily be detected at the armpits, or some other central point. After molecular or absolute death has supervened, the vital current freezes to the very centre.

This is followed by a certain shrinking of the adepose parts, a peculiar marble hardness and coldness of the muscles, subsequently attended with a peculiar odor and change of color, giving unequivocal indications that corruption has laid her hand upon the body.

For such indications, in all cases of possible doubt, we should patiently wait, if we would be sure of not placing the living among the dead. And why should friends be so anxious to bury their dead from their sight, as to commit them to the grave before they have unquestionable evidence that the grave claims them?

During all this time she knew what was taking place, but was unable to make known her condition. Her eyes were closed, her lips sealed, her flesh was cold and stiff, and she was utterly unable to move a muscle. She knew that her husband was absent, and that there was a possibility of his returning about that time, although he was not expected for several days. The utmost time to which it was thought expedient to defer the funeral on his account had arrived, and she endured all the horrors of expecting to be buried alive.

She had the impression that, if her husband arrived before she was buried, he would arrest the proceeding. Just at the agonizing moment, when they were about to carry her to the grave, he drove up to the door in a carriage! The thrill produced in her by his arrival occasioned a slight muscular movement; this was followed by another, and another, until signs of life appeared. She subsequently regained the state of usual health, which she now enjoys.

REMARKS ON THE ABOVE CASE.

In the instance above cited, we observe no suspension of mental activity on the one hand, and no trance on the other. The mind was, throughout, apparently very much in its natural state. She thought, reasoned, judged as usual, and afterwards remembered what had happened. All that was wanting was the *physical power*. The will had entirely lost its ordinary control over the muscles. The body, as an instrument of the mind, had ceased to act. For any thing that appears, the mind might be equally active after the body is laid in the grave.

Still the principle of animal life was there; hence the union of the mind with the body was not actually dissolved. The partnership was still in existence, although one of the parties had for the time ceased to act. The mind willed the eye to open, the eye did not obey; it willed the tongue to speak, the tongue was silent; it willed the hand to make signals, no signals did it make. The mind was on duty; the body was in utter fault.

PECULIARITIES OF THIS STATE.

This state differs from that of *dreaming;* the physical functions being in a condition more like that of death, while those of the mind are the same as we usually have when awake. It is still more unlike that of *insanity;* as in this state the functions of the body are much in their usual condition, while those of the mind are disordered. Yet more, if possible, is it unlike those *artificial* states induced by mesmeric influence.

In the comatose state, the condition of the body bears no strict resemblance to that of death; and the subject, on awaking, has no knowledge of any thing that took place during the state of coma. And when the subject of mesmeric influence becomes somnambulic, and discovers unusual exaltation of the senses and of the muscular energy, he departs yet further from the state now in question.

Nor can we fail to see that this state is utterly unlike that claimed for the supposed subjects of *clairvoyance.* There is claimed for them a certain power of mental vision, by which they see distant and concealed objects, explore the dwellings of others and reveal their secrets, tell the histories of the past and the events of the future.

Nothing of all this pertains to the case now examined. The person to whom we have referred knew only what she was ordinarily wont to know, and what others knew around her. She could not even see her best friend, and had no knowledge of his coming until he actually arrived. The case is therefore divested of all mystery, all marvel, save only that the mind can be so entirely active, when the body is, to all appearance, dead.

Even this ceases to be wonderful, when we consider that the mind is active by virtue of its own nature, independently of the body. In this case, the mind was acting, as usual, and trying to *act itself out,* — that is, to *manifest* its activity, — through the body; but the body was not at the time under its control.

CONCLUSION.

We can explain the operation of this person's mind, during the state of apparent death, on natural principles. There was no apparent violation, no transcending, of the known and established laws of mental operation. During her sickness, her mind was intensely anxious for the return of her husband. This was the one absorbing thought at the time the bodily functions failed. The suspension of breathing and of the circulation of the blood was followed by that paleness, coldness, and fixedness of muscle which so much resemble the state of death.

In the mean time, the train of thought and association was continued in the mind as usual. Her eyes being fixedly closed, she probably saw little or nothing, but her sense of hearing might have continued sufficiently active to hint to the mind what was going on around her. When the mind is awake with anxiety and suspicion, it requires but a feeble hint to tell the whole story of what is passing.

How often do we observe a sick person, whom we imagine sunk below the power of noticing any thing that takes place around him, catching every whisper from the lips of the physician, and interpreting with wonderful exactness every thing said and done! Let us now suppose the breathing and circulation suspended, and the muscular energies paralyzed, and we have a parallel to the case of apparent death above related.

The reader is, perhaps, aware of the great influence of the emotional power of the mind over the body. In some instances, persons all but dead have been roused to action by something addressed to their mental feelings.

I was once called to visit a lady past the age of ninety, who was thought to be dying, and who for some time had been in a state of apparent unconsciousness. Children and friends, weeping around her, were seeking in vain to get the evidence of a single recognition. Her eyes were closed, her muscles set; her pulse was scarcely perceptible; nothing said or done elicited any signs of consciousness. She had been a devoted Christian for threescore years; I had therefore a right to presume what was her ruling passion. Placing my lips close to her ear, I asked her if she knew JESUS CHRIST. Instantly, to the surprise and joy of all, tears stole down her cheeks; emotion began to play on her pale and withered face; one muscle after another began to act; her arms moved; she revived and lived several days, to leave her parting blessing, and then fell sweetly asleep, to awake only in heaven.

To recur to the case of apparent death. The subject of this state, aware of what was passing, naturally became more and more anxious as the hour for burial approached. Her feelings on this subject must have reached a point of extreme intensity when at last they were about to carry her to the grave. All her hopes were suspended on the arrival of her husband; and just at this moment *he arrived!* From a state of most intense *depression*, her mind was suddenly exalted to one of most *transporting joy*. Such mental electricity was adequate to do what no other means could: it started again the suspended wheels of physical life; the heart moved, the blood stirred in the veins, the stubborn muscles became again obedient to the mind.

QUESTIONS ON CHAPTER III.

What is said of suspended animation? Of apparent death? Notice the case mentioned. What is said in the note about death? Remarks on the case cited? Wherein does it differ from *dreaming?* From *insanity?* From artificial *coma?* From artificial *somnambulism?* From *clairvoyance?* What remains that is marvellous? When does this cease to be so? What is said in conclusion?

CHAPTER IV.

TRANCE.

TRANCE is a state of suspended animation, in a greater or less degree, in which the mind passes from its natural condition into an *ecstasy*. It is usually of a religious kind, and implies a special exaltation of the *spiritual* nature. It has no necessary resemblance to clairvoyance; it assumes no divine prerogative; it has nothing to do with discovering stolen property, or revealing a neighbor's secrets, or predicting future events; it is a spiritual perception, a fervid imagination, a glowing heart, communing with the subjects of revealed truth.

Trances are of every degree, from ordinary instances of great religious abstraction to the seraphic ecstasy of Paul. Such was his trance, that, he informs us, he could not tell whether he was in the body or out of the body; but he was caught up into paradise, and heard unspeakable words, which it is not lawful for a man to utter.

Some religious sects abound in trances more than others, owing, probably, to the importance they attach to them. By placing the mind and body in situations favorable to induce them, by ardently seeking and expecting them, they may often be obtained, when they would not come spontaneously.

The following instance occurred at a house in the country where I was at the time boarding: A religious service was held there in the evening, and a Methodist preacher delivered an animated discourse. At the close of the sermon, permission was given to all present to speak. Among others, a lady of about twenty-five arose and spoke. After relating her religious experience, with great apparent emotion, she swooned and fell. As it was presumed she would soon revive, no alarm was felt.

She was removed to a chamber in a state of apparent insensibility, in which she continued two days and three nights, or about sixty hours. During the second day, scarcely a symptom of life appeared. No pulse could be felt, no movement of the lungs could be observed; the body was cold, the eyes were closed, and the mouth so firmly set that it could not be opened. On the morning of the third day, a feeble pulse was observed; some warmth and other signs of animation appeared. Soon after, she suddenly opened her eyes, and commenced singing.

She had no knowledge of what had taken place, and after concluding her song, asked where the people were who had been present at the meeting. She said she had been to heaven, had seen the Savior, had joined in the song of the redeemed, and realized such views of the heavenly world, and such experience of its joys, as she would not exchange for whole years of worldly pleasures. But the whole sixty hours had seemed to her only a few moments. She could, at first, hardly believe that the religious meeting had closed.

The excellent character of this young woman precludes all reasonable doubt of her entire sincerity. She was of a highly nervous temperament, of great religious devotion, and of singular simplicity and purity of purpose. She has since died as she lived, trusting in the Savior, and leaving the best of evidence that she has in truth gone to realize the eternal enjoyments of that world, of which she had in trance, like Paul, received the foretaste.

TRANCE OF REV. WILLIAM TENNENT.

One of the most remarkable trances on record is that of Rev. William Tennent. The following account of it is taken from his Memoir, written by Dr. Boudinot, the late venerable President of the American Bible Society, who was an intimate acquaintance of Mr. Tennent, and had the facts from his own lips. They are also confirmed by others, who were personal witnesses of all the facts, excepting of course those which were known only to Mr. Tennent himself.

"From the very nature of several things, of which an account will be given," says Dr. Boudinot, "they do not indeed admit of any other direct testimony than that of the remarkable man to whom they relate. But if there ever was a person who deserved to be believed unreservedly on his own word, it was he. He possessed an integrity of soul and a soundness of judgment which did actually secure him an unlimited confidence from all who knew him. Every species of deception, falsehood, and exaggeration, he abhorred and scorned. He was an Israelite indeed, in whom there was no guile."*

The reader may be interested to know something of the personal appearance and general religious character of him who was the subject of the following trance. His biographer says, "Mr. Tennent was rather more than six feet high; of a spare, thin visage, and of an erect carriage. He had bright, piercing eyes, a long, sharp nose, and a long face. His general countenance was grave and solemn, but at all times cheerful and pleasant with his friends. It may be said of him, with peculiar propriety, that he appeared, in an extraordinary manner, to live above the world and all its allurements. He seemed habitually to have such clear views of spiritual and heavenly things, as afforded him much of the foretaste and enjoyment of them. His faith was really and experimentally 'the substance of things hoped for, the evidence of things not seen.'

"Take him in his whole demeanor and conduct, there are few of whom it might more emphatically be said, that he lived the life and died the death of the righteous."† He lived to the age of seventy-two, and was for half a century a distinguished and eminently useful minister of the gospel in Freehold, N. J. Such was the man of whom the following extraordinary trance is related.

* Memoir, p. 7. † Ibid. p. 64.

"His intense application," says his biographer, "affected his health, and brought on a pain in his breast and a slight hectic. He soon became emaciated, and at length was like a living skeleton. His life was now threatened. He was attended by a physician, a young gentleman who was attached to him by the strictest and warmest friendship. He grew worse and worse, till little hope of life was left. In this situation his spirits failed him, and he began to entertain doubts of his final happiness. He was conversing one morning with his brother in Latin, on the state of his soul, when he fainted and died away.

"After the usual time, he was laid out on a board, according to the common practice of the country, and the neighborhood were invited to attend his funeral on the next day. In the evening, his physician and friend returned from a ride into the country, and was afflicted beyond measure at the news of his death. He could not be persuaded that it was certain; and on being told that one of the persons who had assisted in laying out the body thought he had observed a little tremor of the flesh under the arm, although the body was cold and stiff, he endeavored to ascertain the fact.

"He first put his own hand into warm water, to make it as sensible as possible, and then felt under the arm and at the heart, and affirmed that he felt an unusual warmth, though no one else could. He had the body restored to a warm bed, and insisted that the people who had been invited to the funeral should be requested not to attend. To this the brother objected as absurd, the eyes being sunk, the lips discolored, and the whole body cold and stiff. However, the doctor finally prevailed, and all probable means were used to discover symptoms of returning life.

"But the third day arrived, and no hopes were entertained of success but by the doctor, who never left him night nor day. The people were again invited, and assembled to attend the funeral. The doctor still objected, and at last confined his request for delay to one hour, then to half an hour, and finally to a quarter of an hour. He had discovered that the tongue was much swollen, and threatened to crack. He was endeavoring to soften it by some emolient ointment put upon it with a feather, when the brother came in, about the expiration of the last period, and mistaking what the doctor was doing for an attempt to feed him, manifested some resentment, and in a spirited tone said, 'It is shameful to be feeding a lifeless corpse,' and insisted, with earnestness, that the funeral should immediately proceed.

"At this critical and important moment, the body, to the great alarm and astonishment of all present, opened its eyes, gave a dreadful groan, and sunk again into apparent death. This put an end to all thoughts of burying him, and every effort was again employed, in hopes of bringing about a speedy resuscitation. In about an hour the eyes again opened, a heavy groan proceeded from the body, and again all appearance of animation vanished. In another hour life seemed to return with more power, and a complete revival took place, to the great joy of the family and friends, and to the no small astonishment and conviction of very many who had been ridiculing the idea of restoring to life a dead body.

"Mr. Tennent continued in so weak and low a state for six weeks, that great doubts were entertained of his final recovery. However, after that period he recovered much faster, but it was about twelve months before he was completely restored. After he was able to walk the room, and to take notice of what passed around him, on a Sunday afternoon, his sister, who had staid from church to attend him, was reading in the Bible, when he took notice of it, and asked her what she had in her hand. She answered, that she was reading the Bible. He replied, 'What is the Bible? I know not what you mean.' This affected the sister so much that she burst into tears, and informed him that he was once well acquainted with it.

"On her reporting this to the brother when he returned, Mr. Tennent was found, upon examination, to be totally ignorant of every transaction of his life previous to his sickness. He could not read a single word, neither did he seem to have any idea of what it meant.

"As soon as he became capable of attention, he was

taught to read and write, as children are usually taught, and afterwards began to learn the Latin language under the tuition of his brother. One day, as he was reciting a lesson in Cornelius Nepos, he suddenly started, clapped his hand to his head, as if something had hurt him, and made a pause. His brother asking him what was the matter, he said that he felt a sudden shock in his head, and it now seemed to him as if he had read that book before. By degrees his recollection was restored, and he could speak the Latin as fluently as before his sickness. His memory so completely revived that he gained a perfect knowledge of the past transactions of his life, as if no difficulty had previously occurred.

"This event, at the time, made a considerable noise, and afforded not only matter of serious contemplation to the devout Christian, especially when connected with what follows in this narration, but furnished a subject of deep investigation and learned inquiry to the real philosopher and curious anatomist.

"The writer of these Memoirs was greatly interested by these uncommon events; and, on a favorable occasion, earnestly pressed Mr. Tennent for a minute account of what his views and apprehensions were while he lay in this extraordinary state of suspended animation. He discovered great reluctance to enter into any explanation of his perceptions and feelings at this time; but being importunately urged to do it, he at length consented, and proceeded with a solemnity not to be described.

"'While I was conversing with my brother,' said he, 'on the state of my soul, and the fear I had entertained for my future welfare, I found myself, in an instant, in another state of existence, under the direction of a superior being, who ordered me to follow him. I was accordingly wafted along, I know not how, till I beheld at a distance an ineffable glory, the impression of which on my mind it is impossible to communicate to mortal man. I immediately reflected on my happy change, and thought, "Well, blessed be God! I am safe at last, notwithstanding all my fears."

"'I saw an innumerable host of happy beings surrounding the inexpressible glory, in acts of adoration and joyous worship; but I did not see any bodily shape or representation in the glorious appearance. I heard things unutterable. I heard their songs and hallelujahs of thanksgivings and praise with unspeakable rapture. I felt joy unutterable and full of glory.

"'I then applied to my conductor, and requested leave to join the happy throng; on which he tapped me on the shoulder, and said, "You must return to the earth." This seemed like a sword through my heart. In an instant, I recollect to have seen my brother standing before me, disputing with the doctor. The three days during which I had appeared lifeless seemed to me not more than ten or twenty minutes.* The idea of returning to this world of sorrow and trouble gave me such a shock, that I fainted repeatedly.'

"He added, 'Such was the effect on my mind of what I had seen and heard, that if it be possible for a human being to live entirely above the world and the things of it, for some time afterwards I was that person. The ravishing sounds of the songs and hallelujahs that I heard, and the very words that were uttered, were not out of my ears, when awake, for at least three years. All the kingdoms of the earth were in my sight as nothing and vanity; and so great were my ideas of heavenly glory, that *nothing which did not in some measure relate to it could command my serious attention.*'

"The author" [Dr. Boudinot] "has been particularly solicitous to obtain every confirmation of this extraordinary event in the life of Mr. Tennent. He accordingly wrote to every person he could think of likely to have conversed with Mr. T. on the subject. He received several answers; but the following letter from the worthy successor of Mr. T. in the pastoral charge of his church will answer for the author's purpose." †

As the facts stated in this letter are in substance the same as stated above, only a brief extract will be inserted. "I said to him," says the writer, "Sir, you seem

* This accords with the universal experience, that a state of happiness makes time seem to pass quickly.

† Memoir, pp. 16–18.

to be one indeed raised from the dead, and may tell us what it is to die, and what you were sensible of while in that state." He replied in the following words: "As *to dying*, I found my fever increase, and I became weaker and weaker, until *all at once* I found myself in heaven, as I thought. I saw no shape as to the Deity, *but glory all unutterable!*" Here he paused, as though unable to find words to express his views, and lifting up his hands, proceeded, "I can say as St. Paul did, I heard and I saw things all unutterable. I saw a great multitude before this glory, apparently in the height of bliss, singing most melodiously. I was transported with my own situation, viewing all my troubles ended, and my rest and glory begun, and was about to join the great and happy multitude, when one came to me, looked me full in the face, laid his hand upon my shoulder, and said, '*You must go back.*' These words went through me; nothing could have shocked me more. I cried out, 'Lord, must I go back?' With this shock I opened my eyes in this world. When I saw I was in the world, I fainted, then came to, and fainted for several times, as one probably would naturally have done in so weak a situation."

"Mr. Tennent further informed me, that he had so entirely lost the recollection of his past life, and the benefit of his former studies, that he could neither understand what was spoken to him, nor write, nor read his own name; that he had to begin all anew, and did not recollect that he had ever read before, until he had again learned his letters, and was able to pronounce the monosyllables, such as *thee* and *thou;* but that, as his strength returned, which was very slowly, his memory also returned.

"Notwithstanding the extreme feebleness of his situation, his recollection of what he saw and heard while in heaven, as he supposed, and the sense of divine things which he there obtained, continued all the time in their full strength, so that he was continually in something like an ecstasy of mind. 'And,' said he, 'for three years, the sense of divine things continued so great, and every thing else appeared so completely vain when compared to heaven, that could I have had the world for stooping down for it, I believe I should not have thought of doing it.' "*

The distinguished biographer subjoins the following remark: "The pious and candid reader is left to his own reflections on this very extraordinary occurrence. The facts have been stated, and they are unquestionable. The writer will only ask, whether it be contrary to revealed truth, or to reason, to believe that, in every age of the world, instances like that which is here recorded have occurred, to furnish *living testimony* of the reality of the invisible world, and of the infinite importance of eternal concerns." †

A few remarks will be added, respecting the philosophical bearings of the above facts upon religion.

1. They do not absolutely *prove* the conscious activity of the soul beyond death; for in all such instances the body is not actually *dead.* The principle of animal life still remains. Some of the vital organs are still alive. There is some vitality at the heart; the law of animal life is still in force, however feebly and imperceptibly; the body has not passed under the law of chemical and mechanical changes.

2. Such facts, however, so far as they go, *favor* the doctrine of the soul's continued life and activity after the death of the body. Here, as elsewhere, philosophy carries us to a certain point, and there leaves us to the revealed light of Christianity. If the more active states of the soul have been enjoyed when the body was at its nearest approach to death, it is reasonable to conclude, that, when the body actually *reaches* the state of death, the soul will reach its state of most absolutely free and glorious activity. But it remains for Christianity finally to settle this point.

3. It is perhaps a question, whether the experience of persons in such trances is *subjective* merely, or *objective;* that is, whether the soul is still in the body, and whatever is seen and felt is merely the result of an inward experience; or whether the soul actually *leaves* the body, and passes for a time into the heavenly world, to hold communion with objects there.

* Memoir. Springfield edition, 1822, p. 20. † Ibid. p. 23.

If we have taken the right view of animal life, as the medium through which the soul acts upon the body, we cannot suppose that persons while in trance are ever actually *dead.* They may be in the incipient stages of *somatic* death, but never in a state of *molecular* or *absolute* death. The soul may either remain in connection with the principle of animal life, making no manifestations to this world through the body, on account of its suspended animation, in which case its experience of the heavenly glories is subjective; or the soul may for a time *leave* the body, pass into heaven, actually see and realize the objects of that world, and then return to its earthly tenement: as the principle of animal life revives, and the organs of sense come into play, the soul may resume her dominion over the body, and through it again commune with the objects of this world.

Paul says, that, when he was in trance, he could not tell whether he was "*in* the body or *out* of the body;" and if an inspired apostle could not tell, even in respect to himself, we may as well not attempt to decide the question.

4. These facts throw interesting light upon the subject of *memory.* They prove, that although men may forget all that they have ever learned or experienced for a long period, it may be subsequently recalled. When Mr. Tennent was apparently dead, he remembered and reflected upon the events of his past life. His memory was then in full vigor. After he was resuscitated, his memory failed him. As his strength returned, his memory revived.

This shows, that although, through the infirmities of sickness or age, a man's memory may fail, when he shall have done with the body as an instrument, and entered upon a spiritual state, like that of the soul in trance, he may have a wakeful and perfect recollection of all the events of this life.

5. These facts conspire with Christianity to teach us the immense *value of the human soul.* Some may be disposed to disregard them as the dreams of a distempered imagination; but this is not the part of a true philosopher. Here are *incontestable facts;* and it is the

true business of philosophy to meet all facts, whatever they may be, and give them a thorough consideration.

If, when excluded from all possible connection with this world, the soul can have such exalted communion with another; if it can see, hear, feel, and in the highest degree *realize*, things so far transcending all that the natural eye hath seen, or ear heard, or heart known; if such a man as Paul, in this state, could say, "that he was caught up into paradise, and heard unspeakable words, which it is not lawful for a man to utter;" * if, in a similar state, such a man as William Tennent could say, "The ravishing sounds of the songs and hallelujahs that I heard, and the very words that were uttered, were not out of my ears, when awake, for at least three years; all the kingdoms of the earth were in my sight as nothing and vanity; and so great were my ideas of heavenly glory, that nothing, which did not in some measure relate to it, could command my serious attention," — it surely becomes us, scarcely less as profound philosophers than as enlightened Christians, to put an infinite value upon our spiritual nature, and to make it the great object of this brief existence to prepare for a higher and an endless life to come.

* 2 Cor. xii. 4.

QUESTIONS ON CHAPTER IV.

What is *trance?* Are trances of various degrees? How may they be induced? Relate the instances here mentioned. What is said of the person? What is one of the most remarkable trances on record? What is our authority for it? What is said of the subject of it? Relate the trance as recorded by the biographer. What was the condition of the subject after the trance? The state of his mind? The incidents in connection with his brother? His narration to the writer of his Memoir? Substance of the letter to the author? *First* remark on the above? *Second? Third? Suggestions? Fourth? Fifth?* Concluding thoughts?

PART VI.

SUMMARY VIEW OF THE LEADING PHILOSOPHICAL SCHOOLS.

CHAPTER I.

ORIGIN AND PROGRESS OF PHILOSOPHY.

THE remaining chapters will be devoted to a summary view of the principal advocates and doctrines of the leading philosophical schools. To give any thing like a history of philosophy, in so short a space, would be impossible; I design merely to give an outline of the most important historical facts connected with mental science.

PHILOSOPHY LESS ANCIENT THAN POETRY.

In the early ages, men were more poetic than philosophic. Opening their eyes upon a universe of unexplored wonders, imagination was roused; wonder fired the soul; the glowing language of poetic inspiration fell spontaneous from all lips. Hence poetry is the earlier offspring of the human mind; philosophy is of later birth.

The ancient Egyptians were a comparatively learned

people; but vainly we interrogate their hieroglyphic scrawls, and even the more legible records of history, to learn much of their philosophy. The ancient Jews and Arabians were eminently poetic; but while time has transmitted some of the sacred histories and seraphic lyrics of the former, and a few fragments from the fairy dreams of the latter, she has left us next to nothing by which to learn the results of their philosophical inquiries, or whether, indeed, such inquiries were any very serious part of their studies.

Among the still more eastern nations of India and China, we find the same preponderance of imagination.

PHILOSOPHY ORIGINATED WITH THE GREEKS.

Subsequently, in the palmy days of Greece, her thoughtful sons began to look earnestly into the nature and reason of things. "*The Greeks seek after wisdom*" became a proverb, which divine inspiration has handed down to us. This proverb seems to single out the Greeks as the only people at that time engaged in philosophical inquiries; at least, it gives them prominence in this particular.

PLATO AND ARISTOTLE.

PLATO was the father of Grecian philosophy, and, about the year 400 before Christ, became the founder of a school. He was soon followed by ARISTOTLE, his pupil, who became also the founder of another school. Let me not be understood to say, that all the peculiar doctrines of these schools *originated* with these patriarchs in philosophy. They collected and arranged thoughts suggested at various times and places by others, adding thereto the fruits of their own great genius and research, so as to institute the *beginnings* of well-defined *systems of philosophy*.

SYSTEMS OF PHILOSOPHY OF SLOW GROWTH.

Profound and enduring systems of philosophy are of slow growth. It is not for any one man, or the men of any one age, to monopolize the honor of both laying the foundation and raising the superstructure of a philosophical system to endure the protracted ordeal of time. Great men are rendered such by circumstances, not less than by genius and industry. They are the happy men who spring into being at the right point of time, to avail themselves of the unappropriated fruits of others' minds, and to bring them into systematic and enduring relation to their own thoughts and to those of coming generations. "If we look back steadfastly upon the past history of philosophy," says Morelle, "we may see that it has ever had a progressive development; that each age has contributed its portion, greater or less, and that the agitation between the different schools has been, as it were, the pulsations of this forward movement. Thales and Pythagoras combined the vague theories of their age into their own respective systems. Without the former, Democritus and the Atomists would have been impossible; and without the latter, Parmenides and Zeno had never embodied, in regular form, the tenets of the Eleatic philosophy. The struggle of these two schools paved the way for Socrates, and thus rendered Plato and Aristotle possible. Without the former of these, the early Christian philosophy would not have seen the light; and without the latter, the scholastic philosophy could not possibly have arisen." *

The two philosophical schools, the one founded by Plato, and the other by Aristotle, have continued, variously modified, to this day, dividing the thinking world, in certain fundamental particulars, into two classes.

* An Historical and Critical View of the Speculative Philosophy of Europe, in the Nineteenth Century, by J. D. Morelle, A. M.

LEADING PECULIARITIES OF THESE SCHOOLS.

The PLATONIC school maintains that the mind is created with *innate principles or ideas*, corresponding to the essence of things, from which knowledge is *directly generated.* The ARISTOTELIAN school maintains that the human mind is created *without any ideas or knowledge whatever*, and is incapable of originating any, *without the aid of the senses.* Of the former school are Des Cartes, Leibnitz, Kant, and most of the modern German, with some modern French philosophers. Of the latter school are Bacon, Locke, Reid, and the Scotch and English philosophers generally.

It must not be supposed that the philosophers of the former school attach *no* importance to the senses, as means of knowledge, nor that those of the latter allow *no* place to the original teachings of the mind; still there is between them a radical difference of views on this point—a difference more real in its nature, and serious in its effects, than any other that has divided philosophers.

NAMES OF THE SCHOOLS.

The *Platonic* school is called also the *Cartesian*, in honor of one of its principal advocates; it is called the *rational* or metaphysical, as opposed to giving prominence to the senses, as means of knowledge; it is called the *transcendental*, as making claims to knowledge by means transcending the supposed ordinary operations of the understanding.

The *Aristotelian* school is also called the *Baconian*, in honor of one of its principal advocates and in part a founder; it is called the *inductive*, *empirical*, or *experimental*, (from the Greek *empeiro*, to search or prove;) it is also called *sensuous* or *sensational*, because it maintains that human knowledge originates in sensation.

As LORD BACON may be considered the modern father of the one, and DES CARTES of the other; and as British writers generally have followed in the steps of Bacon, in the essential particulars, and German writers in the steps of Des Cartes; we may properly call the one the GERMAN, and the other the BRITISH school.* French philosophers have been divided between these two schools, having in mental science no peculiar school of their own.

MORELLE'S CLASSIFICATION.

Morelle makes four philosophical schools — the *sensational*, the *ideal*, the *sceptical*, and the *mystical*. In a critical view, this classification has some importance, as it is intended to indicate certain distinctions actually existing, and deserving of notice. But it has its disadvantages, and, in a general view, is quite objectionable. It unites men who differ on points more important than those on which they agree; and it separates men who agree on points more important than those on which they differ. For instance, it separates Reid from Locke and Brown, and transfers him to Germany, "which, from Königsberg to Basle, is still advocating the most profound systems of idealism." † It occasions not a few other divorces and alliances equally strange and unfortunate. It exalts subordinate differences to the rank of generic ones, and of course depresses generic differences to the rank of subordinate ones.

It is true, the author says he uses the word *idealism* in its broadest signification. This he has a right to do, if he abides by his definition, — and few writers are more faithful than he to their definitions, — but adopting this signification, Locke is as much an idealist as Reid. As applied to the German philosophy, idealism is quite different from what it is as applied to the Scotch and English philosophy. The term *rational* has acquired a world-wide currency, as indicating that phase of the metaphysical school which Morelle had in view. But

* There seem to be certain peculiarities in the structure, circumstances, or habits of the German, as distinguished from the English and Scotch intellect, which incline the former to favor the rationalistic and contemplative philosophy, rather than the inductive and practical.

† History of Philosophy, p. 797.

he was afraid to use it, lest it might prove injurious to the school towards which his sympathies seem, on the whole, most inclined. "The term rationalism," he says, "would certainly have been better adapted to express a philosophy starting from conceptions of reason, rather than intimations of sense; but then it has acquired such notoriety in the religious world, that I well knew the penalty of pressing it into my service. On the whole, therefore, as the term *idea* is now frequently used to signify a mental conception, in opposition to a sensational feeling, I thought it not inappropriate to apply the word *idealism*, in the general sense in which it is found in the following pages." *

His reason, then, for making Reid an idealist, and Locke a sensationalist, is, that "the term *idea* is now very frequently used to signify a mental conception, in opposition to a sensational feeling." But did not Locke mean by an *idea* a *mental conception?* Does he not expressly say, "By an *idea*, I mean that which a man has in his mind when he is thinking about something"? And what is this but a mental conception? Does Locke ever call "a sensational feeling" an idea? He calls it an occasional *cause* of ideas. So does Reid. The only difference between them here is, that while Reid advocates the immediate perception of things, Locke, in accordance with the current theory, speaks of perceiving through the medium, or by means of ideas. Locke considered an idea an entity, distinct from the mind itself, and so do all the soundest philosophers of the British school, Brown excepted.

If Reid is an idealist, Locke is equally one. On minor points they differ, as I have shown on former pages; but the points of their difference are of little moment, compared with those in which they agree. The same is true of the difference between Reid and Brown, although more serious in this case than in the other.

If Morelle did injustice to Locke, in considering him, in distinction from Reid, a champion of an exclusive sensationalism, he did it only as he was misled by

* Preface to History of Philosophy, p. 5.

Cousin.* There must be, in all true systems of philosophy, a *sensational*, as well as an *idealistic* element; and they whose spectacles do not allow them to see but one of these elements, or how to blend them, cannot be received as faithful expounders of the philosophy of John Locke. No writer ever did more than he, in his day, to elevate the mind to its true position as a spiritual, thinking essence; to turn its thoughts inward upon itself, as the subject matter of philosophy; and, in short, to expound and defend the principles which lie at the very basis of all true idealism.

An admirable writer, in a review of Morelle, says, "A philosophical system may assume a positive form, when it is wholly negative in its character and mission; and its protest against the errors of previous systems may be accepted, and never need to be repeated, while its affirmations shall be rejected almost as soon as proffered, or, if adopted, shall lead to errors only less gross than those which it supplanted. Thus the true value of Locke's Essay on the Human Understanding is as a protest against *objective* philosophy, which had prevailed alike among the ancients and in the scholastic ages. Ideas had, down to his day, been regarded and treated as detached and independent essences, so much so as the objects of physical science. The effort had been to analyze, not the states, but the products of the intellect; not to sound the source, but to define the forms, of ideas. That the mind itself is the subject matter of true philosophy, was a discovery the honor of which is due to Locke alone. He is the father of *subjective* philosophy. With this discovery, his positive system gained extensive and enduring currency; and its sensationalistic divorced from

* In some particulars, Morelle is at present as much in favor of Cousin, as, a few years since, he was of Brown. He is yet a young man; ten years more added to his learning and candor will probably give him the same impartiality towards Locke, which characterizes what he has written in relation to most others.

Cousin undertook to annihilate Locke, and verily thought he had done so. What is more, he has succeded in making some others, for a time, think so too. But the name of the great English thinker is still bright on the read pages of philosophy, and will continue to be so, long after those of the French critic shall have passed to the dull pages that are turned over and forgotten.

its idealistic element, led, by routes which he neither indicated nor contemplated, to infidelity, naturalism, and fatalism. But Kant was as much indebted to him as Condillac; and modern idealism, no less than sensationalism, has pursued the truth in the route which he first opened." *

SCEPTICISM AND MYSTICISM.

Nor are the terms *scepticism* and *mysticism*, as applied to designate distinct and permanent philosophical schools, entirely unexceptionable. The term *scepticism* does not so much indicate a *distinct school*, as certain *results* of schools which may be essentially different. The ultra rationalist on this hand, and the ultra sensationalist on that, educated in different schools, meet together on the ground of a common scepticism. It is the place where extremes meet; the ground of malecontents. Dissatisfied with their past views, tired of the dogmas imposed by false or partial conceptions gathered from their respective schools, they are looking about for something better. They usually move off in a direction the opposite to that from which they came.

On this point, the reviewer above cited justly remarks, "Scepticism cannot be regarded as a permanent form of philosophy. It marks the transition epochs, when old dogmas lose their hold on reflective minds, and are just going to yield place to more profound and comprehensive theories. It is the protest against false and inadequate views which is needed to prepare the way to further developments of philosophical truth.

"Scepticism being an epoch rather than a normal state of philosophical speculation, must necessarily have

* North American Review, April,. 1849. Thus our excellent reviewer ascribes to Locke the honor of modern idealism. It is curious to observe that Morelle refers this same honor to Des Cartes, a philosopher of exactly the opposite school. "Des Cartes, looking more deeply beneath the phenomenal world, and with an intense power of reflection, gazing upon the mind itself as the instrument and medium by which all truth is perceived, gave a new impetus to the rationalistic method of philosophizing, and thus laid the basis of the modern idealism." —*History of Philosophy*, p. 64.

a reaction towards some positive system. This may take place in favor of idealism, if the sceptical movement had its rise in the inconsequent reasonings or untenable conclusions of the sensationalists, or *vice versa.* Or it may assume the divine agency, as not only the virtual, but the sole proximate cause of all mental phenomena, and seek the conclusion of all intellectual problems in the attributes and ideas of the Supreme Intelligence. Hence *mysticism*, which, in its various modifications, resolves the administration of the intellectual universe into a theurgy, pervaded by laws or principles corresponding to the individual inquirer's peculiar dogmas."

The term *mysticism* indicates a peculiar phase of mind, in certain stages of inquiry, at which the explained is reaching towards the inexplicable, and the natural towards the spiritual, rather than a distinct philosophical school. As we live in a universe of wonders, which no philosophy can fully fathom, the Creator has implanted that in our constitution which, when excited, tends to mysticism; and its phenomena must needs constitute a part of all true mental science.

We can enter no school where we do not sooner or later overtake the unexplained and the wonderful, and where mysticism does not, of course, become an element. When this element becomes absorbing or excessive, the subject of it is called, by way of eminence, a *mystic.* There are as profound mystics among the followers of Locke as among those of Kant. At the same time, it must be conceded, that some systems of philosophy nourish the mystic element more than others.

ECLECTICISM.

The term *eclecticism* may, perhaps, with some propriety, designate a philosophical school; but I should prefer to dissent from Cousin, in this respect, and consider it a term indicating those who belong to no particular school; those who prefer to stand apart, and select from each school as their judgments dictate. So far as the term is

ative, it of course indicates no bond of union; so far it is positive, it may indicate elections so opposed as place its subjects in quite opposite schools.

An eclectic may be a materialist, a transcendentalist, nystic, or a sceptic. Cousin professes eclecticism; so s Morelle; so did Hume; so did Shaftesbury. Yet o would consider these men as truly belonging to one l the same school? Both Locke and Kant, so far as y went from home after thoughts, are eclectics. All n profess to be, and really ought to be, such. But y must finally be judged by what they *actually think l teach.*

CONCLUSION.

I have, therefore, concluded to consider mental philosy as descending to us in two generic schools — the annt Platonic and modern German on the one hand, the cient Aristotelian and modern British on the other. th of these schools are really sensational, as both rely the latter more than the former — upon the teachings sensation; both are alike ideal; both have their sceps, and both their mystics.

But the German school is the more rationalistic and nscendental; the British, the more inductive and exrimental. The former assumes most; the latter proves ost. The former relies most upon innate ideas and d spontaneous suggestions of the mind itself; the latter on what the mind learns by a slow and cautious inction of facts. The former begins with principles, and ds with facts; the latter begins with facts, and ends th principles.

QUESTIONS ON CHAPTER I.

Subject of remaining chapters? What is proposed? Comparative anaity of philosophy? With whom did it originate? Proverb? Who s the father of Grecian philosophy? Who succeeded him? What is said of them ? What of the growth of philosophical systems ? State the leading peculiarities of the two schools ? Who are mentioned of the former school ? Who of the latter ? By what names is the Platonic school called ? The Aristotelian ? What reasons for calling the one the German, and the other the British school ? Remark in the note on peculiarities of German mind, &c. ? Morelle's classification ? Objections to it ? His reasons for considering Reid an idealist, and Locke a sensationalist ? Remarks on them ? Substance of the remarks from the Review ? What is said of scepticism and mysticism ? What of sceptics ? Of mystics ? Of eclecticism ? Conclusion ?

CHAPTER II.

THE ANCIENT PLATONIC AND MODERN GERMAN SCHOOL.

PLATO, the father of this school, was scarcely less renowned for his poetry and eloquence than for his philosophy. It is fabled, that, while in his cradle, bees shed honey upon his lips; thus presaging the future powers of his eloquence.* In his youth he composed several tragedies and elegies, which, when he determined to devote himself to philosophy, he gave to the flames. Still the poetic inspiration followed him, and became an important element in his philosophy. Like Coleridge, who has been called the modern Plato, he may be styled the *poetic philosopher*.

It is interesting to notice the mental peculiarities of the two fathers of philosophy, and to trace them through the respective schools, down to the present time. Aristotle was cool, cautious, plodding; Plato was ardent, confiding, ready: with the former, knowledge came by *searching*; with the latter, it seemed to *gush up spontaneously*. With the one, it was severe knowledge; with the other, a mixture of imagination.

The mental habits of Aristotle were characterized by objectivity; those of Plato by subjectivity. By this is meant, that the former relied mostly upon what he learned

* Most of the writings of Plato are translated into English. As their original form is beautiful classic Greek, the scholar will prefer to read them as they fell from the great author's pen. There is a fine edition of his argument against atheism, in the original Greek, published by the Harpers, with valuable notes, by Dr. Lewis, of the University of New York city.

from without; the latter, upon the spontaneous promptings of his own mind. Yet Plato was a scholar as well as a genius. The laborious pupil of Socrates, and teacher of Aristotle and Demosthenes, his mind took a wide range over the fields of literature, and gathered fruits from every clime. His philosophy strikes not a few notes, to which there are responsive chords in the human soul; and, by the aid of his learning, he gave it an enduring name and place among men.

RENE DES CARTES.

The Platonic philosophy subsided into a state of dormancy, in which it mostly remained, through a long period, until the early part of the seventeenth century, when it was revived by DES CARTES. He was a French nobleman, of distinguished talents and extensive learning. Commencing with the knowledge of his own mind, of which he found evidence in the consciousness of thinking,* he ascended to the conception of the Infinite Mind — the perfect and Supreme Being.

Finding what he was thus led to conceive verified in the evidences of design around him, he inferred the infallibility of human reason; since it was not presumable that such a being as God would give us reason to mislead us. In the old Platonic philosophy, he found some of the elements of what he conceived to be the right mode of thinking.

This philosophy does not, like the Aristotelian, proceed by an induction of particulars to establish general principles. It *starts* with general principles, deduced directly from the mind, and proceeds to apply them to the scientific classification of particulars. Principles innate to the mind being assumed as a type of all that is to be learned without, what is taught by the senses is considered secondary to what is learned directly by inward teachings. Reason teaches us how things *must* be, rather than things

* "*Cogito; ergo sum.*"

themselves how they *are*. Reason gives laws to objective facts, rather than facts to reason.

Philosophizing in this way, his fine genius naturally struck out rich and original thoughts, and formed visionary theories. A comprehensive and logical reasoner, he framed a metaphysical system which has been the basis of many subsequent speculations. He supposed the *essence of mind* to consist in *thinking;* the *essence of matter*, in *extension;* that as extension is every where, the universe is, of course, an infinitely-extended *plenum;* hence the heavenly bodies do not revolve in empty space, but in *vortexes* or *whirlpools.* Holding to the natural immortality of the soul on the ground of its indecomposability, and to the mortality of brutes, his theory made them mere machines, without soul, thought, emotion, volition.

To explain the mode of communication between the soul and the body, he supposed a very subtile fluid, secreted from the blood, and called "*animal spirits*," to circulate in the nerves, and to convey intelligence from every part of the body to the soul resident in the *pineal gland* of the brain; and thence, also, to convey the commands of the soul to all the muscles employed in voluntary motion.*

"His writings excited much attention, and they prompted many to engage in philosophical studies; but they also met with great opposition. Gassendi, and the adherents of the Baconian method, of course, rejected his views. The Jesuits in France, and many of the Protestants in Holland, did the same. In England, he scarcely had a follower. His principal adherents in France were several of the Messieurs de Port-Royal, especially Malebranche; and in Holland, Spinoza and a few others." †

* "Des Cartes, observing that the pineal gland is the only part of the brain that is single, all the other parts being double, and thinking that the soul must have one seat, was determined by this to make that gland the soul's habitation, to which, by means of the animal spirits, intelligence is brought of all objects that affect the senses." — *Reid's Works*, vol. ii. p. 104.

† Sketches of Modern Philosophy, especially among the Germans. By James Murdock, D. D.

BENEDICT SPINOZA.

The next conspicuous name in this connection is that of Benedict Spinoza, a learned Jew of Amsterdam. He was born in 1632, and, unlike most philosophers, died at an early age, being only forty-five. A warm admirer of Des Cartes, he yet thought to improve upon his system. Assuming Des Cartes' definition of a substance,—"a thing which so exists as not to depend on any thing else for its existence,"—he legitimately inferred that God alone is that substance, since of him alone independent existence is predicable.

"There is, then," said he, "but one real substance, and that substance is God. As universal substance is God, all creatures, all things, are but parts of God. In the idea of substance, he includes both mind and matter. When God creates mind, he sends forth a portion of his own mind; when he creates matter, a portion of his own material substance. The mind and the matter thus created do not become separate existences, but are still only God himself extended or reproduced. This is *pantheism*. God is in every thing, and every thing is God.

"By virtue of the divinity in man, we are competent to know all truth. The object which we can most easily know and most perfectly comprehend is God, since he is perpetually dwelling and developing himself within and around us. To know that of which we are conscious, is to know God; to know that which is about us, is to know God. Every thing within and around us reveals to us God, whom to know is our highest happiness; to obey, our most perfect freedom." It would seem, in this view, that man can hardly fail to be a very *happy* being, whatever might be the fate of his *freedom*.

"It is manifest," says Murdock, "that he carried his speculations quite beyond the bounds of human knowledge, and ran into downright *transcendentalism*, in which obscurity must ever reign." *

* Modern Philosophy, p. 29

NICHOLAS MALEBRANCHE.

Of the same school was NICHOLAS MALEBRANCHE, of Paris, a devout Jesuit, whose *Inquiry after Truth* was published in 1673. He has been considered one of the most original and profound thinkers of France.* His work was published in a revised and enlarged form but three years before he died, in 1712. With Spinoza, he supposed the soul to be a portion of the divinity, or the divine *reason*, (Logos,) and all matter to be a development of the one infinite substance. Sometimes, however, his language seems to import nothing more than a mystical union of our souls with God. Holding the source of error to be in the senses, and the source of truth in God, if we would aspire to pure truth, we must rise superior to the senses, and view things in the position of the divine Mind.

In common with others of this school, he supposed the immediate objects of our knowledge to be only the *ideas* of things, not the *things themselves*.† As these ideas existed in the divine mind before any thing was created, in proportion as we commune with the divine mind, we apprehend the true ideas of things as God does, and not as they are furnished by the uncertain senses. Maintaining God to be the object of our immediate vision, while all other objects are seen indirectly, he completely reversed the common doctrine on this subject.

He went even beyond his own school; for supposing that we see all things in God, he saw no necessity for holding the theory of innate ideas, since knowledge is more surely obtained directly at the source than by any thing that can represent it. Hence the theory of innate ideas fell out of his philosophy. Malebranche was a *religious enthusiast.* The marks of sincerity, simplicity,

* "Malebranche, with a very penetrating genius, entered into a more minute examination of the powers of the human mind than any before him." — *Reid*, vol. ii. p. 128.

† "It is obvious that the system of Malebranche bears no evidence of the existence of a material world from what we perceive by our senses; for the divine ideas which are the objects immediately perceived were the same before the world was created." — *Ibid.* vol. ii. p. 150.

devoutness of soul, pervade his writings, and prove that a spirit averse to all infidelity, rather than a love of daring speculation, became the occasion of his philosophical errors. His style is easy and inviting, affording some of the finest specimens of the French language at that period.

LEIBNITZ AND WOLF.

The name of GODFREY WILLIAM VON LEIBNITZ is of world-wide renown.* He led on the German mind in the track of its modern philosophy. He was contemporaneous with JOHN LOCKE. These two philosophers were the principal antipodes of their day on the main question that divided the schools. Leibnitz was an extensive scholar, a deep thinker, a rare genius. Although following mainly in the remote steps of the great Plato, he had the courage to do his own thinking. It was his ambition and his aim to make philosophy as perfect a science of reason as the pure mathematics, thereby to settle all disputes and put the world at rest.

He began by laying down the principles of pure reason, drawn directly from the mind's original furniture, and proceeded to build thereon his logical demonstrations. He labored at the same great idea that had descended from Plato — the competency of the mind to educe from itself a perfect system of philosophy. To settle the truth of abstract and general principles, he applied the mathematical tests of identity or contradiction ; to settle the question of facts, the proof deduced from the relations of cause and effect. He hence differed from Des Cartes in this particular, that while Des Cartes held the proof of ideas to be *in themselves*, whenever they are clearly perceived,

* "He was highly respected by emperors, and by many kings and princes, who bestowed upon him singular marks of their esteem. He was a particular favorite of Queen Caroline, consort of George II., with whom he continued his correspondence by letters after she came to the crown of Britain till his death. The famous controversy between him and the mathematicians of Great Britain, whether he or Sir Isaac Newton was the inventor of that noble improvement in mathematics, called by Newton the *Method of Fluxions*, and by Leibnitz the *Differential Method*, engaged the attention of the mathematicians in Europe for several years." — *Reid's Works*, vol ii. p. 233.

he held that they require and may have *logical* proof; first, directly from the innate principles and spontaneous conceptions of the mind itself; secondly, by reasoning from effects to causes.

For his curious and ingenious theories respecting Monads, Preëstablished Harmony, and the Best System, the reader is referred to his writings; or, for a lucid condensation of them in English, to Murdock's Modern Philosophy of the Germans. A notice of them would require too much room here, and would not comport with the general design of this work.

The philosophy of Leibnitz encountered some opposition, which it soon surmounted, on its way to universal ascendency over Protestant Germany. Its great expounder and defender was Christian Wolf, himself also a German, born in 1679. He lived to the age of seventy-five, devoting most of his life to explaining and improving the Leibnitzian philosophy. He pushed the plan of Leibnitz to the extreme, of carrying the strictly mathematical method into all his investigations.* To him mainly the Germans are indebted for their copious list of technical terms, derived mostly from the Greek language.

"This Leibnitzian-Wolfian philosophy reached its culminating point about the middle of the eighteenth century. Soon afterwards, from various causes, it began to decline. Many had all along questioned the soundness of its principles, and still more the tendencies of some of its doctrines. The downright pedantry of most of its advocates, who dogmatized ostentatiously, and stuffed their writings with formal demonstrations of the simplest truths, rendered it disgusting to well-informed minds. About the same time, Locke's principles, or those of the empirical school, found their way into Germany. And these principles were propagated in and along with the writings of the English and French deists and sceptics, (Hume, Voltaire, Rousseau, &c.,) which began now to circulate extensively, and to produce in that country a set of free thinkers and contemners of long-established

* See his "*Psychologia Rationalis*," also "*Psychologia Empirica*."

opinions. The friends of revealed religion were alarmed at the progress of infidelity and scepticism, under the assumed name of philosophy; and they anxiously inquired, What is true philosophy? It was amid this state of things that EMANUEL KANT appeared on the stage as a master spirit, controlling and guiding public opinion by his superior talents." *

EMANUEL KANT.

This illustrious philosopher was born at Königsberg, in 1724. His whole life was spent in that city; he is said, indeed, never to have travelled from it more than twenty-two miles. He lived to the advanced age of eighty. Of great acutenesss, patient study, profound thought, and of most pure and amiable character, through a long life his name became every where the synonyme of whatever is great and worthy.

The system of Kant is called the Critical Philosophy. It is decidedly of the rationalistic school, although it calls to its aid some of the principles of the inductive. He held philosophy to be a science of pure *Reason*, at whose bar all questions must be tried. Yet the senses and the understanding have their importance. He supposed that man possesses three distinct faculties, rising one above the other in the following order of importance — SENSATION, UNDERSTANDING, REASON.

He considered *Sensation* a mere *receptive* faculty, conveying to the mind only impressions made by the objects around us. From this source we learn only the *phenomena* of things within the range of the senses; nothing of the essential nature of the things themselves. The *Understanding* is the faculty which apprehends the materials furnished by the senses, and of them forms conceptions and judgments respecting whatever may be learned from without. It is restricted in its operations to the *sensible* world, and all the knowledge acquired by it is empirical.

* Modern Philosophy, by Dr. Murdock, p. 43.

REASON is the grand attribute distinguishing man from the brute creation. The sphere of its operations is the supersensible world. It has to do directly with spiritual and essential truths, general laws, abstract principles. The knowledge which it supplies has respect to the *universal* and the *necessary*, in distinction from the *local* and *contingent*. It is called *rational* and *pure* knowledge, to distinguish it from *empirical* knowledge, acquired through the senses by the understanding, and liable to be diluted with error. It is called *transcendent*, or *transcendental*, because it is from a source transcending the sensual world. The decisions of Reason are considered superior to all others. All things must be arraigned, tried, and finally settled at her bar. What she knows is certain; what is learned by the understanding may be doubted. Reason is fixed; understanding is discursive.

Reason is both *speculative* and *practical;* the former imparting to us rational *knowledge*, the latter enjoining upon us rational *conduct*. The former is, as it were, the eye of the soul; the latter, the moral law within. The former teaches what we *must believe;* the latter, what we *ought to do.**

Many of the truths which Kant recognizes as taught by reason are what I have called *intuitive;* but he extends the province of reason quite beyond what I have supposed to be strictly intuitive truths. In his REASON we recognize again the LOGOS of Plato, the RATIO of Cicero, the supposed *divinity* within us of his various predecessors.

In Kant's philosophy, the distinction between *reason* and *reasoning* is not merely the distinction between what is indicated by a noun and its participle. Things are supposed to be *directly* known by *reason*, which cannot be known by *reasoning*. Reason is sure; reasoning may be fallacious. For instance, reason teaches the existence of an infinitely perfect Being, because she speculatively needs this ideal of absolute excellence, and because her

* *Kritik der reinen Vernunft*, pp. 800–830. The writings of Kant are translated into clumsy English. Persons familiar with the German will obtain more clear and satisfactory knowledge of his views in the original than from the translation.

moral wants demand it; but all reasoning to prove the existence of such a Being is uncertain. The *fact* is certain, because directly proclaimed by *Reason herself;* the mode of reaching it, by *reasoning*, may be false.

Upon this infallible REASON — the finite image of God within us, aspiring to the infinite in knowledge, and the moral law within us, directing to the Infinite in goodness — this philosopher erects his sublime system of *Natural and Moral Theology.*

EFFECTS OF KANT'S WRITINGS.

The writings of this great thinker aroused the German mind to high enthusiasm for metaphysical studies, to urgent inquiries into the foundation of rational knowledge, and to sanguine anticipations of the speedy millennium of philosophy. He was followed by various authors, laboring to subvert, amend, or enlarge his system, or to establish other rational systems.

Amid the various lights of reason, the light of revealed truth faded away; the Bible was either laid upon the shelf, or not opened until reason had first decided what it must teach.

In France, some philosophers went with the German transcendentalists, others with the extreme and sceptical followers of Locke; the former mounting upwards into the clouds, on the wings of etherial Reason; the latter plodding earthward, at the sluggish heels of Understanding.

OTHER PHILOSOPHERS OF THIS SCHOOL.

Our limits do not admit a particular notice of all the writers of this school. Among the most distinguished which we have not noticed are Jacobi, Fichte, Schelling, Hegel, and Herbart.

Jacobi was born in 1743, and devoted most of his life to authorship.

Fichte was born in 1762, was professor of philosophy at Zurich, and afterwards at Jena.

Schelling was born in 1775, succeeded Fichte in the chair of philosophy at Jena, and was afterwards professor at Würzburg.

Hegel was born in 1770, became first a professor at Jena, and afterwards at Berlin.

Herbart was born in the year 1776, and was at different periods professor at Gottingen and Königsberg.

Jacobi is classed with the mystics; and all these philosophers, with their pupils, are among the more transcendental of the German school.*

VICTOR COUSIN.

We must pass on to notice a single name, as a representative of others, in France. The name of Victor Cousin is familiar to all ears. This noted philosopher was born in Paris, November 22, 1792. He is still living. He claims to belong to no positive school, but to proceed upon the principles of an impartial *eclecticism*. We do not read far, however, without finding his tendencies setting strongly towards the rational school.

He supposes that the first aberration from the true philosophical method comes from Bacon; and as to Locke, although a great and ingenious thinker, his Essay on the Understanding is wrong in point of method, false to the true origin of our most essential ideas, replete with solecisms and contradictions, and always, of course, inclining too much to the sensuous.

* "That is called *transcendental* which surpasses the limits of sensible or empirical knowledge, and expatiates in the region of pure thought or absolute science. It is therefore truly scientific; and it serves to explain empirical truths so far forth as they were explicable. On the other hand, that is called transcendent which not only goes beyond empiricism, but surpasses the boundaries of human knowledge. It expatiates in the shadowy region of imaginary truth. It is therefore falsely called science; it is the opposite of true philosophy." — *Murdock's Modern Philosophy*, p. 168.

The terms are, however, now used indiscriminately, or, rather, only the term *transcendental* is used, and is applied to all those whose fundamental views are of the rational school. Hence Jacobi, Fichte, Hegel, Schelling, Rauch, and Coleridge are, alike with Kant, usually called transcendentalists, although differing from him and from each other in more or less of the particulars formerly indicated by these several terms.

Cousin supposes, not without reason, that the extreme doctrine of Locke, on the one hand, led to the extreme doctrine of Condillac on the other. Assuming to take the neutral stand, his antagonism with the errors of the English school became so earnest, and that with the German school so feeble, that he unconsciously falls quite into the arms of the latter.

He accuses Locke of beginning at the wrong point,—the origin of ideas,—instead of beginning with the psychological *facts;* that is, the *phenomena* of mind, in its mature state. He therefore begins with psychology, reasoning, *à posteriori*, from facts to causes; and ends with reasoning, *à priori*, from causes to facts. He thus, in a measure, confounds the methods of the metaphysical and of the empirical schools.

Cousin considers reason a *general*, not a *personal* attribute. All men have *one and the same reason*, of which they are at liberty to avail themselves. He does not professedly admit the theory of innate ideas, and indeed denies that any writers ever really held it, as understood by Locke; but, in his philosophizing, he virtually admits all that the theory has been assumed to maintain. Supposing that reason is not personal to man, but the same in man as in God, by the very constitution of our minds,—that is, by virtue of what is original to our reason,—we must, of course, in so far as we have this divine endowment, view things as God views them. The principles of knowledge are then inherent and original with the human mind.

This is not the same as maintaining that the mind is so constituted as to *admit* certain first truths when presented to it, which is a principle of the British school; it is maintaining that the mind itself spontaneously *produces* them, from its innate furniture, which is a principle of the German school.

Among the orignal ideas of reason, Cousin places those of space, time, infinity, substance, cause, good and evil, and the essential and absolute generally. As the writings of this philosopher are now extensively read, I do not deem it best to occupy our limited space with a particular notice of them. They are in easy modern

French, written in flowing and rather careless style. Among many fine original thoughts, the reader finds some absurd and extravagant ones, and not a few specimens of loose and incoherent reasoning.

As a whole, however, to all who are fond of philosophical studies, and can think for themselves, they are both interesting and instructive. Those who do not embrace his views will at least honor his industry, learning, and genius, and will be delighted with the easy and prompt way in which he speaks out his mind. To those not familiar with the French, his Elements of Psychology, translated by Dr. Henry, of New York, will be found a valuable substitute for his original writings at large.

We have thus glanced at the leading peculiarities and advocates of the German school of philosophy. That its general *tendency* is *to displace the teachings of revealed religion, to give undue exaltation to human reason, to feed the fires of vanity, and to substitute, for* THE ONE LIVING AND PERSONAL JEHOVAH, *the dreams* of A PAGAN PANTHEISM, facts have abundantly proved.

Yet these facts ought not to bear unkindly upon the *men* who have espoused and advocated this philosophy. It is a wise and just maxim, that men ought not to be held responsible for the *consequences* of their doctrines, when they do not intend and cannot foresee them. Among the philosophers of this school are some of the richest thinkers, the purest spirits, and the brightest ornaments of humanity. Besides, the philosophy itself embodies many of the loftiest truths and noblest sentiments within the range of the human intellect.

QUESTIONS ON CHAPTER II.

The father of this school? What is said of him and Aristotle? Des Cartes? His philosophy? Spinoza? Peculiarities of his philosophy? Malebranche? His views? His character? What is said of Leibnitz? Of him and Locke in connection? What did he propose to do? Wherein did he differ from Des Cartes? What was the success of his philosophy? Who expounded and defended it? What can you say of Wolf? When was Kant born? What is said of him? What distinctions does he make in philosophy? Effects of Kant's writings? Mention other writers of this school. Definition of *transcendental* in the note? What is said of Cousin? Of his philosophy? What does he think of Bacon, Locke, &c.? How does he consider reason? Mention some of the original ideas of reason. Tendencies of the German philosophy? Remark?

CHAPTER III.

THE BRITISH SCHOOL.

ARISTOTLE, the ancient founder of this great school, was born at Stagira, 384 years before Christ. Inheriting a fortune, it was his early ambition to devote his life and means to philosophical studies. At the age of seventeen, he commenced attendance on the instructions of Plato, at Athens. The brilliancy of his genius soon outshone that of all his associates, insomuch that Plato considered him the intellect of his school. He continued to prosecute his studies with Plato twenty years, deaf alike to the calls of pleasure and of courtly ambition.

On the death of Plato, he was by Philip chosen preceptor of his son Alexander, which office he discharged eight years, until his pupil's accession to the throne. He was of a spare habit, ate and slept but little, was retiring and simple in his manners, and was wholly devoted to study.

An alienation of feeling is said to have arisen between Aristotle and Plato, towards the latter part of Plato's life, owing to their different philosophical views. Aristotle had the boldness to institute a new theory and enter upon a new track of thought. This awakened the jealousy of Plato, who became subsequently as bitter towards him as he had previously been friendly. It is hoped, for the honor of philosophy, that this is not true, although the current developments of human nature look very much as though it may be.

The writings of Aristotle have sometimes been compared with those of Plato; but they are really very unlike them. The writings of Plato are characterized by glowing imagination and embellishment of style, while those of Aristotle are remarkable for their simplicity. "The philosopher of Stagira," says his biographer, "studied nature more than art, and had recourse to simplicity of expression more than ornament."

Aristotle died at the age of sixty-three. His writings, in chaste and classic Greek, are many of them read, with ease and advantage, by most scholars. Persons not familiar with the Greek language are favored with translations of this great philosopher's works, in every form and variety.

Aristotle's *Logic* reigned in the schools for many centuries; but it has yielded to modes of reasoning characterized by greater simplicity. The ascendency which his *philosophy* early obtained it has continued to hold, in various degrees, down to the present day.

FRANCIS BACON.

Although the Aristotelian philosophy held the ascendency, yet it made little progress during the dark ages, and even down to the time of FRANCIS BACON. This was the beginning of the seventeenth century. Philosophers had generalized too hastily, relying on few facts and first impressions, thus foreclosing the inlets of sound knowledge.

Lord Bacon published his Chart of the Sciences, and New Method of pursuing them, in 1620. In these he sets forth, in strong light, the importance of very careful observation and experiment, as the only true basis of scientific conclusions. His writings gave a new impulse to the Inductive school, and led the way to vast and sure accessions of philosophical knowledge.

He was the first to set aside the Aristotelian logic of the schools, and to institute methods of arriving at truth more simple and satisfactory. Of the same philosophical school with Aristotle, as to the principle that all knowledge is *acquired*, rather than *innate*, he yet took more direct methods to obtain it.

"Retiring as he did from the court and the senate

house into his study, from the busy scenes of political life to the pursuit of philosophical truth, he could hardly fail of becoming more and more convinced of the practical uselessness of the scholastic logic to a mind that requires sagacity in seizing analogies, and needs experience in collecting facts. He saw that in ordinary cases, where we have to deal with mankind, the keenest logic could not supply the place of accurate observation; and proceeded, with that comprehensiveness of mind for which he was remarkable, to generalize his views, until he evolved the conclusion that pure scientific knowledge, as well as all other of a more ordinary and practical kind, must take its start from a diligent observation of facts."*

By the "inductive method" is meant a careful observation of facts in their relations to each other, as constituting genera and species, and contemplating them in view of the great central truth, that, under similar circumstances, the same causes will uniformly produce the same results. Thus, from a comparatively few observations, carefully made, wide conclusions may be drawn. But to render our conclusions both ample and certain, they must be ultimately verified by extended observation, and by facts gathered from every department in nature. The mind thus rises, by a gradual and sure ascent, from facts to principles, and from specific principles to general laws.†

Lord Bacon was to the British school what Des Cartes was to the German. Both were leading minds; both were great; both thought profoundly and earnestly; the one after the English method, the other after the German.

Bacon put forth all his energies to examine and to prove; Des Cartes fell back upon the inborn ideas of his own mind, to contemplate and to reason. Bacon *proved* all things, and held fast that which is good; Des Cartes

* Morelle's History of Philosophy, p. 65.

† "Duæ viæ sunt, atque esse possunt ad inquirendam et inveniendam veritatem. Altera a sensu et particularibus advolat ad axiomata maxime generalia, atque exiis principiis corumque immota veritate judicat, et invenit axiomata media; atque hæc via in usu est. Altera a sensu et particularibus excitat axiomata ascendendo continenter et gradatim, ut ultimo loco perveniatur ad maxima generalia, quæ via vera est, sed intentata." — *Novum Organum*, 1 aph. 61.

thought he knew by virtue of *à priori* principles; hence he sometimes held the true and the false together. Nor did Bacon limit his method of investigation to the outward world; he contemplated their ultimate application to all the phenomena of mind.

That Bacon in some respects carried his views to extremes, and that he came short, in others, of setting sufficiently forth all the considerations that bear upon the investigation of subjective philosophy, is freely admitted; but although Cousin ascribes to him the first aberration from the true philosophical method, I cannot but think the time far off when the great voice of British and American intellect will agree with him.

JOHN LOCKE.

It was in 1698 that this great philosopher issued his renowned ESSAY ON THE HUMAN UNDERSTANDING. It is said to have almost annihilated what then remained of the Platonic philosophy in Great Britain, and to have brought it into extensive disrepute, or greatly to have modified it in many parts of the continent, especially in France.

As so much has been said of this philosopher on our former pages, a few words here will suffice. The leading doctrine of his Essay is, that the mind has no innate ideas — that all its knowledge is *acquired* by sensation and reflection. Our knowledge comes, first, in the form of ideas received through the organs of sense; and, secondly, by the reflections awakened in the mind by these sensuous ideas.

Maintaining the objective reality of knowledge, Locke supposes all our ideas to be either simple or complex — the former being derived directly from sensation and reflection, the latter being compounded of simple ideas by the understanding. When these ideas are legitimate, they correspond exactly with the object which they are supposed to represent. By this is meant, that when a person has what Locke calls an *adequate* idea of an object, that object really is what it appears to him to be.

To persons not conversant with the ancient theory of ideas, this seems little short of a truism; and yet volumes have been written on this single debated point.

SCEPTICAL RESULTS.

Locke's Essay was intended for a protest, not only against the objective philosophy of the scholastic ages, but also against the current *à priori* reasonings of the continent, which were flooding the schools with error. It was intended to make the mind humble and cautious in its search for truth; and to summon it forth from the little world of bright dreams and pleasant fancies of its own creation, to the sober task of proving the realities of the world that God had made. It has, therefore, more to do with the sensational than with the rational; more with the understanding, as empiricizing by the senses, than with the reason, as operating by virtue of its unaided intuitions.

That Locke never taught an exclusive sensational philosophy; that he as truly made the world within the subjective matter as he did the world without the objective matter of philosophy; and that he designed ample scope to all the legitimate intuitions and spontaneous teachings of the mind, has been shown on former pages.

But some of Locke's followers laid an *exclusive* hold on the *sensational* part; and as his philosophy was strictly inductive, cautious, distrustful, admitting nothing without *proof*, it tended in them to produce scepticism. As pupils are wont to go beyond their teacher when they deviate from the right path, some of this school pushed off to avowed scepticism or deism.

In this list, the names of Hume, Collins, Shaftesbury, Bolingbroke, Gibbon, and others, are familiar to all. Among the French are Voltaire, Rousseau, Buffon, Condorcet, D'Alembert, Diderot, and others of less note. Some passed on to *materialism;* of whom were Shaftesbury and Priestley, of the English; and De la Mettrie and Helvetius, of the French. Others went quite over to avowed atheism.

It has been already said, that Morelle would not have laid the blame of this at the door of Locke, had he not been misled, by Cousin, in making him an exclusive sensationalist; for Morelle's views in regard to the necessity of combining the two elements, the sensational and the ideal, are in the main just; and the following sentence, with slight modifications, so well expresses my own views, that I am induced to insert it in this connection:—

"The whole process of sensation, we are conscious, is passive; the moment, therefore, we attempt, like Condillac, to reduce all our notions to different species of transformed sensations, we virtually deny the liberty or energy of the mind, and make humanity itself but an ingenious piece of mechanism, which is moved hither and thither by forces impressed upon it from the outward world. Human freedom accordingly perishes under the hands of a bold sensationalism. Nor is it alone the *moral* nature which is stripped of its grandeur by these principles; the foundations of truth itself are likewise undermined, and the road to scepticism prepared. Knowledge, which comes to us simply through our sensations, can have nothing fixed and absolute about it. Its truth must be relative to the construction of our material organs, and can never attain to a necessary and universal character. In other words, there can be no such thing as truth, which may not at some time prove error; so that the whole framework of our knowledge is rendered insecure." This last clause needs qualifying.

"Idealism, on the contrary, leads us just as far from the truth in the other direction. Neglecting the peculiar element which exists in all our perceptions, and by which we are inseparably linked to the material world, it first of all attempts to deduce the notion of matter by a logical process from our purely rational ideas: failing, however, to afford satisfaction by this process, it begins to undermine the reality of the notion itself, and ends at length in its positive denial. Both sensationalism, therefore, and idealism, when exclusively pursued and developed to their furthest results, lead us into a labyrinth of error, from which it appears impossible for any philosophy to extricate us; they both give us the thread by which we may enter into the very centre of the metaphysical maze, but, having conducted us there, they snap it asunder, and leave us in perplexity which way to turn, in order to retrace our steps. The consequence infallibly is, that philosophy becomes distrusted, that the conclusions of reason are set at nought, and a boastful scepticism is engendered, which magnifies itself against all science, and builds itself up upon the metaphysical errors which it can deride, but not correct."*

The friends of Christianity became alarmed at the results of the prevailing philosophy, and naturally concluded that either there must be something wrong in the philosophy itself, or that it had been misapprehended in some material point. They did not strike for a divorce of Christianity, but for a revision of philosophy.

BISHOP BERKELEY.

Among the attempts to revise philosophy, that of Bishop Berkeley is most conspicuous. As an offset to the writings of Priestley, who had virtually annihilated the soul, having reduced all mental phenomena to modifications of sensation, the learned bishop published a book, in which he maintained that God himself is the immediate cause of all our sensations.†

What we call material objects, being, as he supposed, the *results* of our sensations, and not their *causes*, he considered it most rational to conclude that they exist *only in our minds*.‡ In his view, as God was to be regarded as the direct efficient cause of our sensations, he could as well produce them without any external objects as with them; all that was necessary was to produce in us the *idea* of them, in order to make us *realize* them as truly as though they did actually exist.

* History of Philosophy, pp. 191, 192.

† See the Works of George Berkeley, D. D., Bishop of Cloyne, &c. London edition, 1837.

‡ As, according to this theory, objects have no existence excepting in *ideas*, those who embraced it were sometimes called *idealists*.

The excellent bishop thought that, by thus improving upon the current philosophy, he should banish infidelity, recall the soul, and place it again under the benignant care of its Maker. Of the two errors, — that of Priestley and that of Berkeley, — if we must have either, we should not hesitate to take the latter; but we may congratulate ourselves that a more generous philosophy casts us upon neither alternative. We are privileged to enjoy *both* the material and the mental world, embraced alike in the ample arms of Christianity.

THOMAS REID.

A strange mingling of faith and scepticism, in respect both to philosophy and religion, pervaded the English and many of the continental institutions at the time THOMAS REID appeared to confute the scepticism of Hume, on the one hand, the idealism of Berkeley, on the other, and to restore harmonious confidence in philosophy, as by him expounded, in its relations both to natural and revealed truth. He was born in 1710, not far from Aberdeen, in Scotland, and became professor of Moral Philosophy in the University of Glasgow.

This may be called the era of *common sense.* She was called in, by this excellent philosopher, to curb ultra tendencies in either direction, and to serve as a standard of ultimate appeal. What he called *common sense* is, in fact, much the same as what we designate by spontaneous intuitions. His main force seems to have been directed against the *representative* theory, so called; that is, the theory of intervening ideas between the mind and objects viewed; and he succeeded in clearly expounding the doctrine of immediate and direct perception. The truth is, as I have stated on former pages, that ideas are *results*, not *means*, of perception.

Reid was not so remarkable for originality as for good sense. In several instances, however, his usually good sense fails him; as if to impress upon us the time-honored maxim, that even wise men are not always wise. His writings are classics in mental science, and have contributed an enviable share towards advancing the interests of sound knowledge. In point of style, they are among the finest models of philosophical composition in the English language — lucid, simple, chaste.

BEATTIE and others followed in his track, adding something to his views. These writers did not allow any fellowship with the Platonic theory of innate ideas, yet they placed great confidence in the instinctive promptings of our nature to correct errors incidental to philosophical speculations. This is certainly a very *convenient* method of disposing of difficult points; whether it is always fair, or in the highest degree honorable to the intellect of him who adopts it, is another question.

However this may be, the writers in question proceeded on the assumption that the sober dictates of common sense are often more trustworthy than the results of the most accurate philosophical reasoning. There was a truth in the thought, but it stood too much alone. That philosophy and common sense should ever *seem* to be at variance, argued something still to be learned; for, when rightly expounded, their teachings must always agree.

DUGALD STEWART.

Some French writers, such as Condillac, Bonnet, and others, did something in the way of disabusing, expounding, and improving the philosophy of Locke; but it remained mostly for DUGALD STEWART to elaborate, and in a measure reconstruct, the entire system, on the essential Baconian basis. Without the highest pretensions to originality, by his candor, his great good sense, and his extensive and profound learning, to say nothing of the elegance of his style, he claims a rank among the first philosophical writers in our language.

His books are among the best classics in the schools of Britain and America. If we are constrained sometimes to dissent from his positions, or to point out inaccuracies and contradictions in his statements and reasonings, we must remember that the soundest thinkers sometimes err, and that no man is so wise as not to leave something to be done. It must be added, moreover, that this accomplished writer has done far less in the way of elementary investigation, or of correcting existing errors, than of setting forth, in graceful diction, the thoughts elaborated by other minds.

Dugald Stewart was born in 1753. He was at first professor of Mathematics, afterwards of Moral Philosophy, in the University of Edinburgh. "Respecting Stewart's ability as a writer, there never has been," says Morelle, "so far as I know, but one opinion, and that decidedly favorable. His reading upon all metaphysical subjects (with the exception of the more modern German philosophy) appeared to be almost as extensive as the literature itself; his judgment upon the merits of the different authors was, for the most part, clear and comprehensive. His own mind exhibited all the traces of the scholar and the man of taste, while his easy and attractive style seemed to throw a charm and an interest around the most abstruse and forbidding subjects. There can be little doubt but that the Scottish metaphysics, while they derived their bone and sinew from Dr. Reid, yet owed to the labors of his successor all that mould and system, that order and beauty, which have given them a popularity greater than any philosophical treatises in the English language which have appeared in modern times." *

THOMAS BROWN.

Of the same philosophical school, and of the same university, was THOMAS BROWN. He was born in 1778, and having received a liberal education in England, entered, while young, upon the studies of the University of Edinburgh. He commenced the study of moral philosophy under Dugald Stewart, at the age of sixteen, and soon evinced great acuteness in the investigation of metaphysical subjects. He became colleague professor with Stewart in 1810; and died in 1820, "beloved by many, regretted by all, in the very ascendency of his genius and reputation."

* History of Philosophy, p. 366.

In Brown, we scarcely know which most to admire, the originality of his method, the boldness of his speculations, or the luxuriance and splendor of his diction. Proceeding on the essential Baconian basis, he yet carried the process of simplification beyond any of his predecessors, proposed new theories, — especially in relation to cause and effect, — struck out new thoughts, and made some actual advances in the science of mind. His writings are by no means a substitute for those of Locke, Reid, and Stewart, but are a valuable accompaniment.

OTHER WRITERS.

Neither our space nor object admits the notice of all the writers who have contributed, in some form, to this school. One of the greatest of human productions — Butler's Analogy — is at once a debtor to this school for its origin, and a contributor to its intellectual wealth. Among the most noted of the ultra sensationalists were HARTLEY, PRIESTLEY, and DARWIN.

In quite recent times, the name of JOHN STUART MILL has become considerably known in England, in connection with a work by him, entitled "A System of Logic, Ratiocinative and Inductive," a work of no ordinary merit. The writings of ABERCROMBIE are in most of our schools. Many valuable contributions to mental science have been made by writers in our own country, whose names need not here be mentioned.

PRESENT STATE OF THIS SCHOOL.

Although the distinguishing peculiarities of the two great leading philosophical schools are traced down through all ages, yet each has had its mutations, and many interchanges have been made between them. The Aristotelian school is not now just what it was under the teaching of Aristotle, or Bacon, or Locke. Although still as severely inductive as ever, it is yet more idealistic, more rational, and less sensational. It has made an approximation towards the rational school; it has taken from that school some valuable truths, without, however, compromising its own fundamental principles.

In its present improved condition, it is at once a proud monument of Anglo-Saxon thinking, and a noble tower of defence against the infidelity resulting from an overweening rationalism on the one hand, and an exclusive sensationalism on the other. In the *natural* sciences, it is now triumphant over all the educated world. In the departments of *mental* science, it holds the ascendency in Great Britain and America, and has extensive sway over the continent. There are, however, many in England and America who sympathize with the German school; and on the continent its disciples are yet numerous.

The British philosophy has become incorporated with the classical writings of our language upon physical and medical science, physiology, natural theology, ethics, civil polity, the laws of nations. What is most important, its affinity with the Christian religion has been practically demonstrated; and, in its present improved state, it is found to be a safe depository of revealed truth. It serves to hold the mind in that posture of calm and patient inquiry, which, with proper guidance, conducts to sound knowledge in all departments, both human and divine.

Yet philosophers have ordinarily stood too far apart from Christianity. They have fixed their stand point too low in the earth. If philosophy begins with the earthly, she ought not to end there. She ought to aim heaven-high. All sound systems of philosophy are parts of Christianity, as all mountains, valleys, rivers are parts of our globe. Nor is any philosophic system but partially developed, until its relations to revealed religion are clearly shown.

QUESTIONS ON CHAPTER III.

Ancient founder of this school? What is said of him? What of him and Plato in connection? With whose writings have those of Aristotle been compared? What is said of the success of his philosophy? What is said of Bacon? At what time did he publish? What was he the first to do? What is meant by the inductive method? What is needful to render it sure and comprehensive? Lord Bacon and Des Cartes compared? What does Cousin ascribe to Bacon? What does the reader think of this? When did Locke issue his famous Essay? What is said of it? Its leading doctrine? Sceptical results? Did Locke teach an exclusive sensationalism? What is said of some of his followers? Remarks and quotation? What did the friends of Christianity? Berkeley? His philosophical views? What did the bishop hope to accomplish? Remark? State of things when Reid appeared? When was this? What may this era be called? What is said of it? What was Reid's main force directed against? Did he succeed? For what was he most remarkable? Beattie? Remarks? Dugald Stewart? What is said of his writings? Brown? His philosophy, &c.? Other writers? Present state of this school? With what has this philosophy become incorporated? What, in its present improved state, is it found to be? What does it serve to do? Remark?

A

WINSLOW'S

INTELLECTUAL PHILOSOPHY.

This valuable book is designed for the use of Schools and for Private Reading. The following table of contents will give some idea of the plan of the work:—

Contents. — Life. — Difference between Men and Animals. — Instinct. — Nature of the Human Mind. — Immortality of the Human Mind. — Origin of Human Knowledge. — Primary Knowledge of two Kinds. — Sense of Touch. — Additional Senses. — Sensation. — Improvement of our Sensations. — Perception. — Conception. — Primary Rational Knowledge. — Intuition. — Consciousness. — Attention. — Association. — Memory. — General Views of Man's Superiority. — Abstraction. — Classification. — Induction. — Reason. — Moral Reasoning. — Judgment. — Imagination. — Imagination as related to Morals and Religion. — Dreaming. — Insanity. — Mesmerism. — Suspended Animation. — Trance. — Philosophical Schools. — The German School. — The British School.

The work is highly recommended by some of the most distinguished educators in the country. The following are some of the

RECOMMENDATIONS.

From Jared Sparks, D. D., President of Harvard University.

"The plan of the work appears to me judiciously conceived, and the style and train of thought are clear and natural, and well adapted to excite the interest and secure the attention of young minds. I concur in its estimate of the general principles advanced by Locke, and of the preference they claim to the more recent theories and speculations of the French school."

From Mark Hopkins, D. D., President of Williamstown College.

"I have read the book with great satisfaction, and think it well adapted to the purpose for which it is designed. It is a work containing much original and just thought, and I regard it as a valuable addition to our literature in this department."

From Simeon North, D. D., LL. D., President of Hamilton College.

"I have examined with care the Elements of Intellectual Philosophy, by the Rev. Hubbard Winslow, of Boston, and take great pleasure in saying, that I deem it a work well fitted to subserve the study of that highly important department of knowledge. Its exhibition of the principles of Metaphysical Science, as developed by the most eminent writers on the subject in our language, is clear, concise, and comprehensive; and in a form well adapted to facilitate the progress of those who are just entering upon the study of the mind. In preparing it, its author appears to have had special reference to its use as a text book, and as such I deem it especially worthy the favorable consideration of instructors in this department of learning."

From Mr. Thomas Sherwin, Principal of the English High School, Boston.

"I have examined the treatise on Intellectual Philosophy, by the Rev. Hubbard Winslow, and have been much gratified by the manner in which the subject is treated. This branch of knowledge is very important, and should be so regarded in all our higher institutions of learning. But, unfortunately, it is often presented in a manner so dry and abstract, as to afford but little interest to the youthful mind. This work has presented the study in a form at once agreeable and easy of comprehension; and, I believe, it will be studied with no small degree of interest, as well as with much profit. With great confidence I commend it to all engaged either in learning or teaching intellectual philosophy."

From Mr. M. P. Case, Principal of the High School, Newburyport, Mass.

"I can truly say, after considerable attention to its method and its merits, that it is, in my judgment, better adapted to the business of teaching than any similar work with which I am acquainted. The fulness of the discussion; the clearness with which the topics are presented and illustrated; and the fairness with which the opinions are stated, so decidedly mark its superiority for the teacher and the scholars, that I shall introduce it into my school as soon as the time arrives in which our senior class pursue that particular study. I hope and believe that this work on Intellectual Philosophy will awaken a deeper interest in a most important though too much neglected science."

From Mr. Charles D. Cleveland, Principal of an Institution for Young Ladies, in Philadelphia.

"I am thankful for the valuable addition recently made to our school literature, in the Elements of Intellectual Philosophy, by Mr. Winslow. I have examined it with care, and consider it the best text book for my first class that I have yet seen; and I shall soon show my faith by my works, (the only test of faith that is worth any thing,) by introducing it into my school. It has laid the fraternity of teachers under great obligations. I have heretofore given my pupils but little instruction in this department, for the want of a suitable text book."

From Mr. Francis Bowen, Editor of the North American Review.

"I have examined the work with some care, and I think the author has been very successful in the difficult task of so presenting the great truths and problems of Intellectual Philosophy as to make them intelligible to youthful minds, and to those who have had little previous acquaintance with the subject. The style is very clear and simple, but concise, and the illustrations are well chosen, being such as will interest the reader, and throw light upon the theme of discussion. He has avoided the easily besetting sin of elementary writers upon this subject — that of cumbering the statements and the process of the argument with many words, with wire-drawn discussions and extraneous matter. He has supplied hints and suggested topics, which the judicious teacher and careful thinker will expand and pursue with more profit than if there were nothing left for him to do. The general tone of the book is excellent, the problems of mental science being always viewed in their proper relation to the inestimable truths of Christianity, so that Philosophy appears as the handmaid of Religion, not as its opponent, or as a substitute for it."

From the Boston Transcript.

"The volume forms one of the most valuable and complete text books in Intellectual Philosophy ever published; and every intelligent person should be in possession of the knowledge here to be found, systematically arranged and clearly set forth. The book is not only well adapted to the purposes of colleges and the higher order of schools, but contains an amount of information which will be found very useful for reference to the advanced scholar and the general reader."

From the Christian Witness and Advocate.

"This volume is worthy the attention of parents and teachers, and we shall be disappointed if, after a thorough trial, it does not rank high as a text book in the important science of which it treats."

From the Christian Examiner.

"The author evidently had in view the preparation of a good philosophical manual for the use of the pupils of a well-taught school, and designed to make his work of the most intelligible and useful character to them. His aim was highly commendable, and we think he has accomplished it with very marked success. Mr. Winslow judges wisely in attaching great importance in education to that mode of disciplining the powers of thought and reason which is found in distinguishing the differences and relations of things. There is scarcely any defect more common, even among the pupils that have enjoyed our best means of education, than that of *discrimination* — a word which cannot be fairly and fully defined without meaning almost the same as philosophy. We regard this volume as eminently well adapted to cultivate the faculty of *discrimination* in pupils, for it is intended to make them philosophize — to answer questions as well as to receive instruction. The main effort of the author seems to have been to render philosophy a matter of practical utility; to show that, so far from having no bearing upon things of daily use and value, as a vulgar prejudice judges of philosophy, it is eminently a guide to all that is actually useful and precious beyond a merely animal existence."

www.ingramcontent.com/pod-product-compliance
Lightning Source LLC
LaVergne TN
LVHW021142110826
845150LV00005B/1104

* 9 7 8 1 4 2 5 5 4 7 1 1 0 *